Teaching Young Children Through Their Individual Learning Styles

RELATED TITLES OF INTEREST

Teaching Young Children Through Their Individual Learning Styles

Practical Approaches for Grades K–2

RITA DUNN
St. John's University

KENNETH DUNN
Queens College

JANET PERRIN
Harborfields School District

ALLYN AND BACON
Boston London Toronto Sydney Tokyo Singapore

67.99

Photographs provided courtesy of the Center for the Study of Learning and Teaching Styles, St. John's University, were taken by Dr. Kenneth Dunn.

Copyright © 1994 by Allyn and Bacon

160 Gould Street
Needham Heights, Massachusetts 02194

Library of Congress Cataloging-in-Publication Data

Dunn, Rita Stafford
    Teaching young children through their individual learning styles: practical approaches for grades K–2 / Rita Dunn, Kenneth Dunn, Janet Perrin.
        p.   cm.
    Includes bibliographical references (p.   ) and index.
    ISBN 0–205–15271–6
    1. Individualized instruction. 2. Education, Primary.
    3. Cognitive styles. I. Dunn, Kenneth J. II. Perrin, Janet.
    III. Title.
    LB1031.D83   1994
    371.3'94--dc20   93–13944
                                                                           CIP

Printed in the United States of America

10 9 8 7 6 5 4 3   97 96 95 94 93

ABOUT THE AUTHORS

Rita Dunn, Ed.D., is Professor and Chairperson, Division of Administrative and Instructional Leadership, and Director, Center for the Study of Learning and Teaching Styles, St. John's University, New York. She is the coauthor of 13 textbooks and more than 300 published chapters, research papers, booklets, and other manuscripts. Dr. Dunn is the recipient of numerous honors, including New York University's Research Scholarship Award (1967); National Academy of Education Research Management Scholarship (1979); College Teacher of the Year (1980); Association for Supervision and Curriculum Development's Outstanding Consultant of the Year (1982); American Association of School Administrators' Distinguished Lecturer (1985); St. John's University's Outstanding Faculty Achievement Gold Medal (1985) and Merit Awards every year they were offered (1989–1993); National Association of Elementary School Principals' Educator of the Year (1988); and Mensa Education Research and Foundation Award for Excellence in Research (1992).

Kenneth Dunn, Ed.D., is Professor and Coordinator of Administration Programs in the Department of Educational and Community Programs, Queens College, New York. He has served as superintendent of schools in selected suburban school districts and is the coauthor of 13 books and more than 150 published manuscripts. He and Rita Dunn received the Education Press of America Award for ". . . the best series in an educational journal . . . " (1979) and were the first married couple simultaneously elected to the Hunter College Hall of Fame (1987).

Janet Perrin, Ed.D., is principal, T. J. Lahey Elementary School, Harborfields School District, Greenlawn, New York. She was the recipient of the American Association of School Administrators' Research Award (1985) for the quality of her doctoral dissertation, for which Dr. Rita Dunn served as mentor. Dr. Perrin is the author of articles published in *Early Years, Educational Leadership, Teaching K–8,* and other national journals.

DEDICATION

To those scholars and researchers at more than eighty institutions of higher education throughout the world (see References) and to those educators in hundreds of schools across the United States who have reported results and provided feedback:

We thank you, with the deepest appreciation, for your consistent energy and willingness to experiment, accept difficult challenges, persist, test this model of learning style, improve it, and share what you learned for the benefit of students everywhere. We recognize your valuable contribution and dedicate this book to you.

Among those outstanding professionals are the following colleagues who have worked with us over the decades to develop a quality instructional program for students:

- Professor Gene Geisert, St. John's University Faculty, Administration and Supervision
- Professor Josephine Gemake, St. John's University Faculty, Reading
- Professor Shirley A. Griggs, St. John's University Faculty, Counseling
- Professor John B. Murray, St. John's University Faculty, Psychology
- Professor Louis Primavera, St. John's University Faculty, Psychology
- Professor Gary E. Price, University of Kansas, Lawrence
- Professor Peter Quinn, St. John's University Faculty, Instructional Leadership
- Professor Richard Sinatra, St. John's University Faculty, Reading
- Professor John N. Spiridakis, St. John's University Faculty, Bilingual Education
- Professor Donald Treffinger, State University College at Buffalo
- Professor Jennie Venezzia, St. John's University Faculty, Research and Statistics
- Professor Robert Zenhausern, St. John's University Faculty, Psychology

CONTENTS

PREFACE

Research on the Dunn and Dunn model of learning styles is more extensive and more thorough than the research on most previous educational movements. As of 1993, that research had been conducted at more than 85 institutions of higher education; in every grade from kindergarten through college; and with students at most levels of academic proficiency, including gifted, average, underachieving, at-risk, dropout, special education, vocational, and industrial arts populations. Furthermore, the experimental research in learning styles conducted at the Center for the Study of Learning and Teaching Styles, St. John's University, New York, received two regional, thirteen national, and two international awards/citations for its quality between 1980 and 1992.

That wealth of well-conducted research verifies the existence of individual differences among students—differences so extreme that identical methods, resources, or grouping procedures can promote achievement for some and inhibit it for others.

This book is designed to help teachers, administrators, college professors, and parents discover the learning style of each youngster and then to suggest practical approaches for teaching students through their individual learning style strengths. Each chapter presents practical, tried and tested ideas and techniques that can be used as quickly as the personnel in a given school can absorb them and put them into practice. The ideas and strategies include the following:

- A thorough analysis of each of the 21 elements of learning style and an instrument and observational methods for recognizing them
- Detailed blueprints for redesigning early childhood school classrooms to accommodate a wide variety of learning style differences
- Step-by-step guidelines for creating instructional spaces for young children, such as Interest Centers (for global students), Game Tables (for tactual/kinesthetics), Media Corners (for youngsters with specific perceptual strengths), and a Reading Corner (for those who cannot concentrate on printed text in an environment containing classmates' movements, sounds, or other distractions)
- Descriptions and examples of small-group instructional strategies for peer-oriented students, such as Team Learning, Circle of Knowledge, Brainstorming, and Case Study

- Detailed explanations for designing Programmed Learning Sequences, Contract Activity Packages, Multisensory Instructional Packages, and tactual and kinesthetic instructional resources—different methods for teaching the identical information to children with different learning styles
- Sample individual printouts that permit readers to test their developing ability to diagnose and prescribe for individuals with diverse learning styles
- New approaches for teaching young children to read based on their global versus analytic processing styles
- Suggestions for grouping auditory, visual, tactual, and kinesthetic youngsters for reading based on their perceptual strengths

In a practical sense, these tried and tested techniques, all based on valid and reliable research findings, may be used by all people concerned with the instructional process at the early childhood level.

- Teachers can use the text as a how-to guide to respond to the learning style requirements of individual students.
- Administrators can use the descriptions of methods and approaches as supervisory tools when assessing and aiding teachers to respond to the learning style characteristics of their students.
- Central office personnel can use the separate chapters as a basis for staff development to build instructional skills among faculty.
- Colleges and university professors can use the text as a basis for a course in theory and its practical translation into responsive methods for the preparation and retraining of teachers—who, increasingly, are being required to diagnose and prescribe on the basis of individual learning style differences.
- Parent groups can use this book to understand, monitor, and support improved instructional programs and to assist their own offspring at home.
- School districts can protect themselves against the increasing number of educational malpractice suits by accurate identification of student learning differences and provision of instructional prescriptions based on accurate data.
- Motivated young children can use the strategies included herein to teach themselves how to do their homework through their learning style strengths.

This book, then, was written to translate accepted research theory into practical techniques that any teacher, administrator, professor, or parent can use and try immediately. It also includes the first guidelines for teaching young children how to teach themselves based on their unique learning style areas, and the provision of varied and style-responsive resources and approaches will, relatively quickly, build an instructional process that will respond directly to the individual learning styles of each of your students.

Previous Books by Rita and Kenneth Dunn

Tanzman, J., & Dunn, K. (1971). *Using Instructional Media Effectively,* Prentice-Hall.

Dunn, R., & Dunn, K. (1972). *Practical Approaches to Individualizing Instruction; Contracts and Other Effective Teaching Strategies,* Prentice-Hall.

Dunn, R., & Dunn, K. (1975). *Educator's Self-Teaching Guide to Individualizing Instructional Programs,* Prentice-Hall.

Dunn, R., & Dunn, K. (1977). *Administrator's Guide to New Programs for Faculty Management and Evaluation,* Prentice-Hall.

Dunn, R., & Dunn, K. (1977). *How to Raise Independent and Professionally Successful Daughters,* Prentice-Hall.

Dunn, R., & Dunn, K. (1978). *Teaching Students through Their Individual Learning Styles: A Practical Approach,* Prentice-Hall.

Dunn, R., & Dunn, K. (1983). *Situational Leadership for Principals: The School Administrator in Action,* Prentice-Hall.

Carbo, M., Dunn, R., & Dunn, K. (1986). *Teaching Students to READ Through Their Individual Learning Styles,* Prentice Hall.

Dunn, R., & Griggs, S. A. (1988). *Learning Styles: Quiet Revolution in American Secondary Schools,* National Association of Secondary School Principals.

Dunn, R., & Dunn, K. (1992). *Teaching Elementary Students Through Their Individual Learning Styles,* Allyn and Bacon.

Dunn, R., Dunn, K., & Treffinger, D. (1992). *Bringing Out the Giftedness in Every Child: A Guide for Parents,* John Wiley and Sons.

Dunn, R., & Dunn, K. (1993). *Teaching Secondary Students Through Their Individual Learning Styles,* Allyn and Bacon.

The Dunns' Books Translated into Foreign Languages

Dunn, R., & Dunn, K. (1975). *Procedimentos Practicos para Individualizar la Ensenanza,* Prentice-Hall.

Dunn, R., & Dunn, K. (1977). *Programmazione Individualizzata: Nuove Strategie Practiche per Tuitti,* Prentice-Hall.

Dunn, R., & Dunn, K. (1978). *La Ensenanza y el Estilo Individual del Aprendizaje.* Prentice-Hall.

Rita and Ken also are co-authors of six children—Robert, Rana, Richard, Kerry, Kevin, and Keith—and one grandson—Ryan.

ACKNOWLEDGMENTS

Our deep and continuing appreciation to three very special people:

- **Mrs. Madeline Larsen,** who typed four textbooks simultaneously and maintained her normal charm, civility, and nurturing attitude throughout. In addition, she smiles lovingly *every* day!
- **Mrs. Pamela Brady,** who, with persistence and dedication, graciously typed hundreds of thoughts and afterthoughts. We are certain that *she* is smiling at this book's publication.
- **Dr. Angela Klavas,** assistant director of the Center for the Study of Learning and Teaching Styles, St. John's University, New York, who gallantly assumed many of the responsibilities of the director while that person was co-authoring the four books, performed them admirably, and rarely complained. She, too, smiles every day—a smile that says, "Don't worry! *I'll* take care of it!" And she *does*.
- **Professor Shirley A. Griggs,** whom we treasure as a friend, colleague, and respected associate. *She* makes *us* smile!

Rita and Ken Dunn and Janet Perrin appreciatively acknowledge the insights provided by Susan Trostle of the University of Rhode Island and Ann Marie Leonard of James Madison University.

1

Understanding Learning Style and the Need for Individual Diagnosis and Prescription

Introduction to Learning Style and Brain Behavior

The research on learning styles explains why, within the same family, certain children perform well in school whereas their siblings do not. It demonstrates the differences in style among members of the same class, culture, community, profession, or socioeconomic group, but it also reveals the differences and similarities between groups. It shows how boys' styles differ from girls' and the differences between youngsters who read well and those who read poorly.

More important than its documentation of how conventional schooling responds to certain students and inhibits the achievement of others, the research on learning styles provides clear directions for teaching individuals through their style patterns and for teaching them to teach themselves by capitalizing on their personal strengths.

Everybody has strengths, although a parent's strengths tend to differ from those of the other parent, from those of their offspring, and from those of their own parents. Thus, mothers and fathers often learn differently from each other and also from their children. Nevertheless, parents commonly insist that children study and do their homework as they themselves did when they were young. That approach is not likely to be effective for at least some of the siblings because, within the same family, different individuals usually learn in diametrically opposite ways.

What Is Learning Style?

When a child is ill, a competent physician examines more than just the part of the anatomy that hurts—the throat, the eyes, or the chest. Professionalism requires that the child be examined thoroughly to determine what might be contributing to the health problem; thus, doctors get at the *cause,* not just the symptoms. So it is with learning style. Although some pioneers identified style as only one or two variables on a bipolar continuum (Dunn, DeBello, Brennan, Krimsky, & Murrain, 1983; De-Bello, 1990), style is a combination of many biologically and experientially imposed characteristics that contribute to learning, each in its own way and together as a unit.

Thus, learning style is more than merely whether a child remembers new and difficult information most easily by hearing, seeing, reading, writing, illustrating, verbalizing, or actively experiencing; perceptual or modality strength is only one part of learning style. It also is more than whether a person processes information sequentially, analytically, or in a so-called left-brain mode rather than in a holistic, simultaneous, global right-brain fashion; that, too, is only one important component of learning style.

It is more than how someone responds to the environment in which learning must occur or whether information is absorbed concretely or abstractly; those variables contribute to style but, again, are only part of the total construct. We must look not only at the apparent symptoms but also at the whole of each person's inclinations toward learning.

Learning style, then, is the way in which *each* learner begins to concentrate on, process, and retain new and difficult information. That interaction occurs differently for every individual. To identify a person's learning style pattern, it is necessary to examine each individual's multidimensional characteristics to determine what is most likely to trigger each student's concentration, maintain it, respond to his or her natural processing style, and lead to long-term memory. To reveal that, it is necessary to use a comprehensive model of learning style because individuals are affected by different elements of style and so many of the elements are capable of increasing academic achievement for those to whom they are important within a short period of time—often as little as six weeks. Only three comprehensive models exist, and each has a related instrument designed to reveal individuals' styles based on the elements included in that model (DeBello, 1990). It is *impossible* to obtain reliable and valid data from an unreliable or invalid assessment tool. The instrument with the highest reliability and validity, the one used in most research on learning styles, is the Dunn, Dunn, and Price Learning Style Inventory (LSI).

Teachers cannot identify correctly all the elements of learning style (Dunn, Dunn, & Price, 1977; Marcus, 1977a; Beaty, 1986). Some aspects of style are not observable, even to the experienced eye. In addition, teachers often misinterpret behaviors and misunderstand symptoms. Chapter 2 explains which instruments are appropriate at different age levels and how to prepare students to answer their questions. Chapter 2 also describes how to administer a learning style instrument to obtain accurate information.

The Dunn and Dunn Learning Styles Model

Evolution of the Model

In 1967 Professor Rita Dunn was invited by the New York State Department of Education to design and direct a program that would help "educationally disadvantaged" children to increase their achievement. Freed from teaching responsibilities and, thus, able to focus on how individuals responded to alternative instructional approaches, she observed the widely diverse effects of exposure to identical methods and teaching styles on same-age and same-grade youngsters. She and Dr. Kenneth Dunn then scrutinized the educational and industrial literature concerned with *how* people learn. They found an abundance of research accumulated over an eighty-year period that repeatedly verified the individual differences among students and how each begins to concentrate on, process, absorb, and retain new and difficult information or skills.

Initially, the Dunns identified twelve variables that significantly differentiated among students (Dunn & Dunn, 1972); later they reported the existence of eighteen (Dunn & Dunn, 1975); by 1979 they had incorporated hemispheric preference and global/analytic inclinations into their framework. Over the past two decades, research conducted by the Dunns, their colleagues, doctoral students, and graduate professors and their students throughout the United States have documented that, when students are taught through their identified learning style preferences, they evidence stratistically increased academic achievement, improved attitudes toward instruction, and better discipline than when they are taught through nonpreferred styles (Andrews, 1990, 1991; Brunner & Majewski, 1990; Stone, 1992; Sullivan, 1993).

Currently, research is being focused on additional variables, such as the amount and kind of space that people need when concentrating on new and difficult information or the effects of color. By 1990, however, the Dunn and Dunn model included twenty-one elements that, when classified, revealed that learners are affected by (1) *their immediate environment* (sound, light, temperature, and furniture/seating designs); (2) *their own emotionality* (motivation, persistence, responsibility (conformity versus nonconformity), and need for either externally imposed structure or the opportunity to do things their own way); (3) *their sociological preferences* (learning alone, in pairs, in small groups, as part of a team, with either an authoritative or a collegial adult, and wanting variety as opposed to patterns and routines); (4) *their physiological characteristics* (perceptual strengths, time-of-day energy levels, and need for intake of food and drink and/or for mobility *while* learning); and (5) *their processing inclinations* (global/analytic, right/left, and impulsive/reflective) (see Figure 1–1).

Theoretical Cornerstone of the Model

Learning style is a biologically and developmentally determined set of personal characteristics that make the identical type of instruction effective for some students and

FIGURE 1-1 Learning styles model

Designed by Dr. Rita Dunn and Dr. Kenneth Dunn

ineffective for others. Though initially conceived as an outgrowth of practitioners' observations combined with university researchers' studies, this learning style model traces its roots to two distinct learning theories—cognitive style theory and brain lateralization theory.

Cognitive style theory suggests that individuals process information differently on the basis of either learned or inherent traits. Many previous researchers investigated the variables of field dependence/independence, global/analytic, simultaneous/successive, and/or left- or right-preferenced processing. As we conducted studies to determine whether relationships existed among these cognitive dimensions and students' characteristics that appeared to be more or less responsive to environmental, emotional, sociological, and physiological stimuli, we found that selected variables often clustered together. Indeed, relationships appeared to exist between learning persistently (with few or no intermissions), in quiet and bright light, in a formal seating arrangement, and with little or no intake, and being an analytic left processor (Dunn, Bruno, Sklar, & Beaudry, 1990; Dunn, Cavanaugh, Eberle, & Zenhausern, 1982). Similarly, young people who often requested breaks while learning and who learned more, more easily in soft lighting, with sound in the environment, seated informally, and with snacks, often revealed high scores as right processors. Field dependence versus field independence correlated in many ways with a global versus an analytic cognitive style and, again, seemed to elicit the same clustering as right- and left-preferenced students did.

In some cases, more attributes allied themselves with global/right tendencies than with their counterparts'. Thus, although global/rights often enjoyed working with peers and using their tactual strengths, analytic/lefts did not reveal the reverse, nor did their sociological or perceptual characteristics evidence consistent similarities.

As the relationships among various cognitive style theories were evidenced, brain lateralization theory emerged, based to a large extent on the writing of the French neurologist Paul Braco, whose research had led him to propose that the two hemispheres of the human brain have different functions. Subsequent research by the Russian scientist Alexander Luria and the American scientist Roger Sperry demonstrated that the left hemisphere appeared to be associated with verbal and sequential abilities, whereas the right hemisphere appeared to be associated with emotions and with spatial, holistic processing. Those conclusions, however, continue to be challenged. Nevertheless, it is clear that people begin to concentrate, process, and remember new and difficult information under very different conditions.

Thus, the Dunn and Dunn model is based on the theory that:

1. Most individuals can learn.
2. Instructional environments, resources, and approaches respond to diverse learning style strengths.
3. Everyone has strengths, but different people have very different strengths.
4. Individual instructional preferences exist and can be measured reliably (see Appendices A and B).
5. Given responsive environments, resources, and approaches, students attain sta-

tistically higher achievement and attitude test scores in matched rather than mismatched treatments (Dunn & Dunn, 1992, 1993).

6. Most teachers can learn to use learning styles as a cornerstone of their instruction.

7. Most students can learn to capitalize on their learning style strengths when concentrating on new and/or difficult academic material.

Assessing the Elements of Style

What Do We Know about Processing New and Difficult Information?

Dunn, Beaudry, and Klavas (1989) discuss the different ways people learn new and difficult information. The terms *analytic/global, left/right, sequential/simultaneous,* and *inductive/deductive* have been used interchangeably in the literature; the descriptions of these variables tend to parallel each other. Analytics learn more easily when information is presented step by step in a cumulative sequential pattern that builds toward a conceptual understanding. Globals learn more easily when they either understand the concept first and then can concentrate on the details, or are introduced to the information with, preferably, a humorous story replete with examples and graphics. What is crucial to understanding brain functioning, however, is that both types reason, but by different strategies (Levy, 1979; Zenhausern, 1980); each strategy "is a reflection of a trend toward optimalization of efficient use of neural space" (Levy, 1982, p. 224).

Thus, whether youngsters are analytic or global, left or right, sequential or simultaneous, or inductive or deductive processors, they are capable of mastering identical information or skills if they are taught through instructional methods or resources that complement their styles. That conclusion was documented in mathematics at the elementary (Jarsonbeck, 1984), high school (Brennan, 1984), and community college (Dunn, Bruno, Sklar, & Beaudry, 1990) levels, in high school science (Douglas, 1979) and nutrition (Tanenbaum, 1982), and in junior high school social studies (Trautman, 1979). Processing style appears to change. The majority of elementary school children are global, but the older children get and the longer they remain in school, the more analytic some become.

What is fascinating is that analytic and global youngsters appear to have different environmental and physiological needs (Cody, 1983; Dunn, Bruno, Sklar, & Beaudry, 1990; Dunn, Cavanaugh, Eberle, & Zenhausern, 1982). Many analytics tend to prefer learning in a quiet, well-illuminated, formal setting; they often have a strong emotional need to complete the tasks they are working on, and they rarely eat, drink, smoke, chew, or bite on objects *while* learning. Conversely, globals appear to work with what teachers describe as "distractors"; they concentrate better with sound (music or background talking), soft lighting, an informal seating arrangement, and some form of intake of food or drink. In addition, globals take frequent breaks while studying and often prefer to work on several tasks simultaneously. They begin a task,

Ryan enjoys the introductory *global story in the Programmed Learning Sequence (PLS) "Rocks: A Hard Topic" (see Chapter 7). He then reinforces through the MIP's colorful tactual and kinesthetic games and materials. The PLS is one of several instructional strategies included in a Multisensory Instructional Package (MIP). Other primary students prefer to work step-by-step sequentially through analytically structured resources. (Photograph courtesy of Center for the Study of Learning and Teaching Styles, St. John's University, New York.)*

stay with it for a while, stop, do something else, and eventually return to the original assignment.

One set of procedures is neither better nor worse than the other; they are merely different. Globals often prefer learning with their peers rather than either alone or with their teacher, and also often prefer to structure tasks in their own way; they tend to dislike imposed directives. What is interesting is that most gifted children with IQs of 145 or higher are global (Cody, 1983)—and so are most underachievers. The difference between the high-IQ and underachieving global students tends to be motivation and perceptual preferences.

It is understandable that the motivation levels of underachievers would be lower than those of achievers, but what may separate the two groups is the biological development of their auditory, visual, tactual, and kinesthetic senses. Although we do not yet know how to intervene in their biological development, we have been successful in teaching them through their existing perceptual preferences (Carbo, 1980;

Gardiner, 1986; Ingham, 1989; Jarsonbeck, 1984; Kroon, 1985; Martini, 1986; Urbschat, 1977; Weinberg, 1983; Wheeler, 1983).

Beginning Steps for Practitioners

Teachers need to know how to teach both analytically and globally. Chapter 4 describes that process and will help develop beginning skills in teaching both ways. However, global students often require an environment that differs from the conventional classroom. They also appear to need more encouragement and short, varied tasks because of their apparent lower levels of motivation and persistence. Most children learn more easily when lessons are interesting to them, but globals *require* that new and difficult information be interesting, be related to their lives, and permit active involvement. Hart (1983) insists that these are requirements for all youngsters; without doubt, they are necessary if globals are to master academic requirements.

What Do We Know about Students' Environmental Needs?

Although many children require quiet while concentrating on difficult information, others literally learn better with sound than in silence (Pizzo, 1981, 1982). For the

Katie concentrates best when "reading" her story book with background music playing. Other youngsters prefer to block out normal classroom noises with headphones that do not actually work. (Photographs courtesy of the Center for the Study of Learning and Teaching Styles, St. John's University.)

latter group, words without lyrics provide an atmosphere more conductive to concentrating than do melodies with words, and baroque music appears to promote better responsiveness than rock (DeGregoris, 1986). Similarly, although many people concentrate better in brightly lit rooms, others think better in soft light than in bright light. Indeed, fluorescent lighting can overstimulate certain learners and cause hyperactivity and restlessness (Dunn, Krimsky, Murray, & Quinn, 1985).

Temperature variations affect individual students differently. Some achieve better in warm environments and others in cool surroundings (Murrain, 1983). Similar differences are evidenced with varied seating arrangements. Some prefer studying in wooden, plastic, or steel chairs, but many others become so uncomfortable in conventional classroom seats that they are prevented from learning.

Few educators realize that, when a person is seated in a hard chair, fully 75 percent of the total body weight is supported by just 4 square inches of bone (Branton, 1966). The resulting stress on the tissues of the buttocks causes fatigue, discomfort, and frequent postural change—for which many youngsters are scolded on a daily basis. Only people who happen to be sufficiently well padded exactly where they need to be can tolerate conventional seating for long periods of time.

Teachers everywhere testify to the fact that boys tend to be more hyperactive and restless than girls, and seating arrangements contribute to this phenomenon. However, when students are permitted to learn and/or take tests in seating that responds to their learning style preferences for either a formal or an informal design, they achieve significantly higher test scores than when they are mismatched with their design preferences. That occurred in high school English (Nganwa-Baguma, 1986; Shea, 1983) and mathematics (Orsak, 1990), junior high school word recognition (DellaValle, 1984; Dunn, DellaValle, Dunn, Geisert, Sinatra, & Zenhausern, 1986; Murrain, 1983) and mathematics (Hodges, 1985), and elementary school reading (Krimsky, 1982; Lemmon, 1985; MacMurren, 1985; Miller, 1985; Nganwa-Bagumah & Mwamenda, 1991; Pizzo, 1981, 1982) and mathematics (Lemmon, 1985) (see Table 1–1).

Beginning Steps for Practitioners

Redesign conventional kindergartens and first- and second-grade classrooms with cardboard boxes and other usable items placed perpendicular to the walls to allow for quiet, well-lit areas and, simultaneously, sections for controlled interaction and soft lighting. Permit children who want to do so to work in chairs; on carpeting, beanbags, or cushions; and/or seated against the walls—as long as they pay attention and perform as well as or better than they have previously. Turn the lights off and read in natural daylight with underachievers or whenever the class becomes restless. Establish rules for classroom decorum as you feel comfortable—for example, no feet on desks, no shoes on chairs, do not distract anyone else from learning. You also may require improved test performance and behavior. You will be surprised at the positive results (Dunn, 1987).

For easy-to-follow suggestions for redesigning classrooms quickly and at no cost, see Chapter 3.

TABLE 1–1 Experimental Research Concerned with Learning Styles and Instructional Environments

Researcher/ Date	Sample	Subject Examined	Element Examined	Significant Effects	
				Achievement	Attitudes
DeGregoris, 1986	Sixth-, seventh-, eighth-graders	Reading comprehension	Kinds of sound needed by preferents	+ [a]With moderate talking	Not tested
DellaValle, 1984	Seventh-graders	Word recognition memory	Mobility/passivity needs	+	Not tested
Hodges, 1985	Seventh-, eighth graders	Mathematics	Formal/informal design preferences	+	+
Krimsky, 1982	Fourth-graders	Reading speed and accuracy	Bright/low lighting preferences	+	Not tested
Lemmon, 1985	Third-sixth-graders	Reading and mathematics	Design and time	+	Not tested
MacMurren, 1985	Sixth-graders	Reading speed and accuracy	Need for intake while learning	+	+
Miller, 1985	Second-graders	Reading	Mobility/ passivity needs	+	Not tested
Murrain, 1983	Seventh-graders	Word recognition/ memory	Temperature preference	*[b]	Not tested
Nganwa-Baguma, 1986	High schoolers	English	Formal/ informal design	+	Not tested
Nganwa-Bagumah & Muramenda, 1991	Second-fifth-graders	Reading comprehension	Formal/ informal design	+	Not tested
Pizzo, 1981, 1982	Sixth-graders	Reading	Acoustical preferences	+	+
Shea, 1983	Ninth-graders	Reading	Formal/informal design preferences	+	Not tested
Stiles, 1985	Fifth-graders	Mathematics testing	Formal/informal design preferences	0	Not tested

Source: Adapted by permission form "Survey of Research on Learning Styles" by R. Dunn, J. S. Beaudry, and A. Klavas, March 1989, *Educational Leadership, 46*(6), p. 51. Copyright © 1989 by the Association for Supervision and Curriculum Development.

Note: Price (1980) reported that the older students became, the less they appeared able to adapt to a conventional setting. Thus, design may be far more crucial to secondary students' ability to concentrate than to that of fifth-graders, who may be better able to adjust to this element (Stiles, 1985). Dunn and Griggs (1988) described the importance of design to high schoolers throughout the United States.

[a]+ represents significant positive findings at $p < .01$ or greater; 0 = no differences or slight trend.

[b]* represents trend toward significant findings at $p < 1.00$.

This student is most productive in low *light. Katie often snuggles under a table in a fairly dark corner when reading. Other children require bright light; some need to be near a window, whereas others concentrate well under overhead illumination. (Photograph courtesy of the Center for the Study of Learning and Teaching Styles, St. John's University, New York.)*

What Do We Know about the People with Whom Students Learn Most Easily?

For years, many teachers directly taught their students whatever had to be learned. When youngsters had difficulty in acquiring knowledge, teachers believed that their charges were not paying attention. Few realized that despite the quality of the teaching, some children were incapable of learning directly from an adult. These young people were uncomfortable when under pressure to concentrate in either teacher-dominated or authoritative classes. They were fearful of failing, embarrassed to show inability, and often too tense to concentrate. For such little ones, learning either alone or with peers is a better alternative than working directly with their teachers in either an individual or group situation. Indeed, research demonstrates that when students' sociological preferences were identified and the youngsters then were exposed to multiple treatments—both congruent and incongruent with their identified learning styles—each achieved significantly higher test scores when taught in congruent pat-

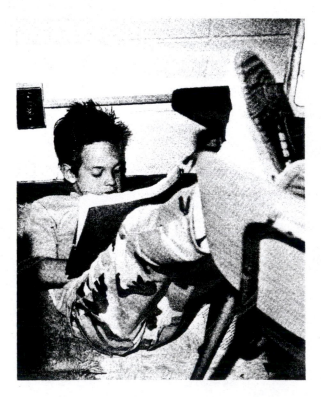

The positions in which youngsters learn best vary from upright, formal seating in chairs and at desks to informal reclining on couches, carpeting, beanbags, soft chairs, and cushions. Some students kneel, sprawl, or prop their feet up onto chairs. The students shown here are studying or working intensely and productively. (Photographs courtesy of P. K. Yonge Laboratory School, Gainesville, Florida and Northwest Elementary School in Amityville, New York.

*When the academic content is difficult for them, some children prefer to learn
alone. (Photograph courtesy of West Seneca Central School District, West Seneca, New York.)*

terns (Dunn, Beaudry, & Klavas, 1989). Four studies also examined the effects of
sociological preferences on attitude toward learning and found statistically higher
attitude scores when students were taught in matched situations (DeBello, 1985;
Dunn, Giannitti, Murray, Geisert, Rossi, & Quinn, 1990; Miles, 1987; Perrin, 1984
(see Table 1–2). Indeed, gifted students strongly prefer to learn by themselves rather
than with others (Cross, 1982; Griggs & Price, 1980; Kreitner, 1981; Price, Dunn,
Dunn, & Griggs, 1981). These research data were supported in schools throughout
the United States when site visits, observations, and evaluation collection documented that students achieved more, behaved better, and liked learning better when
they were permitted to learn through their sociological preferences as revealed by the
Learning Style Inventory (Andrews, 1990; Dunn & Griggs, 1988b; Harp & Orsak,
1990; Lemmon, 1985; Sinatra, 1990). Since 1984, schools have been experimenting
with teaching students to teach themselves by capitalizing on their sociological and
other learning style preferences (Dunn, 1984); the results to date are very promising

TABLE 1–2 Experimental Research Concerned with Sociological Preferences

Researcher/Date	Sample	Subject Examined
Cholakis, 1986	106 underachieving, inner-city, parochial school seventh- and eighth-graders	Vocabulary development was provided through three strategies—by the teacher, alone by themselves, and in a peer group treatment.

Findings: Those who preferred learning alone scored significantly higher (.01) than those who preferred learning either with peers or the teacher. However, all students attained significantly higher acheivement (.001) and attitude (.01) scores when learning with an authority figure.

DeBello, 1985	236 suburban eighth-graders	Students wrote social studies compositions and then experienced revision strategies that were congruent *and* incongruent with their sociological preferences.

Findings: Peer learners scored significantly higher when matched with the peer-conferencing technique (.01). Authority-oriented learners, when revising through the teacher-conference, achieved statistically higher (.01) than when revising either through peer conferencing or self-review. And those who preferred to learn alone scored significantly higher (.01) when matched, rather than mismatched, with self-review. No learning style group achieved better than any other, but a significant interaction occurred between individual sociological style and the matched method of revision (.001). In addition, the attitudes of students who preferred to learn alone or with an adult were significantly more positive (.01) when they were assigned to approaches that matched their styles.

Giannitti, 1988	104 suburban, parochial and public school sixth-, seventh-, and eighth-graders	Social studies was taught through both a mini-Contract Activity Package (CAP) and a small-group strategy, Team Learning.

Findings: Peer-oriented students achieved significantly higher test and attitude scores when learning through Team Learning than through the mini Cap (.01). Learning-alone preferents attained significantly higher test and attitude scores (.01) through the mini-CAP than with their peers. Nonpreferenced students acheived better through the mini-CAP than through the Team Learning and liked working alone better than in groups. A significant interaction occurred between learning alone and peer-preferenced learning and the method of learning (mini-CAP and Team Learning).

Miles, 1987	40 inner-city fifth- and sixth-graders	Twenty-two who preferred to learn alone and 18 who preferred to learn with peers were assigned randomly to two instructional groups that taught career awareness and career decision-making concepts in conditions both congruent and incongruent with their preferences.

Findings: The matching of sociological preference with complementary grouping patterns increased achievement significantly on career awareness (.01) and career decision making (.01). In addition, students' attitude scores were statistically higher when they were taught career awareness (.01) and career decision-making concepts (.05) in patterns accommodating their sociological preferences. With the exception of career awareness achievement, neither sociologically preferenced group achieved better than the other, but learning-alone preferents scored higher (.05) than peer-preferenced individuals.

TABLE 1–2 Experimental Research Concerned with Sociological Preferences

Researcher/Date	Sample	Subject Examined
Perrin, 1984	104 gifted and nongifted, suburban first-and second-graders	Problem solving and word recognition were taught through both individual and peer-group strategies. Learning with the teacher was eliminated as a strategy when not a single gifted child preferred to learn that way.

Findings: Analysis of the mean gain scores revealed that achievement was significantly higher (.05) whenever students were taught through approaches that matched their diagnosed sociological preferences. Although the gifted tended to prefer to learn alone in their heterogeneously grouped classes, a small group of seven gifted, who previously had known each other from participation in a special, part-time program for the gifted, actually performed best when learning in isolation with other gifted children.

Source: Adapted by permission from "Survey of Research on Learning Styles" by R. Dunn, J. S. Beaudry, and A. Klavas, March 1989, *Educational Leadership, 46*(6), p. 54. Copyright © 1989 by the Association for Supervision and Curriculum Development.

Some students learn most effectively with one partner, whereas others are most productive in teams of three, four, or five. (Photograph courtesy of West Seneca Central School District, New York.)

(Clark-Thayer, 1987, 1988; Dunn, Deckinger, Withers, & Katzenstein, 1990; Griggs, 1991; Nelson, 1991; Mickler & Zippert, 1987).

Beginning Steps for Practitioners

It is easy for teachers to post an assignment with specific objectives and/or tasks and say to the entire class: "You may work on this alone, in a pair, in a team of three, or with me. If you wish to work alone, sit wherever you will be comfortable in the room. If you wish to work in a pair, take a moment to decide where you want to work, but allow privacy to classmates who need to be by themselves." After a momentary pause, students who want to work cooperatively may move together quietly. Then those who wish to work directly with the teacher or with an aide may move to a specifically designated area of the room.

We strongly recommend, however, that Team Learning and Circle of Knowledge—specific small-group strategies to *introduce* and to *reinforce* difficult information—should become an integral part of the class's repertoire *prior* to permitting many sociological choices. Those strategies enable students to work efficiently with a tape recorder and printed illustrated materials, either alone or in a small group, for a lengthy period. Thus, once youngsters are familiar with these strategies and can function independently with a peer or two, teachers have sufficient time to teach the smaller group while others are engaged in Team Learning or independent study. These small-group instructional strategies, as well as others, can be found in Chapter 5.

What Do We Know about Triggering Concentration and Increasing Retention through Perceptual Strengths?

When students were *introduced* to new material through their perceptual preferences, they remembered significantly more than when they were introduced through their least preferred modality. That was true for primary (Carbo, 1980; Urbschat, 1977; Wheeler, 1980, 1983), elementary (Hill, 1987; Weinberg, 1983), *and* secondary (Garrett, 1991, Kroon, 1985; Martini, 1986) students. It was true for adults (Ingham, 1989).* Furthermore, when new material was reinforced through students' secondary or tertiary preferences, they achieved significantly more than when materials merely were introduced correctly—an additional .05 (Kroon, 1985) (see Table 1–3).

Considering that most primary children are not auditory (they rarely remember at least three-quarters of what they hear in a normal 40- or 50-minute period), lectures, discussions, and talking are the *least* effective way of teaching. Few teachers, however, know how to *introduce* difficult new material tactually or kinesthetically—the sensory preferences of most young or underachieving students. Easy-to-make tac-

---

*It is important to note that the Carbo (1980), Ingham (1989) and Martini (1986) studies won national awards for best research during the year each was published. Each demonstrated that statistically higher test scores occurred when students were introduced to new and difficult academic information *initially* through their perceptual preferences—rather than through a less-preferred modality.

Only 10 to 12 percent of primary school students remember approximately 75 percent of what they hear during a 40- to 50-minute period; those who do are called auditory learners. (Photograph courtesy of the West Seneca Central School District, New York.)

tual resources are described in Chapter 6 and should be used *before* discussing new content.

Using all four modalities in sequence does not ensure that each youngster is *introduced* to difficult material correctly (through his or her perceptual strength or preference); nor does it ensure that each will be *reinforced* correctly—and that is what caused the gains in achievement and/or retention in the studies cited here.

Young children or underachievers are almost exclusively tactual/kinesthetic learners (Crino, 1984; LeClair, 1986; Keefe, 1982; Price, 1980). Teaching them new and difficult information auditorially at the onset almost ensures confusion and/or difficulty for many. If their auditory skills are to be developed, we must *reinforce* in that way and patiently wait for the day when, as usually happens, their modalities mature and they are "ready" to learn in our way. Meanwhile, they absorb and understand only a small percentage of what we say. As a general guideline, it is better to teach underachievers tactually and experientially first and then to speak in order to emphasize and reinforce.

Underachieving, at-risk, and dropout students almost exclusively are tactual/kinesthetic learners; when they have auditory preferences, they usually are only tactual/kinesthetic/auditory—lacking the visual, aspect which often is a typical learning-disabled profile. Students with learning disabilities often are tactual/kines-

TABLE 1–3 Experimental Research on Perceptual Learning Styles

Researcher and Date	Sample	Subject Examined	Perceptual Preference Examined	Significant Achievement
Bauer (1991)	Learning-disabled and emotionally handicapped junior high school underachievers	Mathematics	Auditory, visual, tactual	+
Buell & Buell (1987)	Adults	Continuing education	Auditory, visual, tactual	+
Carbo (1980)	Kindergartners	Vocabulary	Auditory, visual, "other" (tactual)	+
Garrett (1992)	9th-, 10th-, 11th-, 12-graders	Vocabulary	Auditory, visual, tactual	+
Ingham (1989)	Adults	Driver safety	Auditory/visual, tactual/visual	+
Jarsonbeck (1984)	4th-grade underachievers	Mathematics	Auditory, visual, tactual	+
Kroon (1985)	9th-, and 10th-graders	Industrial arts	Auditory, visual, tactual, sequenced	+
Martini (1986)	7th-graders	Science	Auditory, visual, tactual	+
Urbschat (1977)	1st-graders	CVC trigram recall	Auditory, visual	+
Weinberg (1983)	3rd-grade underachievers	Mathematics	Auditory, visual, tactual	+
Wheeler (1980)	Learning-disabled 2nd-graders	Reading	Auditory, visual, tactual sequenced	+
Wheeler (1983)	Learning-disabled 2nd-graders	Reading	Auditory, visual, tactual	+

Source: Adapted by permission from "Survey of Research on Learning Styles" by R. Dunn, J. S. Beaudry, and A. Klavas, March 1989, *Educational Leadership, 46*(6), p. 52. Copyright © 1989 by the Association for Supervision and Curriculum Development.
Note: + represents significant positive findings.

thetic or tactual/auditory, but it is easier for them to learn tactually than in other ways. Introducing them to new material with Flip Chutes, Pic-A-Holes, Multipart Task Cards, and/or Electroboards (see Chapter 6), and then reinforcing with auditory and visual supplements, is likely to help them achieve almost on grade level and in approximately the same amount of time that most average achievers require.

A system for introducing each student to new material through his or her perceptual strengths and reinforcing through his or her secondary or tertiary modality is available (see Chapters 6 and 11), is easy to use, costs little or nothing, and does not require repetition through various forms or whole-class instruction provided at different times in four different ways.

Most young children learn by manipulating objects such as Flip Chutes, Electroboards, multipart Task Cards, and Pic-A-Holes (see Chapter 6). (Photograph courtesy of the Center for the Study of Learning and Teaching Styles, St. John's University, New York.)

Beginning Steps for Practitioners

Identify students' primary perceptual preferences with the Learning Style Inventory: Primary and use the sequence for introducing new material through individuals' strengths and reinforcing through their secondary and tertiary modalities whenever you teach by talking or discussing (see Chapter 11). *Before* you lecture, introduce tactual students to the new content tactually—with Electroboards, Flip Chutes, Pic-A-Holes, Multipart Task Cards, and so on, as described in Chapter 6. If you need help remembering which youngster needs what, obtain or design your own Homework Charts, available from St. John's University's Center for the Study of Learning and Teaching Styles (see Chapter 12). Use Programmed Learning Sequences to *reinforce* for essentially tactual children. Tape record the printed material for poor or slow readers (see Chapter 7).

What Do We Know about Time-of-Day Preferences?

Task efficiency is related to each person's temperature cycle (Biggers, 1980); thus, it is related to *when* each student is likely to learn best. For example, junior high school math underachievers became more motivated, were better disciplined, and produced a trend toward statistically increased achievement when they were assigned to afternoon math classes that matched their chronobiological time preferences—*after* they had failed during their energy lows (Carruthers & Young, 1980). One year later,

*Other resources that trigger the concentra-
tion of tactual children include writing, manipulative games, and puzzles. (Photograph
courtesy of Brightwood Elementary School,
Greensboro, North Carolina.)*

Lynch (1981) reported that time preference was a crucial factor in the reversal of
chronic initial truancy patterns among secondary students.

Later, the matching of elementary students' time preferences and instructional
schedules resulted in significant achievement gains (.001) in both reading and math
(Dunn, Dunn, Primavera, Sinatra, & Virostko, 1987). The following year, teachers'
time preferences were identified and inservice sessions were conducted in both
matched and mismatched sessions (Freeley, 1984). Interestingly, teachers implemented innovative instructional techniques significantly more often (.01) when they
were instructed at their preferred times. Then Lemmon (1985) administered the Iowa
Basic Skills Achievement Tests in reading and math to elementary school students
whose time preferences matched their test schedule—either morning or afternoon.
She reported significantly higher test gains in both subjects compared with each
youngster's previous three years' growth as measured by the same test.

Most students are *not* alert early in the morning. Primary school children experience their strongest energy highs between 10:00 A.M. and 2:00 P.M.: Only approximately 28 percent are "morning" people (Price, 1980). Approximately one-third of
junior high schoolers are alert in the early morning when academics are accented,
but, again, the majority first "come alive" after 10:00 A.M. In high school, almost 40
percent are "early birds"; a majority, however, continue to be late morning/afternoon
preferents, and, for the first time since infancy, 13 percent are "night owls" (Price,
1980). There are exceptions to these data, but test *your* pupils to determine their individual style patterns.

The largest group of primary students is made up of kinesthetic *learners, those who learn most effectively through movement and real-life involvement. These youngsters re-member best when they are* actively *rather than passively involved. Teacher Marie La Bianca developed a Floor Game similar to Twister to teach second-graders Danielle Maurina, Amanda Kama, and Danielle Nunziata subtraction facts. The left and right foot must touch a subtraction example and its* correct, *matched answer. (Photograph courtesy of Otsego Elementary School, Half Hollow Hills, New York.)*

Beginning Steps for Practitioners

Advise students to do all their studying during their energy highs at their best time of day. Offer demanding subject material at varied times of the school day, and assign underachieving, at-risk, and dropout students to their most important subjects when they are most alert. Time is one of the more crucial elements of learning style and demands attention, particularly for potential underachievers (Gardiner, 1986; Gadwa & Griggs, 1985, Dunn & Griggs, 1988; Johnson, 1984; Thrasher, 1984), for whom learning at their energy high increases achievement.

What Do We Know about Restlessness and Hyperactivity?

Most students referred to psychologists are not clinically hyperactive. Often, they are normal youngsters in need of mobility (Fadler & Hosler, 1979). In addition, the less interested the children are in what is being taught, the more mobility they need. A disquieting point is that such youngsters are "almost always boys" (p. 219).

The seated students are spelling words aloud and, simultaneously, moving the ball from one to the other. The word must be spelled correctly before the ball rotates through the circle twice—or the next child has a chance to "Spell and Score"! (Photograph courtesy of the West Seneca Central School District, West Seneca, New York.)

Restak (1979) substantiated that "over 95 percent of hyperactives are males" (p. 230) and that the very same characteristic, when observed in girls, is correlated with academic *achievement*. He deplored the fact that boys are required to be passive in school and are rejected for aggressive behaviors there, but are encouraged to engage in typical male aggressions in the world at large—a situation that Restak suggested might lead to role conflict. He added that conventional classroom environments do not provide male students with sufficient outlet for their normal movement needs and warned that schools actually cause conflict with societal expectations that boys not be timid, passive, or conforming.

Tingley-Michaelis (1983) corroborated Restak's warnings and affirmed that boys labeled "hyperactive" in school often were fidgety because their teachers provided experiences for them "to think about something" when what they needed was "to do something" (p. 26). Tingley-Michaelis also chastised educators for believing that activities prevented—rather than enhanced—learning!

When researchers began equating hyperactivity with students' normal need for mobility, they experimented with providing many opportunities for learning while engaged in movement. Reports then began to document that, when previously restless youngsters were reassigned to classes that did not require passivity, their behav-

Leslie and Sara prefer to learn addition facts by using a Floor Number Line.
This kinesthetic game requires that they progress through the continuum by add-
ing an agreed-on given amount to each number they walk on in sequence—for
example, 7 and 8, 7 and 9, 7 and 10—and then the correct answer. (Photograph
courtesy of Sharon Barton, Lee Elementary School, Corsicana, Texas.)

iors were rarely noticed (Fadley & Hosler, 1979; Koester & Farley, 1977). Eventually, teachers began indicating that, although certain students thrived in an activity-oriented environment that permitted mobility, others remained almost exclusively in the same area, despite frequent attempts to coax them to move (Hodges, 1985; Miller, 1985). That supported Fitt's (1975) conclusions that no amount of persuasion would increase selected students' interest in movement, whereas others found it impossible to remain seated passively for extended periods. "These are cases of a child's style . . . governing his interactions with and within the environment" (p. 94).

Add to all that the knowledge that almost 40 percent of youngsters require informal seating while concentrating, and it is not difficult to understand why so many—particularly boys—squirm, sit on their ankles and calves, extend their feet into the aisles, squirrel down into their seats, and occasionally fall off their chairs.

DellaValle (1984), in research that won three national awards, documented that almost 50 percent of students in a large, urban junior high school could not sit still for any appreciable amount of time. Twenty-five percent could remain immobile if they were interested in the lesson, and the remaining 25 percent preferred passivity. Della-Valle clearly demonstrated the importance of the mobility/passivity dimension of learning style. When students' preferences and their environment were matched, they achieved significantly higher test scores (.001) than when they were mismatched.

Students who required mobility moved from one part of the room to another in order to master all the information in the lesson and performed better than when they sat for the entire period. On the other hand, students who disliked moving performed worse when required to learn while walking and significantly better when permitted to sit quietly and read. Table 1–4 reports the post hoc analysis used to determine exactly where the interaction occurred. This analysis was conducted after the initial repeated measures design indicated a significant interaction at the .001 level.

Beginning Steps for Practitioners

Establish varied areas in the classroom so that mobility-preferenced youngsters who complete one task may move to another section to work on the next. See Chapter 3 for easy-to-follow guidelines for redesigning a conventional classroom so that it responds to multiple learning style characteristics.

Whenever possible, incorporate kinesthetic activities into each lesson so that, while demonstrating points, acting, role playing, brainstorming, interviewing (whether simulated or real), or observing phenomena, students may move. Permit those who can be trusted to behave *and* who require mobility (as revealed through their behavior and/or the LSI) to move to the varied areas you have established in the classroom. Some may need only the space available in their own "office" or "den"; others may require movement to one classroom area (such as a Library Corner, an Interest Center, a Media Section, or a sectioned-off space near the door in a hall). One or two responsible students might be permitted to work in the corridor immediately outside the classroom under the supervision of a volunteer parent, older student, or aide. Children become increasingly trustworthy when they see that you recognize their needs and know that they will lose a privilege if they abuse it. Many difficult-to-contain youngsters are precisely those who cannot sit still and thus require opportunities to stretch (Dunn, Della Valle, Dunn, Geisert, Sinatra, & Zenhausern, 1986; Miller, 1985).

In addition, do not forget to experiment with some form of independent study such as Programmed Learning Sequences (see Chapter 7) or Contract Activity Pack-

TABLE 1–4 Analysis of Preference × Environment Interaction

	Means	
	Passive b₁	*Active b₂*
Passive a₂	8.70	5.45
Active a₂	7.15	9.10

Source: Adapted by permission form "Survey of Research on Learning Styles" by R. Dunn, J. S. Beaudry, and A. Klavas, March 1989, *Educational Leadership, 46*(6), p. 51. Copyright © 1989 by the Association for Supervision and Curriculum Development.
Note: a = preference; b = environment.

ages (see Chapter 8) that allow students to move as they concentrate without disturbing others. Finally, be certain to experiment with small-group techniques such as Team Learning for *introducing* new and difficult material and Circle of Knowledge for *reinforcing* it (see Chapter 5). Peer-oriented learners who need mobility will function well with these instructional strategies because of their responsiveness to both the sociological and physiological characteristics.

What Are Some Important Ramifications of Style?

Both Restak (1979) and Thies (1979) ascertained that three-fifths of learning style is genetic; the remainder, apart from persistence, develops through experience. Individual responses to sound, light, temperature, seating arrangements, perceptual strengths, intake, time of day, and mobility are biological, whereas sociological preferences, motivation, responsibility (which correlates with conformity), and structure versus need for providing self-direction are thought to be developmental. The significant differences among the learning styles of students in diverse cultures tend to support this theory (Dunn, 1989; Gemake, Jalali, & Zenhausern, 1990; Dunn, Gemake, Jalali, Zenhausern, Quinn, & Spiridakis, 1990; Dunn & Griggs, 1990; Guzzo, 1987; Jacobs, 1987; Jalali, 1988; Lam-Phoon, 1986; Mariash, 1983; Roberts, 1984; Sims, 1988; Vasquez, 1985).

Persistence is one variable over which there is disagreement concerning its origin—whether it is biological or developmental. Analytics tend to be more persistent than globals; globals tend to concentrate on difficult academic studies for relatively short periods of time, need frequent breaks, and work on several different tasks simultaneously. Once strongly analytic students *begin* a task, they appear to have an emotional need to complete it.

Within any culture, socioeconomic stratum, or classroom there are many within-group differences. Indeed, within one family, some members may be analytic and others global—each with many of the learning style traits that tend to correlate with one processing style or the other.

Every person has a learning style pattern and every person has learning-style strengths. People tend to learn more when taught with their *own* strengths than when taught with the teacher's strengths (Buell & Buell, 1987; Cafferty, 1980).

No learning style pattern is better or worse than another. Each style encompasses similar intelligence ranges. Students tend to learn and remember better and to enjoy learning more when they are taught through their learning style preferences. There must be more than fifty studies that document that statement (see Annotated Bibliography, 1993.

Beginning Steps for Practitioners
Ask the teachers and administrators in your building or district to take the Productivity Environmental Preference Survey (Dunn, Dunn, & Price) (see Appendix A) to identify their learning styles. Compare your style and the learning style of the teacher

you like best—and least—or wish most or least to emulate. Notice where the two individual printouts differ.

Decide to learn a little more about learning style. Administer the appropriate test to those children about whom you are most concerned. Examine their styles. Discuss their individual printouts with them. Ask questions about how they believe their styles have affected their attitudes toward school and why. If possible, visit a learning styles school (Andrews, 1990; DellaValle, 1990; Dunn & Griggs, 1988, 1989a, 1989b, 1989c, 1989d, 1989e; Orsak, 1990; Sinatra, 1990).

Next, decide which students are of most concern to you. If you are *visual,* read the chapters in this book that help you work with the styles of those youngsters. For example, if you want to attend first to bright, high-achieving children and enhance their ability to teach themselves more rapidly than could occur in a heterogeneous class, read Chapters 1, 2, 8, 3, 4, 6, 7, 5, 9, 11, and 10 in that order, and you will be able to help those little ones. However, if you are more concerned with an at-risk and potentially dropout population, read Chapters 1, 2, 3, 6, 5, 8, 7, 9, 10, and 11 in that order. If you are global or nonconforming, pay no attention to *our* sequence; we know you will design your own! If you prefer a structure for learning and can identify a specific type of student you wish to help, you probably will adhere to our suggested pattern (see Table 1–5). It does not matter where you start and how you proceed; what is important is that you *do* start and experiment with the suggestions so that you can determine for yourself whether, in fact, students achieve higher test scores when they are taught through their styles than when they are not.

If you are *not* a visual learner, examine Chapter 11's resources and purchase one of the Teacher Inservice Packages (TIPs) available for learning tactually or auditorially. You will learn kinesthetically as you begin to implement the methods you choose. Study in an environment that complements *your* style for sound, light, tem-

TABLE 1–5 A Guide to Reading This Book for Visual Learners

Students with Whom You are Concerned	Chapters to Read in Indicated Sequence										
	One	*Two*	*Three*	*Four*	*Five*	*Six*	*Seven*	*Eight*	*Nine*	*Ten*	*Eleven*
Slow learners	1	2	3	6	4	7	8	—	5	9	10
Gifted but underachieving learners	1	2	7	4	5	10	9	3	6	8	11
Fidgety children who do not concentrate	1	2	3	10	5	4	7	6	8	9	11
Dropouts and the turned-off	1	2	5	3	4	6	8	—	9	7	10
Behavior problems	1	2	4	9	3	5	6	8	7	10	11
Bright, achieving learners	1	2	4	5	8	6	7	3	9	11	10
All	1	2	3	4	5	6	7	8	9	10	11

perature, and design. Examine your sociological preference and decide to work either by yourself, with a friend or colleague (or two), or with an authority—another teacher, an administrator, a college professor.

If you have no strong primary perceptual preference, you can use this book *if you are motivated;* if not, you are likely to learn better with one of the videotapes described in Chapter 11 or through an on-site visit.

Figure 1–5 may be a good guide for involving you in learning styles–based instruction. Once you decide with which children you are most concerned, find that group on the figure and then follow the itemized chapter sequence.

Meanwhile, if you want to begin *tomorrow* and have little time to read and absorb today, experiment with those of the following suggestions *that most appeal to you.* Almost any effort to complement students' learning styles produces positive effects. Try—and encourage your colleagues to experiment with—one or more of the following suggestions. Look for improvements in students' behaviors, attitudes, and test scores.

- Tell them what is "important." As you mention items you want students to remember, use verbal clues: "Make note of this!" "Write this down!" "This is important!" "This could be on your test!" It provides STRUCTURE for those who need it.
- When you mention important items, walk to the chalkboard and, in big print, write a word or two that synthesizes that content so that *visual* learners can see it and others can copy it onto their papers.
- When you write on the chalkboard, illustrate important information. Stick figures are fine. If you can't draw, ask students to do it for you. Encourage *global* students to illustrate their notes. *Visual Left* processors seem to respond to words and numbers; *Visual Rights* pay attention to drawings, symbols, and spatial designs. *Global rights* often are strongly *tactual;* they are the doodlers who pay attention better if they use their hands while they are listening. Use colored chalk on blackboards or colored pens on overhead transparencies for global learners.
- Give strongly *visual* children a short assignment to read to introduce new and difficult material. Then they should listen to you speak or participate in a discussion of the topic. Strongly *auditory* students should hear your explanation first and then read materials that will reinforce it. Visual children should copy notes while they listen; auditory learners should copy notes while they read.
- When working with youngsters who read poorly, read in natural daylight. If necessary, turn off the classroom lights or darken a section of the room. Low light relaxes and permits better concentration for 8 out of 10 children who do not read well.
- Write a three- or four-word illustrated outline of the lesson on the chalkboard at the beginning of each period. That overview helps the *visual* learner who cannot focus well to keep track of the lesson's emphasis. From time to time, draw attention to the outline and say, "Now we're moving into this part of the topic."

- Laminate 30 or 40 numbered, colored footprints and 6 or 8 handprints. With masking tape folded against itself to provide two sticky surfaces, place the prints into a Twister Game pattern in a less busy part of the classroom, so that walking on it in sequence requires body contortions. When youngsters with short attention spans lose interest in a task they should be doing, give them a chance, one at a time, to "walk the footprints." *Kinesthetic* youngsters, or those in need of *mobility*, will benefit greatly. After just one minute, they will be able to return to their seats and concentrate for another ten minutes or more. These kinesthetic prints can be designed to incorporate educational games, as well.
- Encourage highly *kinesthetic* children to walk back and forth while they read their assignments. Somehow, the movement helps them understand better.
- Encourage youngsters to study at their best time of day, either early in the morning *before* they leave for school, during lunch or free periods, immediately after school, or in the evening before they go to bed.
- Permit children who need *intake* while they are concentrating to bring raw vegetables to school. Establish firm rules: They cannot make noise while eating (you need quiet!); no leftovers should remain in the class the custodian must never know what you are permitting; what is not wanted must be placed into waste baskets; and they must get better test grades than they ever have before (otherwise it's not helping!)
- Begin reading this book tomorrow, if you can't possibly begin today! Experiment with the suggestions made in each of the chapters you read!

2

Identifying the Learning Style Characteristics of Young Children

Why Use an Identification Instrument?

Every child can learn—but not the same way as every other child. If young children are to feel and be successful in school, it is important that they understand their own uniqueness and how to capitalize on their personal strengths. It is equally important that teachers correctly identify and then accommodate their pupils' unique learning style characteristics. The extensive research on learning style verifies that students describe their learning style preferences accurately when they are assessed with a comprehensive and valid instrument (see Appendix A).

The Learning Style Inventory: Primary (LSI:P) is a valid, reliable, simple to use, hand-scorable questionnaire that assesses the learning style preferences of young children. This inventory consists of twelve charts, each containing pictures and a series of questions to determine students' environmental (sound, light, temperature, and design); emotional (persistence, responsibility, structure versus alternatives, and motivation); sociological (working with an adult, alone, or with peers); and physiological (visual, auditory, tactual, or kinesthetic perceptual strengths, intake, time of day, and mobility) preferences. After you have administered and scored the LSI:P, an Individual Learning Style Profile is generated for each child. When completed, this information, combined with observations and experimentation, permits the designing of an instructional program based on the characteristics of every child—a program in which many children learn how to teach themselves and each other!

Research Conducted with the Learning Style Inventory: Primary

The LSI:P has been used in many studies that have revealed that students can achieve significantly more when their learning style preferences are matched than when they are mismatched to appropriate resources and strategies. The learning style character- istics of children can be observed, but observation alone is limited and often incorrect (Beaty, 1986; Dunn, Dunn, & Price, 1977; Marcus 1977). Although students with learning disabilities and identified gifted children differ from their counterparts in selected variables, learning style preferences remain consistent over a two- to three- year period (Copenhaver, 1979; Miles, 1987; Virostko, 1983). It is important to retest primary children every two or three years, for that is the period during which their perceptual strengths are most likely to mature (Crino, 1984; LeClair, 1986).

Achievement of Nongifted Children

Spires (1983) reported that, as a result of administering the Learning Style Inventory in grades 3 through 6 and the LSI:P in kindergarten through grade 2 and then imple- menting a learning styles instructional program, significant gains in both reading and math resulted at all levels.

Miller (1985) identified second-graders' learning styles with the LSI:P. She then administered two comparable forms of the Gates–MacGinities Reading Test. During the first administration, she did not permit the students to move about; during the second administration the students were permitted mobility. For the youngsters who needed mobility, results revealed significantly higher scores (.05) when they were permitted to move while concentrating than when they were required to remain passive.

Damian (1988) developed instructional strategies to accommodate the socio- logical preferences of her third-graders as identified by the LSI:P. She then taught three units of vocabulary words, matching and mismatching her students' preferences with three varied formats—one corresponding to self-instruction, another to cooper- ative learning, and the third to teacher-directed instruction. Analyses of the students' mean pretest–posttest score growth revealed that achievement was significantly higher when the youngsters's preferred style was accommodated.

Fox (1989) investigated the relationship of first-graders' expressed motiva- tional and perceptual preferences and their achievement on math concepts of subtrac- tion after instruction through: (1) computer assistance, (2) cooperative learning, (3) direct teacher instruction, and (4) manipulatives. Results indicated that children whose motivational sources and perceptual preferences were accommodated through complementary instructional resources and strategies achieved higher posttest scores than those whose learning styles were not accommodated.

Achievement of Gifted Children

Perrin (1984) administered the sociological subtest of the LSI:P to 140 first- and sec- ond-grade students, 30 of whom had been identified as gifted. Not one gifted child chose to work with adults as a preferred learning style, but Perrin reported that many nongifted children preferred learning directly with an adult. She then taught each student problem solving and word recognition through both individual and peer group strategies. Analysis of the mean gain scores revealed that achievement was significantly higher (.05) and attitudes were significantly more positive (.05) whenever students were taught through approaches that matched their diagnosed sociological preferences.

Although the gifted tended to prefer to learn alone in their heterogeneously grouped classes and, indeed, performed significantly better that way, a small group of seven gifted children actually performed best when learning in isolation with other gifted children! Thus, when instruction was matched with students' individual sociological preferences, they achieved significantly better than when it was not matched—with the sole exception of the group of seven gifted youngsters who learned very well alone but equally well with their intellectual peers.

Correlational Research

LeClair (1986) corroborated Perrin's (1983) findings concerning the preferred perceptual modalities of young children. She assessed 80 kindergartners'; Perrin reported on 75 first-graders. The preferred modalities of both samples, in descending order, were first tactual, followed by visual and kinesthetic co-preferenced, and finally by auditory. LeClair also reported that girls preferred tactual learning more than boys, whereas boys preferred kinesthetic learning more than girls.

Lockwood (1987) obtained parallel results when she administered the LSI:P to 50 youngsters with learning disabilities (LD) and 50 without learning disabilities (non-LD) in kindergarten through grade 2. She analyzed the styles of the two groups and reported that those classified as LD differed significantly from their counterparts in four ways. They were less conforming, they were less persistent, they required less mobility, and they preferred to learn directly with adults more often, whereas the non-LD youngsters preferred learning alone and/or with peers.

Coleman (1988) also reported no evidenced similarities between gifted and nongifted first-graders on their sociological preference responses to the LSI:P. That research indicated, however, that preferences for intake, time of day, motivation, and responsibility and persistence were similar for both groups of students but that the nongifted required more mobility and structure and had fewer perceptual strengths.

Comparisons of Teachers' Observations and Instrumentation Data

Emery (1990) observed and recorded on a teacher observation checklist various learning style behaviors of 40 kindergartners. She then administered the LSI:P to the same youngsters to determine the correlations between teacher observation of learning style and students' expressed preferences on the instrument. She found, on average, that 33 of the possible 40 student responses to each element tested on the LSI:P also were observed marginally by the teacher. She indicated that the use of the LSI:P positively involved the youngsters in the process of identifying their learning style preferences and yielded approximately 83 percent more accurate data than through observation alone. Beaty (1986) revealed essentially similar findings with the Learning Style Inventory (LSI) (Dunn, Dunn, & Price).

Those findings parallel those of an earlier study by Crino (1984), who determined degrees of consistency between observations of 50 kindergarten children's behaviors and their responses to the LSI:P. As stated by the author, however, valid observations were difficult during the seven-month time span because the kindergarten classroom instruction was essentially teacher-dominated, with few allowances for student choices. The researcher concluded that kindergarten curriculum planning should reflect the learning style preferences of the students.

Observing Learning Style Preferences

Early childhood teachers' understanding of the developmental stages of young children often tempts them to make decisions about youngsters' learning style characteristics solely on the basis of observation. But observation alone may be inaccurate or may yield insufficient information to permit correct accommodations to individual strengths (Beaty, 1986; Crino, 1984; Dunn, Dunn, & Price, 1977; Emery, 1990; Marcus, 1977a). To illustrate that point, examine the following scenario.

It is important to prepare *students for answering the* Learning Style Inventory: Primary. *Teacher Marguerite Ballow first explains what "learning style" means and then reads* Elephant Style *to the entire class. Afterward, the children dramatize the story and discuss the ways in which they are similar to and different from each other. (Photograph courtesy Sheridan Hill Elementary School, Williamsville, New York.)*

Peter, a first-grade student, was sitting in his usual position, his back to the window and his legs sprawled in the aisle. "Peter," said Ms. Johnson, "I've asked so many times before, please don't sit that way at your desk. Someone will trip over your feet. Face the front of the room."

Ms. Johnson continued the vocabulary lesson. "Who wants to write the missing word on the blackboard?" she asked. "I do! I do!" Peter called out as he wildly waved his arm and leaped from his seat. He was halfway down the aisle when Ms. Johnson reminded him that he had to wait to be called on when he raised his hand. "Now the whole class will have to wait while you go back to your desk and sit up straight," she said.

Peter frowned, shuffled back to his desk, and slouched in his chair. He immediately started to poke his fingers in and out of the spiral binding on his notebook, counting the number of spirals two by two. He was so involved with this activity that he did not notice Ms. Johnson standing next to him.

"Peter," she chided, "repeat the answer that Amy just gave." Peter's face reddened. "Uh, I don't know." "You don't know because you weren't listening. Please pay attention." Peter raised his hand. "Yes, Peter, do you know the next answer?" He responded, "Ms. Johnson, may I have my snack now?" "Peter, please, we're in the middle of a lesson! Try to pay attention!"

Later that morning, Ms. Johnson observed Peter standing at the math table with Mark. They were absorbed in working out addition computation with the abacus. She wondered why Peter seldom became as involved during formal lessons with the class. In fact, Peter frowned when Ms. Johnson asked the children to return to their desks and take out their reading workbooks. Before the teacher finished reading the directions for the last page, Peter was at her side asking, "What do I do on this page?" "Peter, I just read the directions for that page. You weren't listening again!"

Unaware of the impact of learning styles on an individual's ability to concentrate, Ms. Johnson might describe Peter this way:

Peter seldom pays attention while I am teaching. He is off-task much more often than on. The only time he seems to concentrate is when he is at the Math Learning Center. He is hyperactive—constantly up and out of his seat. When he does sit—which is seldom—he sprawls. I often have to repeat directions for him, and then I usually have to go to his desk and show him what to do. I'm concerned that he has either an attention-deficit disorder or an auditory-processing disability. I am recommending him for testing.

With a knowledge of learning styles, and based on her observations prior to testing with the LSI:P, Ms. Johnson might describe Peter this way:

Peter needs an informal design; he works well when paired with another student and when working one on one with an adult. He is motivated and persistent in some areas but requires a great deal of structure in others. He does not learn well auditorially but has tactual strengths. He requires both intake and frequent mobility.

Only *after* Ms. Johnson assesses Peter's learning style characteristics will she be able to accommodate his strengths. Her observations were, indeed, accurate in

Name: **PETER**   Grade: **1**   Teacher: **Ms Johnson**   Date: **10/90**

SOUND

Not Acceptable	1	1	1	1		3/5
Acceptable	2	2	2	2	2	2/5

LIGHT

Low	1	1	1	1	1	4/5
Bright	2	2	2	2	2	1/5

TEMPERATURE

Cool	1	1	1	1	1	3/5
Warm	2	2	2	2	2	2/5

DESIGN

Formal	1	1	1	1	1	4/5
Informal	2	2	2	2	2	1/5

MOTIVATION

Teacher		1			1		1	3/3
Adult			2	2			2	1/3
Self	3					3	3	2/3
Unmotivated	4	4	4	4	4	4	4	0/7

RESPONSIBILITY & PERSISTENCE

Is not	1	1	1	1	1	1/5
Is	2	2	2	2	2	4/5

STRUCTURE

Needs	1	1	1	1	1	4/5
Needs little	2	2	2	2	2	1/5

SOCIOLOGICAL

Alone	1	1			1	1	1	4/5
Adult		2	2	2	2		2	0/5
Peers	3		3	3		3	3	1/5

PERCEPTION

Tactual		1		1		1	1	1	5/5
Auditory	2		2	2	2			2	0/5
Visual	3	3	3	3				3	2/5
Kinesthetic		4		4	4	4	4		2/5

INTAKE

Does not require	1	1	1	1	1	0/5
Requires	2	2	2	2	2	5/5

TIME

Morning	1		1	1	1	3/4
Afternoon	2	2		2	2	2/4
Evening		3	3	3	3	0/4

MOBILITY

Does not require	1	1	1	1	1	1/5
Requires	2	2	2	2	2	4/5

COMMENTS:

FIGURE 2–1 Student Profile—Learning Style Inventory: Primary

some areas, but some aspects of style are not observable even to the experienced eye, and behaviors associated with other aspects often are misinterpreted.

While interviewing Peter with the LSI:P, Ms. Johnson learned that he needed low light in addition to an informal design. After she moved his desk away from the window to a softly lit area of the classroom, Peter was able to accomplish some tasks while seated for 15- to 25-minute periods. For the remainder of the day, he worked on the floor in a small carpeted area of the room. There, when he was relaxed, his "hyperactivity" was reduced dramatically and he worked without frequent interruption.

Ms. Johnson also discovered that Peter preferred to work alone rather than with an adult. Previously, she always had assigned partners to work with the math manipulatives because of the limited supply. She had never observed Peter working alone with tactual materials. Because of his strong tactual preferences, she provided Peter with Electroboards, Flip Chutes, and Task Cards to use in subjects other than math; she also taught him how to create his own. She was pleased when she noticed how those resources helped Peter to stay on task for longer periods of time.

Peter's LSI:P Profile (see Figure 2–1) confirmed his high need for structure, but Ms. Johnson was surprised to learn that he also was highly teacher-motivated. She began to check on him while he was working, called him to the chalkboard to illustrate directions for the class, gave him short-term activities to complete, and corrected them as soon as time permitted.

Her observations of Peter's need for mobility and intake also were confirmed by his profile. Ms. Johnson now provides a *bottomless* bowl of air-popped popcorn with small serving cups. Peter and other students who need intake now can help themselves whenever they choose as long as they do not disturb their classmates, can complete their tasks, and perform better than previously on their tests.

Ms. Johnson reviewed Peter's LSI:P Profile with him, his parents, and his art and physical education teachers. Peter kept a copy of the Profile taped in the front of his notebook and often referred to it during the day. He also referred to the Class Profile displayed on the bulletin board, which illustrated the environmental, sociological, and physiological learning style strengths of all the children in the class (see Figure 2–2).

Generating Peter's Learning Style Profile from his responses to the LSI:P, combined with Ms. Johnson's observations and classroom experimentation, all contributed to providing a blueprint for an instructional program in which Peter could succeed.

Preparing Students for the Learning Style Inventory: Primary

Before administering the LSI:P, it is important that the children understand the following:

1. What learning style is and how it helps individuals concentrate on, absorb, and retain new and difficult information

STUDENTS	WHO	WHERE	HOW
Matt	Alone	Formal	A-V-T-K
Krista	Peers	—	T-K-V-A
Nicky	—	Informal	K-V-A-T
Amanda	Adult	Informal	T-V-A-K
Liz	Adult	Formal	V-K-T-A
Henry	—	Formal	K-V-A-T
Kevin	Peers	Formal	K-T-V-A
Karen	Alone	Informal	K-V-A-T
Timothy	Adult	Formal	A-K-V-T
Kelly	—	Informal	V-A-K-T
Gary	Alone	—	K-V-A-T
Julie	—	—	T-K-V-A
Tom	Peer	Formal	K-T-A-V

The teacher and children together compile the poster-size class profile from the results of the LSI:P individual student profiles. The class profile reflects the WHO (Sociological—Adult, Alone, Peers); the WHERE (Design—Formal, Informal); and the HOW (Perceptual Patterns—Visual, Auditory, Tactual, Kinesthetic). The children often refer to the chart when beginning a task or selecting a resource during the school day.

FIGURE 2–2 Learning Style Inventory: Primary Class Profile—The Way We Learn

2. Why you and they should know their style preferences
3. That you appreciate all styles and that each style is valuable
4. That the Inventory has no *right* or *wrong* answers

Thus, it is important to prepare the students before they answer the LSI:P's questions.

You can explain learning style in your own words or read *Elephant Style* (see Chapter 11) to the entire class. It is a storybook that describes the different ways in which two elephants, who are best friends, learn. The last page of the book encourages children to talk about resources that help them learn in their classroom and describes how people's styles are alike and also different.

A six-month study of the effectiveness of reading *Elephant Style*, prior to an-

Teacher Sharon Barton has first-graders Melodi and Jonathan play a classification game with Ellie and Fonte, the two characters in Elephant Style *(Photograph courtesy Lee Elementary School, Corsicana, Texas.)*

swering the questions on the *LSI:P* (Perrin, 1981) revealed that young children often reflected behavioral assumptions imposed on them by their parents and teachers concerning how they should learn in school. After reading *Elephant Style* and discussing the different learning style characteristics of each of the two elephants, Elly and Fonty, the children were able to express their own style preferences accurately. Once the children are aware of their learning styles, read *Kids in Style* (Lenahan, 1991) (see Chapter 11). This second storybook explains the concept of global and analytic thinking to young children. *Kids in Style* describes how different people *see* exactly the same thing but understand it differently. It also can be used as both a coloring book *and* a reader!

Next, propose an experiment. Have students examine the classroom together. Point to the lighter and darker areas, the warmer and cooler sections, places where they can work alone or in small groups, and the conventional desks and chairs as opposed to a section or two where you might place some carpeting or pillows. Ask them to think about whether they might feel better about learning in one place than in another and why they would feel that way. Then allow the children to spend an hour working in an area where they believe they would feel most comfortable. Observe the children as they work in their newly selected places and, after some time, discuss their reactions with them in a group. Emphasize that all the places they chose were good; what is best is whatever makes it easy for each child to concentrate. Repeat the experiment several times over a two-week period. Encourage the children to select a different section, explore a new resource, or work alone instead of with a friend. Always discuss their reactions after each experiment.

Next, display the picture charts from the LSI:P and explain the illustrated differences in style (see Appendix B). Announce that, during the next few weeks, you will use the charts to "interview" (ask questions of) each youngster. Tell them that you are interested in discovering *their learning style preferences* so that you can help each one to learn easily and enjoyably. The best way is to use a large calendar, posted on a bulletin board, to mark an appointment date and time with each child. You need approximately 20 to 30 minutes per student.

Before the first interview, acquaint the entire class with the concept of an inventory. Emphasize that there are no right or wrong answers. As an example, you can conduct an inventory on favorite flavors of ice cream. Start by saying, "Today, we are going to find out which flavor of ice cream most children in our class prefer. Pretend we have only two flavors to choose from—vanilla or chocolate. Both are good, but you must choose which one you prefer or like better. You may choose only one." Record each student's response on a graph on the chalkboard and then tally and discuss the results. Suggest that the children conduct an inventory at home to discover one or two learning style preferences of their parents or siblings. For a homework assignment, have them ask members of their family to answer the following questions:

If you had to concentrate or learn something difficult would you be able to do it better:

- Sitting on a hard chair _____ or a soft chair? _____
- In the morning _____ or in the afternoon _____ or in the evening? _____

The next day, graph the responses of mothers, fathers, sisters, and brothers. Emphasize that all places and times are good for learning; the ideal is wherever or whenever it is easiest for each person to work. Compare the responses of (1) children versus their parents, (2) girls versus boys, and (3) mothers versus fathers. Develop a graph to show comparisons. Be certain the children understand that *all* styles are valuable.

Then use the twelve LSI:P charts (pictures and questions) to conduct a personal interview with each student. During the individual interview process, you will learn more about the children than just their learning style preferences. Young children use this opportunity to talk to you about their interests, learning environment at home, and relationships with other adults and peers. Many teachers have reported that, because they learned so much about their students during the LSI:P interviews, they scheduled additional appointments just to talk with children about a variety of topics.

Administering and Scoring the LSI:P

Reproduce an LSI:P Profile form for each student in your class. Using the twelve illustrated charts, interview each student individually and secure verbal responses to each question. It takes approximately 20 minutes per child to complete all the questions. The LSI:P may be administered during one or several sittings, depending on the pupil's attention span.

As they answer, mark their responses on the profile form by shading the appropriate box. If a student responds, "It doesn't matter to me," or, "Sometimes I do and sometimes I don't," do not record that response. Leave the box unshaded and proceed to the next question.

Afterward, compute a fraction score for each sequence of questions by adding the shaded boxes in that section and using the total number as a numerator. The denominator—the number of questions asked on each chart—is indicated in the last box. Interpret the scores for sound, light, temperature, design, structure, intake, mobility, responsibility, and persistence; the closer the fraction is to 1, the more important that learning style element is to the child. If the fractions are almost evenly—divided for example 2/5 and 3/5—then either alternative is acceptable and this element is not very important to that child. For the elements of time, motivation, sociological, and perception, the fractions usually will be divided. Consider the largest fraction the most important for that element. Do not be concerned when children report that an element is not important to them. No one is affected by *all* elements; most children reveal that somewhere between 6 and 14 have an impact on their learning. Some children are affected by fewer than 6 and some by more than 14.

Responding to Students' Preferences Instructionally

After you have scored and interpreted the LSI:P Profile form for each student, you will have sufficient data to design an instructional program based on each student's unique learning style characteristics. Several chapters in this book explain how to manage a variety of individual resources and programs in a single class.

The following are broadly based instructional prescriptions related to LSI:P responses.

1. Sound
   a. *Not acceptable:* Provide quiet work areas such as carrels; design a section of the classroom for a Magic Carpet or Quiet Garden area where silence is the rule (use rugs, pillows, curtains, stuffed furniture, and other sound absorbers).
   b. *Acceptable:* Establish small-group areas where students may work and talk quietly.
2. Light
   a. *Low:* Establish areas where lights can be dimmed or shades drawn; use curtains, shaded lamps, or fireproof tissue paper over lights or windows to diffuse the illumination. Permit youngsters to use sunglasses or caps with visors.
   b. *Bright:* Provide extra lamps; allow students to work near the windows.
3. Temperature

These two students scored high on their need for sound-while-learning. Their teacher located an old set of headphones and allowed them to listen to baroque background music (without lyrics) while reading. (Photograph courtesy of the Amherst School District, Amherst, New York.)

    a. *Cool:* Permit students to work in the cooler sections of the room (near an open door, next to the windows, if not sunny).

    b. *Warm:* Permit students to work away from the cool sections of the room (the warmest area is usually in the center of the room); allow them to wear sweaters or extra clothing.

4. Design

    a. *Formal:* Provide wooden, steel, or plastic desks and chairs.

    b. *Informal:* Permit students to work in the Magic Carpet area (see "Sound, Not acceptable"); lying on a rug, cushions, or pillows; in a comfortable easy chair; or on a bean bag.

5. Sociological

    a. *Alone:* Permit child to work alone at any time in the classroom environment in which he or she feels comfortable. Place the child away from others; assign Multisensory Instructional Packages, independent Contract Activity Packages, or Programmed Learning Sequences based on perceptual and other strengths.

    b. *Adult:* Provide frequent teacher interaction and direction; place the youngster near the teacher whenever possible or appropriate; assign at-home projects that involve parents or other adults.

    c. *Peers:* Allow students to work in pairs; use small-group activities; encourage peer interaction; provide small-group work areas.

Children who concentrate in a global processing style often seek a dimly lit corner or become comfortable in soft lighting beneath *desks, tables, or chairs. As long as Jason does not distract classmates whose style differs from his, completes his work, and scores as high or higher on tests than previously, his teacher permits him to learn in* his *way. (Photograph courtesy of Otsego Elementary School, Half Hollow Hills, New York.)*

6. Structure
   a. *Needs:* Provide clear, simple objectives; give directions visually (in words and in pictures) and auditorially (repeat if necessary); limit choices; provide immediate feedback, check work while the student is working and/or immediately after; assign one page of work or a project at a time instead of several; establish reasonable time limits; assign Programmed Learning Sequences, Multisensory Instructional Packages, structured Contract Activity Packages, or Song Boards as appropriate.
   b. *Needs little:* Permit choices and options; establish objectives with the child; assign several tasks at one time; permit the student to choose what to do first, next, and so on; establish flexible time limits; assign Contract Activity Packages with several choices of Activity Alternatives.
7. Responsibility and persistence
   a. *Is not:* Provide short assignments; check work often; provide high-interest materials. Explain why what you want the child to do is important to you. Speak collegially rather than authoritatively. Give choices.

Primary youngsters may reveal that they prefer to work alone, in a pair, or in a group of three or four. Some need to work directly with a teacher and others prefer to vary their social groupings from day to day. These children's teachers permit every assignment to be done "alone, in a pair, with a small group of three or four, or near my desk." The last alternative is for youngsters who are very teacher-motivated. The only thing every child is required to do alone is test-taking. Even homework is permissible in their preferred learning style. (Photographs courtesy of Brightwood Elementary School, Greensboro, North Carolina and the West Seneca Central School District, West Seneca, New York).

    b. *Is:* Be specific; permit self-pacing and self-checking; provide feedback as needed; assign Contract Activity Packages with a wide choice of Activity Alternatives.

8. Motivation

    a. *Teacher-motivated:* Allow students to work near the teacher; provide frequent teacher interaction and feedback; assign teacher-made materials; provide encouragement and praise when appropriate, but as often as possible.

    b. *Adult-motivated:* Assign at-home projects that will involve parents if they can help; communicate often with parents regarding the student's progress; permit Multisensory Instructional Packages, Contract Activity Packages, Song Boards, and other resources to be taken home and used there.

    c. *Self-motivated:* Provide a variety of instructional resources; permit student-initiated projects and activities; provide praise and encouragement when needed; permit self-pacing and self-checking; provide Contract Activity Alternatives on a variety of topics.

    d. *Unmotivated:* Establish specific, attainable short-term goals based on ability and level; provide frequent praise and feedback; assign projects and activities based on student interest; keep assignments brief; provide interesting and varied learning resources; assign instructional resources that will provide success.

9. Perception

    a. *Visual:* Provide films, filmstrips, books with pictures; allow children to work in the Media Center and library; encourage visual activities; use visuals (transparencies, chalkboard, charts) while lecturing; emphasize literature, whole word, and language experience approaches to reading. Assign Contract Activity Packages, high-interest Multisensory Instructional Packages, or Programmed Learning Sequences (if structure is needed).

    b. *Auditory:* Provide tapes, records, tape-recorded books; allow children to work in the Media Center; permit tape-recorded book reports; use discussion and lecture methods; emphasize phonics and linguistic reading approaches; assign Contract Activity Packages and resources accompanied by tapes.

    c. *Tactual:* Provide manipulative learning materials such as Flip Chutes, Task Cards, Electroboards, Pic-A-Holes, puzzles, sandpaper letters and numerals, lotto games; use art projects in reading, math, and social studies; permit frequent use of the chalkboard, flannel board, magnetic board, typewriter, computer; encourage tracing of letters and words; encourage students to write their own stories; assign Multisensory Instructional Packages and Song Boards; permit frequent use of sand table and water table.

    d. *Kinesthetic:* Provide large-muscle learning materials such as Floor Puzzles, large blocks, step-on number lines, and alphabet squares; provide cooking and building experiences; encourage concrete experiences such as trips, walks, and community projects; permit dramatizing, role playing, and puppet shows; assign Multisensory Instructional Packages.

Many youngsters learn best by seeing words or pictures; some must manipulate tactual materials to learn effectively; still others learn quickly through kinesthetic Floor Games; relatively few learn easily by listening. Teachers who understand children's diverse perceptual strengths capitalize on that knowledge when teaching them to read (see Chapter 10). (Photographs courtesy West Seneca Central School District, West Seneca, New York, and Brightwood Elementary School, Greensboro, North Carolina.)

The Learning Style Inventory: Primary reveals which students work best when permitted nutritious snacks while learning. Teachers who are aware of certain children's need for Intake permit youngsters to bring raw vegetables to school as long as they (a) do not open their snacks anywhere except in the classroom, (b) do not distract their classmates when eating, (c) cook the vegetables for at least two minutes to diminish the sounds of chewing, and (d) earn test scores as high or higher than previously. For this youngster, a carrot or string bean should be substituted for his sweater! (Photograph courtesy Brightwood Elementary School, Greensboro, North Carolina.)

10. Intake
    a. *Does not require:* Permit students to choose their own snack time if they wish.
    b. *Requires:* Make available nutritious snacks such as fruit, raw vegetables, nuts, sunflower seeds; permit frequent snack breaks during the day and particularly while learning new and difficult material.
11. Mobility
    a. *Does not require:* Provide uninterrupted work or leisure-reading periods; encourage children to gather instructional resources before starting an activity or project.
    b. *Requires:* Allow frequent breaks during concentration; permit children to work at various Learning Stations and Interest Centers. If possible, provide a rocking chair or rocking horse for use while reading or working.
12. Time
    a. *Morning:* Assign morning reading and math groups; administer tests in the morning; encourage homework to be done in the morning.
    b. *Afternoon:* Assign afternoon reading and math groups; administer tests in the afternoon.
    c. *Evening:* Assign projects and activities to be completed at home.

Although many girls cannot do their best work while sitting, the need for frequent Mobility, kinesthetic instructional resources, and an Informal Design are decidedly male *characteristics. Teachers should experiment with several different Centers (see Chapter 3) to provide for children's need for periodic movement and a rocking horse or rocking chair in the classroom. Youngsters who previously were behavior problems will calm down and complete assignments when permitted movement while studying or concentrating. (Photograph courtesy Center for the Study of Learning and Teaching Styles, St. John's University, New York.)*

Designing Individualized Educational Plans Based on Children's Learning Style Strengths

When designing an individualized educational plan (IEP) for a student, it is essential to consider how the elements of learning style interact with each other. For example, examine the Learning Style Inventory: Primary Profile of Alison (see Figure 2–3).

Alison is a six-year-old first-grader who completed both a half-day kindergarten and a half-day preschool program. Scan the first four environmental elements of the profile. Highlight any score that indicates a strong preference (i.e., 4/5 or 5/5). Alison responded that she prefers bright light (4/5) and cool temperatures (5/5).

Suggest that she move her desk toward the front of the room, away from the radiators and sunny windows and nearer the door. Because she has no strong preference for either quiet or sound in the environment, she probably is able to screen out any sounds from the hallway while benefiting from the cool air through the opened doorway. Alison also may be able to concentrate on tasks while either stretched out on the floor in the brightly lit carpeted area of the classroom or seated at her desk, because she indicated no strong preferences for either a formal or an informal design (3/5, 2/5).

Next, review the emotional elements to determine motivation, persistence, and responsibility levels, and her need either to be self-structured or to have structure

Name: **Alison**   Grade: **1**   Teacher: **Ms Nagle**   Date: **9/21/90**

SOUND

Not Acceptable	1	1	1	1	1	2/5
Acceptable	2	2	2	2	2	3/5

LIGHT

Low	1	1	1	1	1	4/5
Bright	2	2	2	2	2	1/5

TEMPERATURE

Cool	1	1	1	1	1	5/5
Warm	2	2	2	2	2	0/5

DESIGN

Formal	1	1	1	1	1	3/5
Informal	2	2	2	2	2	2/5

MOTIVATION

Teacher		1		1			1	2/3
Adult			2	2			2	2/3
Self	3					3	3	3/3
Unmotivated	4	4	4	4	4	4	4	0/7

RESPONSIBILITY & PERSISTENCE

Is not	1	1	1	1	1	0/5
Is	2	2	2	2	2	5/5

STRUCTURE

Needs	1	1	1	1	1	1/5
Needs little	2	2	2	2	2	4/5

SOCIOLOGICAL

Alone	1	1			1	1	1	5/5
Adult		2	2	2	2		2	2/5
Peers	3		3	3		3	3	0/5

PERCEPTION

Tactual		1		1	1	1	1	2/5
Auditory	2		2	2	2		2	3/5
Visual	3	3	3	3			3	3/5
Kinesthetic		4		4	4	4	4	0/5

INTAKE

Does not require	1	1	1	1	1	3/5
Requires	2	2	2	2	2	2/5

TIME

Morning	1		1	1	1	0/4
Afternoon	2	2		2	2	3/4
Evening		3	3	3	3	2/4

MOBILITY

Does not require	1	1	1	1	1	5/5
Requires	2	2	2	2	2	0/5

COMMENTS:

FIGURE 2–3 Student Profile—Learning Style Inventory: Primary

imposed externally. First-graders tend to be only adult-motivated; that is, their success in school is related to parental encouragement. Alison's profile indicates adult and teacher motivation (2/3) but also some self-motivation (3/3). She probably will approach most tasks with enthusiasm and successfully complete them, as indicated by her high levels of persistence and responsibility (5/5). Provide her with guidelines for tasks, but encourage her input and offer choices, as she tends to be self-structured (4/5). If she asks for direction, however, give it, because she also is conforming (5/5). This score also suggests that it is not necessary to check on Alison when she is working. Instead, encourage her to check in with you when she has completed several tasks or whenever she has a question.

Although Alison does not need step-by-step directions from you, her profile shows that she would rather work with adults than with peers (2/5, 0/5). Thus, she will respond to directed-teaching activities with you, but it is important that she be allowed to complete independent activities by herself rather than in a small group (alone 5/5). She needs time and space to complete tasks on her own. Alison might be most responsive to Contract Activity Packages designed by you—just build in many choices.

Next, review Alison's perceptual preferences and note the pattern she prefers when learning new or difficult information. Perceptual patterns are determined by rank-ordering the scores from highest to lowest. Alison's pattern is auditory-visual-tactual/kinesthetic (A-V-T/K). Few first-graders exhibit strengths in the auditory perceptual area; that is, they do not learn best through listening activities alone and usually prefer a combination of kinesthetic-visual activities (Perrin, 1983; Crino, 1984). Alison, however, has indicated a strong preference in the auditory area (4/5), which suggests that she remembers verbal instructions and recalls information she hears. If she also is analytic, she probably responds positively to phonetically based reading strategies and benefits from listening to taped books, as well as from making her own book tapes. She also is likely to develop a sight vocabulary and to recall details she sees, as demonstrated by her secondary visual strength (3/5).

Alison has indicated that intake is not important to her and she does not need to move about once she is involved in a task. She does indicate that morning is not her best time of day (0/4); she is more alert in the afternoon and evening. This, again, suggests that Contract Activity Packages (CAPs) should be part of Alison's instructional prescription because she could work on them at home in the evening.

A Final Word

This chapter explained the need for using a reliable and valid instrument to identify young children's learning style characteristics. It introduced the Learning Style Inventory: Primary and recommended steps for preparing kindergarten through second-grade youngsters for taking the Inventory. The case study of Peter provided an overview of how learning style traits might be misconstrued and then suggested ways of responding to an individual's preferences.

If you are an experienced teacher with a great deal of sensitivity to young children, use these suggestions as a guide to teaching little ones effectively on the basis of their unique strengths. As long as children behave with decorum, achieve well, enjoy learning, and do not violate any other child's learning style, permit them to concentrate, study, and learn in their way. Learning style–responsive instruction is for *everyone,* especially:

- Children whom we used to categorize as *immature* because their biological traits were different from what conventional schooling requires of youngsters in kindergarten through second grade
- *Average* children who *wanted* to please the adults in their lives but just *couldn't*

    a. sit still—they needed mobility, an informal design, or kinesthetic learning.
    b. raise their hands when they wanted to speak—it was their *bodies* that required involvement.
    c. finish their work without interruption—they were globals who enjoyed doing multiple activities simultaneously and who needed many breaks in between their periods of concentration.
    d. stay in their seats—they needed a great deal of mobility, adult feedback, and support.
    e. remember what they had been told—they were biologically not yet auditory.
    f. look where they were going—they were biologically not yet visual.
    g. pay attention—academics were boring, and life itself—everything around them—was so exciting. Besides, how could low auditory children listen all day?
    h. keep their hands to themselves; they were so tactual or kinesthetic and, perhaps, peer-oriented—why weren't they permitted to learn through Flip Chutes, Electroboards, Pic-A-Holes, Multipart Task Cards, and with a classmate or two with Team Learning, Brainstorming, or Circle of Knowledge?
    i. stop nibbling or asking for water; they needed intake.
    j. understand what you so painstakingly had explained sequentially—*you* are analytic, and *they* processed new and difficult information *backwards* from the way you taught them.
    k. stop asking questions—they needed *more* structure than you were providing.
    l. do things in the exact way you wanted them done—they needed *less* structure than you were providing.
    m. do what you insisted on—they were nonconforming and the more you insisted, the less they were able to conform. You might have tried: (1) explaining why the thing you wanted them to do was really important to *you;* (2) giving them choices from among options you approved; and (3) speaking to them as if you really respected the youngsters (collegially). Nonconformists *need* your approval.

- *Gifted* children who can learn so much more, so much more quickly and enjoyably, when you teach them in the way they learn.

We are not asking that you cater to children. We are asking that you *try* to use their learning style strengths as much as you can. We *promise* you will love what happens to your class!

_3_

Redesigning the Educational Environment

Classroom Redesign Based on Individual Learning Styles

Many teachers alter the seating assignments in their classrooms in response to discipline problems. But moving a child to another seat without changing his or her total learning environment is a little like playing Russian roulette—you never know what will happen.

For example, a child who likes to work with one or two classmates might be moved away from friends because their frequent discussions disturb others. That youngster may become very unhappy and, as a result, may not be able to concentrate on his or her studies. How much better it would be to establish ground rules for when, how, and under what circumstances children may teach each other and discuss what they are learning, so that peer-oriented students may have time to learn together.

In other classrooms, teachers who feel comfortable with small-group cooperative learning strategies often require that all students engage in learning in teams. The youngster who thinks best alone, in quiet, without the interactions of others, becomes frustrated and is unlikely to perform at his or her maximum potential. Thus, identifying children's learning styles and then redesigning the classroom to become responsive to their personal strengths is an excellent way to go!

Planning Step 1: Identifying Students' Learning Styles

To begin redesigning your classroom to respond to diverse learning styles, first identify each of your students' important characteristics with the Learning Style Inventory: Primary (LSI:P) (Perrin) for K–2 (see Chapter 2). In addition to *individual* strengths, develop a *group* profile and look for large clusters of children with similar styles. Identify the number of children who need:

Classrooms should be redesigned to respond to students' environmental, sociological, and physiological learning style needs. (Photographs courtesy Brightwood Elementary School, Greensboro, North Carolina and Christa McAuliffe Elementary School, Lewisville, Texas.)

- Dimly lit versus well-illuminated spaces
- Sound versus quiet
- Informal versus conventional seating
- Cool versus warm sections
- More than average motivational resources
- Structure *and* choices within structured assignments

- "Breaks" because they cannot stay on task without interruptions
- An understanding of *why* an assignment is important to the teacher, options within a structure, and collegial adult interactions because they tend to be non-conforming
- To work by themselves, in a pair, as part of a small group, with certain, special classmates because of similar interest or intellectual levels, or near the teacher
- A collegial versus an authoritative adult
- A variety of resources and learning experiences versus those who require routines and patterns
- Auditory, visual, tactual, and/or kinesthetic initial introductions to difficult information
- Intake *while* learning
- Afternoon versus morning or late-morning instruction
- Mobility and opportunities for moving *while* learning
- Global versus analytic introductions to difficult information

When you have a fairly good idea of the many different types of students you have in your class, consider the kinds of areas you eventually will need to create—for example, single seats permitting a bit of privacy; paired seating; small dens or alcoves for peer-oriented youngsters who like to work in teams; table surfaces for students who will need hands-on instructional resources; and so forth. Do not become overwhelmed with this initial planning consideration. We are going to lead you by the hand through this entire adventure, and we *promise* that both you and your students will enjoy the newly created environment.

Planning Step 2: Assessing the Classroom for Its Redesign Possibilities

Using the following checklist, identify the areas in the room that might lend themselves to each of the following:

- Places where several students may meet to quietly discuss what they are learning
- Well-lit reading areas
- Warmer areas
- Desks or tables and chairs
- Private "dens" that permit responsible students to work without direct supervision
- "Office" or "conference enclosures" for working alone, with a friend or two, in a small group, with an adult, or in any combination thereof, provided the children show academic progress
- Essentially quiet and screened study areas for individuals or pairs
- Darker sections for media viewing, photography, or dramatizations for low-light preferents

- Cooler areas
- Carpeted, informal lounge furniture such as easy chairs, a couch, beanbags, and/or pillows
- Sections that permit close supervision for less responsible students
- An area where snacks may be available (preferably raw vegetables, fruits, and other nutritious foods)

Some teachers can visualize an entire room redesign merely by closing their eyes. Others must move one seat or section at a time. Still others must try several alternatives before deciding on a relatively permanent arrangement. Experiment with whichever pattern best suits you—but *do* try responding to your students' learning styles by varying the classroom environment so that each pupil can find a place within it that permits the greatest amount of concentration with the least amount of personal stress!

Planning Step 3: Locating Dividers

The third planning step is to identify and locate as many things as possible that can be placed perpendicular to walls, unused chalkboards, and spaces between windows. Such items include file cabinets, desks, bookcases, tables, shelves, material displays, screens, charts that can stand without additional support, and cardboard cartons or boxes that can be attractively painted or decorated. Even your desk can be used as a divider. Do not overlook bookcases that may be partially fixed to a wall or those, such as library stacks, that may seem too unstable to extend into the room.

The school custodians may enjoy the experience and novelty of acting as your "design engineers" and assisting you in this venture. To enlist their support, tell them why you are changing your room and that it will be easier to move around in and to

Dividers that can be placed perpendicular to walls include such items as bookcases, decorated cardboard boxes, filing cabinets, mobile bulletin boards, and so forth. (Photograph courtesy Otsego Elementary School, Half Hollow Hills, New York.)

clean—because it *will* be. The custodians also should respond positively to the need to build supports and add backings to rickety bookcases. They may have good suggestions and, once involved, might be able to obtain that extra table that you need.

These are only a few examples of dividers. Use your imagination to add to this list.

Examples of Dividers Used by Teachers

Cardboard boxes	Cardboard carpentry
Bookshelves	Homosote
Filing cabinets	Movable wardrobes
Wooden crafts	Colored yarn
Bulletin boards	Fish nets
Coat racks	Fish tanks
Streamers	Yarn or beaded strings
Plastic six-pack holders	Voting booths
Shower curtains or liners	Curtains
Plastic wall covering	Styrofoam sheets
Bed sheets	Plastic piping sections
Burlap	Summer lawn or pool furniture
Drop cloths	Covered wire
Art easels	Planters
Dress cutting boards	Bath or "math" tubs
Real or artificial plants	Tree houses
Boards on wheels	Awnings
Bunk beds	Couches or chairs
Display cases	Tables
Tents	Plastic bins or crates
	Car sun shields

Planning Step 4: Clearing the Floor Area

Look at your room. Walk around. There are likely to be boxes of science equipment, art supplies, reading materials, and other assorted items stacked on the floor. Temporarily place this material outside the room or in a closet or corner. Later you will locate these resources on top of the perpendicular units you create to provide additional screening and separation of instructional areas, such as the Learning Station, Interest Center, Magic Carpet Section, Media Corner, Little Theater, Science Corner, Game Table, Author's Hideaway, Taped-Book Center, Listening Lounge, Conference Center, Post Office, Computer Office, Artist's Alcove, Concentration Closet, Thinking Tower, Reflection Loft, Block-Building Area, Tactual/Kinesthetic Center, Reading Section, and so forth. (See the section at the end of this chapter for descriptions of sample Centers.)

When moving the furniture and developing the physical environment, it is usually wise to do it with the students. They should be aware of what is going to be created and why, and that it will take a while to become acclimated to the change. Their involvement in developing the design invariably creates acceptance of the revision, and, more important, the youngsters' suggestions and reactions help with the correct placement of those with specific learning styles.

Planning Step 5: Involving the Students

If you decide to involve all your students, begin your conversation by explaining that, as in their own homes, the way the furniture is arranged in a room should make sense for the people who live there. Some of the boys and girls who "live" in the classroom (and they are living there for four or five hours each school day!) may enjoy the arrangement just as it is, but others may feel uncomfortable because people are different from each other and some need things that others do not.

For example (and here begin to personalize with them), everyone in the present arrangement is seated, in a sense, out in the open, even if there are separations between groups. With many students at close range, it must be difficult for some of them to concentrate as they see and hear the door opening, chairs and people moving, and materials being used and then replaced. Some people need a quiet, cozy place to think when they study; for those children, you would like to create small offices, dens, or alcoves where they can be by themselves or with a friend or two to complete their work.

At this point, you are certain to have their undivided attention; they will be curious, stimulated, intrigued, and individually motivated to redesign the classroom. You might ask how many students would like to serve as assistant interior decorators to aid you in rearranging the room to create spaces in which they will enjoy doing their schoolwork.

One of the first things you can suggest is the establishment of some areas where small groups of students can literally turn their backs on what is happening in the room and become absorbed in their work. They can do this by facing their chairs toward any available wall space. You may add, "If I told you that you were going to face a wall, you might think, 'Who wants to look at bare space?' But you might change your mind if I then said that each person facing a wall would be able to create his or her own bulletin board. You could display your work on it—the things you draw, write, paint, or sew; the models you build; photographs of your pets—wouldn't you like that?" Many students enjoy having a bulletin board in their seating area and making it attractive with personalized decorations.

To develop bulletin board motivation, use sheets of colored construction or drawing paper to form a rectangular wall area as wide as the desk adjacent to it. Scallop a border to complement the paper, and vary the colors so that bulletin boards that are next to each other reflect individual decorating preferences. Frequently, there is not enough wall space in the room for each student to have a bulletin board, and some may not want the responsibility of keeping one attractive and current. Establish rules for what may or may not be displayed, but, within the confines of good taste, permit wide variation based on students' choices.

You can increase the amount of bulletin board space in the room by using the backs of file cabinets, bookcases, closet doors (which can be left closed), and rarely used chalkboard sections. Plywood, cardboard, wallboard, and other building materials can be added to one side of bookcases that are open in both directions or to the side of a file cabinet, or taped to a student's desk or table.

An active primary program involves a great deal of movement to different Learning Centers with provision made to hold students' belongings and materials in closets, cabinets, "cubbies," or decorated boxes. In some classes, teachers may wish to establish more permanent home bases or desk areas with assignments to other centers as the day progresses. Usually, a large area near a chalkboard or overhead projector and screen is designed for planning group instruction as needed. Next, refer to the classroom Learning Style Profile Chart (see Chapter 2) as you discuss the need for some children to work alone in a Center, for others to work in a Center with a buddy, and for still others to be with a small group, depending on individual sociological preferences.

In this preredesign discussion, mention to your students that, just as they are used to the placement of the furniture in their homes, they are currently "at home" with the placement of the various items in the classroom. Explain that it takes time for people to adjust to new things, but that the more flexible they are, the faster they will adjust. (This will encourage many of the pupils to experience positive reactions to the emerging redesign. In turn, they will help others become acclimated to the new arrangement.)

Planning Step 6: Considering Other Ramifications

The major objective of creating centers in the primary classroom is to provide different types of areas to permit children to function through patterns that appear to be natural for them and to their learning styles. Some students, however, may not know how they work best or where they prefer to sit; they can only try new placements and determine whether the arrangement is good or appropriate for them on the basis of how they react after the change. Therefore, rather than asking students where they would like to sit, begin by establishing the areas. Then, one by one, explain the advantages and disadvantages of each, describing the responsibilities of those who elect to work or are assigned to that den, alcove, office, corner, or section. The Centers are in addition to "home bases" (desks or tables) where students keep their things and begin and end the day.

Planning Step 7: Designing Instructional Centers

The Magic Carpet

The Magic Carpet area for reading can be created either in a corner or against a far wall. It should be carpeted and surrounded on at least two sides by bookshelves that face in toward the readers. This area is a quiet, casual, reading-meditating section where students may go to concentrate in silence or to rest if needed. If possible, nat-

Game Tables, Puzzle Places, Authors' Alcoves, Space Stations, and Reading Tree Houses are but a few of the many motivating instructional centers that can be designed for young children who often enjoy study areas that permit mobility and variety. (Photographs courtesy Sheridan Hill Elementary School, Williamsville, New York, and Christa McAuliffe Elementary School, Lewisville, Texas.)

ural light from windows or lamps should be provided for one such area, and a second Magic Carpet hideaway should be on the opposite side of the room in a section with low light and no glare.

Computer Offices and/or Media Centers

Most schools have limited equipment and must distribute their resources equitably among all classes in a given building. It is necessary, however, to provide each large group (25 to 35 students) with enough hardware so that students may use the media to obtain information, study concepts, and develop skills. At the same time, it is inefficient and unnecessary to carry heavy equipment from place to place.

In preference (or in addition) to either the totally centralized Multimedia Instructional Resource Center or the building-centralized Learning Center, teachers may establish a Media Center in each room. This area can house one to three computers, one overhead projector, one or two single-viewer filmstrip machines, a VCR and videotapes, one sound projector (desirable but optional), three or four cassette tape recorders, and many blank tapes. Equipment may be exchanged among clusters of three or four classes joined together as "learning pods" or Media Instructional Areas (MIAs) when needed. The larger, more affluent Media Centers could be used as library resources to provide special materials.

Students should be free to take a software item (filmstrips, videotapes, audiotapes, slides) to their home base or to other Centers when needed and should be taught to return all items carefully when they no longer are needed. Cadres of students should form Team Task Forces to take responsibility for demonstrating how to use, care for, repair, replace, and organize the equipment and resources that make up the Media Center.

When one student begins to view materials, others are drawn into the procedure by interest, curiosity, or social awareness. Students should be permitted to join each other in viewing, discussing, studying, or analyzing the resources, provided each participant is receptive to the cooperative effort. In some cases, individuals require privacy and perhaps quiet while working with either instructional resources or media. Other youngsters are most productive while studying with a partner or with two or three classmates in a cooperating group with consistent verbal and/or physical interaction.

Game Tables

Educational games are used extensively in schools today. Their major contributions to the learning process include: (1) interesting introductions of a topic or concept; (2) applications of information or concepts; (3) increasing motivation and stimulation; (4) provision of an alternative teaching method or device; (5) opportunities for either individual or small-group focus on information through alternative resources; (6) opportunities for independent concentration; (7) activities for small-group and interage shared experiences; (8) review or reinforcement of previously discussed or studied information; (9) remediation; (10) relaxation as a break in the school day; (11) responsiveness to tactual youngsters who often need to *begin* concentration on difficult information through a hands-on, high-interest approach; and (12) a global focus.

Games are available for all age levels (preschool through adulthood), in all curriculum areas, and as interdisciplinary approaches to study. A repertoire of these instructional devices provides alternative resources, methods, and activities for students and increases their options for learning. You and the students may be able to invent new games or redesign existing ones to meet instructional goals or to take advantage of individual learning styles. When you begin using Contract Activity Packages, designing their own games to demonstrate mastery of difficult information is a perfect Activity Alternative for those students who are capable of developing them. Many young children can design games in pairs or as part of a group.

Game tables should be available to students in different sections of the classroom for use at appropriate times. When students share their completed assignments, need or decide to use the games as learning resources or activities, or merely wish to relax for a while, they should be able to go quietly to the table and select whichever resource is appropriate to their tasks or abilities. Games should be cataloged according to their level of difficulty and/or their relationship to the curriculum. Students then will know which games will suit them best.

Little Theaters

Another area guaranteed to provide an exciting, dynamic learning atmosphere is called the Little Theater—an imaginative title for a creative and stimulating center. Here, in a section of the room that may be darkened or partitioned when necessary, students are free to become involved in a series of projects that require applications of the information they have learned through the use of the available Resource Alternatives. Pupils should be encouraged to make slides, filmstrips, films, negatives, photographs, scenery props, costumes, backdrops for productions, rolled-paper "movies," multimedia presentations, transparencies, books, scrapbooks, and games for the Game Tables that require knowledge of the subject matter being studied and applications through personal creativity.

These projects are, of course, appropriately related to the class curriculum, Contract Activity Packages, Programmed Learning Sequences, or Multisensory Instructional Packages. Becoming involved with Little Theater productions requires review, reinforcement, and synthesis of ideas among the students. Children may write dialogue, act out scenes in stories or plays, assume roles, or simply improvise, mime, or critically analyze what they have learned. The Little Theater is especially appealing to youngsters with strong kinesthetic abilities; they literally can show what they have learned. Some will dance or sing; others will make something and show it to a group who wish to listen. Expect to see original plays, puppet dramas, and even family-created videotapes.

Interest Centers

These are particularly appropriate for global students who learn holistically and enjoy humor, anecdotes, pictures, and other illustrations while learning. This section of the learning environment should house interdisciplinary resources concerned with a selected theme—family helpers, nutrition, fairytales, money, calendar, dinosaurs, and so on. Here, items related to many curriculum areas may be found, but they are focused on one central sphere of interest.

In addition to the media resource materials related to the topic (objects, books, magazines, pictures, videotapes, filmstrips, slides, cassettes, audiotapes, loops, cartridges, or study prints), youngsters might find: (1) assignment sheets (machine copies or workbook-type pages); (2) small-group strategies (Circles of Knowledge, Team Learning, Brainstorming, Case Studies, Simulations, Role Playing, or Group Analyses) (see Chapter 5); and (3) games (crossword puzzles, fill-in-the-missing-letter assignments, task cards, and others) on which individuals or small groups might work. A Programmed Learning Sequence, Contract Activity Package, or Multisensory Instructional Package on the topic also could be available.

Interest Centers serve many purposes: (1) they are available as another option for youngsters—an alternative way of obtaining information and concepts about a given theme; (2) they provide young children with a means of gathering facts and concepts independently; and (3) they build small-group activities into the learning process to provide social interaction and group achievement. Interest Centers, therefore, permit a teacher to take advantage of individual learning styles by providing students with a choice of either working independently or with one or more classmates. Although self-pacing is an important instructional goal, many youngsters prefer working with others. For them, isolated studying and learning are not always desirable. Conversely, some students who seem to think best while working independently sometimes need to interact with others to test ideas and to mature intellectually.

Learning Stations

Learning Stations are best suited to analytic students who learn sequentially, step by step. Most primary children are global in their learning orientation but a few—those who usually are strongly auditory and work oriented—often benefit from a detailed, sequential approach to a specific curriculum area such as number facts, number concepts, blends, digraphs, decoding, historical events and dates, or the parts of a plant. Thus, math and reading subjects that must be mastered by all children should be taught both globally and analytically—necessitating the establishment of both Interest Centers that teach globally and Learning Stations that provide analytic resources.

Math Tubs

Locate one or two old-fashioned, discarded bathtubs. Have the students scour and decorate them. Place them into the Math Learning Station or Interest Center, and seek donated pillows or make some large, colorful, comfortable ones with the class. Fill the tub with the pillows and establish a schedule for "swimming in math." Both globals and analytics will respond positively.

The students should be told that, once in the tub, they must be totally immersed in mathematics. They may think only of the mathematics they are reading, learning, or doing inside this hideaway. The "magical waters" of the Math Tub will help them to learn, and you will be able to chart their progress across an "ocean of objectives" that can be attached to the inside and outside of this innovative instructional area.

Reading Tree Houses

Salvage old lumber, bolts, nails, sandpaper, packing cases, and other materials that will allow you to design a Reading Tree House right in your classroom. Involve the custodians, local fire marshal, skillful or willing parents, and anyone else who can help. First, design it and carefully measure where it will go. Construct steady, safe ladders, platforms, and spaces for three or four children. Primary school youngsters will love to read or study quietly, away from the rest of the class. Carpeted bunk beds can be used for this purpose as well.

Office Building

Large sheets of cardboard or the sides of discarded appliance boxes can be used to construct separate compartments or "offices" for individual students. Those youngsters who need to be alone to study or concentrate can crawl or climb into these spaces and screen out the rest of the class or their neighbors in adjacent offices. The cardboard offices may be built in layers (two stories or levels) or in a maze to separate students. The Office Building can be painted either with windows or with solid-colored walls.

Conference Center

The Conference Center is a place where large groups of students can share, small groups of students can confer, or teacher and student can quietly discuss a reading log or writing journal (for those youngsters who can do either or both!). Frequently, an author's chair is placed in the center so that eager authors can exchange their writing or small groups of students can plan together. The Conference Center can be tucked away in a corner of the classroom or in the center of the room, as in the kindergarten sample (see Figure 3–3).

The Taped-Book or Listening Center

Sometimes this Center can be combined with a Media Center. It houses both hardware (tape recorders, headsets, and filmstrip projectors) and software (tapes, taped books, and filmstrips). The best sources of taped books are teacher-read materials. Each time you read aloud to students (at least once each day), turn on the tape recorder. When you have completed a book, glue a zip-lock plastic bag onto the back of the book to store the tape. In a very short time, you can have a selection of taped books that your students will enjoy over and over again. Be certain that this Center has a wall space for viewing filmstrips. Also, you may store a selection of Song Boards here (see Chapter 6).

Artist's Alcove

Locate this center near a sink. Provide one or two easels, paper, a selection of water paints and finger paints, brushes of various sizes, and mixing jars. Mount charts nearby that show how to use various primary colors to create pastels and tones. Encourage youngsters to mix their own colors, and be certain to provide coverups and dropcloths. Clay, play dough, clayboards, and sculpting tools can be found in this area.

Writer's Table

Provide various sizes and colors of lined and unlined paper, envelopes, pencils, pens, and markers. Add a basket to store students' writing journals. Establish a "send me a line" rope strung between two corners, and add clothespins for attaching completed notes, essays, and other creative writing projects for viewing and reading by classmates. House the Center in a quiet area of the classroom, and provide a small lamp for students who need more light than is available.

Tactual/Kinesthetic Center

The materials in this Center include table games, Flip Chutes, multipart Task Cards, Pic-A-Holes, Electroboards, Learning Circles, Wrap Arounds, sandpaper letters, geoboards, pegboards, and other small-muscle manipulative materials, as well as kinesthetic Floor Games. Locate this Center near tables and chairs for those students who need a formal design, and provide floor space and a few cushions for those who prefer an informal setting.

Adding Creative Dividers and Designer Touches

When the basic room redesign nears completion, you may wish to supplement furniture dividers, such as bookcases and file cabinets, with decorative floor-to-ceiling, see-through partitions to further the illusion of separation and to add interest and color. Unique divider materials such as yarn, knotted string, beads, or bottle tops are attractive to young people. Plants, too, make an excellent separation between the various instructional sections.

On a day when you are feeling especially creative, nonconforming, or impulsive, you may be willing to experiment with a single wire tautly stretched across a section of the room (in any direction that makes sense to you!). When firm, it will hold several transparent plastic shower curtains or liners, which can be opened or closed to create either one large get-together area or several smaller alcoves. The plastic liner/dividers can double as kinesthetic Floor Games if you design them with crossword grids, number lines, maps, or large circular, rectangular, or square pockets into which questions can be inserted. Hang them with clip-on loops so they can be removed and rehung easily. These inexpensive dividers also can be used to display student work or to post rules, objectives, and names of the various instructional areas and Centers. Create attractive name signs for each Center, and ask the custodian or a few willing parents to drop them from the ceiling with colored yarn, string, or twine.

Decorative Wall Coverings and Dividers

Leftover holiday wrappings, colored construction paper, unused paint, plastic wallcovering or wallpaper, clear food wrappings, or aluminum foil twisted into sculpted forms can be used effectively to decorate walls, bulletin boards, cardboard dividers, and the backs and sides of file cabinets. Remnant wallpaper, shelf liner, and sections of carpeting, burlap, or cut-up old jeans can be used to create montages and attractive backs for dividers, walls, shelves, and mounted objectives. In addition to creating an attractive learning environment, you will promote interest and enthusiasm if you allow students and their parents to help in the interior decorating process.

Obtain colored yarn from local merchants as a donation or from parents as a contribution. Stretch floor-to-ceiling lengths between two areas in straight, triangular, or other patterns (see Figure 3–1). This attractive wall of yarn can be used to display student work or to post directions. Thumbtacks, pieces of wood, blocks, staples, masking tape, or loops around metal ceiling supports can be used as anchors at the top and bottom. Invite custodians to help you design the wall covering and tie the yarn down. They will know what will work with minimum damage.

Plastic Beverage Tops and Paper Rings

Have the students save the plastic (nonmetal) rings from six-pack beverage containers. These may be attached to each other with colored string or covered wire to form see-through wall dividers similar to the colored yarn partitions. When these are weighted at the bottom, they need not be anchored to the floor, but you will find that they hold their shape better when they are. Colored chains consisting of construction paper rings, like those often made for holiday seasons, may also be used although they are not as permanent as the plastic rings. These should be anchored and repaired as soon as they break (see Figure 3–2).

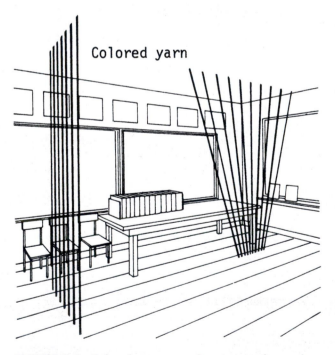

Colored yarn

FIGURE 3–1   Colored yarn or sturdy string can be used as dividers to provide see-through but partially separated areas for privacy and concentration.

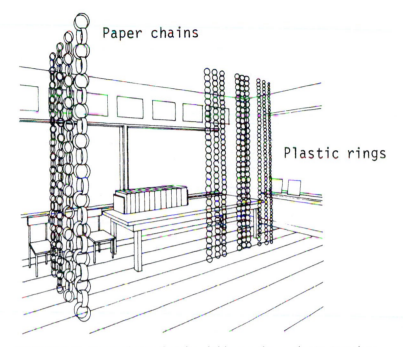

FIGURE 3–2 Paper chains that the children make or plastic rings they collect can also serve as dividers to provide a colorful classroom atmosphere and, simultaneously, permit small areas in which individuals, pairs, or small groups can work together on assignments or tasks of their choosing, such as during the "Self-Teaching Time" intervals.

Alternative Room Designs

Teachers who are just beginning to redesign their classrooms may be hesitant about creating a variety of instructional areas because they fear that students will misbehave and cause discipline problems and a loss of control. Most of the time, whole-class instruction through lecture dominates teaching. Teachers often cannot imagine how to teach unless everyone learns the same material simultaneously.

If that is your concern, experiment with designing only one or two innovative areas in the room while maintaining most of your current environment. Permit those who need informal seating and mobility to experiment, provided they: (1) obey your rules, (2) complete their assignment, (3) do not interfere with anyone else's learning style, (4) pay attention whenever you *are* addressing the class, and (5) earn better test scores than they did previously. If one or two individuals do not follow these rules, judiciously remove the privilege of sitting informally or using mobility from those children. Do *not* punish those students who are abiding by your regulations.

For both small-group and large-group lessons, use an overhead projector to assist in teaching. Place the screen up toward the ceiling so that everyone can see whatever you write or illustrate. Using a projector with all or most of the class with the room's lights off will increase attentiveness *and* good behavior during a lecture or discussion.

Redesign as much as you believe you can and still feel secure with the changes. Do it either in stages or all at once, as you feel most comfortable. As long as *you* are comfortable with the steps, the interior decoration will go a long way toward helping children learn more quickly and retain whatever you have taught them longer than previously. Have the courage to experiment before you decide whether you can or cannot be successful with this type of environment. Ask the students how *they* feel in their new headquarters, and be certain to watch for rises in their test scores as you permit controlled options in the classroom environment.

Whichever Centers or areas you decide to establish, adding a perceptual strength sequence pattern will improve student success. Design each of the Learning Centers in your classroom to capitalize on each individual's perceptual modality. Keep a classroom chart mounted in clear view labeled Visual, Auditory, Tactual, and Kinesthetic Strengths. Print each student's name clearly, and, next to it, state that child's perceptual strengths—primary (strongest) first, followed by secondary and then tertiary. Assign the children to work in the Centers according to the order of their perceptual patterns. Begin with the strongest, reinforce with the next two, and finish with the weakest modality.

Use a keyboard system to assign students to a specific Center. Cut large key shapes from bright-colored oaktag, using a different color for each of the four perceptual strength centers. You will need at least one oaktag key for each child in your class. Next, cut a hole at the top of the key so that it can slip comfortably over a child's head. The children wear the keys when they are working in the appropriate Center so you can be certain that each child is exactly where he or she should be.

This system will enable you to quickly spot-check that youngsters are working in the correct Center, manage the numbers of students assigned to each workplace, and reinforce for the children that they should sequence their work whenever possible according to their perceptual strengths—their first, then second and third combined and, finally, their weakest modality. Give the children enough time to explore the resources in their first assigned Center. Then direct them to the other Centers containing the most resources that match their secondary and tertiary perceptual preferences.

After working with this system several times, the children quickly learn which materials best accommodate them. If you are willing to experiment for 15 minutes twice a day, offer the students "free" Center time. Tell them that this is their "self-teaching time" and that they may choose to work in any Center to teach themselves (or a classmate) their required work. Invariably, they will self-select according to their perceptual pattern because that is how they learn most efficiently. During these short intervals, they might teach themselves new vocabulary, the week's spelling words, math problems, or some other required material. They may use any of the available Centers' resources or create their own. They must, however, use the time *productively*—or lose the privilege. This wonderful respite for both students and teachers permits a few quiet moments whenever something requires your immediate attention. Children need to be *taught* how to use their "free" self-teaching time advantageously.

Gaining Parental Support

Now that you have redesigned your room to base your instructional program on individual learning styles, it is important to gain the support of your students' parents. Parents are interested in and often concerned about the concepts and strategies to which their children are being exposed, especially if those are new. Once the class has become adjusted to the redesigned room, invite parents in to visit and to discuss the rationale of the room or area redesign. Explain the advantages of capitalizing on each youngster's learning style, and describe how the students participated in the developing arrangement. When parents understand why the instructional environment has been altered, they usually are willing to support the effort until sufficient time has elapsed to yield both objective and subjective results, such as students' attitudes, the teacher's reactions, academic progress, and the effects on behavior of responding to learning styles. Actually, the students themselves will presell the change with the enthusiasm they express at home concerning their new interior decoration.

If you are inclined to use media to win parental support for a learning styles–responsive environment, see the book and filmstrip and accompanying audiotape specifically designed to acquaint parents with an understanding of learning style (see Chapter 11).

As you read subsequent chapters and experiment with having students create their own tactual resources, Contract Activity Packages, Programmed Learning Sequences, and Multisensory Instructional Packages, remember that any or all of these may be placed into classroom instructional areas when appropriate. Also, having students *create* their own learning materials is one of the best ways we know of helping them master information. First, however, the youngsters should experience using samples of those different resources, so that they understand how to learn through them and the degree to which each responds to their unique style strengths.

Examples of Redesigned Classroom Possibilities

The secret of building your own instructional Taj Mahal without cost (or for very little), involves using what you already have in new patterns. Desks, chairs, tables, bookcases, file cabinets, and other furniture are moved to take maximum advantage of the available space and the students' individual learning styles.

Begin slowly, be flexible and receptive to new ideas and approaches, plan carefully, and continually evaluate how well the new design meets your objectives for each of the students in the class.

A Redesigned Kindergarten Classroom

Figure 3–3 depicts one kindergarten room specifically redesigned to permit options in accordance with each student's learning style strengths. It is suggested as a possibility, an alternative, a beginning to spark your own imagination. Take from the illus-

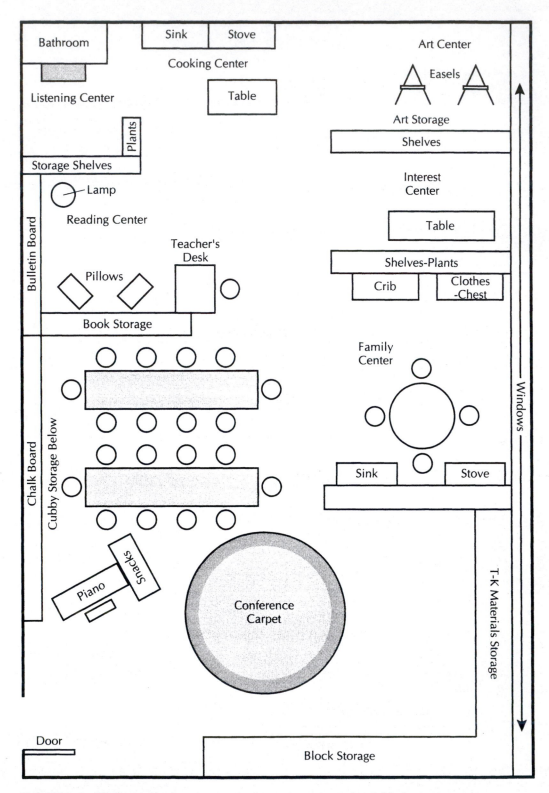

FIGURE 3–3 Kindergarten class. Notice the 10 × 12 open area available for large-group conferencing, chalkboard, and/or overhead projector use; four students' desks can be subdivided with painted cardboard dividers; Magic Carpet reading area also may be used as a Reading and Writing Center.

trations those features that appeal to you and discard those that may be inappropriate for your situation. Be aware that the more immature the kindergartners, the more they require this kind of environment. Asking young, physically energized, academically unfocused children to "sit still," "pay attention" (by listening), "follow directions," and "work by yourself" is unrealistic; those are the very youngsters who need to learn through *movement, with options,* and often with peers or directly with you on a one-to-one basis—which is virtually impossible.

We are going to train these little ones to learn through instructional resources and in redesigned environments that complement their learning style strengths. After they have learned to use the most appropriate resource (for each individual) efficiently, they gradually will learn to teach themselves. Eventually, they will develop the independence skills that permit them to convert textbook information into a mini–Contract Activity Package, a mini–Programmed Learning Sequence, or tactual-kinesthetic resources—whichever best suits the individual.

In this kindergarten room, the "home base" student tables and chairs have been placed near the chalkboard for large group chalk-talks. They are next to the Tactual Kinesthetic (T/K) Center so that they can be used for table games, puzzles, and peg-boards; they also are close to the snack table. The T/K Center has enough space so that a Floor Game can be spread out and played there. This room also houses an Interest Table.

The Family Center can easily be changed, depending on student interest and/or thematic approach. It houses a play refrigerator, sink, stove, small table, and two chairs. With a touch of imagination, it quickly can become a "hospital," an "office," a "shoe store," or a "mini-market."

The Conferencing Carpet is an area where small groups can meet for an informal discussion, where teachers and students can meet for a reading/writing conference, or where impromptu performances or large-group sharing can occur. The Listening and Media Center houses several tape recorders and headsets, as well as filmstrip projectors. The back of the Reading Center divider has a white curtain tacked to it to permit viewing a filmstrip.

Several small lamps have been placed in different areas for students who seek extra light or for those who prefer only the lamp light with the overhead lights turned off.

A Redesigned First-Grade Classroom

This sample first-grade room design provides home base desks or small tables and chairs with bookshelves or decorated cardboard dividing various areas (see Figure 3–4). All dividers are about three feet high, so the teacher can see all the children at a glance. The bookshelves face the students or open into a space such as the Magic Carpet area for reading. Note that a large-group instructional area is available for planning or presenting new topics on a chalkboard or screen. The overhead projector is desirable because the teacher can face the students and everyone can see the screen when it is placed high on the wall or in a corner near the ceiling on braces.

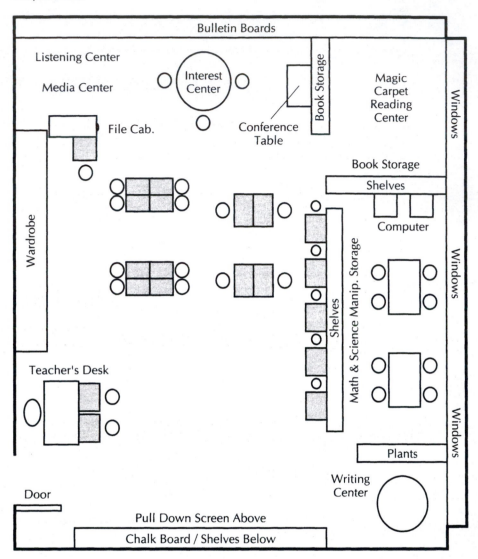

FIGURE 3–4   First-grade classroom. Notice the 10 × 12 open area available for large-group conferencing, chalkboard, and/or overhead projector use; 4 students desks can be subdivided with painted cardboard dividers; Magic Carpet Reading area also may be used as a Reading and Writing Center;

A Redesigned Second-Grade Classroom

This sample second-grade room design provides 27 home base desks or small tables and chairs with bookshelves or decorated cardboard dividing various areas, as described in the first-grade sample design (see Figure 3–5). All students can be seen over the three-foot-high dividers, and bookshelves are accessible in various areas. Teachers usually require whole-group instruction for some topics and for planning. As before, this is provided at the front of the room at an angle with a portable chalkboard or a hanging screen for an overhead projector. When a hanging screen is unavailable, the image should be projected well above the children's eye level so that those in the rear can see well. In addition, children should be allowed to move closer to the screen if they wish.

Developing Skills for Using Centers Effectively

Various Centers were described earlier in this chapter. The types of Centers you can design are unlimited, depending only on your creativity, your needs, the abilities of your students, and especially their learning styles. Follow the models we suggested, or design your own!

As students begin to use any instructional area, they gradually will need to be taught how to:

- Locate, use, share, repair, and replace the available resources.
- Recognize materials that are appropriate to their individual reading and comprehension levels.
- Make selections from among approved alternatives.
- Evaluate their own and their peers' progress.
- Maintain accurate records of those objectives and activities that they have completed successfully.

These skills are essential for functioning in any program that requires students to become increasingly independent. This is the point at which students are most likely to learn the study skills they need for their continued academic growth. They are actually using materials and must begin to depend on their own ability to assess and complete their tasks correctly, to locate appropriate resources and information, to record what they need to remember, to select ways of demonstrating accomplished skills and tasks, and to evaluate their progress. Opportunities for creative experiences or performance demonstrations may be built into evaluation procedures.

Obviously, many students will need either your assistance or the aid of other students while learning how to use instructional areas effectively. The skills listed previously will take some students much longer to acquire than others, but they are goals worth striving for during the primary years.

Experimenting with Your Redesigned Classroom

As you begin to establish varied instructional areas, collect cushions, beanbags, carpet squares, rugs, summer lawn furniture, a couch, a rocking chair, or easy chairs. Permit children to experiment with these items, and establish firm rules for working

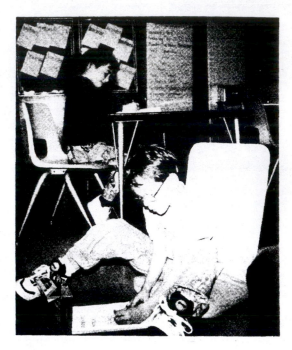

Permit children to sit at desks, in rocking chairs, under tables, at Family Group Centers, and or in specifically planned-for informal areas. The classroom should reflect individual students' differences as revealed by the Learning Style Inventory: Primary Version. *(Photographs courtesy Otsego Elementary School, Half Hollow Hills, New York, and Christa Mc-Auliffe Elementary School, Lewisville, Texas.)*

in the redesigned classroom. Specifically, take one or more of the following steps to determine their effects on students' learning, attitudes, and behaviors.

- Only those students whose Learning Style Inventory: Primary Version printout confirms that an *informal* design is advantageous may use the informal areas.

- No student's learning style should interfere with or distract anyone with a different style.
- Any student who abuses the privilege of working in his or her learning style will forfeit that privilege.
- The grades of each student permitted to sit informally must be at least as good or better than his or her grades prior to this experiment. Otherwise, it is not working, and there is no reason to continue.
- All assignments must be completed, but they may be done anywhere in the classroom as long as: (1) these rules are maintained, (2) everyone can be seen by the teacher, and (3) children behave politely.
- Keep one bank of lights on and the other off. Permit students to sit wherever they feel most comfortable.
- Turn the lights off in a single corner of the room. Permit poor readers to sit in the low-light area. Observe differences in behavior and attention spans during the first six-week period; look for achievement gains.
- Make colored acetate (used for writing on overhead projectors) available to poor readers. Encourage individuals to select a color of their choice (green, blue, red, pink, or lilac; avoid yellow, brown, and black) and to place the acetate on top of each page being read *while* reading. Look for changes in attention span, focusing, and behavior. (Such changes may be observable in 5 to 10 percent of poor readers.)
- Use colored, fireproof paper (available in greeting card stores) between the ceiling light bulb and the glass that covers it in one corner of the room to disperse illumination effects.
- Turn the lights off entirely in a classroom of underachievers and teach in natural daylight. Examine the effects.
- Permit students to wear sun visors or sunglasses when they squint, appear uncomfortable, or ask for that privilege. Many children cannot concentrate in "normal" lighting.
- Create a space with dark curtains where children who need soft illumination may work, *or* permit them to partially block their chosen dens or offices with transparent but dark-toned fabrics.
- Place students who require quiet away from traffic and activity patterns.
- Permit the use of clean, soft cotton balls; rubber ear plugs, joggers' earmuffs; or nonfunctioning listening sets during tests for those who need quiet. Permit listening to music without lyrics for those who need sound.
- Cover a small area of the floor with carpeting beneath students who are distracted by sounds.
- Separate the children who need frequent breaks from those who prefer to work without interruptions. Provide self-contained spaces with the view of class activities blocked for those who are distracted easily; place those who function best with sound near the hub of involvement.
- Locate desks and chairs in several different sizes suitable to your students' varying heights and girths.

- Allow youngsters to stand or stretch out in the informal sections; do not always require that they sit while concentrating.
- Allow kinesthetic children (those who rarely sit still) to walk back and forth quietly along separate paths in designated sections of the room *while* they are reading or completing assignments. They will not take advantage of you.
- Structure assignments to permit those who need variety, mobility, breaks, and

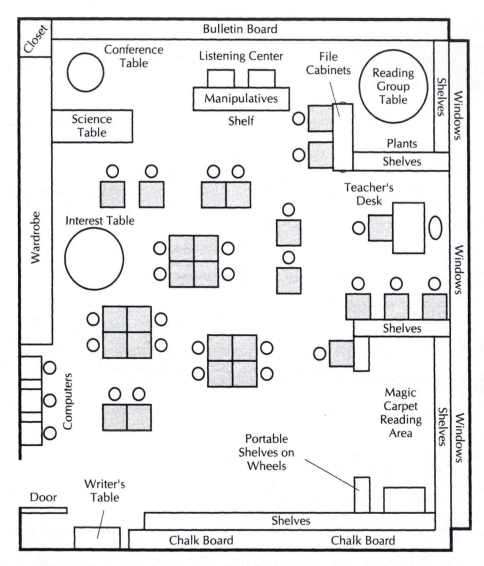

FIGURE 3–5 Second-grade classroom. Shelf dividers are three feet high each. Conference carpet can be rolled to the side for kinesthetic floor games, block building, and dancing.

peer interactions to move about the room purposefully, go from one activity to another, or migrate from one section to another as needed.

- Permit students to complete all or most assignments (with the exception of tests) alone, in a pair, in a small group, or with the teacher. Some classroom spaces should accommodate individuals, pairs, small groups, or large groups.
- Provide curtains that block out afternoon sun, a fan, and water and paper cups on warm days.
- Allow children to keep sweaters in their desks or the closet for when they feel cool.
- Encourage students to wear layers of clothing that may be removed or maintained, depending on the temperature and their individual reactions to its variations.
- Remember that the warmest part of most rooms—with the exception of being near a window in warm weather or next to a heater—is the center.

A Final Word on Room Redesign

As your students gradually become accustomed to working in instructional areas that are responsive to their individual learning styles, they will suggest ways of improving the classroom to make it even more complementary to their strengths. When that happened in Depew, New York, Carolyn Brunner, coordinator of the Instructional Development Center at Erie 1's Board of Cooperative Educational Services, created the classroom furniture illustration in Figure 3–5. She encouraged students to consider every classmate's learning style and to design an environment that would improve on what existed at that time. Youngsters worked alone, in pairs, or in small groups and developed sample classrooms by cutting out the various forms and pasting them onto colored oaktag. Transparencies then were made of those charts and were displayed on an overhead projector so that all the children could see them at the same time. Each transparency was explained, and the class then voted on the sections or parts that appealed to the most participants. The children redesigned a few sections of the classroom and worked in them for a week before deciding whether to keep or alter them. Teachers in the school expressed admiration for the creative, practical, and attractive results. Perhaps you can permit your students to plan their instructional environment on the basis of their increasing understanding of their own and their classmates' styles. Before they are given that responsibility for classroom redesign, they need to understand that: (1) people learn in different environments; (2) it is important that people concentrate where each feels comfortable; and (3) each person needs to respect the differences among class members.

4

Global and Analytic Approaches to Teaching

Forward Can Be Backward for Many Students

Have you ever analyzed your own teaching style—not through an observation form, your supervisor's evaluation, or even a peer conference but, rather, by focusing on how you *begin* a lesson? Most of us initially consider the content objectives, what was taught previously, which items need reinforcement, and what might constitute a motivating opening. Sometimes the introduction is humorous, is interestingly related to a recent event, or seizes students' attention because it reflects something that has happened at the school or in their lives.

Even when we have planned well, however, some students do not respond to what we consider to be motivating. Others drift off into their own thoughts as the lesson sinks into a dull, fact-by-fact development of a concept. Often, the problem is that we are teaching in a way that is *backward* in terms of how many students learn.

Do you introduce new concepts with one fact after another until, gradually, your students begin to understand the idea? If you do, you are engaged in *analytic* teaching. This requires analytic processing, which means that a youngster's mind must be able to absorb many small pieces of information and then synthesize them into an overall understanding. That's the way many people learn, but it is *not* the way most young children learn. In fact, the younger the children, the more likely they are to be *global* processors. Even at the secondary level, between 50 and 60 percent of all students tend to be global. An even higher percentage of slowly achieving students or those having difficulty in school—as many as 85 percent—cannot learn successfully in an analytic mode.

*This chapter is based on R. Dunn and K. Dunn "Presenting Forwards Backwards," *Teaching K-8* (Norwalk, CT: Early Years, Inc., October 1988), *19*(2), 71–73.

As you probably know, analytic students are concerned with details, rules, procedures, and directions; they like specific, step-by-step instructions. Global students, on the other hand, are concerned with end results; they need overviews—the "big picture"—as well as general guidelines, variety, alternatives, and different approaches.

Does their inability to remember facts mean that globals are less intelligent than analytics? Not at all. Several studies have verified that globals and analytics are equally able academically but each group achieves best when taught with instructional approaches that match its individuals' learning styles. Unfortunately, of the thousands of teachers we have tested, fully 65 percent are analytic. Thus, far too often, a serious mismatch between analytic teaching styles and global learning preferences occurs, resulting in disaffected students with low scores, poor self-discipline, and damaged self-image (Andrews, 1990, 1991; Brennan, 1984; Dunn, Bruno, Sklar, & Beaudry, 1990; Jarsonbeck, 1984).

What about you? How do you begin a lesson? If you don't know, just listen to yourself as you introduce each new topic. Do you begin with one detail followed by another? If you do, you are teaching analytically. Or, instead, do you tell a story that gives your students the major focus of the lesson, and then fill in the gaps with the pertinent details? That's a global approach. Neither approach is better than the other, but matching the instructional strategy to the student is crucial.

Many teachers, either intuitively or by design, use both global and analytic approaches when introducing lessons. If you do not, you would do well to examine the results in your classroom. First, test your students to determine which are global and which are analytic. The Learning Style Inventory: Primary Version (LSI:P) (Perrin, 1982) offers an easy way to tell which is which (see Chapter 2). Next, analyze your teaching style to see which approach you tend to use most often. Then compare the scores of those students who match your style with the scores of those who do not. You'll find that the children who learn best in the way you naturally tend to teach will achieve better test scores and progress more easily than those who do not.

Guidelines for Teaching Global Students

If you are analytic but wish to teach your global students in ways that make it easier for them to understand and remember, try the following:

1. *Introducing material:* Begin the lesson with either a story, an anecdote, a humorous incident, or a joke that is directly related to the content you are teaching. If possible, relate the introduction to the students' experiences. If that is not feasible, relate the introduction to something that is realistic to them.

2. *Discovery through group learning:* Avoid telling the students too many facts directly; instead, get them to unravel the information by themselves. To do this, suggest that they divide into small groups, rather than working as individuals, unless specific students prefer to work toward solutions by themselves. Usually, global students find it less threatening and more fun to solve problems with others. For four

Begin each reading lesson for global students with a short story or anecdote rather than alphabetical letters or individual vocabulary. Accent the introduction with illustrations or symbols. Relate the content to the children's experiences or interests. (Photograph courtesy Amherst Central School District, Amherst, New York.)

easy-to-use small-group techniques that enable students to learn together in an organized, controlled way, see Chapter 5.

   3. *Written and tactual involvement:* In addition to encouraging global students to think about and solve learning tasks by themselves or in a small group, have them graph or map those details that they are supposed to learn and, if they can, illustrate them. Globals tend to draw meaning from pictures, photographs, symbols and other visual representations; they respond less well to words and numbers. Have them demonstrate their mastery of specific objectives by developing dioramas, graphs, charts, games, and so on. It helps globals to dramatize what they are learning, so you might also suggest pantomimes, plays, and puppet shows to demonstrate what has been learned. In addition, encourage students to develop their own teaching devices—such as Flip Chutes, Pic-A-Holes, Task Cards, or games—to share with classmates so that others can learn through alternative strategies.

Guidelines for Teaching Analytic Students

If you are global and wish to reach your analytic students, try the following:

   1. *Explanations and visual reinforcement:* Explain the procedures and approaches to be used in reaching specific objectives. Write key words on the chalk-

Global children often perform best when solving problems with others; they tend to be people- or peer-oriented. (Photograph courtesy West Seneca Central School District, West Seneca, New York.)

board as you speak. (Analytics respond to words and numbers.) Answer questions about details directly, and use printed visuals on either an overhead projector, slides, or the chalkboard. Print the words on large sheets of oaktag. Illustrate them if you can, or ask a pupil to do that for you.

2. *Directions:* Write all assignments, directions, test dates, and specific objectives in large letters, and provide a copy for each student, or list the directions on a chart and have students copy them if they are able. Read the directions to the others, and have them repeat the information.

3. *Learning through direct teaching or related resources:* Proceed step by step through the details that need to be assimilated to reach understandings or acquire skills. Put key words on the chalkboard; distribute duplicated materials and fact sheets; underline important sections; check homework and notebooks daily. Teach students how to use learning materials independently and how to find and use reinforcing items and books directly related to the specific objectives of the sequence.

4. *Testing and feedback:* Test frequently; provide instant feedback on details in the sequence; respond to questions as soon as possible; itemize your expectations and requirements; if you give an assignment, check it; when you say you will test, do so.

For analytic students, begin each lesson with clearly stated objectives, key words, and directions printed on a chalkboard, chart, or transparency. Globals pay attention to those items toward the end of the lesson, during the review. (Photograph courtesy Sheridan Hill Elementary School, Williamsville, New York.)

A classroom environment responsive to global students includes soft lighting, music, an informal design, snacking, and activities in which children can solve problems and choose to learn together. (Photograph courtesy Amherst Central School District, Amherst, New York.)

Clues to Recognizing Analytic and Global Students; What They Are Likely to Say to You

Analytics	*Global*
Does spelling count?	Why are we doing this?
Should I use a pen or a pencil?	I'll do it later!
Should I skip lines?	I need a break!
Will this be on the test?	He messed up the stuff on my desk.
When do I have to do this?	Why does it really matter?
Can't I have some more time?	Let's start this—and that one too!
What comes first? second?	Why can't I skip around in the book?
Why can't we do one thing at a time?	I'll come back to this later!
Please check my work.	Who cares?!
What do you want done?	

Analytic and Global Lesson Starters

In each of the following lesson starters, Teacher 1 and Teacher 2 are introducing the same lesson. One teacher is using an analytic approach, the other a global approach. Can you tell who is using which? Even more important, do you recognize your own teaching style? The answers are at the bottom of the quiz. Remember—one approach is not "better" than the other. Matching the technique to the strength of the student is crucial to the learner's success.

Quickie Quiz: Global or Analytic?

Community Helpers

Teacher 1	*Teacher 2*
Boys and girls, today we're going to learn about the people in our community who help us. Who remembers what the word *community* means? That' right, Betty! Now, let's learn about four of the people who help us where we live in our own neighborhood. They are the firefighter, the police officer, the garbage collector, and the doctor. This is a picture of a firefighter in uniform. He is on the way to a fire. After he gets there, he aims a hose at the fire and shoots the water onto the fire until it goes out. Sometimes he has to go inside a house that is on fire and help people get out. We	Yesterday, I was walking near the movie theater in town and I saw black smoke coming from the tall building across the street. Two little children were hanging out of a window and crying. I saw flames come shooting out of a corner window. I ran to the telephone on the corner and called the emergency Fire Department number. In just a few minutes, a big red fire engine came racing around the corner with its horn wailing. Firefighters in black raincoats jumped off the engine, attached hoses to the fire hydrants, and began pumping water through hoses aimed at the windows.

say he *rescued* them. Now, see if you can find the words that describe the firefighter's uniform and what he does on these story sheets.

Reading a New Story

Teacher 1

Today we're going to read a story with some new long words. Before we begin to read, try to become familiar with these new words so that you can recognize and say them when you see them in the story. I have the words printed on Task Cards with the word on one side and a picture of it on the other. The cards are scrambled or mixed up. You can figure out what they are by matching all the shapes that fit together. There are six words—or twelve parts—that have to fit together. You will know that you have the right answers when each word is matched with its picture. For example, you've probably seen a camel in the movies, on television, or at the zoo. This Task Card tells you the word that goes with the camel picture. See how the word and picture fit together? When you make your own set of Task Cards, print each word neatly and draw what that word means to you!

Shapes

Teacher 1

Boys and girls, today we're going to learn about shapes. You have four sheets on your desk. One is for the square, another is for the circle, the third is for the triangle, and the last one is for a rectangle. Let's learn about the square first.

Another fire truck sent a ladder and carried the children down. Have you ever seen the firefighters fight a fire? Next week we're going to visit Firehouse Number 10 and hear what fighting fires is really like!

Teacher 2

Today we're going to read a story with some new words. Before we begin to read, I want you to learn all these new words so that you can recognize and say them when you see them in the story. Now I'm going to write some words on the chalkboard that you know and then some that you may not have seen before. After I say and spell them, I want you to say them and spell them out loud with me.

Last week we learned the word cup: C-U-P. Say it with me: "cup"—"cup"—"cup." A new word in the story is pup: P-U-P. Say it with me: "pup"—"pup"—"pup." Let's find the pictures of the *cup* and the *pup* in the story. Say the words as you point to the picture. Now spell each word as you point to its letters.

Teacher 2

Boys and girls, I would like to tell you a story about a place where the families were named after shapes. These shape families all looked exactly like their names! Right on the corner lived the square family! They had to live on the corner because their bodies were made up of all corners! They had four sides and four corners, and each side was exactly the same size. Papa square is four inches on top, four inches on bottom, and four inches on each side. Mama square is three inches on all sides, and the twins, one is for a rectangle. Let's learn about the square first. Notice that each line meets in a corner? Now take your rulers and draw two more squares, each with four-inch lines. Can you draw one with two-inch lines? If you can, you are a good "square" artist!

Sally and Sammy, are two inches on all sides. Can you draw the square family on the special sheets I gave you? First, connect the dots. Then see if you can measure them with the ruler I gave you. Color them, and give them faces, legs, and arms, too. Next we'll go around the corner and meet the circle family.

Answers: "Community Helpers," Teacher 1 (Analytic), Teacher 2 (Global); "Reading a New Story," Teacher 1 (Global), Teacher 2 (Analytic); "Shapes," Teacher 1 (Analytic), Teacher 2 (Global)
Try teaching globally at least part of the time. More than half your students will be motivated and interested in what happens next. Do not be surprised when analytics indicate displeasure with your global lessons. For them, global teaching is just as backward as analytic teaching is for globals. Note the youngster who becomes impatient with your storytelling and asks, "Is this important? It is going to be on a test?" Chances are, you have an extreme analytic on your hands, and you probably will have to teach that lesson both ways.

Lessons and topics will appeal to both processing styles when they are begun with an activity that appeals to global and analytic youngsters' tactual and kinesthetic strengths. (Photograph courtesy Amherst Central School District, Amherst, New York.)

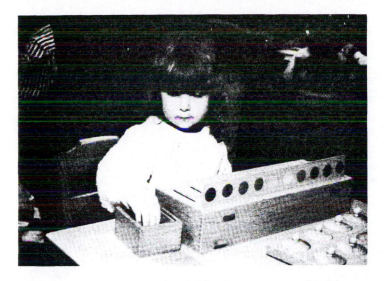

When (a) lessons relate to the children's experiences, (b) they understand why *they need to learn the content,* and *(c) they have an overall understanding of what they need to remember, they then can concentrate on facts and details. (Photograph courtesy Amherst Central School District, Amherst, New York.)*

Well, why not? It certainly isn't fair to teach to one style and not to the other. In addition, you will be successful with more students because you will be teaching forwards for *both* groups. When you teach globally to globals and analytically to analytics, the lesson will move more quickly than when one group is, in effect, being mistaught.

Teaching to Both Groups Simultaneously

If you are willing to experiment once or twice to see the effects of teaching to each group correctly, try giving global students a Team Learning with creative assignments, inference questions, and factual material in that order at the beginning of a period while, simultaneously, you teach exactly the same information to analytics in reverse order. Succinctly instruct the analytics, and then direct them to do the same Team Learning. Then bring the globals together and *elicit* the answers from them. After that, ask students to describe their reactions to the dual, matched instruction. Pay particular attention to the test results on the unit involved. Chances are strong that most students will perform better after being *introduced* to the information through their correct processing styles. They also should enjoy learning better than in nonmatched teaching.

Lessons and topics can be made to appeal to both analytic and global youngsters through the "Learning Person" (LP)—an Independent Contract (see Chapter 8). Analytics who require structure and sequence can proceed through each separate step in order, from "What I Want to Learn" to "How I Feel about Learning." Globals may complete the requirements out of sequence or do two or more at the same time. In addition, the LP graphic permits them to see the "whole thing," at once and the activities permit them to show creatively what they have mastered. (Courtesy Amherst Central School District, Amherst, New York.)

A Final Word on Global and Analytic Approaches to Teaching

Before beginning each lesson, print on the board exactly what you expect the children to learn during that period. Point out those objectives to the analytics, and urge them to concentrate on learning the information. Then begin the lesson with an anecdote, a hands-on activity, or a dramatic or humorous story that directly relates what has to be learned to the children's lives. Next, include everything important in a Team Learning (see Chapter 5) to emphasize the objective.

After the children have completed the Team Learning, either individually or in small groups, discuss their answers in a large-group review. Reemphasize the objectives on the chalkboard for the global youngsters. As homework, require each child to provide answers to those objectives by making a set of Task Cards, a Pic-A-Hole, a Floor Game, an Electroboard, or a game—either independently or in a pair or a small group (their choice). The children will enjoy learning *and* remember more than they ever did before.

5

Designing Small-Group
Instructional Techniques

Importance of Small-Group Techniques

Many primary children respond best to a learning situation that involves between two and five of their peers. Some of these youngsters may not be authority- or teacher-oriented for a variety of reasons. They may feel intimidated, anxious, or too strongly directed by adults or those in charge. Some may need the interaction of friends to stimulate them to learn; others are motivated by a team effort. Many relax when a group, rather than each of them individually, is responsible for a task, contract, or project. There also are students who gain persistence through group goals or who can deal more effectively with a short, specific portion of an assignment rather than with an entire task. Such youngsters often feel more responsibility to their peers than to either themselves or adults. For these reasons, or to satisfy their simple gregariousness, approximately one-third of K–2 youngsters' learning styles are best served if they often are permitted to work in groups.

First Concrete Step toward Individualization of Learning

Diagnose your students' sociological elements with the Learning Style Inventory: Primary Version (LSI:P) (Perrin). Print the information concerning those with whom each learns best—their sociological preferences—on a Class Wall Chart (see Chapter 12). Explain their sociological styles to the youngsters, and suggest that *some* of them will learn best alone or in a pair, but that others will learn more, more easily, in a small group of three to five children. Then assign the peer-oriented students to a few small-group experiences and examine the results.

Students who have been parent- or teacher-directed for most of their lives should first learn to make simple decisions and to assume the responsibility for completing tasks free of constant adult supervision. Use selected techniques such as Circle of Knowledge, Team Learning, Brainstorming, Case Study, and Simulation to provide a structure wherein learning occurs through cooperative small-group effort without the teacher serving as a constant guide or fountain of knowledge.

Small-group interactions also permit youngsters to avoid feelings of failure or embarrassment by solving problems in cooperation with other students. When they make errors, sharing the responsibility with a group of peers sharply reduces the tension or trauma. Further, the small-group techniques help students to understand how other people reach decisions and work toward solutions. Finally, interaction with peers creates sounding boards on which to reflect ideas, build solutions, and suggest conclusions to the group and to the teacher.

Greater Learning through Sociological Preferences

Over the years, a number of researchers examined teams and groups as they strove toward achievement. Homans (1950) postulated that groups were separate entities and results could be viewed simply as the sum total of their individual members. Argyris (1957), Lorge, Fox, Davitz, and Brenner (1958), Hankins (1973), and others both in and out of education reported that small teams often obtained better results than the individuals might have accomplished if working along or with an adult. Poirer (1970) studied students as paired partners and reported increased learning, as did Bass (1965), who pointed to group recognition, respect, and affection, as well as fun, as motivating factors toward higher achievement.

According to Slavin (1983), the discrepant outcomes in cooperative learning research, where no clear small-group strategy produced better results than another, were due to intervening variables inherent in the research designs, setting, subject areas, and evaluation measures. Five years later, Slavin (1988) concluded that a fifth variable was concerned with whether individual or group accountability was required. However, the major intervening variable, which neither Slavin, the Johnsons (1975), nor their predecessors addressed, was the one of individual differences— which they neither identified nor analyzed in their work.

Another deficiency of their studies was that they did not expose students to a variety of sociological experiences so that they then could determine whether, indeed, all children performed best in cooperative small groups. Their designs did not permit analysis of how well individuals achieved when permitted a variety of treatments, and whether those same children *consistently* performed best in one condition or another. Another concern is that they did not address *initial* teaching to determine how effectively children could teach themselves, as opposed to learning with peers, learning with adults, or learning best in the same way consistently when mastering new and difficult information through their learning style strengths.

Research revealed that when students' sociological preferences were identified and the youngsters then were exposed to multiple treatments both congruent and incongruent with their identified learning styles, each achieved significantly higher test scores in matched conditions and significantly lower test scores when mismatched (DeBello, 1985; Dunn, Giannitti, Murray, Geisert, Rossi, & Quinn, 1990; Giannitti,

Although small-group techniques are appropriate for approximately 28 percent of the students in grades 3 through 12 who do concentrate when working with peers, at least 13 percent of primary children consistently achieve best when working alone. Some prefer studying in a pair, but almost 30 percent strongly prefer learning with an adult. (Photographs courtesy West Seneca Central School District, West Seneca, New York, and Brightwood Elementary School, Greensboro, North Carolina.

1988; Miles, 1987; Perrin, 1984). In the three studies where attitudes were included as a dependent variable, those scores also were significantly higher as an outcome of matched conditions. In the one investigation where an interaction effect did not occur (Cholakis, 1986), the population consisted of students who had attended a parochial school for their entire education. The researcher suggested that these youngsters' history of strong orientation to authority may have skewed the results. Those students, however, learned equally well in other conditions. The studies listed here indicated that students learned more and liked learning better when they were taught through their identified learning styles.

Learning Style Characteristics Responsive to Small-Group Techniques

Many small-group techniques can be designed to accommodate differences in students' learning styles, but they are especially appropriate for students who are peer-oriented. They provide structure as well as both auditory and visual experiences. Students who serve as Recorder will gain additionally by writing (a tactual method).

Small-group techniques will accommodate the elements of light, temperature, design, time, intake, and mobility. Motivation, persistence, and responsibility may be enhanced by the group process; members can exert positive peer pressure on those who are peer-oriented but not strong in these areas.

Those who prefer to work alone or with adults and those who do not require structure are less likely to benefit from small-group techniques. Teachers can post assignments with specific objectives or tasks and tell the class: "You may do this alone, in a pair, in a team of three, or with me. If you wish to work in a pair, decide where you want to work, but stay away from your classmates who need to be by themselves." After a brief pause, students who wish to work in small groups may move together quickly. After that, those who want to work directly with the instructor may move to a previously designated area of the room.

We strongly recommend, however, that Team Learning and Circle of Knowledge—specific small-group strategies for teaching and reinforcing difficult information—should become an integral part of the class's repertoire *prior* to permitting sociological choices. These strategies enable students to work efficiently either alone or in a small group for a long period of time. Thus, they give teachers enough time to teach the smaller group without interruption. These two easy-to-master instructional strategies are good ways to begin to teach students through their individual learning styles.

Descriptions and Samples of Small-Group Techniques

Circle of Knowledge

The Circle of Knowledge technique is highly motivating and is ideal for reinforcing skills in any subject area. It permits students to do the following:

- Review previously learned information in an interesting way
- Focus thinking on one major concept at a time
- Contribute to a group effort as part of a team
- Serve as catalysts for additional responses
- Develop ingenuity in helping team members to contribute
- Be exposed to and learn information without becoming bored

Procedures

Several small circles of four or five chairs (no desks) are positioned evenly about the room. One student in each group must serve as the Circle's Recorder. One way to designate a Recorder is to say, "The person wearing the most of the color *red* will serve as Recorder this time. If no one is wearing red, go to the person with the most *orange;* if no one is wearing orange, go to *yellow.*" Keep adding colors until each Circle has a Recorder. Colors, of course, are not the only way to choose a Recorder. Other possibilities include the person who:

- Lives closest to or farthest from the school
- Has the most alphabetical letters in his or her first name
- Has the most buttons on his or her clothing
- Has a birthday closest to Halloween, Thanksgiving, New Year's Day, Lincoln's birthday, Valentine's Day, Columbus Day (any holiday), or today

This technique is a fair, objective way of drafting youngsters who do not volunteer and protects younger and less aggressive children who may be "chosen" repeatedly by their classmates. It avoids the elitism—or stigma—of *electing, appointing, drafting,* or *volunteering* out of desperation or pressure. All children have a chance—if they happen to have . . . the longest pencil, . . . smallest eraser, . . . longest hair, . . . lightest-colored eyes, . . . longest fingernails, . . . largest notebook, . . . brightest-colored clothing, . . . most bleached-out jeans, . . . most members in their family.

Everyone participates by providing answers to a single question—one that has more than one possible response. Each person responds in rotation, one at a time, either *clockwise* or *counterclockwise.* To help the children remember in which direction the Circle moves (left to right or right to left), walk to the chalkboard or a blank wall. Say, "Make believe that you can see a clock right here on this wall. If you *do,* the 12 is here." Point to where the 12 would be located on a clock (upper center of the imaginary—or real—circle you drew). Continue: "If the 12 is here (pointing), the 3 is here." Move your hand to the right-center, where the 3 normally would be found. "If the 12 and the 3 are here (point again, moving in rotation), then the 6 is here." (Point to where the 6 would be on a clock.) "Then the 9 is here (move to left-center), and if we keep going, we are moving around the clock, from left to right. We call that movement, from left to right, *clockwise.* The members in each Circle of Knowledge will give one answer at a time, *clockwise!*"

Only the Recorder writes the answers that each person, in turn, contributes to the Circle's list. Only the Recorder writes, but *everyone* thinks of answers—as many as possible. With young children who may not yet be writing, use a tape recorder in the center of each group, and show the youngsters how to get their mouths close so that their answers will be recorded. If you do not have enough tape recorders, use those that you *do* have and substitute older children, aides, parents, a volunteer, or a community member to record the answers. It also is possible for children to *draw* their answers—for example, "Draw all the fruits (shapes, community workers' hats, animals that can be pets, flowers, types of houses, etc.) that you can!"

When a Circle member gives an answer that others know is wrong, they can tell the Recorder not to add that response to the Circle's list—because they believe it is incorrect. The group decides whether to keep an answer (if it is correct) or discard it (if it is incorrect). When there is disagreement among the members, the Recorder writes the *majority* decision; the minority may write its own answers. *Tell* the children that majorities can be wrong. If they have different beliefs than their teammates, they should take a chance and write their own answer.

A single question or problem is posed, and—whether written and reproduced or printed on a chalkboard—it must have many possible answers. Examples include naming all the community helpers you can, all the words you can think of that start with "C," foods that are starches, and so forth.

Each Circle of Knowledge team will respond to the same question simultaneously (but quietly). Children are urged to *whisper* their answers so that no one else can hear them. One member of each group is designated as the first to begin, and the answers then are provided by one member at a time, clockwise or counterclockwise, as explained before. No member may skip a turn, and no one may provide an answer until the person directly before has delivered a correct one. Therefore, the answers stop being recorded while a member is thinking or groping for a possible response. No teammate may give an answer to another, but anyone in the group may act out, draw, or pantomime hints to help the person remember an item, an answer, or a possible response. Only the Recorder may write, and he or she jots down (in a word or a phrase) the suggestions (answers, responses, thoughts) of each participant as the Circle of Knowledge continues.

At the end of a predetermined amount of time, usually two to five minutes, the teacher calls a halt to the knowledge sharing, and all Recorders must stop writing the groups' answers. The number of responses produced by each group may be noted, but credit is not given for quantity.

The teacher divides the chalkboard or overhead transparency into columns and numbers the columns so that each represents one of the groups. In turn, a representative from each Circle is called on to report one of the answers suggested by that group. When an answer is provided, the teacher writes it in the group's column, and all the recorders in the room look at the list of answers developed by their group. If that answer is on their Circle's list, the Recorder—or any member of the Circle—crosses it off, gradually decreasing the length of the list until only the answers that have not yet been reported to the group and written on the board remain. This procedure continues until no Circle has any remaining answers on its list. Recorders should cross off reported answers immediately because there is a penalty for reporting a duplicate answer.

The answers given by each Circle of Knowledge can be awarded points that then are recorded on the board to produce competition among the teams. The teacher might decide that each correct response will earn 1 point (or 5 or 10 points) and that the Circle achieving the most points will be the winner. Whenever an answer is challenged by a rival Circle, the teacher must decide whether it is right or wrong. If the answer is correct, and the challenger is incorrect, the challenger's Circle loses one point. If the answer is incorrect and the challenger is correct, the Circle that sponsored the answer loses the potential point, and the challenger's Circle gains one.

The important thing to remember about Circles of Knowledge is that they may be used only to review something that already has been introduced and taught. Because the information required has been taught to the students previously, the time span permitted is usually a short one (2 to 5 minutes) as previously indicated.

Sample Primary Circle of Knowledge Questions

- List all the clothes you would wear on a cold winter day (3½ minutes).
- Name all the community helpers you can (3 minutes).
- List all the jobs each community helper does in your neighborhood (5 minutes).
- Name all the words that start with the letter M (4 minutes).
- List all the sweet-tasting foods that are healthful for you (5 minutes).
- Name all the vegetables you can (2⅙ minutes).
- List all the colors you can (4⅓ minutes).
- Tell all the things you can do to make your mother happy on Mother's Day without spending one penny (5 minutes).
- List all the baby animal names you can (3 minutes).
- List all the different kinds of furniture you would find in a house (4¹/₁₀ minutes).
- Name all the songs you can remember that are about animals (4⅑ minutes).
- Draw all the things you can that are round (4½ minutes).
- Write all the words that *rhyme* (sound like) with *eat* (5¹/₁₂ minutes).

Children often pay attention to the amount of time permitted for a Circle of Knowledge if an unusual fraction is added to the number of minutes. Try using "2 and 11/13 of a minute" and see whether the youngsters react to it.

Team Learning

Team Learning *introduces* new and difficult material successfully because it:

- Presents it in either printed or pictorial form.
- Poses one or more of each of three different types of question—factual, inference, and creative.
- Permits children to work either alone, in pairs, in a small team, or in a group with their teacher, based on each child's sociological preference as revealed by the LSI:P.
- Allows children to sit anywhere in the classroom they wish *as long as they*

Team Learning is an instructional strategy for introducing new and difficult *academic information. It may be completed by a group of three or four youngsters* or *by a pair or by a single student who prefers working alone. (Photograph courtesy West Seneca Central School District, West Seneca, New York.)*

behave well, work quietly and with decorum, complete their work, and achieve well on the test directly related to the material being taught with the small-group technique.

- Uses a multisensory approach—seeing, talking, hearing, writing, and hearing again when the teacher elicits the answers and confirms responses.
- Tape-records the entire Team Learning—the material to be learned, the three types of questions, and the directions for working cooperatively.
- Reduces the tension that occurs when individuals are responsible for mastery of materials they may not be able to learn by themselves.

Procedures

1. Begin by writing a paragraph or two to teach what you want the youngsters to learn. You may take the information from commercial publications such as books, paraphrase existing materials, or create your own original text. Do not teach too much at one time. For primary youngsters, one or two paragraphs is sufficient unless you are teaching highly motivated or gifted children. If that is the case, experiment by adding a little more for each of several small-group sessions, and determine the appropriate length and complexity of the information by observing how well the children handle it.

2. Add the three kinds of questions to what you have written. (You may pose more than one of each type.) Begin with the factual ones so that the students can (a) find the answers, (b) develop awareness of how they find them, and (c) be successful. Because the children can combine their strengths and talk things through, most teams perform and retain well when involved in Team Learning.

3. Tape-record everything so that your more independent children can work together, but apart from the group, if they wish. Gradually, these youngsters will begin to self-pace themselves and will be able to use Team Learning to learn a great deal more, more quickly, than they would if they maintained the class's pace.

4. Explain the rules to the children. Each must decide on the person or persons with whom he or she wishes to learn. They may *not* verbally ask someone else to work with them. Instead, they can make eye contact and pantomime an invitation to work together. Individuals either may accept (by nodding their heads vertically) or decline (by turning their heads from side to side.)

Children who choose to work alone merely need to withdraw from the larger group, move to the part of the classroom where each wants to work, and get started. If they choose to work in a pair, their mutual acceptance will be demonstrated by nodding, and the two then can determine where they wish to work, stand behind their chairs, lift them, move them quietly to the preferred section, and—keeping their voices *very* low—begin to work together.

5. All others can be divided into groups of three to five children—the maximum number of students for *any* small-group strategy. For peer-oriented students, learning occurs through their interaction; having more than five in a group *prevents* real involvement. Four is more effective than five; three may be better than four.

6. Establish a time frame during which the assignment should be completed. Periodically, note the amount of remaining time on the chalkboard to keep the youngsters on task. You may walk around, helping those who request your assistance and observing what occurs.

7. Tell the Recorders that they need to elicit the answers from their team members. When one person gives an answer, the Recorder may *not* write it before asking, one at a time, whether each member agrees with that answer. When there is a consensus, the Recorder writes the answer. When there is *not,* discussion continues, with Team members explaining why they think the answer is correct or incorrect. If agreement does not come readily, the ones who disagree with the majority write their own answers, while the Recorder writes or draws the majority's answers.

For example, to the assignment, "Describe the feelings some big sisters and brothers sometimes have when the new baby gets a lot of attention from everyone," some children might describe anger, resentment, irritation, feeling "bad," or wanting to cry or hit; others might describe feeling happy and pleased. There is no right or wrong answer, and disagreement can easily occur within the team. The Recorder writes or draws what the majority reports; the minority records its response. When you call on the various team members after the teams have completed their work, and hear the different responses, explain that people *do* differ in their reactions to the same situation and that it is all right if your feelings differ from others'.

8. Tell the children that, within each team, all members should contribute and help each other develop answers to the assignment. It is to the team's advantage to help the Recorder get all the answers recorded (in writing or drawing). To promote quiet and order, advise the children that anyone who hears another team's answers has your permission to *use* them. Children need to work quietly to avoid giving away their responses!

9. When the allocated amount of time has been exhausted, or if most groups complete the task in less time, tell the children that you all will work together on checking the answers the teams developed. Read the first question aloud, and ask for a volunteer from any group. Call on one, hear the team's response, discuss it if that is warranted, and write the correct answer on either the chalkboard or an overhead projector. *Seeing* material on the board or on a transparency for reinforcement after reading, hearing, and discussing it will help develop the children's word recognition ability and expand their reading and speaking vocabularies. It also will help them retain the information.

10. Proceed through all the answers, calling on different Recorders and other team members alternately. The answers do not "belong" to the Recorders, who merely record the *team's* agreed-on decisions. Thus, if you call on someone other than the Recorder, that person may extend a hand, and the Recorder can pass the team's answers to that youngster. As the children become familiar with the procedures for Team Learning and recognize that they may be called on to deliver an answer or two, they will urge their team Recorders to write or draw neatly so that they can decipher what has been noted.

11. Soon thereafter, review what was introduced through the Team Learning with a Circle of Knowledge. After the two small-group strategies, peer-oriented students will remember much more than they have in the past.

After one or two Team Learning experiences, groups of students will develop team relationships and begin to question and analyze the material with enthusiasm and animated but productive conversation. Walk around and help with the process the first time or two. You will discover newly found freedom to work with individuals or groups who need you once the students have gained initial experience with this teaching strategy.

Time limits may be imposed or left open, depending on the learning style and need for structure of the members of each class. An alternative to strict time limits would be to assign some Team Learning prescriptions to a group as homework or as a self-teaching activity.

For purposes of comparison, participation, and reinforcement, the Recorders of teams working on the same assignment can be asked to share with the entire group those responses to the material that were developed and approved by their membership. Number the groups, and then ask Team 1 for a response to a question, Team 2 for a second response, and so on.

Write each Team's responses on the chalkboard or overhead projector as they are given, and instruct students to cross an answer off their Team's list if the one just recorded on the chalkboard duplicates theirs; they will be left with only answers that have not yet been reported. Other Team members may be called on to respond during the second or third round. The Recorders should pass their lists to the students who are called on to answer next. Eventually, you and the class will proceed through all the answers, permitting many of the team members to participate. In this way, errors and misinformation are not likely to be retained. Moreover, all questions will be answered, and many will have had one or more chances to participate actively. Younger students, or those who don't yet read or write well, can respond by holding up the right answer or a drawing or picture of the item requested.

As with the Circles of Knowledge, you and your class may elect to use a team competition approach, with points based on the correct number of answers given by each team. Competition among teams is usually friendly and stimulating; often, different teams win. Furthermore, the competition does not put self-image at risk by pitting one individual against another.

Team Learning responds to the important learning style elements of structure, design, time, mobility, intake, learning with peers, motivation, persistence, responsibility, and visual and auditory perceptual strengths. Kinesthetic and tactual resources can be added to Team Learning exercises for those who require them. Sample Team Learnings are shown in Figure 5–1, 5–2, and 5–3.

Brainstorming

Brainstorming is an exciting group participation designed to develop multiple answers to a single question, alternative solutions to problems, and creative responses. It is an associative process that encourages students to call out—one of the few times this is permitted in our schools. Thus, it responds to personal motivation and does not suppress spontaneity.

In addition to increasing motivation, brainstorming offers many practical advantages.

- It is *stimulating*. It offers a unique, freewheeling, exciting, and rapid-fire method that builds enthusiasm among many participants.
- It is *positive*. Quiet, shy students usually become active participants because they do not feel put down; their contributions are masked by the group process. Conversely, those who usually dominate discussions are structured into offering succinct suggestions.
- It is *focused*. Diversions and distractions are eliminated. Irrelevant stories and speeches are eliminated.
- It is *spontaneous* and *creative*. Students serve as a sounding board that generates new ideas. Creativity is released by the momentum of the process.
- It is *efficient* and *productive*. Dozens of suggestions, facts, ideas, or creative

Sample: Team Learning #1*

Team Members

1. _____   3. _____

2. _____   4. _____

             5. _____ Recorder

Use the tape recorder to help you sing along with this song.

Ann and Andy

Ann and Andy went for a walk.
Ann and Andy liked to talk.
They said, "Hello!" to an alley cat,
to a little black ant and an ailing rat.

The alley cat smiled and said, "Have a good day!"
The ant laughed out loud and the rat came to play.
They sang and they danced and they all had fun,
And liked each other when the day was done!

Ann and Andy and the alley cat,
The little black ant and the happy rat,
They ate green apples and asked, "Say when
Can we get together and meet again?"

1. Can you name at least two (2) words that begin with the letter *a*?

   _____ _____.

   If you can name three (3) words—one more—you are sensational!

   _____

2. Find at least two (2) more words that were *not* used in this song

   that begin with the letter *a*. _____ _____

3. Write at least one (1) person's name that begins with the letter *A*.
4. Do you think that Ann and Andy had fun that day? Why?
5. With whom did Ann and Andy play that day? Write what they
   were.

   _____ _____ _____

*This Team Learning was designed by Alyse Ritchie, kindergarten teacher, Public School #156, Brownsville, New York. It is part of her Contract Activity Package, "Knowing Your ABCs from A to E."

FIGURE 5–1 Sample Format for Team Learning

6. Why did they want to "get together again"?
7. Why do you think they ate green apples?
8. Draw a picture of what they all must have looked like while dancing. Draw Ann, Andy, the cat, the ant, and the ailing rat.
9. What is another word for *ailing?*
10. Why do you think the "ailing rat" became happy?
11. Make up your own sentence about Ann, Andy, the cat, the ant, and the rat.

FIGURE 5–1   Sample Format for Team Learning (continued)

Sample: Team Learning #2*

Team Members

1. _____   3. _____

2. _____   4. _____

5. _____ Recorder

(Read or Listen to the Tape)

How Can Foods Help You Stay Healthy?

Your eating habits affect how you feel during the day. For example, what happens if you have no breakfast or a poor breakfast? You are likely to be tired or cross, and you may be hungry by midmorning. What might also happen to the way you do your schoolwork?

Some good food choices for breakfast are fruit, fruit juice, cereal, bread, milk, and eggs. Cheese, peanut butter, and potatoes are other good breakfast foods that can add variety to your meal. All these foods give you energy for your schoolwork and help you grow as you should. They contain *nourishing substances,* or *nutrients*, that your body needs. Candy, cookies, and other sweetened foods and drinks do not supply the *nutrients* you need.

1. List two (2) things that could happen if you often eat a poor breakfast.

_____

_____

_____

2. Another word for *nourishing substances* is: _____

FIGURE 5–2   Nutrition or Neat Treats

3. What word in the last sentence means things that are healthful for you?

   _____

4. Do you think boys and girls who do well in school usually eat a good breakfast? Why?

   _____

   _____

   _____

5. Write a menu that would describe a good breakfast.

   _____

   _____

   _____

6. Write a poem naming good foods a person could eat when having a nourishing breakfast.

   or

   Draw a picture of at least eight (8) *nutritious* breakfast foods.

   _____

   _____

   _____

*This Team Learning was designed by Carolyn Bovell, teacher, Portledge School, Locus Valley, New York.

FIGURE 5–2   Nutrition or Neat Treats

solutions are generated in a matter of minutes. Additional steps or plans for an activity can be brainstormed, as well as more specific answers for general responses (subset brainstorming).

- It is *involving* and builds *self-image*. Seeing their ideas listed enhances self-image. Group pride and cohesiveness increase as members begin to feel part of the unit that created the lists.
- It is *ongoing* and *problem solving*. The results are recorded and may be modified and used in new situations.

Procedures

The Brainstorming leader also acts as Recorder. He or she records all responses, asks for clarification or repetition, synthesizes large phrases into short key ideas, and keeps the group focused on each single topic. The leader should not comment, editorialize, or contribute, but should concentrate on creating an effective and productive

Sample: Team Learning #3*

Team Members

1. _____   3. _____

2. _____   4. _____

    5. _____ Recorder

Read the following paragraphs or listen to the tape and discuss the questions with your group. Answer all the questions together. If you do not agree, you may write your own answer.

What does the word *dinosaur* mean? *Dinosaur* means "terrible lizard." Those terrible lizards lived 225 million years ago. Dinosaurs were *reptiles*. Their body temperature changed all the time. They had *scaly skin*, laid eggs, and could walk without dragging their bellies on the ground.

Most dinosaurs grew to be taller than a two-story 2-story building. Although they could weigh as much as seventy (70) cars, some dinosaurs were only as small as a chicken.

1. What does the word *dinosaur* mean? _____

2. How were dinosaurs like reptiles? _____

3. How were dinosaurs different from reptiles? _____

   _____

4. Why do you think some dinosaurs grew so large? _____

   _____

5. Write a story about finding a baby dinosaur and keeping it as your pet. Name your dinosaur!! _____

*This Team Learning was designed by Jo Anne Dobbins, doctoral student, St. John's University, New York.

FIGURE 5–3   Team Learning: Dinosaurs

session. Act as leader-recorder yourself until some of the more mature students can serve in this capacity. For younger children, use a tape recorder to capture their answers. Then write them on an overhead projector transparency or on the chalkboard. The youngsters will be proud to see their answers displayed.

Setting for Independent Students Who Can Read and Write
From five to ten students should form a fairly tight semicircle of chairs facing the leader. (Larger groups can be effective at times.) Behind the leader should be a wall

Very young children may require the teacher to conduct initial Brainstorming sessions. After many experiences with this small-group technique, many may be able to partici-pate with the aid of a tape recorder rather than an adult. (Photograph courtesy West Seneca Central School District, West Seneca, New York.)

containing three to five large sheets of lecture pad paper or newsprint double folded to prevent strike-through marks on the wall (see Figure 5–4). Attach these sheets (approximately 20 to 24 inches wide and 30 to 36 inches high) to the wall with mask-ing tape, and place them a few inches apart at a comfortable height for recording. The leader should use a broad-tipped felt marker for instant visibility by the entire group. A timekeeper should be appointed for the two- or three-minute brainstorming seg-ments, but he or she may participate. Have additional sheets available, as well as an overhead projector to permit groups to analyze, plan, or do subset brainstorming for specific aspects of general answers. Figure 5–5 presents the rules for Brainstorming. Reproduce these and post them in the classroom to remind students of how to engage in this problem-solving technique. Figures 5–6 and 5–7 provide sample Brainstorm-ing exercises for primary-grade children.

Setting for Younger Children Who Do Not Yet Read or Write
Have from five to eight students sit in a tight circle with a tape recorder placed in the middle to pick up and capture all students' answers and comments. Then write the words on the board, on oaktag, or on a transparency on the overhead projector for discussion and praise.

FIGURE 5–4   For optimum results, a brainstorming session consists of a tight semicircle of five to ten participants. The teacher serves as Recorder until one or more children mature sufficiently to serve in that capacity.

1.	Concentrate on the topic—"storm your brain."
2.	Fill the silence—call out what pops into your head.
3.	Wait for an opening—don't step on someone's lines.
4.	Record the thoughts in short form.
5.	Record everything—no matter how far out.
6.	Repeat your contribution until it is recorded.
7.	Be positive—no putdowns, body language, or editorial comment.
8.	Stay in focus—no digressions.
9.	Use short time spans—one to three minutes.
10.	Analyze later—add, subtract, plan, implement.
11.	Brainstorm from general to specific subsets.

FIGURE 5–5 Rules for Participation

Describe all the problems people could avoid by eating *nutritious* foods instead of junk foods. (3 minutes)

_____   _____

_____   _____

_____   _____

_____   _____

_____   _____

_____   _____

_____   _____

Carolyn Bovell designed this Brainstorming strategy for her second-grade unit on nutritious foods.

FIGURE 5–6   Sample: Brainstorming: Nutrition or Neat Eats

Name all the different ways you can of getting from one place to another.
(2 9/10 minutes)

_____   _____

_____   _____

_____   _____

_____   _____

_____   _____

_____   _____

_____   _____

_____   _____

_____   _____

_____

FIGURE 5–7   Brainstorming: Transportation

When used either as a class assignment or for homework, a Case Study permits children to work together and to see how each perceives events, solves problems, or creates novel end products. (Photograph courtesy Center for the Study of Learning and Teaching Styles, St. John's University, New York.)

Case Study

A Case Study stimulates and helps to develop analytic skills. Four to five students can spend considerable time discussing and interpreting short, relevant stories that each of them finds interesting

Case Studies provide:

- A strategy for developing material within the student's frame of reference. The characters, situations, and events can, if constructed properly, strike responsive and understanding chords.
- An approach that can be stimulating and meaningful if student identification is fostered and debate is structured to understand different points of view on recognized problems and situations
- Safe, nonthreatening situations for students who can enter the analysis without being affected personally
- Training and development in problem solving, analytic skill development, arriving at conclusions, and planning for new directions in learning situations and in real life

Guidelines for the Development of Case Studies

Format   Case Studies may be written as very short stories, audio- or videotaped dramatizations, films, psychodramas, news events, or historical happenings—real or fictional. The use of chronological sequence helps students follow the flow of events and analyze key issues. Avoid flashbacks and other complex approaches except for the most advanced students.

Focus   The case should focus on a single event, incident, or situation. Ability to analyze is aided by a high degree of concentration on the factors that precipitated the event, the attitudes prevailing during a given incident, or the sharply defined points of view of those dealing with a problem.

Relevance   Reality or "potential credibility" related to the frame of reference of the students is crucial to the success of this small-group technique. The participants involved in analyzing the case must be able to recognize, understand, or even identify with the people in the situation because what they do or say seems authentic or possible. The style of writing should attempt to capture the flavor of familiar places, people, and their actions at a level that is equal to or slightly above the levels of understanding of the participants.

Increasing Motivation   After initial training in the analysis of Case Studies, involve students in actually writing and acting out roles in subsequent cases. Both relevance and motivation will increase as students become involved and begin to feel a sense of ownership of either their new creation or a variation of an older case.

Procedures

Select, seek volunteers, or appoint a leader and a Recorder from among four or five participants. Have the group read or listen to the case at the beginning of the session. As the students become more familiar with this approach you may wish to assign the materials as prior reading or listening exercises to increase the amount of time devoted to group discussion.

The leader should not dominate the session but should keep the group on target for the allotted time. The Recorder should participate and also concentrate on capturing the essence of the group's responses to various analytical questions. He or she must periodically check with the group to obtain consensus.

Develop key questions for the Case Study or short story in advance. Other questions may be suggested by the group as it delves deeply into the problem or situation. Questions may begin with factual checkpoints but then should move quickly into possible reasons, alternative motives, and analysis of the subtleties and complexities of human experiences and interactions as well as values, standards, and other abstractions. Finally, ask students to reach conclusions and to apply developing insights to new situations.

Analyzing Case Studies should build student powers of interpretation, synthesis, description, observation, perception, abstraction, comparison, judgment, conclusion, determination, and prediction. Obviously, the difficulty of the material will depend on the ability, experience, and sophistication of the group.

Sample Case Study for Primary Grades: Values

Purpose   Understanding some of the factors that cause others to behave as they do when they want to be accepted.

The New Student

Ryan arrived with his family from up-state in the beginning of November. He felt strange and alone. How was he going to make new friends? Could he learn to read in his new school? All the kids seemed to be so smart. And they all had their own friends; his were back where he used to live.

Ryan was quiet at first but then tried to talk to some of the other boys. He asked a question or two. Jim seemed to like him. He asked Ryan if he wanted to play catch after school. But before Ryan could answer, two of Jim's friends pulled Jim away and yelled at Ryan, "Hey Dumbo, go away." Then they pushed him. Ryan was angry. He kicked one boy and hit the other. Soon they were all wrestling on the ground. A teacher came, stopped them, and took them to the principal's office.

Case Study Analysis Questions

- Why did the boys fight?
- How would you help Ryan?
- Who was right? Who was wrong?
- What would *you* say to Ryan? To Jim? To the other two boys?
- Why did the other two boys call Ryan names and push him away?
- What are three things you could do to help Ryan become part of the class and feel welcome?

Scores of cases like this one and their analyses can be developed about a variety of situations dealing with values, attitudes, interactions, or preferences. Others can be generated dealing with curriculum areas such as health, safety, colors, or vowels.

A Final Word on Small-Group Techniques

These four small-group techniques and others you use or devise are essential to building independence and responding to those youngsters whose learning style clearly indicates a need to work with peers.

- Circle of Knowledge reviews and reinforces previously learned material. It is always a *review* technique.
- Team Learning introduces new material and requires both factual and higher

Whenever planning to use small-group or cooperative learning strategies, it is crucial *to remember that some children* need *to learn by themselves, others work well only in a pair, some need a small group, and others need the periodic, direct supervision of a teacher. (Photograph courtesy Lee Elementary School, Corsicana, Texas.)*

level cognitive questions as well as creative applications. It is always an *introductory* technique.

- Brainstorming releases creative energy and aids in planning and solving problems. It can be an *introductory* technique.
- Case Studies develop analytic skills and build empathy and understanding among children as they work together to solve problems or cope with crises. It can be used to either *introduce* or *review* new or difficult information.

Each of the techniques suggested in this chapter focuses on one or more specific objectives. The rules for each strategy tend to contain the impulsivity of peer-oriented children who want their classmates' approval. Select or develop those strategies that respond to the learning styles of the youngsters with whom they will be used. Teaching will become more rewarding than ever for both you *and* the youngsters who respond well to these techniques.

This chapter on small-group techniques provides suggestions for helping young children begin to shift their dependence on direct instruction from the teacher to cooperative learning with peers. The aim is that, in due course, many children will be able to assume the responsibility for teaching themselves. Should that occur, they will be able to master any content and increase their rate of achievement. Small-group strategies are just one step in the long road toward independent learning. It is a good step—but not for everyone. Some young children come to kindergarten with the independence skills that permit them to transfer instructional dependence from the teacher to themselves easily. Those youngsters need not participate in peer learning for, in effect, they have matured beyond that state; small-group techniques restrict them to a level of instruction they have outgrown. Some of them, however, may work well with *one* classmate but may not function well in a group. Other pupils will remain adult-oriented for many years, and some may never overcome that stage. Approximately 30 percent of the school-age population, however, are *peer*-oriented. For that group, these instructional strategies will prove extremely effective.

This chapter does *not* suggest that small-group techniques are appropriate for everyone; they are *not*. Research demonstrates that students achieve statistically higher test and attitude scores when they are permitted to learn through their sociological preferences (DeBello, 1985; Dunn, Giannitti, Murray, Rossi, Geisert, & Quinn, 1990; Gadwa & Griggs, 1985; Giannitti, 1988; Miles, 1987; Perrin, 1984).

6

Designing Tactual and Kinesthetic Resources to Respond to Individual Learning Styles

The Importance of Recognizing Tactual and Kinesthetic Learners

Young children learn by touching, feeling, moving, and experiencing. Indeed, we have to protect them from being injured by sharp objects, electricity, hot water, and pointy items, which they eagerly grasp, squeeze, or put into their mouths. During the school years, however, educators often ignore these tactual and kinesthetic preferences. Instead, classroom instruction focuses on auditory and visual teaching strategies.

Restak (1979) and others have indicated that many students do not become strongly visual before third grade, that auditory acuity first develops in many students after the sixth grade, and that boys often are neither strongly visual nor auditory even during high school. Therefore, since most young children are tactual and kinesthetic learners, such resources should be developed and used, particularly for those who are experiencing difficulty learning through lectures, direct verbal instructions, "chalk talks," and textbook assignments. Instruction should be introduced through an individual's strongest perceptual strength and reinforced in the two next strongest modalities (Bauer, 1991; Carbo, 1980; Dunn, 1990a; Kroon, 1986; Ingham, 1989; Martini, 1986; Weinberg, 1983; Wheeler, 1980, 1983). Further, because many K–2 youngsters are enthusiastic about designing and building tactual/kinesthetic games and materials, they can easily teach themselves through this procedure. Use the easy-to-follow directions in this chapter to help primary youngsters gradually achieve instructional independence.

Students who do well in school tend to be those who learn either by listening in class or by reading. This leads most of us to believe that the brighter students are

When children who need either informal seating or a great deal of mobility use tactual or kinesthetic instructional resources in sections of the classroom where they feel comfortable, their concentration, memory, and behavior improve. (Photograph courtesy Otsego Elementary School, Half Hollow Hills, New York.)

auditory and/or visual learners. In reality, however, we usually teach by telling (auditory), assigning readings (visual), or explaining and writing on a chalkboard (auditory and visual). Youngsters who are able to absorb through these two senses are the ones who retain what they have been taught. They also respond well on tests, which are either auditory (teacher-dictated) or visual (written or printed).

Two decades of research have verified that many students who do not do well in school are tactual or kinesthetic learners (Dunn, 1990c); their strongest perceptual strengths are neither auditory nor visual. These boys and girls tend to acquire and retain information or skills when they can either handle manipulatives or participate in concrete, real-life activities. Because so little of what happens instructionally in most classes responds to the tactual and kinesthetic senses, these students are, in a very real sense, handicapped. Once they begin to fall behind scholastically, they lose confidence in themselves and either feel defeated and withdraw (physically or emotionally) or begin to resent school because of their repeated failures.

Many young children appear to be essentially tactual or kinesthetic learners. As they grow older, some youngsters begin to combine tactual and visual preferences; for them, the resources suggested in this chapter will be helpful. Eventually, some youngsters develop auditory strengths and can function easily in a traditional class where much of the instruction occurs through discussion or lecture. But this group does not represent the majority of K–2 children.

We have found some parallels between age and perceptual strengths among students. Even among high schoolers, however, many continue to be unable to learn well either by listening in class or by reading. Sensory strengths appear to be so individualized that it is vital to test each student and then recommend resources that teach to that student's strengths rather than his or her weaknesses. When you recognize that selected youngsters are not learning well, either through readings or from class discussions or lectures, experiment with several of the following resources to provide tactual or kinesthetic instruction that may reverse their underachievement.

Learning Style Characteristics Responsive to Tactual and Kinesthetic Resources

Because tactual and kinesthetic materials tend to be gamelike, they usually are motivating, particularly for underachievers. When they are perceived as being babyish, however, they can cause embarrassment and turn off many youngsters. It is important that the children to whom these resources are assigned feel positive about them and therefore be willing to follow directions for their use, care, and replacement. If they

Tactual instructional resources may be used alone, in pairs, or in a small group—dependent upon individuals' sociological preferences. They also may be used at either a table, a desk, or on the floor—for students so inclined. (Photograph courtesy Joe Wright Elementary School, Jacksonville, Texas.)

enjoy learning in this way, they will be persistent and will continue using the materials until they have achieved the goals or objectives that have been outlined for them.

All the materials are self-corrective so that youngsters can manipulate them to find correct answers. Nevertheless, the motivation for using these materials is necessary if students are to be responsible for them—because the parts or sections of each set need to be kept intact, returned to holders or boxes, and maintained in good condition. Often however, we observed previously apathetic tactual students become highly motivated *because* of their interest in and enjoyment of Learning Circles, Task Cards, Electroboards, Pic-A-Holes, and Flip Chutes. Floor Games had the same effect on kinesthetic learners.

Other than the taped and printed directions for using the resources, little structure is provided through these materials. Students using them may, therefore, need *some* structure—but not too much. Beyond the need for motivation, persistence, responsibility, and structure, these resources respond to students who have visual/tactual, tactual/kinesthetic, or visual/kinesthetic inclinations and who do not learn easily either by listening or by reading. Emphasize to the entire class that all students will be responsible for learning and mastering exactly the same objectives, but that each will learn the information through his or her learning style strengths.

Learning Style Characteristics to Which Tactual and Kinesthetic Resources Can Be Accommodated

Because these resources can be used in a classroom, in a library, in a corridor, or in an instructional resource center as well as at home, they can accommodate each student's environmental and physiological preferences. Because they can be used independently, in pairs, with a small group, or with an adult, they also respond to each student's sociological needs.

Step-by-Step Guide to Designing Tactual Resources

Developing tactual resources is easy. Once you have designed one or two samples, most young children can duplicate and create additional samples for themselves. Although many of these materials are available in primary schools, they often are used indiscriminately rather than with those youngsters whose perceptual inclinations they would complement. Usually, they are commercially produced and do not respond directly to either the topics that are taught or the specific objectives on which you wish to focus. After you have made a few samples for experimentation and observed the progress that certain students make through their use, you will become committed to them as an instructional resource for your classroom. They save labor by being adaptable to different levels, questions, and even subject areas—for example, a Learning Circle with interchangeable parts. In the primary grades, however, most children can create their own tactual resources. Once they have learned to do so, they

Students whose primary perceptual strength is tactual *find it interesting and comparatively easy to learn with manipulatives like Learning Circles and picture-sequenced cards that can be moved so that they match the words each represents. (Photograph courtesy West Seneca Central School District, West Seneca, New York.)*

find that they remember difficult academic information more easily than they ever could before.

The ability to take difficult information from a chalkboard or a ditto and translate it into resources that facilitate memory retention is a first important step toward becoming an independent learner—a stage to which most underachievers rarely aspire. Research findings clearly suggest that tactual kinesthetic learners may *become* poor learners because their teachers lecture or require readings *as the basic source of introductory learning* (Andrews, 1990; Bauer, 1991; Carbo, 1980; Garrett, 1991; Ingham, 1989; Kroon, 1985; Martini, 1986; Weinberg, 1983; Wheeler, 1980, 1983). When such students experience initial concentration tactually, it is easier for them to succeed.

Chapter 10 describes how, once teachers and students become aware of individuals' perceptual strengths, they can learn to *sequence* exposure to the teacher's lectures by capitalizing on strengths in the *beginning*. Thus, the lecture may be either an introductory, intermediary, *or* reinforcement strategy based on the child's primary, secondary, and tertiary perceptual strengths. Chapter 10 also describes how many young children can be taught to design their own tactual instructional resources.

Teaching Reading and Spelling through a Variety of Tactual Resources

As described in the review of the elements of learning style in Chapter 1, youngsters learn through different senses determined by their individual perceptual preferences or strengths. When you teach tactually inclined students important skills such as language concepts, word recognition, spelling, or writing, *introduce* these skills through each youngster's strongest modality and *reinforce* through two different modalities. The way to do this is described in Chapter 10, where the process is applied directly to teaching young children to read through their learning style strengths.

When we teach by telling (either personally or on tape), we are trying to attract children's *auditory* (or listening) ability. For them to *remember* at least three-quarters of what they have heard in 40 or 50 minutes, they need strong auditory *memory,* which most youngsters do not develop much before sixth grade. In fact, less than 30 percent of *adults* have strong auditory memory when trying to recall new difficult academic information. At the primary level, this percentage falls to approximately 12 percent.

When we teach by *showing,* we concentrate on the *visual* sense, on *seeing.* Fewer than 40 percent of adults have strong visual memory, and that figure is only about 20 percent among primary children. The learning style element of *processing style* (global and analytic) also enters into the picture. Analytic visuals tend to remember words and numbers; global visuals often remember pictures, illustrations, graphs, maps, and symbols.

When we teach through touching methods, we appeal to the *tactual* sense. When we teach by requiring active participation through experiences (such as teaching inches and feet by building a wagon), we emphasize a *kinesthetic* (whole-body involvement) approach.

Materials that facilitate a tactual approach include clay; sandpaper; fabrics of various consistencies such as felt, velvet, or buckram (you can cut up old, worn-out clothing); sand; water; fingerpaints; or uncooked macaroni. For example, to help your students to learn to spell a very difficult word, you might use any or all of the following activities, depending on their preferences and how long it would take for them to master the word.

1. Say the word. Explain its meaning. Give them an example of how it might be used in a sentence. Ask them to say the word and to use it in a sentence. When each student can do that, spell the word for them. (auditory)

2. Print the word in black on a white sheet of paper; then print it in white on a black sheet of paper. Repeat the spelling, and point to each letter as you say it. Ask the students to look at the spelling and try to memorize the letters in correct sequence. Then ask them to try to write the word without looking at it. (visual, auditory, tactual)

3. Ask the youngsters to write the word by copying the letters that you wrote. If they can copy the letters accurately, ask them to write the word again without looking. If they are correct, praise them. If not, show them the word written by you and point out their errors. (visual, tactual)

4. Empty the contents of a small bag of sand into an aluminum pan. Encourage your students to trace the letters of the word in the sand. Permit them to look at the printed word as they "write" the letters. Then see if they can write the letters without looking at the word. If they can, ask them to spell the word without looking and without writing. (visual, tactual)

5. Ask each youngster to dip one finger into a plastic cup of water, look at the printed word on the chalkboard, then write the word on the chalkboard without looking at it. Then have the student stare at the word as it evaporates. (tactual, visual)

6. Cut the small letters of the alphabet out of heavy sandpaper. Make duplicates of letters that are used often. Place all the letters into an empty shoebox and ask your students to find the letters in the spelling word without looking (strictly by feeling each of the letters and discarding those that are not in the word). When they have found all the letters, ask them to place them into the correct sequence so that the word is spelled correctly. (tactual, visual)

7. Cut the small letters of the alphabet out of old jean fabric. Place them into an unused shoebox. Follow the procedure suggested for using sandpaper letters. (tactual, visual)

8. Press different-colored strips of clay into a pan. Ask your youngsters to write the word in the clay with a toothpick. (tactual, visual)

9. Keep a jar of uncooked macaroni available for spelling. If you have alphabet noodles, ask each student to find each of the letters in the word and to glue them onto a cardboard to make a three-dimensional spelling list. If you have the other types of macaroni, print the word in large letters on an eight-and-a-half- by eleven-inch sheet of writing paper or shirt cardboard, and let them paste the food bits into the letters so that they, too, form the word. (tactual, visual)

10. Have them trace the word in salt, colored or white sugar, or write with fingerpaints. (tactual, visual)

11. Students love to trace letters and words in Jell-O or chocolate pudding with their fingers (or a small spoon) and then fill the resulting changes with milk. The reward for carving the right answer is permission to eat the dessert or lick their fingers. (tactual, visual)

All these activities will not be necessary at one time, nor will all your students require so many tactual experiences. They are listed here to give you some alternatives so that you can approach teaching through varied—and thus interesting—techniques for youngsters who profit from more than an auditory-visual method. For students who learn to read or spell a word merely by hearing it, seeing it, writing it once or twice, and concentrating on or memorizing its letters, you need not introduce these tactual materials. But if learning does not come easily through such reading approaches as phonics, word recognition, or whole language, offer students a choice of these tactual resources and the ones described later in this chapter, and continue experimenting with various options until the children find the method that *best* helps them master the material—and enjoy doing do! Unless your students indicate special preferences, use different resources to introduce new and difficult words so that these young children do not become bored—*unless they reveal a need for patterns and routines!* As indicated previously, introduce new and difficult information with resources that respond to individuals' *primary* perceptual preference and *reinforce* through their secondary and tertiary preferences.

These suggestions may be used to teach numbers, letters, computations, geometric shapes, and other curriculum requirements in addition to spelling, vocabulary, and reading words. Here is a hint to follow before actually introducing several tactual resources: Instead of telling the children, "These words are easy. If you only concentrate (or try), you will learn them," give them three- and four-syllable words to learn, and then dramatize their length and difficulty. "Play" with the youngsters by saying, "I can't imagine what makes me give you fifth- and sixth-grade words to study! These are *difficult!* You'll be lucky if you learn *one* new word each week!" Then, after you permit them three or four Self-Teaching Times of 10 minutes every day for two or three weeks, you will be surprised at the number of really "grown-up" words your little ones will have mastered!

Some of the *best* ways to teach tactually involve the following resources: Learning Circles, Learning Strips, Task Cards, Electroboards, Flip Chutes, and Pic-A-Holes. These tactual materials help young children remember many things they otherwise would forget.

Designing Learning Circles

A Learning Circle is an interesting way for children to review skills. You can teach the formation or recognition of new words, mathematics concepts, historical data, and almost any kind of skill development through them. Try making one or two Learning Circles to see whether your slow achievers respond favorably to them. If they do, let them help you create more. Auditory or visual achievers will enjoy them also and can use them to reinforce information.

Suppose you have been teaching students to add. Begin with a Learning Circle that gives them opportunities to practice completing different number fact problems. You will need the following items:

Materials
- Two pieces of colored oaktag, heavy construction paper, or posterboard
- One wire coat hanger (optional)
- Black fine-line felt-tip pens, colored felt-tip pens
- Eight clip-on clothespins (the colored plastic type are pretty and do not break easily)
- Masking tape or strong glue
- Clear or lightly colored transparent adhesive-backed paper

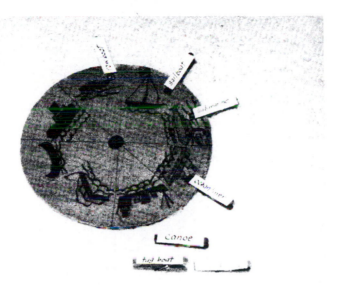

A Learning Circle is an interesting way for children to master many worthwhile skills. By matching color-coded clothespins with answers to related questions, students acquire facts and skills visually and tactually. (Photograph courtesy Center for the Study of Learning and Teaching Styles, St. John's University, New York.)

- Old magazines that may be cut up to either color-code or picture-code the mathematics examples and their answers (optional)

Directions   Figure 6–1 illustrates the steps for making the Learning Circle, as follows:

1. Cut two circles, 18 inches in diameter, for each Learning Circle.
2. Divide each circle into eight sections.
3. In each of the eight sections, print (using a black felt-tip pen) an addition problem that is simple enough to be computed by the students for whom it is intended.
4. Print the answer to one of the math problems on the tip end (rather than the squeeze end) of a clothespin. Follow suit for each of the seven remaining problems and clothespins.
5. Turn the second circle so that its eight sections become its back. Place the front of the second circle against the back of the first circle (spoon-in-spoon fashion or blank sides together).
6. Either color-code or picture-code each correct answer to match its problem. Do

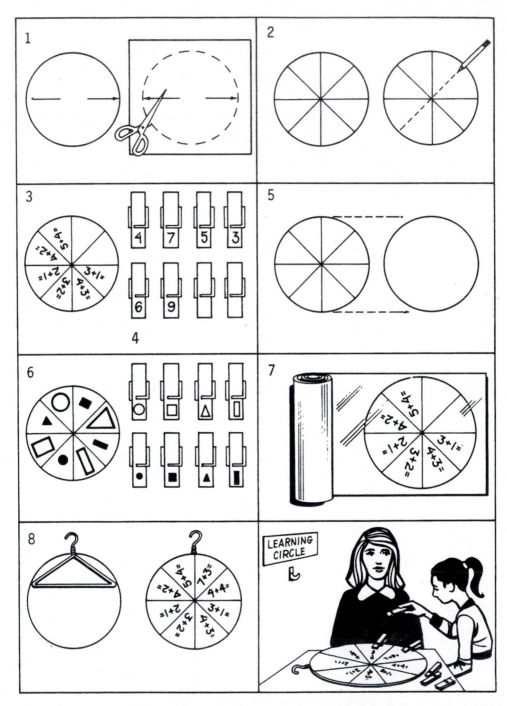

FIGURE 6–1 Constructing a Learning Circle

this by placing an identically shaped and colored symbol (a) underneath the clothespin that provides the answer to the problem and (b) inside the section of the second circle (the bottom one) that will be pasted directly beneath the problem.

7. Cover both circles with clear adhesive-backed paper, or laminate them.
8. Glue the two circles together with a wire hanger securely fastened between them. When laminated or covered with clear contact paper, the Learning Circle will remain in excellent condition despite extensive use and may be stored easily by hanging it on a doorknob or a hook (see Figure 6–1). (You may, of course, omit the wire hanger.)

Store the Learning Circle in a convenient place in the classroom, preferably in or near an instructional area where the students may use this resource during Self-Teaching Time or whenever they are free to do so. Remove the clothespins from their storage niche—either on the lower half of the wire hanger or in an oaktag pocket attached to the back of the Learning Circle. Challenge the students to mix the clothespins and then try to match the answer on each to the related question or problem on the chart. They may work alone or in a pair, by choice.

When the clothespins have been matched and clipped onto what the student believes is the correct section of the chart, show him or her how to turn the entire chart over (revealing the back) to see whether the color-coded or picture-coded symbols match. The design of the underside of the clothespin should be identical to and directly above the same design on the back of the second circle to permit self-correction. When the two symbols match, the answer is correct; when they do not, the matching answer may be found by comparing the paired colors or pictures.

Variations on the Design of Learning Circles

1. *Velcro answers:* Paste Velcro strips near the top of each sector. Attach answers to the matched Velcro strip instead of to clothespins.
2. *Question-and-answer booklets:* Use circles of two layers of clear contact paper stuck together and a circle of blank oaktag. Sew or glue pockets that exactly match the question sections on the front and the answer sections on the back. This blank Learning Circle may be used for different sets of questions or problems, with appropriate attachments to fit into the blank pockets.

You now have a Learning Circle with exchangeable parts so that the same resource can be used for several different problems. For example, one day you can insert math problems, another day language problems, and so on. The pockets on the Learning Circle can be used to hold alternative sets of problems so that you or your students may use different materials as they are needed.

Designing Learning Strips

A similar tactual resource is the Learning Strip, an elongated version of the Learning Circle (see Figure 6–2). It can be made by dividing a long piece of oaktag, construc-

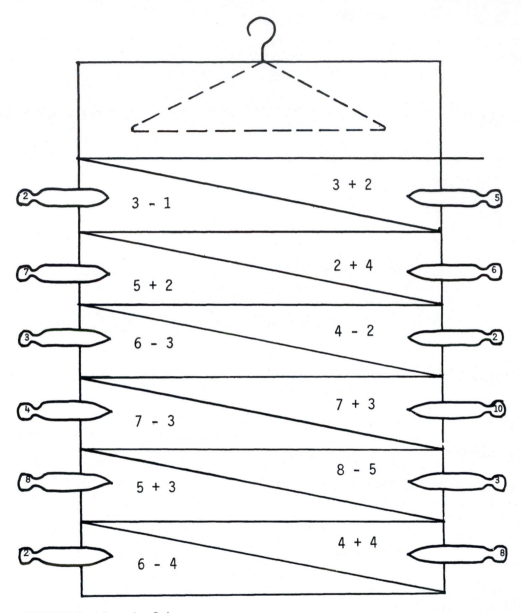

FIGURE 6–2 A Learning Strip

tion paper, or posterboard into eight or ten sections and printing a different number (or problem) in each box. Tape the wire hanger to the top of the back of the board. Place different numbers (within the child's range of addition facts) on each of the clothespins.

If the students for whom you are designing these resources are learning to recognize numbers, a simple match will do. If they are practicing the addition of num-

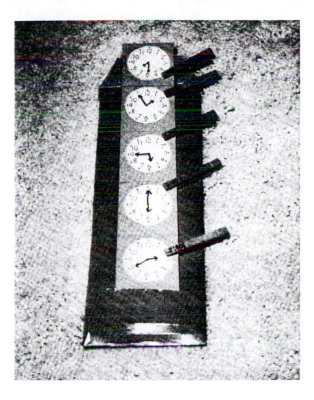

An elongated tactual resource that is similar to the Learning Circle is the Learning Strip. Another variation includes Question-and-Answer Booklets with Velcro tabs on matching cards. (Photograph courtesy Center for the Study of Learning and Teaching Styles, St. John's University, New York.)

bers, then on the back of each section neatly print number combinations that complement the addition of all the numbers of each clothespin that may be added to the number on the front. For example, if the number 3 is placed in the first section on the front of the Learning Strip, and if the numbers 1, 2, 3, 4, 5, 6, 7, or 8 each appears on a different clothespin, then on the back of the section of the Learning Strip that has number 3 on top, print the following:

$$3 + 1 = 4 \qquad 3 + 5 = 8$$
$$3 + 2 = 5 \qquad 3 + 6 = 9$$
$$3 + 3 = 6 \qquad 3 + 7 = 10$$
$$3 + 4 = 7 \qquad 3 + 8 = 11$$

Follow suit for each of the strips, providing the correct answer by printing all the correct number combinations added to the number on the front of the chart. In this case, you do not need to color- or picture-code the answers; they will be apparent.

Learning Circles or Strips are excellent resources for either introducing or reinforcing an endless number of facts or skills that your students may be required to learn. Here are some examples:

1. In each of the sections of the front of the resource, place the letters; *an, and, at, ear, en, end, in,* and *on.* (Any word roots may be substituted.) Place a different letter on the top of each clothespin. By placing one clothespin at a time in front of each of the sections on the circle, your students may be able to form new words and read them. If they are just beginning to read well, they may need you to work with them to be certain that the words they form are correct. When they are independently able, perhaps toward the end of the year, write all the possible words that may be made by adding a single letter or group of letters to the basic letters on the chart. Do this on 3 × 5 inch index cards, which you can store in a pocket on the back of the chart.

2. Print the names of each of eight different geometric shapes on the chart, and paste pictures of the shapes onto the clothespins. Number-code both the pictures and the clothespins to make matched pairs. Your students are likely to learn to recognize, spell, and write the names of those shapes before most of their peers.

3. Print new vocabulary on the chart, and paste pictures of the words onto the clothespins. By matching the pictures to the words, students become familiar with the formation and letter combinations and will read them—first on the chart and then in a text.

By using tactual, self-instructional, and self-corrective materials, students gradually will become increasingly independent. By using Learning Circles or Learning Strips, they will have new material introduced without extensive directions from others. This type of introduction to the facts and skills they need to know will facilitate their academic achievement, both now and in later years when they will need to learn on their own. They will not forget how to convert new knowledge into understandings they can handle!

Understanding Task Cards

Task Cards are easy-to-make multisensory resources that respond to a youngster's need to see and to touch simultaneously. Often designed in sets or as part of a unit, each series teaches related concepts or facts. This resource tends to be effective with children who cannot remember easily by listening or by reading. Task Cards are used both to introduce new material and to reinforce something to which the youngster has been exposed, but did not learn.

The most effective Task Cards are self-corrective. They permit students to recognize whether they understand and can remember the material, while allowing no one other than the youngster using the cards to see errors made, thus preserving the child's dignity and self-image. They enable little ones who do make mistakes in their responses to find the correct answers, and they free the teacher to work with other, more dependent youngsters.

Task Cards can be made self-corrective through one of several methods: color-coding, picture-coding, shape-coding, or the provision of answers. Task Cards for primary children can be either simple or multipart, introductory or reinforcing, and global or analytic at many different comprehension levels. They may be used by individuals, pairs, or small groups and permit self-pacing. Children may continue to use them until they feel secure about their knowledge of the topic. Task Cards can be reused to reinforce specific data that have been forgotten. Their gamelike character often wins and sustains youngsters' attention. They are important because they appeal to young people who cannot learn through other available resources.

Students who select or are assigned Task Cards may work with them at their desks, in an instructional area such as a Learning Station or Interest Center, in the library, on carpeting, or anywhere they prefer, either at school or at home. Task Cards may be used alone by an individual, in a pair, or with a small group provided they follow established rules—for example, "Your learning style must never interfere with someone else's style." "Your grades must be better than they ever have been before." "You need to work quietly and must complete this assignment." "You need to be where I can *see* you."

Designing Task Cards

Task Cards are easy-to-make, effective resources for tactual students at all levels. Begin by listing exactly what you want your students to learn about a specific topic, concept, or skill. Then translate your list into questions and answers concerning what they should learn. For example, if your students are interested in dinosaurs (as many

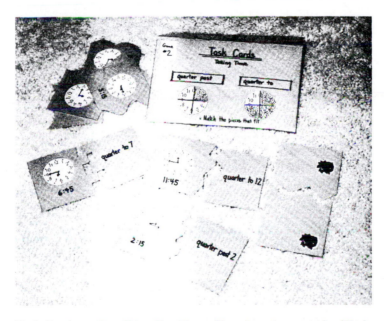

Task Cards work well in all subjects. Here is a photograph of Task Cards on telling time. Other subjects might include dinosaurs, nutrition, insect facts—just about anything. (Photograph courtesy Center for the Study of Learning and Teaching Styles, St. John's University, New York.)

young children are), you might help them to recognize various dinosaurs by creating a set of Task Cards with the name of members of the species printed at the top and an illustration of the particular type illustrated on the bottom (Figure 6–3). After some of the children have become familiar with the words by using the first set of Task Cards and then writing short stories about their "favorite" dinosaur or "The Dinosaur of My Dreams," you might reinforce the names with a second set that has each dinosaur's name on the front of a Task Card and the illustration on the back (Figure 6–4). In that way, children who have become familiar with some of the names might be further challenged by seeing whether they can recognize ("read") the names *without* the illustrations.

Any factual information lends itself to Task Card translation. For example, it is easy to describe animals and their babies (Figure 6–5), number facts (Figure 6–6), or science or literature details (Figure 6–7). In fact, children can be assigned to develop their *own* Task Cards in class or as homework, provided they understand the information and how to create this resource. Use a Basic Task Card outline (Figure 6–8) as a pattern, and show the children how to design original samples in class. Then tell them to create one or two for homework and, eventually, to make a complete set of as many as appear to be appropriate for their age and grade. Develop a few Task Card sets in the *shape* of what they are teaching—some of your students will surely follow suit.

Use Task Cards to engage the children in thinking skills by placing numerals and accompanying illustrations on each Task Card in a set and asking the children to use them either independently or in a pair (or small group) to decide what the numbers really *mean* (Figure 6–6). Children often begin to understand meaning when they need to figure out things for themselves—or with a friend or two.

Materials
- Colored oaktag or cardboard
- Black felt-tip pens for printing
- Colored felt-tip pens for illustrations and attractiveness

Directions

1. Cut the colored oaktag or cardboard into three by twelve-inch rectangles or, if the topic lends itself to being represented by a shape, into shapes approximately three by twelve inches each.

2. On the left side of each of the rectangles, in large, easy-to-read letters, print either information or a question about the topic. On the right side of either the rectangle or shape, print the corresponding answer. Leave space between the two facts or between the question and answer, the word and its meaning, or the numeral and the representative illustration. Illustrate the answer. If you are teaching vocabulary, you might place the printed word on one side of the shape and the illustration on the other.

3. Either laminate the cards or cover each one with clear contact paper.

4. Cut each rectangle or shape into two or more parts by using a different linear separation for each (to code them according to shape) so that only the matched halves fit together (Figures 6–3 through 6–8).

5. Package the set in an attractive box, perhaps a recycled gift box. On top of

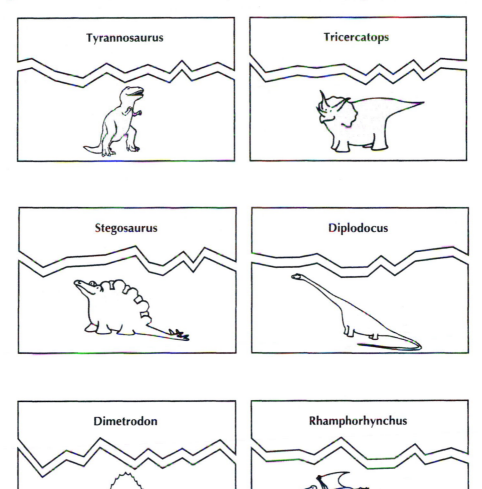

FIGURE 6–3 These Task Cards are one of the tactual resources of a Multisensory Instructional Package on "Dinosaurs: Lifestyles of the Big and Ancient" designed by Jo Anne Dobbins for first-graders. After using this set, the children had a choice of making either their own Task Cards, a Learning Circle, a Flip Chute, *or* a Pic-A-Hole with exactly the same information. They then used the resource they created to teach either themselves or a classmate during their Self-Teaching Time each day.

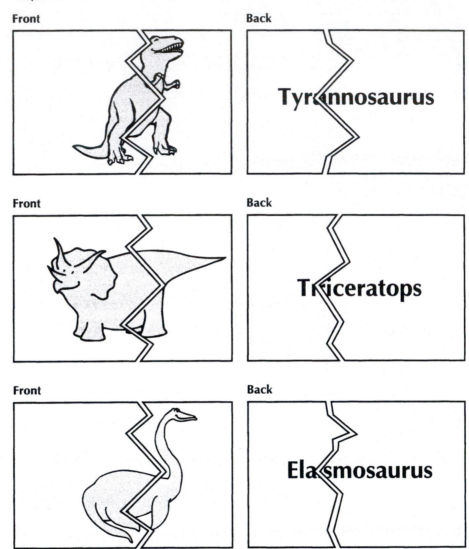

Front   **Back**

Tyrannosaurus

Front   **Back**

Triceratops

Front   **Back**

Elasmosaurus

FIGURE 6–4   Another effective way for children to begin teaching themselves is shown with Carole Solar's set of Task Cards for young children. An illustration of the word is displayed on the front, and the printed word is on the back. Because Task Cards are shape-coded, learning to write each dinosaur's name can be mastered by correctly matching the two sides of each figure and then studying that reptile's name on the back of its card.

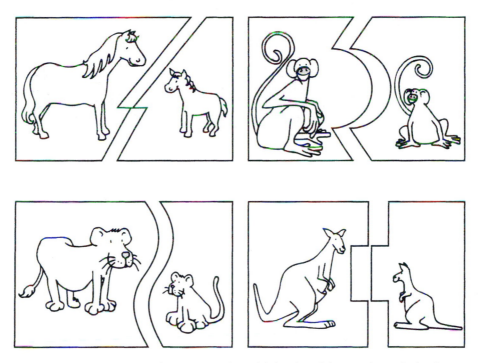

FIGURE 6–5 By matching the correct right and left sides of these Task Cards, kindergartners and many preschoolers can see what the babies of specific animals look like when they are very young. The children begin to identify both the changes that occur during the aging process *and* the relationships between mothers and their offspring.

the box, place a title that describes the Task Cards inside. Take one sample from the set, illustrate it, and glue it onto the top of the box next to the title so that young children can identify the topic of the Task Cards within each box. For example, if the box holds math Task Cards, place a single sample from the set inside the box on top of the box and laminate the entire top—or box. Thus, the tops of the boxes for addition, subtraction, the week's spelling words, and social studies or science Task Cards will all look different from each other.

6. The very *best* Task Cards are made in the *shape* of the topic they are trying to teach. For example, Phyllis Napolitano designed a set of Task Cards on "Butterfly Facts", and Kathy Hazelton designed a set on "Whales: Don't Blow Your top!" in shapes directly related to those creatures (Figure 6–9).

Figure 6–3 shows simple Task Cards designed for very young children. They can be used either to *introduce* or to reinforce new material. They work well in all subjects, including mathematics, social studies, science, vocabulary, sight reading, and spelling. Most children can recognize words that are *visually* different from other words faster than they can words that look alike. Thus, *hippopotamus, dinosaur, dan-*

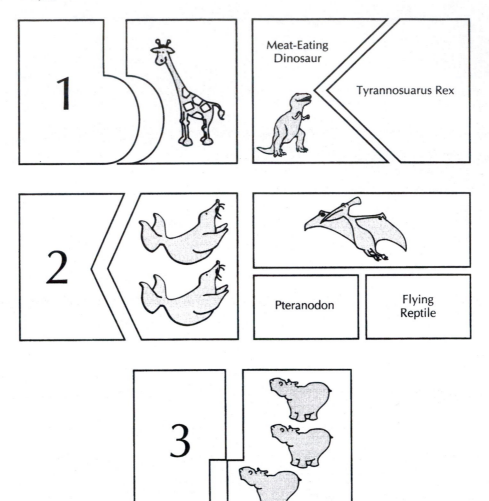

FIGURE 6–6 The same concept can be used to establish an understanding of numbers and what they *mean*. Children can begin by using Task Cards their *teachers* create. After a few experiences with those, they can design their own by tracing a pattern (see Figure 6–7), pasting pictures they collect from old magazines onto one side, and adding the appropriate numeral to the opposite side. This is an excellent assignment because it requires that they: (a) concentrate with both their eyes and hands; (b) respond to factual information (the number of items in each picture) *and* higher-level (the relationship between the number and what the numeral represents) objectives; and (c) *use* the information they are learning in an original way (application-leading-to-transfer).

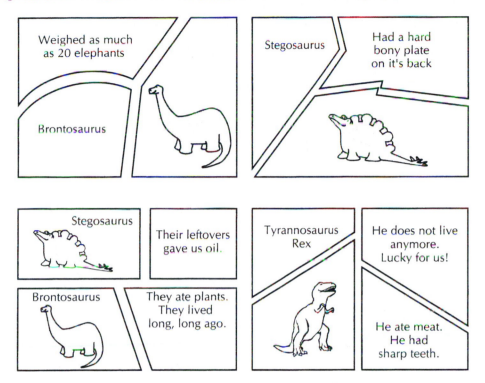

FIGURE 6–7 Teacher-made Task Cards can be used to *introduce* new and difficult in-formation. Then children can create their own personal set to *reinforce* what they learned. Kathleen McLaughlin designed these three-part sections as part of a set to teach about "Dinosaurs: And You Thought Trucks Were Big!" After using Kathleen's set, a second-grader designed his own *four-part* set to show what he had liked most about this topic.

gerous, masquerade, and *idiosyncratic*—when introduced dramatically, with humor and song or dance—are not difficult for kindergarten and first-grade youngsters. In-troduce one or two new words each day, follow up by providing Task Cards with those words and matching illustrations the next day. Tell the children:

> *I have some really* difficult *new words for you on Task Cards. They are words that many* sixth-graders *don't know! I suspect that they are much too difficult for you to learn, but they are here in this Task Card box [show box]. If you feel like "working your poor little head the most it can," experiment! But don't be discouraged if you can't write the new words even after you have really studied them. They are sixth-grade words and proba-bly* no one *in kindergarten (or first grade) can learn them!*

Then leave the Task Card box in an accessible spot and, when the children have Self-Teaching Time, remind them that the things they may work with include the "regular" Task Cards, the Learning Circle, the Flip Chute, the Pic-A-Hole, the read-

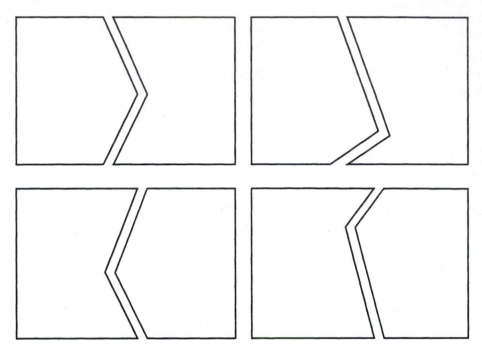

FIGURE 6–8 Sample Task Card pattern created by Dr. Angela Bruno for Lamtex Incorporated, Canton, Ohio.

ing story charts, and *"these really difficult sixth-grade word Task Cards that nobody can learn"*! A few children will exert every effort to master some of those difficult, long words—and many of them will be successful. If they are *not,* just say, "I *told* you those words were **hard**!" When a few children *are* successful, pretend to be astonished, and say something like, "I can't believe it! You *can't* be a kindergartner! You probably are *masquerading* as a kindergartner! You probably are *really* in fifth or sixth grade!" Then, next day, add *masquerading* to the Task Card box—and announce the new word you have added! Explain the word, give a couple of short samples of its use, and dramatize it with the children. Do nothing more, except to use the word (with the other long, difficult words) as often as you can in class when the opportunity presents itself.

When designing Task Cards for primary children, you might experiment with number facts and their answers as making up one set; word blends and possible letter combinations to form new words if you teach through phonics; initial letters that can be combined with "word families" (at, bat, cat, fat, hat, mat, pat, sat, rat, that) if you teach through linguistics; or whole words and their illustrations, which then can be combined into short sentences if you teach through whole language. Of course, you might try all three possibilities to see which children learn the most new words through which method!

For older or more advanced students, you might consider three- and four-part

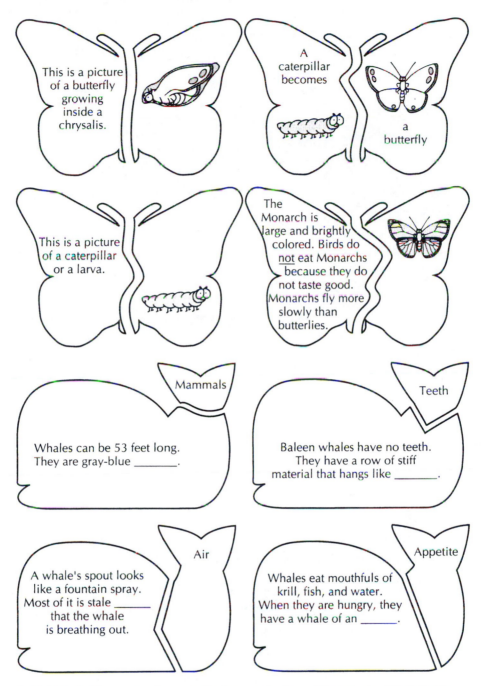

FIGURE 6–9 These are a few samples from each of two different sets of Task Cards. Phyllis Napolitano designed this instructional resource in the shape of a butterfly to accompany a Contract Activity Package (see Chapter 6), Programmed Learning Sequence (see Chapter 7), and Multisensory Instructional Package (see Chapter 8) on "Discovering Butterflies: Come Fly with Me." Kathleen Hazelton designed hers in the shape of a whale for a unit on "Save the Whales: Don't Blow Your Top!"

With a little assistance, most young children are able to design and make an attractive Flip Chute and its Question-and-Answer Cards for any curriculum assignment. Here, a team of five students are writing answers to their teacher's questions on Flip Chute cards to enable them to study through their combined tactual/visual strengths. (Photograph courtesy Otsego Elementary School, Half Hollow Hills, New York.)

(or more) Task Cards (Figure 6–7). However, although you need to *introduce* the youngsters to working with Task Cards through the samples *you* create, they will learn more from designing their own than they will from the ones you make. Thus, teach them to design their own as early as possible. Even if you doubt that most of your class is capable of creating Task Cards, *try* having everyone make a few in class. You will see how quickly the children will learn from—and teach!—each other.

Designing Flip Chutes

Everything that can be taught through either a Learning Circle or Task Cards also can be taught using a Flip Chute. We suggest alternating tactual resources to maintain the interest and enthusiasm of students who need variety. For those who prefer to use the same materials repeatedly, this single device will be a strong reinforcement.

Flip Chutes are attractive, half-gallon orange juice or milk containers decorated to reflect the subject matter being studied. Small question-and-answer cards are designed to be inserted into the upper face of the container. As each card descends on

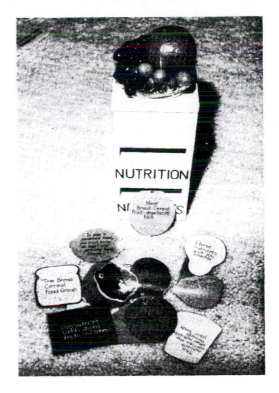

Flip Chutes may be designed to reflect a particular theme or area of study. This photograph depicts a dish of fruit for facts on nutrition. You might use an astronaut for a unit on space, a lighthouse for the topic "Boats Float," a Raggedy Ann doll to represent the storybook character, or a solar system robot for a study of planets. (Photograph courtesy Center for the Study of Learning and Teaching Styles, St. John's University, New York.)

an inner slide, it flips over and emerges through a lower opening with the correct answer face up.

Materials

Directions*

1. Pull open the top of a half-gallon milk or juice container.
2. Cut the side folds of the top portion down to the top of the container (Figure 6–10).
3. On the front edge, measure down both (a) 1½ inches and (b) 2½ inches. Draw lines across the container. Remove that space.
4. Mark up from the bottom (a) 1½ inches and (b) 2½ inches. Draw lines across the container. Remove that space.
5. Cut one 5 × 8 index card to measure 6½ inches by 3½ inches.
6. Cut a second index card to measure 7½ inches by 3½ inches (Figure 6–11).
7. Fold down ½ inch at both ends of the smaller strip. Fold down ½ inch at one end of the longer strip.

*Flip Chute directions were developed by Dr. Barbara Gardiner (1983).

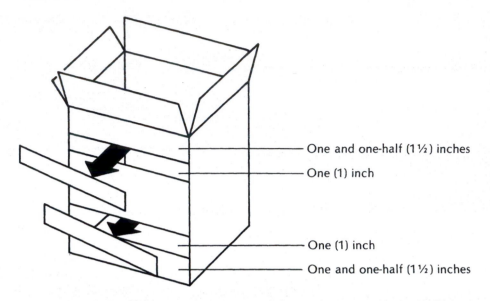

One and one-half (1 ½) inches

One (1) inch

One (1) inch

One and one-half (1 ½) inches

FIGURE 6–10 Flip Chutes are wonderful tactual devices for learning the multiplication tables, new words and vocabulary, and any facts that lend themselves to questions and answers.

8. Insert the smaller strip into the bottom opening with the folded edge resting on the upper portion of the bottom opening. Attach it with masking tape.

9. Bring the upper part of the smaller strip out through the upper opening, with the folded part going down over the center section of the carton. Attach it with masking tape (Figure 6–12).

10. On the longer strip, one end is folded down, and the other end is unfolded. Insert the unfolded end of the longer strip into the bottom opening of the container. Be certain the strip goes up along the back of the container. Push it into

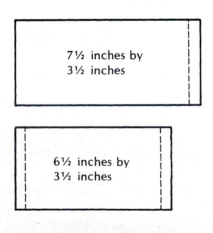

7 ½ inches by 3 ½ inches

6 ½ inches by 3 ½ inches

FIGURE 6–11 Fold down ½ inch at *both* ends of the smaller strip. Fold down ½ inch at *one* end of the longer strip.

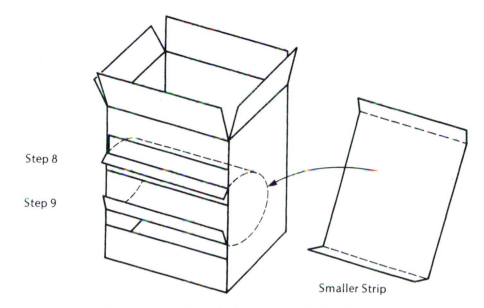

Step 8

Step 9

Smaller Strip

FIGURE 6–12   These are steps 8 and 9 when creating the Flip Chute.

the container until the folded part rests on the bottom part of the container. Attach it with masking tape.

11. Attach the upper edge of the longer strip to the back of the container ⅝ inch from the top, creating a slide. Secure it with masking tape. Follow the next illustration (Figure 6–13).

12. Fold down the top flaps of the container and tape them in place, forming a rectangular box.

13. Use small 2 × 2½ inch index cards to write the question on one side and the answer upside down on the flip side. Notch each question side at the top right to ensure appropriate positioning when the youngster uses the cards (Figure 6–14).

If you want to make the Flip Chute reflect a particular theme or area of study, add a rounded section at the top to represent a head, arms, or other special effects. Paint, color, or cover it with colored contact paper or vinyl wallcovering, and add lettering describing this particular Flip Chute's purpose. When completed, an every-day sample should be similar to the one in Figure 6–15. Figure 6–16 shows how questions are printed on one side (with the upper right-hand corner notched to show which side should be inserted into the Flip Chute top) and the answers are printed on the reverse side—but *upside-down*—so that they come out of the Chute face up and can be read easily. Carolyn Bovell designed several attractive Flip Chute cards in the shapes of various foods to accompany her Programmed Learning Sequence (Chapter 7), Contract Activity Package (Chapter 8), and Multisensory Instructional Package (Chapter 9) on "Nutrition: Neat Treat—or Health Wealth!" (Figure 6–17).

Side View of Container

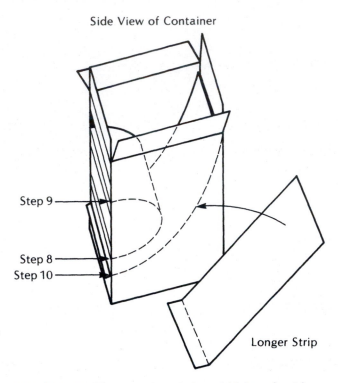

Step 9

Step 8
Step 10

Longer Strip

FIGURE 6–13   These are steps 8, 9, and 10 from the side view.

Flip Chutes are an effective way of helping children learn math combinations, *particularly* the multiplication tables. Do not pressure the youngsters; merely make math Flip Chute cards available to them, and see how well many begin to teach *themselves* and *others!* Self-Teaching Time is a wonderful opportunity for little ones to play school—either alone or with a friend or two, and work toward gaining knowledge without tension or stress. Samples of such cards are available in Figure 6–18.

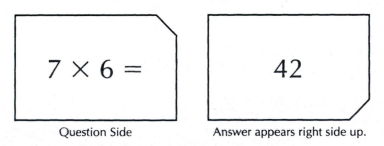

$$7 \times 6 =$$

42

Question Side

Answer appears right side up.

FIGURE 6–14   This is how the index cards should be notched on the upper-right-corner side.

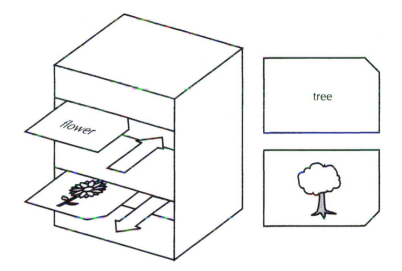

FIGURE 6–15 Sample Flip Chute and cards designed by Dr. Barbara Gardiner, Learning Styles Network, St. John's University, New York.

Finally, Flip Chute cards can be used to take gifted children beyond their classmates and the normal grade-level curriculum. Many bright children enjoy learning independently and can think things through on their own *without* direct instruction. Given a set of Flip Chute cards with a variety of number, word–picture, and word–definition combinations, these youngsters can learn more rapidly than in whole group instruction. In addition, the very fact that children are engaged in teaching themselves and advancing at their own pace and in their own learning style further increases *their* confidence and self-concept and motivates *others* to follow suit!

Cynthia Willett, a New York City artist, created a Multisensory Instructional Package on "Rocks: A Hard Topic." That package included a Flip Chute with challenging cards specifically designed for brighter primary youngsters. Although the most gifted children *initially* were attracted to the materials, others gradually began to use its contents and, to our surprise, more than three-quarters of an "average" first-grade class mastered the information (Figure 6–19).

Designing Pic-A-Holes

Tactual students have used Pic-A-Holes successfully in a variety of subject areas. The attached directions for constructing them initially require measuring and cutting accurately but, when you have constructed the first sample—*before you seal it*—trace the pattern you made. Students then will need only to copy that pattern, and duplicating multiple replicas will be easy for them. On the other hand, many tac-

Question Side   Answer Side (Upside down)

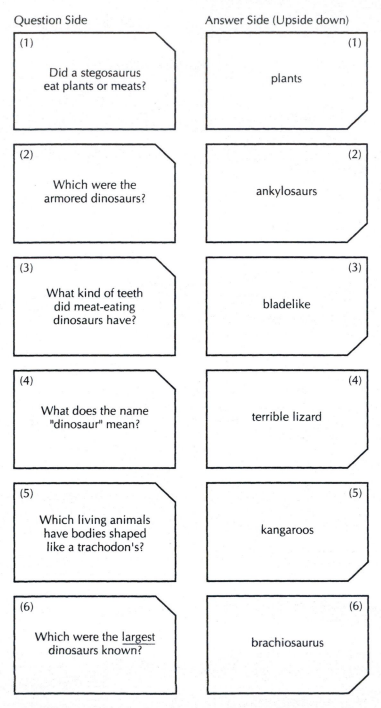

(1)

Did a stegosaurus
eat plants or meats?

(1)

plants

(2)

Which were the
armored dinosaurs?

(2)

ankylosaurs

(3)

What kind of teeth
did meat-eating
dinosaurs have?

(3)

bladelike

(4)

What does the name
"dinosaur" mean?

(4)

terrible lizard

(5)

Which living animals
have bodies shaped
like a trachodon's?

(5)

kangaroos

(6)

Which were the largest
dinosaurs known?

(6)

brachiosaurus

FIGURE 6–16 These sample Flip Chute cards demonstrate one of the types of questions and answers that lend themselves to this format.

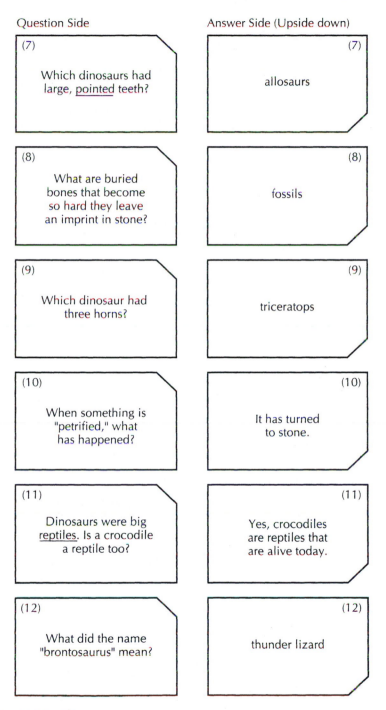

Question Side

Answer Side (Upside down)

(7) Which dinosaurs had large, <u>pointed</u> teeth?

(7) allosaurs

(8) What are buried bones that become so hard they leave an imprint in stone?

(8) fossils

(9) Which dinosaur had three horns?

(9) triceratops

(10) When something is "petrified," what has happened?

(10) It has turned to stone.

(11) Dinosaurs were big <u>reptiles</u>. Is a crocodile a reptile too?

(11) Yes, crocodiles are reptiles that are alive today.

(12) What did the name "brontosaurus" mean?

(12) thunder lizard

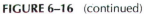

FIGURE 6–16 (continued)

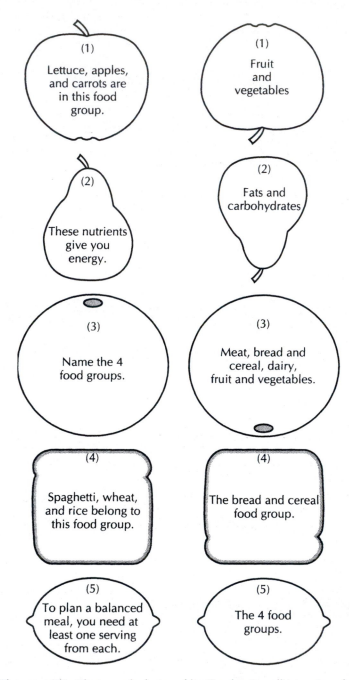

FIGURE 6–17 These are Flip Chute cards designed by Carolyn Bovell in various food shapes to accompany her Programmed Learning Sequence (see Chapter 7), Contract Activity Package (see Chapter 8), and Multisensory Instructional Package (see Chapter 9) on "Nutrition: Neat Treats—or Health Wealth"!

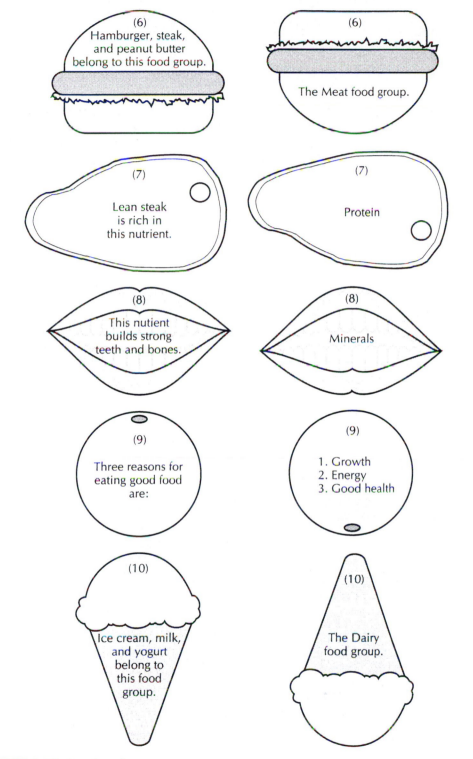

(6)
Hamburger, steak, and peanut butter belong to this food group.

(6)
The Meat food group.

(7)
Lean steak is rich in this nutrient.

(7)
Protein

(8)
This nutient builds strong teeth and bones.

(8)
Minerals

(9)
Three reasons for eating good food are:

(9)
1. Growth
2. Energy
3. Good health

(10)
Ice cream, milk, and yogurt belong to this food group.

(10)
The Dairy food group.

FIGURE 6–17 (continued)

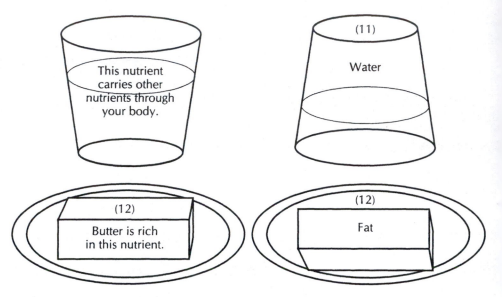

FIGURE 6–17   (continued)

Pic-A-Holes may be used alone, in a pair, at a desk, or in an informal setting as shown here. (Photograph courtesy Center for the Study of Learning and Teaching Styles, St. John's University, New York.)

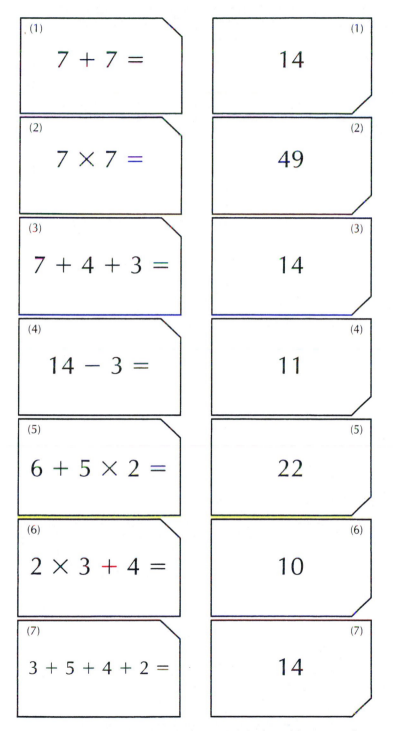

FIGURE 6–18 Flip Chute cards for various math problems, may be used to *introduce* and/or *reinforce* new and difficult material and during "self-teaching" times.

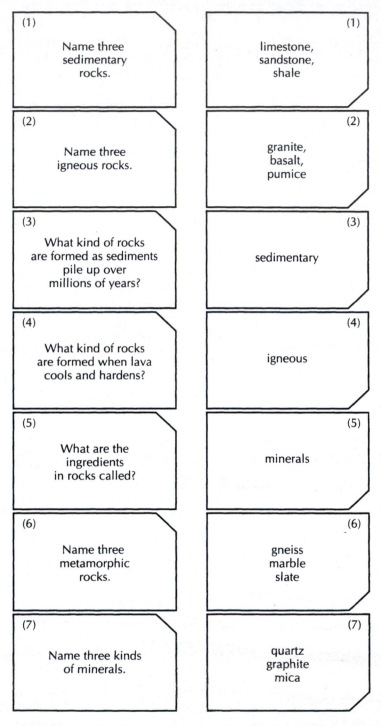

FIGURE 6–19 Flip Chute cards designed by Cynthia Willett to interest gifted students in learning about rocks through a Multisensory Instructional Package on "Rocks: A Hard Topic!"

tual/visual youngsters for whom this resource will be effective are capable of measuring and cutting exactly according to directions.

The Pic-A-Hole (Figure 6–20) is similar to a series of cards with printed questions. Students consider answers and look at three possible options at the bottom. Using a tied-on golf tee, they place the point directly below the option they believe to be correct and then attempt to lift the question card. If the answer selected is correct, the card lifts easily and can be removed; if it is incorrect, the card will not budge (see Figure 6–20).

Directions
1. Cut a colorful piece of cardboard or posterboard 24⅜ inches by 6½ inches.
2. Following the guide in Figure 6–21, measure and mark the cardboard (on the wrong side) to the dimensions given. Use a ballpoint pen and score the lines heavily (Figure 6–21).

Samples Figures 6–22 and 6–23 include examples from each of two different Pic-A-Holes. The first is from a set designed by Jo-Anne Dobbins on dinosaurs; the second is from Carolyn Bovell's unit on "Nutrition—Neat Treat or Health Wealth."

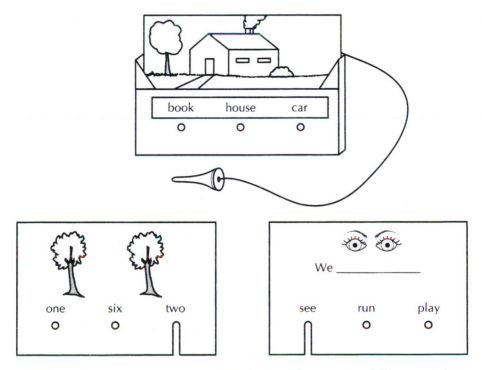

FIGURE 6–20 Dr. Barbara Gardiner (1983) designed this operational illustration of a Pic-A-Hole to show how this instructional resource works. Primary children should be taught to create their own for daily use with required and optional information.

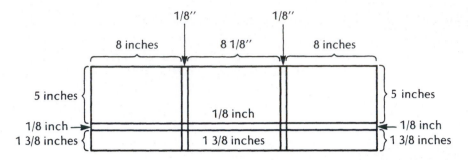

FIGURE 6–21 Graphic description of step 2 in Pic-A-Hole development.

A third sample, Figure 6–24, was designed by Eileen Clark and used by her first-graders in a unit on "Insects—Don't Bug Me!." Figure 6–24 shows a few from that card set.

Because the children for whom Pic-A-Holes and similar tactual resources are recommended are hands-on people, they learn more easily in this way than through other, more conventional approaches. When little ones consider options and then examine the three possible choices at the bottom of each card, they may be conjecturing analytically about the correct answer. When, instead, they look for the answer and

This Pic-A-Hole asks questions about plants. Other topics might be space, insects, or time. (Photograph courtesy Center for the Study of Learning and Teaching Styles, St. John's University, New York.)

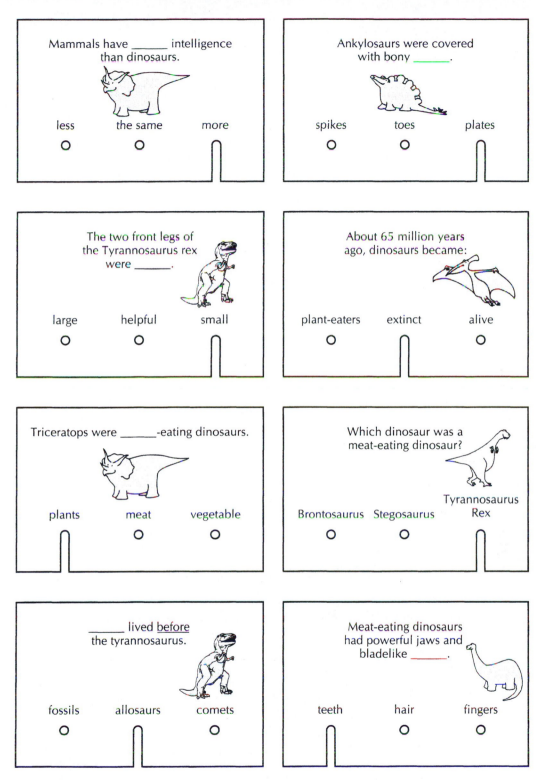

Mammals have _____ intelligence than dinosaurs.

less   the same   more

○   ○

Ankylosaurs were covered with bony _____.

spikes   toes   plates

○   ○

The two front legs of the Tyrannosaurus rex were _____.

large   helpful   small

○   ○

About 65 million years ago, dinosaurs became:

plant-eaters   extinct   alive

○   ○

Triceratops were _____-eating dinosaurs.

plants   meat   vegetable

○   ○

Which dinosaur was a meat-eating dinosaur?

Brontosaurus   Stegosaurus   Tyrannosaurus Rex

○   ○

_____ lived before the tyrannosaurus.

fossils   allosaurs   comets

○   ○

Meat-eating dinosaurs had powerful jaws and bladelike _____.

teeth   hair   fingers

○   ○

FIGURE 6–22 Flip Chute cards on Dinosaurs developed by Jo-Anne Dobbins.

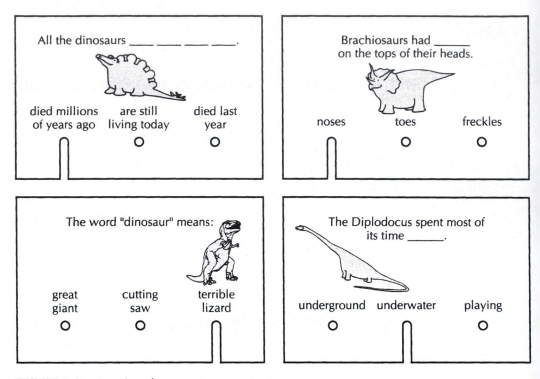

FIGURE 6–22 (continued)

then read the question to determine how that answer is appropriate, they are attacking their assignment globally. When analytics cope analytically and globals cope globally, they gradually learn; one sequence is not necessarily better than the other.

Designing an Electroboard

Electroboards have a bulb that lights up whenever the chosen answer is correct, and—as with a slot machine or a computer—that feature appears to mesmerize children because the lighted bulb provides immediate visual feedback of the student's success. These resources take longer to make but, once completed, are worth every moment devoted to them.

Questions are listed on one side of the resource and answers on the opposite side, but they are out of order, so that they do not match correctly. Students hold a two-part continuity tester in their hands. They attach one prong to the question they are trying to answer and, after reading the list of possible answers on the opposite side of the board, touch what they believe is the correct answer with the second prong. If the answer is correct, the bulb lights up; in some instances a bell rings, but the sound can be disconcerting to some students.

Electroboards and all other tactual resources are particularly delightful when

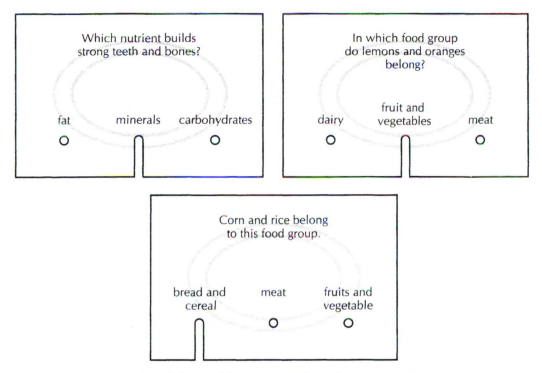

FIGURE 6–23   Carolyn Bovell designed these Pic-A-Hole cards on "Nutrition: Neat Treat—or Health Wealth" to accompany the Programmed Learning Sequence in Chapter 7, the Contract Activity Package in Chapter 8, and the Multisensory Instructional Package in Chapter 9.

their outer shapes are in harmony with the subject matter they are trying to teach. For example, an Electroboard about whales could be designed in the shape of a whale.

Directions   Creatively vary the outer dimension of each Electroboard so that it reflects the theme or unit being studied and is easy for the children to find without assistance. For example, they will learn that an Electroboard dealing with a unit on transportation will very likely have an outline in the shape of a car, a train, or a plane. When they are focusing on a specific theme, all the tactual resources for that theme should have the same shape. The resources on a unit on nutrition might all be in the shape of a fruit; those on community workers might have a Learning Circle, a set of Task Cards, a Flip Chute, a Pic-A-Hole, and an Electroboard all in the shape of a firefighter's or police officer's hat.

    1. Begin with two pieces of either posterboard or oaktag cut into exactly the same size and shape (12×10 inches to 24×10 inches).

    2. List the exact questions you want the Electroboard to ask; then list their answers. Count the number of questions and divide the face of the left side of the Electroboard into evenly divided spaces so that the questions all fit on the left side.

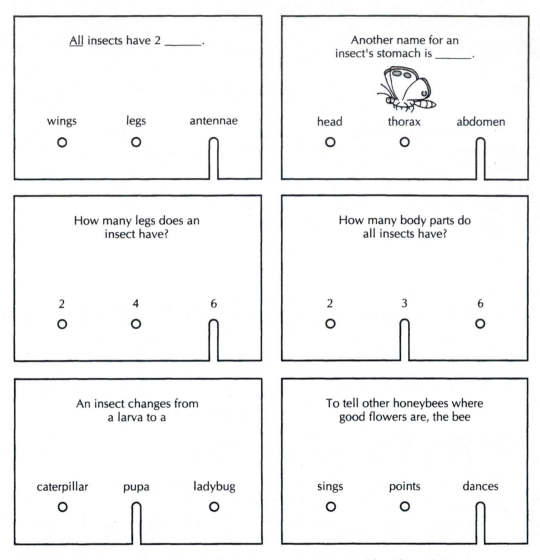

FIGURE 6–24 Excerpts from Pic-A-Hole on "Insects: Don't Bug Me" by Eileen Clark.

3. Use a paper hole puncher to make one hole on the left side of the face of the Electroboard for each question you developed. Then punch corresponding holes on the same horizontal level as the beginning of each question, but on the right side. These holes are for the answers to the questions (½ inch in and 1 to 2 inches apart).

4. Print the questions and answers separately in large, black, capital letters, either directly on the oaktag or posterboard or, to make very neat, attractive lines, onto double lines (2″ × 8″) of opaque correction tape, which can be obtained in most large stationery stores. When you are satisfied with the printing of the questions and

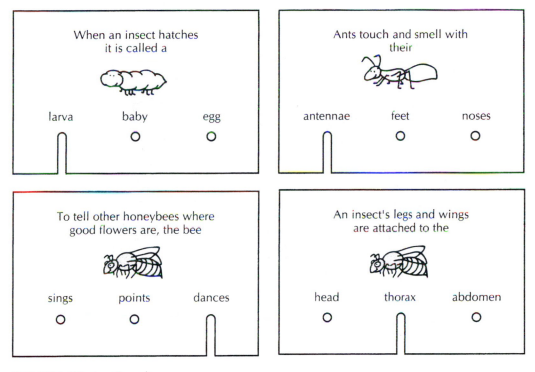

FIGURE 6–24 (continued)

their corresponding answers, peel the correction tape from its base. Carefully place each question next to one of the prepunched holes on the left side of the developing Electroboard's face and each answer next to one of the prepunched holes on the right side. Be certain that each question and answer pair is placed on a horizontal plane with the other and that even spaces remain in between. It is important to randomize the answers so that no answer is on the same horizontal level as its matched question.

5. Turn the oaktag or posterboard over and, on its back, create circuits made with aluminum foil strips and masking tape. One at a time, place quarter-inch-wide strips of aluminum foil connecting each question and its correct answer. Then use masking tape that is wider than the foil strips, cover each foil strip with three-quarter-inch- to one-inch-wide masking tape. Be certain to press both the foil and the masking tape cover so that they: (a) completely cover the punched holes and (b) remain permanently fixed. An easy way to be certain that the foil is covered involves laying the appropriate length of masking tape on a desk or table, sticky side up, and then placing the foil on the tape.

6. Note the positions of each question and its answer so that you can prepare a self-corrective guide in case one is necessary for substitute teachers or aides. Write the name and number of the Electroboard (assuming you have several) at the top of the code. Place the answer key into a secure place where access is available when necessary.

Electroboards are used with a continuity tester that lights up when the child chooses the correct answer (see Chapter 11). The lighted bulb often mesmerizes youngsters, and the answers seem to become imprinted on their memory. They may be used either alone, as shown, or in a pair. (Photograph courtesy Center for the Study of Learning and Teaching Styles, St. John's University, New York.)

7. Using a continuity tester, which can be purchased in any hardware store (see Chapter 11 if you can't locate a tester), check every circuit to be certain that all are working correctly. Touch each question with one prong of the circuit tester and its related answer with the other prong. If the circuits were put together correctly, the tester's bulb should light. Experiment with touching several questions and incorrect answers (one at a time) to be certain that the bulb does not light. Remove sharp points if any exist.

8. Next, tape the second, identically shaped and sized piece of oaktag or posterboard to the back of the first piece on which you have been doing all this tactile work. The second piece will conceal the circuits so that your students do not know which questions are paired with which answers. Tape the entire perimeter of both cards together, or connect the cards using double-faced tape.

Electroboard Variations

For efficiency in developing multiple Electroboards, insert blank circuit boards with room for question-and-answer cards to be placed in the middle and attached with one of the following:

1. Velcro
2. Plastic binder spines
3. Pocket made of oaktag (Figure 6–25).

Additional circuit patterns are presented by turning the Electroboard upside down, turning it over (where the holes have been punched through and show on both sides), or using both sides as well as the top and bottom (Figure 6–26).

Examples of Electroboards

Figures 6–27 through 6–30 are samples of Electroboards. Laminate or use clear contact paper on all boards after questions and answers are completed, but *before* holes are punched. Insert a paper fastener into each hole for permanence.

Designing Tactual-Visual Games

Any games that students play by both seeing and moving them with their hands are, in a sense, tactual-visual; they are not always as tactual as Task Cards, but they often facilitate learning for youngsters who require some manipulative involvement with the learning materials.

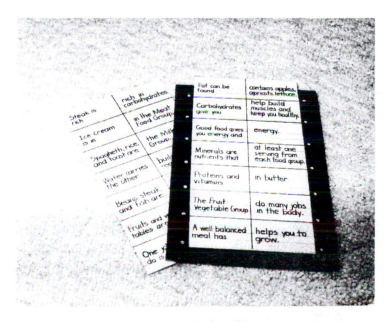

Multiple Electroboards may be developed by designing blank circuit boards with room for Question-and-Answer Cards to be attached in the middle with Velcro. (Photograph courtesy Center for the Study of Learning and Teaching Styles, St. John's University, New York.)

"The Mystery Animal" (Figure 6–31) is one such device and is easy to duplicate at any level. In fact, given an example to study and the following directions, many first- and second-grade students are capable of making their own versions when permitted to work on them with a classmate or two or as a homework option.

Materials
- A photograph or illustration of something connected with what your students are studying; if appropriate, a "Mystery Animal"
- A piece of colored construction paper, preferably light-colored, the same size as the picture or illustration you select
- Black felt-tip pens
- Clear contact paper to cover the front and back of the illustration
- A glue stick

Directions
1. Back the illustration by gluing the construction paper to it.
2. On the construction side, print questions all over the page at different angles. Turn each question upside down and, beneath it, print its answer. (Separate each question-and-answer pair with an outlined shape of different sizes.)
3. With clear contact paper, cover both the illustration and the construction paper side of the game.
4. Cut the illustration into several pieces, with each question separated from its answer. (Test it first using a paper sample.)
5. Cover a box or an envelope with construction paper, and use it to store the question-and-answer pieces. Label it to explain the contents and directions for use. If the box cover is large enough, suggest that the students piece together the question-and-answer sections inside the top of the box. When the written

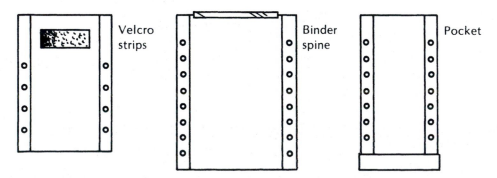

FIGURE 6–25   Three ways of designing blank Electroboards are shown here. Questions and answers can be placed between the aluminum foil contact and points to provide different information for different units without constructing totally new Electroboards. Velcro strips, plastic binder spines or holders, and oaktag pockets all can be used to hold posters with questions on one side and out-of-order, answers on the other.

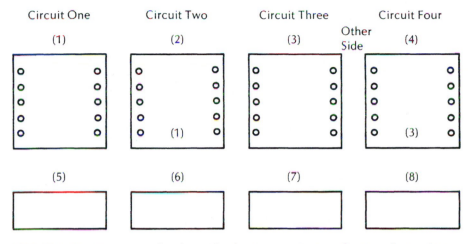

FIGURE 6–26 Circuits can be changed to limit memorization of patterns by turning circuit upside-down (circuits one and two), using the other side (circuits three and four), and then sideways (circuits 5 and 6, and circuits 7 and 8).

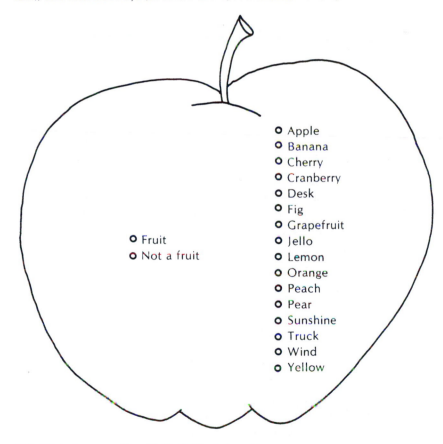

FIGURE 6–27 Samples of a Fruit Electroboard

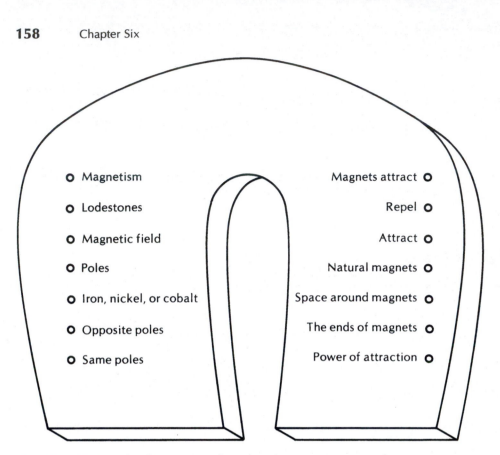

FIGURE 6–28 Sample of Magnetism Electroboard

puzzle has been completed, it can be flipped upside down, and the original illustration should be intact—the Mystery Animal will appear!

6. Cover the box or envelope with contact paper to protect it.

Designing a Touch-Compute Can

Although many teachers have been using a compute can to facilitate addition and multiplication processes for youngsters who need assistance, the added feature of letting the student *feel* the answers may help younger or slower students to commit number facts to memory much faster than they could without the aid of this clever device.

Materials
- 2 sheets of different-colored construction paper
- 1 Pringle's Potato Chips can or a similar-shaped product
- Clear contact paper

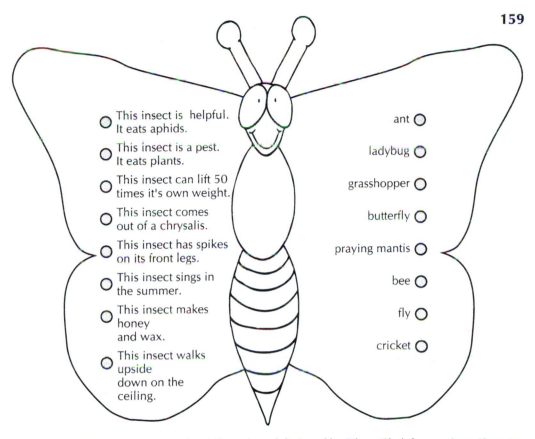

This insect is helpful. It eats aphids.

This insect is a pest. It eats plants.

This insect can lift 50 times it's own weight.

This insect comes out of a chrysalis.

This insect has spikes on its front legs.

This insect sings in the summer.

This insect makes honey and wax.

This insect walks upside down on the ceiling.

ant

ladybug

grasshopper

butterfly

praying mantis

bee

fly

cricket

FIGURE 6–29 Sample of Electroboard designed by Eileen Clark for a unit on "Insects: Don't Bug Me!"

- Black, felt-tip pens for printing; colored pens for illustrating
- Scotch tape
- Dennison glue-stick
- Elmer's glue

Directions

1. Enlarge these samples and then cut out sheet #1 (Figure 6–32) to help your students improve in addition, or sheet #2 (Figure 6–33) to help them improve in multiplication—or both sheets if they need help with the two math processes.

2. Cover sheet #1 with contact paper on its top side and attach it to the can. Cut the clear contact paper (10¾ inches long and 8¼) inches wide to fully cover sheet #1 (addition or multiplication) which is 9¼ inches high and 8¼ inches wide. The additional ¾ inch at the top and ¾ inch at the bottom are used to attach sheet #1 to the can permanently. Use either glue or Scotch tape as you wrap sheet #1 around the can.

3. Outline the numerals with Elmer's glue so that the children can feel the shape of the numbers as well as see them.

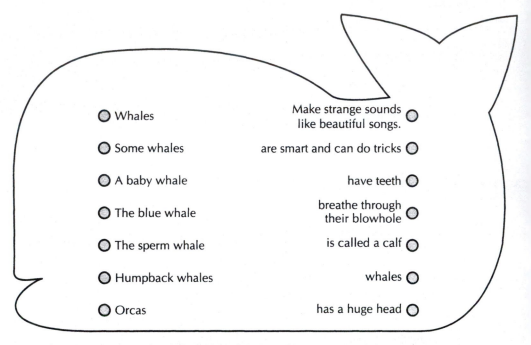

FIGURE 6–30 Sample of Electroboard designed by Irene Kozak for a unit on "The Humpback Whale: Have a WHALE of a Time!"

4. Cut sheet #3, which will rotate around the can, 9⅜ inches long and 7⅜ inches wide. Cut out and remove all the boxes marked with an "X" (see Figure 6–34). Cut contact paper the same size (9⅜ inches long and 7⅜ inches wide). Place the contact paper over the front of sheet #2 even with the top so that the additional 1 inch of length is at the bottom. When curling sheet #2 around the can, this additional inch will attach to the top, forming a sleeve that can rotate around sheet #1, which is at-tached to the can. Sheet #2 may be used for addition *and* multiplication.

5. Place the sheet #2 "sleeve" over sheet #1. The correct answers will appear in the cut-out boxes.

6. Label the Touch-Compute Can, adding the phrase (perhaps at the bottom), "Give Me a Turn!" Demonstrate how to use this device for youngsters who need help with their number facts. Then let them try it. Emphasize that, when they turn to the correct answer in the boxed cut-out, they also touch the numbers.

Designing Scramble Word Games

From time to time, most of us have used word games in which we scramble the letters of an answer to a question and ask students to decode them. To make such a device tactual, secure a set or two of either sandpaper or felt-embossed alphabetical letters

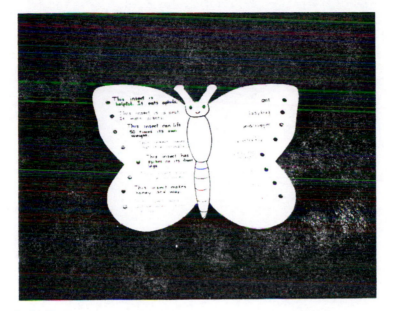

Like other tactual/kinesthetic materials, Electroboards should be attractive and, when possible, shaped like the topic being studied. These photos show Electroboards on insect types and dinosaurs. Pamela Koshuto of the Lowman Elementary School, Idaho designed the dinosaur Electroboard so that it works both front and back, with two different sets of answer keys. (Photographs courtesy Center for the Study of Learning and Teaching Styles, St. John's University, New York.)

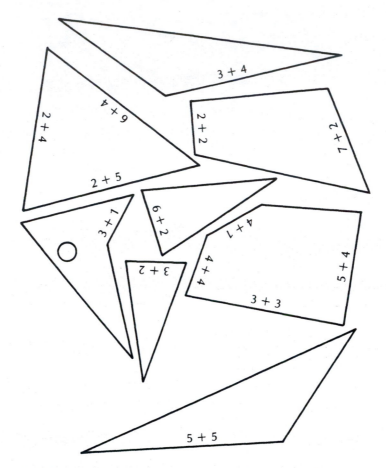

FIGURE 6–31 "The Mystery Animal" title is based on an illustration of Mickey Mouse. The teacher capitalized on children's natural interest in animals with personality to develop a math game in which, once they found the answers to all the problems on the *back* of the construction paper, the picture on the reverse side would have been put together and would no longer *be* a mystery!

that include the answers to specific questions you have in mind. Place all the letters together into one box or a laminated envelope (to keep the envelope from tearing easily with student use). Again, place a title and directions on the box and cover both the letters and the box with clear contact paper. Voilà! A tactual-visual game that will introduce new—and reinforce previously taught—information!

Topic: Animal Pets

Directions Inside this box are 52 alphabetical letters. When placed together correctly, they form the names of 12 animals that different people like to keep as pets.

Find the names of any *10* animals. If you can find the 11th, you are *wonderful!* If you find 12 names, you are brighter than most people your age!

Inside the box, the letters could include:

3	A's	2	I's	4	T's
1	B	2	K's	2	U's
2	C's	3	M's	1	Y
3	D's	1	N		
6	E's	5	O's		
1	F	1	P		
3	G's	5	R's		
3	H's	4	S's		

Answers   bird, cat, dog, duck, ferret, fish, goat, hamster, horse, mouse, monkey, pig.

Designing Word Searches

Place each of the letters in this week's spelling or vocabulary words into boxes in crazy, mixed-up patterns, and ask the children to find and circle them with colored crayons or pens—a different color for each word they recognize. This activity may be done alone, in a pair, in a small group of three or four, or with *you* (for teacher-motivated youngsters). Another alternative is to emphasize one or more particularly difficult words with which you anticipate many youngsters will have trouble, as in Figure 6–35.

Example

Directions   I hid the word *fossil* seven (7) different times in this Word Search. How many can you find? Circle each *fossil* you find with a different colored crayon!

Designing Crossword Puzzles

Emphasizing what is *important* in each unit helps children to focus on what they need to memorize. In a unit on dinosaurs, placing questions that require specific answers on the chalkboard or on a ditto and then requiring that the children (a) find the answers and then (b) convert those answers into a crossword puzzle serves several purposes.

- It emphasizes what needs to be remembered.
- It provides different types of activities for children who prefer to learn in several ways and therefore tend to become bored with routine teaching and learning.
- It permits the youngsters to concentrate using their learning style *strengths* rather than in predetermined ways. For example, they may seek the answers

0 +		0	1	2	3	4	5	6	7	8	9
9 +		9	10	11	12	13	14	15	16	17	18
8 +		8	9	10	11	12	13	14	15	16	17
7 +		7	8	9	10	11	12	13	14	15	16
6 +		6	7	8	9	10	11	12	13	14	15
5 +		5	6	7	8	9	10	11	12	13	14
4 +		4	5	6	7	8	9	10	11	12	13
3 +		3	4	5	6	7	8	9	10	11	12
2 +		2	3	4	5	6	7	8	9	10	11
1 +		1	2	3	4	5	6	7	8	9	10

FIGURE 6–32 Touch-Compute Can Sheet #1 to be used for addition.

from *printed* material, *ask* for the information, use *tactual* resources to gather it, or learn it through a *kinesthetic* Floor Game.

- It enables children to learn in any sociological grouping that is best for them—alone, in a pair, in a small group, or with their teachers.
- It allows reflective learners to think critically and impulsive learners to get their answers down immediately without disturbing others.

0 ×		0	0	0	0	0	0	0	0	0	0
9 ×		0	9	18	27	36	45	54	63	72	81
8 ×		0	8	16	24	32	40	48	56	64	72
7 ×		0	7	14	21	28	35	42	49	56	63
6 ×		0	6	12	18	24	30	36	42	48	54
5 ×		0	5	10	15	20	25	30	35	40	45
4 ×		0	4	8	12	16	20	24	28	32	36
3 ×		0	3	6	9	12	15	18	21	24	27
2 ×		0	2	4	6	8	10	12	14	16	18
1 ×		0	1	2	3	4	5	6	7	8	9

FIGURE 6–33 Touch-Compute Can Sheet #2 to be used for multiplication.

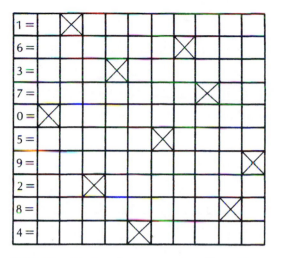

FIGURE 6–34 Touch-Compute Can Sheet #3, to be used for multiplication or addition.

- It allows for learning in any environment that most appeals to the child.
- It increases motivation.
- It permits options and choices for the nonconformist.
- It details structure for those who are externally motivated and choices for those who are internally structured.

Example   Find the answer to as many of these questions as you can. As you find the answer to a question, count the number of alphabetical letters in that answer and the number of spaces in the blank crossword puzzle attached to it (Figure 6–36). If the number of alphabetical letters *and* the number of spaces on the *same numbered* item are the same, neatly print the answer into the correct space—one letter in each space. In this way, you will be doing a crossword puzzle, just as many adults do!

CROSSWORD PUZZLE QUESTIONS

1. The word *dinosaur* means _____.
2. Which dinosaur was called the "King of Tyrants"?
3. Dinosaurs were like reptiles because they *laid* _____.
4. We know about dinosaurs because we saw their footprints and body prints in special rocks. What are those prints called? _____.
5. Dinosaurs lived on _____ 200 million years ago.
6. Dinosaurs are *different* from reptiles because they do not drag their _____ on the ground.

As you find each answer, write it onto the crossword puzzle.

ANSWERS:

FIGURE 6–35 Word Search for a single difficult word.

Step-by-Step Guide to Designing Kinesthetic Activities

Some youngsters can learn only by doing; for them, real-life experiences are the most effective way of absorbing and retaining knowledge. It is easy to teach students to convert pints to quarts and quarts to gallons through baking and cooking, or to teach them inches and feet by helping them to build a scooter or antique dollhouse, but it is not simple to teach all the skills and information that must be achieved through reality-oriented activities. In the first place, such activities are time-consuming; second, many activities require supervision; finally, we are not used to teaching that way, and to do so requires an endless source of creative suggestions. There is, however, a new kind of kinesthetic (whole-body) game that you can design for classroom use and ever-continuing learning by your kinesthetic students.

Designing Body-Action Floor Games

Many teachers save old things and then use them creatively to instruct their students. Now is the time to locate all the large plastic tablecloths, shower curtains, carpet pieces, furniture coverings, and sails that may be hidden away in basements, attics, garages, and wherever else too-good-to-throw-away things are stored. Old sheets and bath towels may also be pressed into service,but they are not as durable as plastic, and when they are washed the printed matter on them often fades and occasionally disappears altogether. If you are not a collector of old valuables,you may need to solicit cast-off materials from others or to purchase a large sheet of plastic from your neighborhood bargain store.

Materials
- One large sheet of plastic or other material, approximately 4 × 5, 5 × 5, or 5 × 6 feet, or within that size range
- Smaller pieces of multicolored plastic that can be cut into decorations and illustrations and then glued or sewn onto the larger sheet
- Black thin-line permanent-ink pens
- Black and brightly colored permanent-ink felt-tip pens
- Glue that will make plastic adhere to plastic
- Assorted discarded items that, depending on your imagination and creativity, you use as part of the game you design
- Pad and pencil for sketching ideas

Directions
1. Identify the information or skills that you want your students to learn.
2. Consider ways in which you either can introduce that information or rein-

FIGURE 6–36 A Crossword Puzzle for Primary Children.

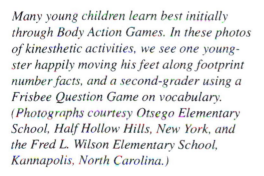

Many young children learn best initially through Body Action Games. In these photos of kinesthetic activities, we see one young-ster happily moving his feet along footprint number facts, and a second-grader using a Frisbee Question Game on vocabulary. (Photographs courtesy Otsego Elementary School, Half Hollow Hills, New York, and the Fred L. Wilson Elementary School, Kannapolis, North Carolina.)

force it through a body-action Floor Game on which kinesthetic students can hop, jump, or merely move from one part of the large sheet to another as they are exposed to the questions on the topic and need to move to what they believe is the answer.

3. Sketch a design on a sheet of paper to work out where you will place the various answers before you begin cutting, pasting, or sewing.

4. When you are satisfied with your conceptualization of the game, plan a layout of the various sections on the plastic sheet that you will use; consider the placement of questions and answers, and list the additional items that you can use to make this lesson gamelike.

5. In pencil, lightly sketch on the large sheet where you will paste each item, the dimensions for which you must plan, and where you will place key directions.

6. Cut smaller plastic pieces into appropriate shapes or figures, and glue them onto the larger sheet.

7. With a felt-tip pen that will not wash off, trace over those penciled lines that you wish to keep.

8. Develop a set of questions and answers or tasks that students may complete as they use the body-action Floor Game. Then either develop an answer card so that students may correct themselves, or color-code or picture-code the questions and answers so that the game is self-corrective.

9. If you teach either very young children or poor readers, develop a tape that will tell them how to play the game, what the game will teach them (the objectives), and how they can recognize that they have learned whatever it is the game is designed to teach (the test).

10. If your students are capable of reading and following printed directions, print or type a set of directions for them and attach them to the sheet (perhaps in a pocket that you cut out and glue or sew onto its underside).

Examples

For an instructional package on "shapes," several activities were designed that taught students to recognize a series of different shapes (Figure 6–37). As the culminating exercise, a body-action game was created with the following directions:

Directions

1. To play this game, you must correctly name each shape as you come to it. Travel along the path according to the direction on the answer side of each card. Begin by naming the first shape that is part of the path.

2. Look at Answer Card 1 in the pocket on the underside of the game. If your answer is correct, hop on one foot to the next shape. If your answer is not correct, take "baby steps" to the next shape.

3. You now should be standing on the yellow shape. It has five sides. What is the name of the yellow shape?

The directions guide students through a series of varied geometric shapes, permitting them to check their answers and, if they name the shape incorrectly, to learn

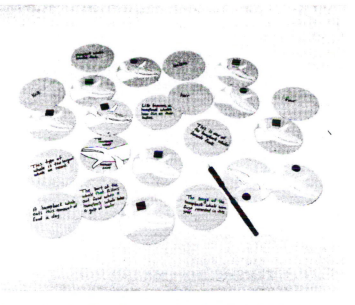

This samples of a Floor Game teaches about humpback whales.
Other topics might be balanced meals, the solar system, or insects.
(Photograph courtesy Center for the Study of Learning and Teach-
ing Styles, St. John's University, New York.)

why the answer is wrong. When the Floor Game is completed, a duplicate sheet attached to the larger package tests them on their ability to identify a variety of shapes. The teacher then checks their final assessment responses.

Kathleen McLaughlin designed a Floor Game on dinosaurs for her first-graders. She Velcroed five different dinosaur drawings onto a clear plastic sheet, made a "path" along the sheet of "dinosaur tracks", and printed the name of each reptile on its own picture. The first member of a playing team could request the cards of any dinosaur on the game but then had to tell at least three facts unique to that particular dinosaur. On each card, Ms. McLaughlin had printed facts about that member of the species. The students' information had to match the facts printed on the card. Only one card could be selected at a time, but all the cards had to be completed to win the game. If the information stated by the player was on the card, the youngster progressed along the path to the next "Dinosaur Information Stop." When the first team had 5 points—one for each card with three correctly stated facts about that dinosaur—it was considered the "winner"! Ms. McLaughlin added facts to the card each week, even when the unit had been completed. Thus, the information the children needed to know to play that game gradually increased during the semester. She also added more dinosaurs to the plastic as the term progressed.

Phyllis Napolitano found that her second-graders learned the stages of a

FIGURE 6–37 A Floor Game that required kindergartners to name various shapes as they followed along "the path to storyland" helped those young students to learn ordinary and unusual forms and their correct nomenclature fairly quickly. Afterward, their teacher substituted reading vocabulary matched with descriptive illustrations and found that the game helped the children recognize new words at a more rapid pace than previously.

butterfly's life quickly when she converted the information into a Floor Game with just four illustrations on it (Figure 6–38). She added directions on a large white card:

> *Let's see how well you remember how a butterfly grows. This circle shows the life of a butterfly. Put the correct label on each picture. When you have finished, turn the labels over and see whether you* knew *the answer! Then place the labels back into the game's envelope.*

Because so many young children *are* essentially kinesthetic, Floor Games, in addition to real-life activities—dividing a pizza into the number of slices needed; taking a trip and accumulating information from the experience; or attending the theater, a museum, or a concert—add more to a young child's knowledge than most lecture-and-listen lessons.

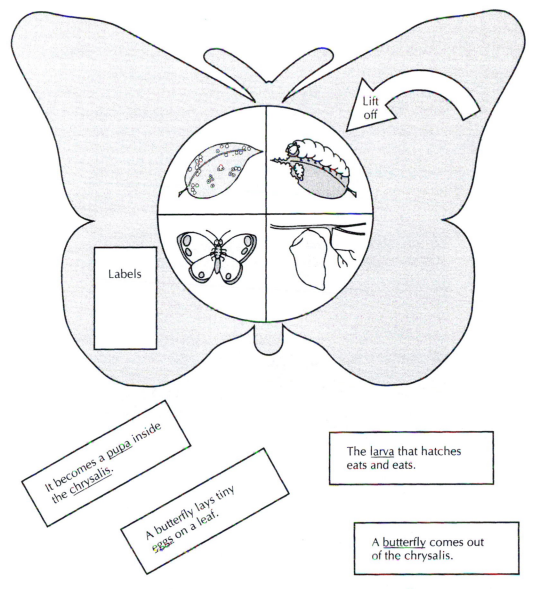

FIGURE 6–38 Floor Game on the "Life Stages of a Butterfly" designed by Phyllis Napolitano for second-graders.

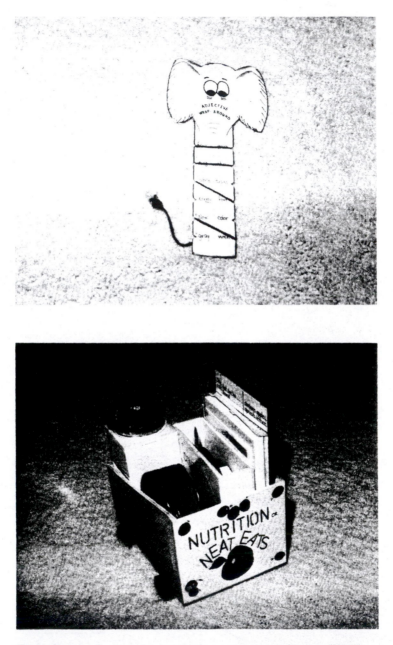

Tactual strategies may be as simple as using an Adjective Wrap-Around or as complex as using an entire Multisensory Instructional Package on nutrition filled with hands-on and move-around-and-learn activities, with directions for using them attached. (Photographs courtesy Center for the Study of Learning and Teaching Styles, St. John's University, New York.)

A Final Word on Kinesthetic Resources

Extensive time and effort is needed to develop the games described here. But if you find that students who rarely achieved before, when exposed to this method, suddenly begin to learn and to enjoy learning, won't you agree that the outcomes are well worth the effort? The plastic sheets can be used over and over again for different sets of facts and skills merely by changing the directions and the cards that are given to the students.

A Final Word on Teaching Tactually and Kinesthetically

Most of us use tactual and kinesthetic activities in our classroom! When we *do,* however, we use them with everyone. Only primarily tactual and kinesthetic children *require* them. Furthermore, most of us teach by talking *first* and *then* using tactuals to reinforce for the youngsters who seem to be having trouble.

We encourage you to do something very different for the next unit you teach. *Start* the unit with the Flip Chutes, Task Cards, Electroboards, and Pic-A-Holes for the tactual children, and *start* the unit with the Floor Game for the kinesthetics. After they have had a chance to become familiar with the concept and vocabulary by working with these resources twice, perhaps for twenty minutes each time, *then* teach them by talking. We are certain that you will *see* the difference in their levels of understanding, attention to the topic, attitude, and behavior. If not, you have lost little. If we are correct, you have gained a great deal.

Try these instructional resources with the children who do not seem to be your best achieving pupils. Try them with the ones who seem to be unhappy, nonconforming, ostracized, or just "not too bright." Identify the few who, if you *had* to guess, might be the potential dropouts eight to ten years from now; you may notice a total reversal in how they perform when they *begin* learning new material through Flip Chutes, Electroboards, Task Cards, Pic-A-Holes, or Floor Games. If these resources do not improve their knowledge base and behavior, stop! If they *do,* you have contributed to these children's ability to achieve well.

7

Designing Programmed Learning Sequences to Respond to Individual Learning Styles

A second basic method for individualizing instruction is to program material so that it may be learned in small, simple steps without the direct supervision of an adult. Like any other method, programmed instruction is responsive only to selected learning style characteristics and, therefore, should not be prescribed for all students. The special types of programming described in this chapter are called Programmed Learning Sequences.

Programmed Learning Sequences (PLS) are designed around preselected concepts and skills, called *objectives*, that must be mastered by each student. Objectives ranging from simple to complex are sequenced so that, after taking a pretest, students are assigned only those they have not achieved before using that particular program. All students proceed through the identical sequence but may pace themselves and use the program when and where they prefer to study.

Programs that have been commercially produced have had only limited effectiveness because they are solely visual—similar to short workbooks—and therefore appeal most to students who either read fairly well or can retain information by seeing. The firms that produce such programs maintain that cassettes and filmstrips occasionally supplement their resources. When multimedia materials are available, they should be used to enhance the program's effectiveness for those youngsters who are auditory, while serving as reinforcement for those who are visual.

In actual practice, students are each given a PLS for which they are responsible. As the various objectives and their related tests are completed, gradual progress is made toward completing the material. Unless learners seek assistance, they can work through the PLS by themselves without adult or peer interaction. The tape, of course, reads the material to them, and the youngster is directed to listen carefully, think of the answers, and record them. They are self-corrected by the material, so there is little danger that the child will make erroneous guesses that will not be corrected.

At each age and grade level, however, there are some children who are peer-oriented; they learn better working with a friend than they do alone. When the LSI:P indicates that certain youngsters are so inclined, there is no reason that two cannot work quietly and cooperatively with the materials. Many teachers have tried permitting peer-oriented learners, whose learning style diagnoses revealed their need to work with another child, to do so and have reported no instances of inappropriate behavior or poor grades. Extensive research indicates that such children attain statistically higher achievement and attitude test scores when they *are* permitted to work with a classmate (DeBello, 1985; Dunn, 1989; Dunn, Giannitti, Murray, Geisert, Rossi, & Quinn, 1990; Fleming, 1989; Giannitti, 1988; "Review of Research," 1991; Miles, 1986; Perrin, 1984). Establish firm, well-understood rules for working together before the children begin—for example, "The words you speak to each other must not be so loud that any other child can tell me what you are actually saying. Speak quietly. Your learning style must not infringe on anyone else's style. Your grades must be equal to a B or better, or this is not working and you two cannot continue."

Learning Style Characteristics Responsive to Programmed Learning Sequences

Because programmed materials usually are used independently, it is important that students to whom this resource is assigned enjoy working alone or in a pair and are motivated to learn the program's contents. They should also be persistent, suggesting that they normally would continue using the materials until the program has been completed. If they experience difficulty, they either should review the previous frames and continue to try to progress, or should seek assistance from appropriate persons.

By organizing everything that should be learned so that only one item at a time is presented, the sequenced materials in each program provide a great deal of structure. A student cannot proceed until what must be achieved at each stage has been fully understood, as demonstrated through a short quiz at the end of each frame or page. Youngsters who prefer to be told exactly what to do will feel at ease with programmed learning, whereas creative students may find it boring and unchallenging.

PLS are ideally suited to youngsters who prefer to work alone and to avoid sound, movement, and interaction with classmates. They are a perfect match for students who learn best by seeing and for those who need to read and, perhaps, reread information before it is absorbed.

Teachers who believe that selected students are neither motivated nor persistent, but who recognize that they are average or slow achievers, visual learners, and in need of structure, should experiment with programmed instruction. Because this strategy presents concepts and skills simply, gradually, and repeatedly, and because

Programmed Learning Sequences (PLSs) permit young children to learn independently, but students who wish to work together may do so. (Photograph courtesy Center for the Study of Learning and Teaching Styles, St. John's University, New York.)

it may be used alone—without causing the embarrassment or pressure that emerges when one has difficulty achieving among one's peers—many youngsters become motivated, persistent, or responsible when using a PLS. When the "right" method is matched with the "right" student, increased academic achievement and improved attitudes toward learning are likely to result. Obviously, a tape of your voice reading each frame slowly may be required for those who do well with Programmed Learning but who do not read well.

Learning Style Characteristics to Which Programmed Learning Sequences Can Be Accommodated

Because a PLS may be used in a classroom, in a library, in a corridor, or in an instructional resource center as well as at home, it can accommodate each student's environmental and physiological preferences. For example, the PLS can be taken to a silent area if quiet is desired, or it may be used in the midst of classroom activity when the learner can block out sound. It can be moved to either a warm section of a room—near a radiator, perhaps—or to a cool area. It can be studied at a desk or on a carpet, in a well-lit space or away from bright sunshine. A student may snack or not as he or she works, may use the package at any time of day that is convenient, and may take a break or two if mobility is necessary.

Because the PLS is visual, it will utilize the perceptual strengths of students who learn best by reading or seeing. For auditory youngsters, a teacher should add a tape that repeats orally what the text teaches visually. Hearing and seeing the words simultaneously will help beginning or struggling readers. When students are either tactual or kinesthetic learners, the teacher should add instructional measures like Pic-A-Hole games to introduce or reinforce the PLS' objectives through those senses. For students who learn slowly or with difficulty, it is wise to supplement a visual Programmed Learning Sequence with three other types of perceptual resources—auditory, tactual, and kinesthetic. When appropriate, a PLS may be completed by pairs or teams of students. When a student is tactually strong, introduce difficult information through tactual resources and *reinforce* through a PLS.

Case Studies Describing Students Whose Learning Styles Are Complemented by Programmed Learning Sequences

Only the sound of his own name was able to break into his thoughts. As Mrs. Diamond's voice repeated the question, Kerry sat up in his seat. He had been so engrossed in contemplating the effects of insects on the environment—an item on which the teacher had been focusing 10 minutes earlier—that he was imagining giant insects roaming through his backyard.

Mrs. Diamond's voice was sympathetic. "Do you know the answer?" Kerry sat up quickly in embarrassment. "I'm sorry," he answered. "I was thinking about something else." "What?" she asked. He merely shrugged. He was reluctant to reveal that he was imagining giant insects at work in the garden. "Please keep up with us," the teacher urged, and slowly shook her head in exasperation.

Students who are motivated to learn, but who need more time to consider items or to concentrate than is usually permitted by group instruction, may learn more effectively through Programmed Learning Sequences.

Mark became upset when Ms. Dobbins announced they only had 10 minutes before lunch. Knowing he would not be able to complete the assignment in time, he began to work more quickly. He knew he was making mistakes because he was rushing. He then asked Ms. Dobbins if he could skip recess after lunch and return to the classroom to complete his work.

Students who are persistent—who continue working toward the completion of an assignment and find ways to do so—usually respond well to Programmed Learning Sequences.

Barbara focused her eyes on page 1 of the new book. It was her favorite time of day. As Mrs. Winter read Alice in Wonderland *aloud, Barbara transformed the words of the story into vibrant pictures in her mind. Mrs. Winter was always so pleased when, days after a section of the story had been read, Barbara could draw a detailed illustration of the events.*

Students who are visual learners—who remember more by reading and seeing than they do by listening—usually respond well to Programmed Learning Sequences. Also, many primary children tend to be either global/tactual or global and responsive to pictures. Therefore, many pictures should be added to all learning materials.

Maria complained to the teacher. "Timothy is bothering us. He keeps making ugly faces." "Timothy!" chastised Mrs. Levant, "this is the third interruption because of you. Your team will never finish its project. I'm sorry, but you will have to work by yourself." As soon as Timothy went back to his own desk, he immediately became involved in his work.

Students who do not work well in groups may work better alone knowing that they, personally, are responsible for completing an assignment. Such youngsters may respond well to Programmed Learning Sequences, Contract Activity Packages, or Multisensory Instructional Packages. Children who *do* work well with classmates should be permitted to work cooperatively, using the best method for both children.

Claire was at her teacher's side again. "Mr. Dawes, is this right?" she asked. "You asked the same question 5 minutes ago!" the teacher responded. "I know,"Claire answered, "but I want to be sure!"

Students who are authority-oriented and/or require structure—who need to know exactly what to do and how to do it—usually respond well to Programmed Learning Sequences.

Basic Principles of Programmed Learning Sequences

Programmed Learning is based on several important principles that facilitate academic achievement for students with selected learning style elements. Programs follow a pattern that includes each of the following characteristics:

1. *Only one item is presented at a time.* A single concept or skill that should be mastered is introduced through a simple written statement. After reading the material, the learner is required to answer a question or two to demonstrate that what has been introduced on that frame (page, section) has been understood. This procedure prevents the lesson from advancing faster than the student, and it does not permit the student to fall behind. The youngster may learn as quickly as he or she is capable of comprehending the material, or as slowly and with as much repetition as needed. Students should not continue to a subsequent frame or phase of the program until each previous one has been mastered.

Presenting one item at a time is effective for the analytic youngster who wants to learn (is motivated), who will continue trying (is persistent), and who wants to do what is required (is responsible/conforming). For students who are not persistent, being exposed to one item at a time divides the content into small phases and the process into short steps that can be mastered gradually. Young children who tend to be more global than analytic will also respond positively to programmed learning when the frames are illustrated and the PLS is introduced by a brief story that summarizes its content and attracts their interest. A PLS is usually inappropriate for those who cannot continue to work with the same set of materials for any continuing amount of time and who need diversity and variety. In addition, it is a method that does not often attract and hold creative students who want to add their own knowledge and special talents to what is being learned before they have accomplished the entire task.

Unlike large-group instruction, where a student may merely sit and appear to be listening, a PLS requires that a response be made to questions related to each introduced item. Youngsters cannot progress through the program without responding, and only accurate answers permit continuation of this instructional process.

2. *The student is required to be an active rather than a passive learner.*

3. *The student is immediately informed of the correctness of each response.* As soon as a youngster has read the frame, he or she is required to answer a question based on the material that has just been read. The moment that the student's response has been recorded, the youngster may turn to the back of the frame, where the correct answer appears. The student, therefore, immediately discovers the accuracy or inaccuracy of the response. This immediate feedback is a highly effective teaching strategy with most learners.

4. *The student may not continue into the next phase of a program until each previous phase has been understood and mastered.* When the program reveals that a student's response to the questions related to each frame are correct, the student is directed to continue into the next section (frame, page, or phase). When students' responses are not correct, they can be directed either to restudy the previously read frames or to turn to another section of the program that will explain in a different way the material that has not been understood. Because each phase of the program must be mastered before students are permitted to continue into the next phase, learners do not move ahead aimlessly while grasping only parts of a concept or topic. Their base of knowledge is solid before they are exposed to either new ideas or related ones.

5. *The student may be exposed to material that gradually progresses from easy to more difficult.* Frames are written so that the first few in a series introduce what should be learned in an uncomplicated, direct manner. Gradually, as the student's correct answers demonstrate his or her increasing understanding of what is being taught, more difficult aspects of the topic are introduced. Through this technique, students are made to feel both comfortable and successful with the beginning phases of each program, and their confidence in their own ability to achieve is bolstered. Youngsters who find themselves achieving are likely to continue in the learning process.

6. *As the student proceeds in the program, fewer hints and crutches are provided.* Programming uses a system of "fading" or gradually withdrawing easy questions or hints (repeated expressions, illustrations, color coding, and similar aids) so that eventually, the student's developing knowledge is tested precisely. This technique also enables the teacher to assess accurately the youngster's progress and mastery of the material.

Step-by-Step Guide to Designing a Programmed Learning Sequence

Developing a program is not difficult, but it does require that you organize the topic that will be taught into a logical, easy-to-follow sequence. Begin with Step 1 and gradually move through each of the remaining steps until you have completed your first program. Each consecutive program will become easier and easier to design. By their questions and responses, students will provide direct feedback on how to revise and improve your initial efforts. Subsequent programs will require fewer revisions.

Step 1. Begin by identifying a topic, concept, or skill that you want to teach. A good choice would be a lesson or unit that most youngsters in your classes need to learn. Because all students are not capable of learning at the same time, in the same way, and at the same speed, a program is one way of permitting individuals to self-pace themselves with materials whenever they are ready to achieve. Thus, some youngsters may use a specific program early in the semester, while others will use it later. Some will use it to learn before the remainder of the class is exposed to a new idea, and others will use it to reinforce an idea that you already have taught—but that they did not master.

Step 2. Write the name of the topic, concept, or skill that *you* have decided to teach as a heading at the top of a blank sheet of paper. Add a subtitle that is humorous or related to a real-life experience. Plan to design the covers—or the entire PLS—in a shape that represents the topics to appeal to the tactual children. If you can introduce some humor, it will appeal to the more global students.

Examples

- Exploring the Planets: Give me Some Space!
- All about Insects: Don't Bug Me!
- Math: Divide and Conquer
- Butterflies: Fluttering Friends
- Going to the Dentist: Getting Your Teeth into It!
- Electricity: The Shock of Your Life

Step 3. Translate the heading that you have written at the top of the sheet into an introductory sentence that explains to the youngsters using the PLS exactly what they should be able to do after they have mastered what it is designed to teach. For

*The Programmed Learning Sequences' unique shapes represent
the topics they teach. Their humorous subtitles and global story be-
ginnings attract children's attention. This photograph shows "Dinosaurs: Make No Bones about It!"; Save the Whales: Don't Blow
Your Top!"; and "Lifestyles of Dolphins: Don't Flip Your Lid!"
(Photograph courtesy Center for the Study of Learning and Teaching Styles, St. John's University, New York.)*

example, in "Plants, Animals, Insects: For the Life of Us," Christine L. Bitalvo
wrote: "By the time you finish this Programmed Learning Sequence, you should be
able to recognize plants, animals, and insects and name at least five (5) of each of
their characteristics."

Step 4. List all the prerequisites for using the program effectively. For example:

> *On the following frames, answer questions by either filling in the blanks, circling, un-
> derlining, or matching answers. The correct answers will be on the back of each frame.
> You may use a marker or wipe-off crayons. Good luck!*
>
> *Be certain that you begin reading this Programmed Learning Sequence either on
> or near a large table so that you have ample room to use the booklet, its materials, and
> the tape recorder at the same time.*

Because you may realize that certain knowledge or skills are prerequisites after
you have moved beyond step 4, leave space on your paper so that you can insert
additions as they come to mind.

Step 5. Create a short global story, fantasy, cartoon, or humorous beginning related to the topic. Place this global opening just before the information-and-question frames begin. (See sample programs for global openings.)

Step 6. Decide which of the two basic types of programming you will use.

Type 1: Linear Programming   This type of programming presents material in a highly structured sequence. Each part of the sequence is called a *frame,* and each frame builds upon the one immediately preceding it. Each frame ends with an item that requires an answer—in either completion, matching, or multiple-choice format. Before the introduction of each subsequent frame, the answer to the previous frame is supplied. To increase program efficiency, the correct answer should be accompanied by an explanation and a humorous comment or cartoon. To develop additional comprehension, incorrect answers also should be accompanied by explanations. You can add other modes of response for variety as you develop additional frames—"Circle the correct answer," "Match the correct answers to each question by connecting them with lines" or "Place the correct answer in the right space."

Type 2: Intrinsic Programming   Intrinsic programming also presents material in a highly structured sequence. The major difference between the linear and intrinsic types is that the latter does not require that each student complete every frame. Intrinsic programming recognizes that some youngsters can move through learning experiences faster than others can, and it permits those who score correct answers to skip over some of the reinforcement frames.

A system that allows students to bypass frames that teach the same aspect of a subject is called *branching*. Branching, in effect, permits a faster rate of self-pacing.

A student who answers a question incorrectly, must continue from one frame to the next, one by one, until every frame in the program has been completed. But if a student studies several introductory frames and then answers the questions correctly, he or she may branch over additional reinforcement frames if the program is intrinsic.

Step 7. Outline how you plan to teach the topic. Use short, simple sentences, if possible.

Most people have two different vocabularies—one for speaking, the other for writing. When you begin to outline your program, pretend that you are speaking to the student who will have the most trouble learning this material. Use simple words and sentences. Then write exactly the words you would use if you were actually talking to that youngster. In other words, use your speaking vocabulary rather than your professional writing vocabulary to develop the Programmed Learning Sequence.

Step 8. Divide the sentences in your outline into *frames.* Frames, which are equivalent to pages, are small sections of the topic that teach part of the idea, skill, or information. After listing the sentences that teach the information, ask a question that relates to that material. The student's answer will demonstrate his or her growing understanding of the subject. Think small! Most people who begin to write programs try to cover too much in a frame. Keep each one a simple, small part of the total knowledge represented by your instructional objectives. For global students, you may wish to start with a simple generalization and move to specific examples and applications.

Pose fairly easy-to-answer questions in the first two or three frames to:

- Build a student's self confidence
- Demonstrate to the student that he or she can learn independently through the PLS
- Provide the student with a couple of successful experiences by using the process of Programmed Learning Sequences.

Step 9. Using five by eight-inch (or larger) index cards or oaktag cards cut into a shape (see the sample PLS later in this chapter) to represent each frame, develop a sequence that teaches a subject and, simultaneously, tests the student's growing knowledge of it.

Step 10. Refine each index card frame.

Step 11. Review the sequence to be certain it is logical and does not teach too much on each frame. Add the answers to the questions you have posed on the *front* of each frame to the *back*. Also on the back of the frame, add a humorous comment, joke, or "human" remark to relax the user.

Step 12. Check the spelling, grammar, and punctuation of each frame.

Step 13. Examine the vocabulary to be certain it is understandable by the slowest youngsters that may use the PLS. Avoid colloquialisms that are acceptable in conversation but are less than professional in written form. Remember to use good oral language as opposed to good written language.

Step 14. Reread the entire series to be certain that each frame leads to the next one, and so on.

Step 15. When you are satisfied with the content, sequence, and questions on the frames, add colorful illustrations to clarify the main point on each index card. If you do not wish to draw, use magazine cutouts or gift wrapping paper to supplement graphically the most important sections of the text. The illustrations should relate directly to the PLS content.

Step 16. Read the written material on each frame onto a cassette so that poor readers may use the PLS by listening to the frames being read to them as they simultaneously read along. (See Chapter 6 for directions on making a tape.)

Step 17. Ask three or four of your students to try the PLS, one at a time. Observe each youngster using the material, and try to identify whether any errors, omissions, or areas of difficulty exist. Correct anything that requires improvement.

Step 18. If necessary, revise the PLS based on your observations of your students' usage.

Step 19. Laminate each of the index cards that make up the program or cover them with clear contact paper. Student use will cause the index cards to deteriorate unless they are protected by a covering. Laminated programs last for years and can be cleaned with warm water and soap. They can be written on with grease, pencils, or water-soluble felt pens and then erased for use by another youngster.

Step 20. Add miniature tactual activities (Pic-A-Holes, Task Cards, or Electroboards) for reinforcement of the most important information in the PLS (see Chapter 6). The PLS, as designed through Step 14, will respond only to youngsters who learn through either their visual or auditory strengths. By adding tactual reinforcements, you provide youngsters who need to learn through their sense of touch with a method appropriate for them. You thus add to the effectiveness of the PLS and increase the number of students who can learn successfully through it.

Step 21. Ask additional students to use the PLS.

Step 22. When you are satisfied that all the "bugs" have been eliminated, add a front and back cover (in a shape related to the topic). Place the title and global subtitle of the program onto the front cover and, if possible, shape and illustrate the cover to represent the subject matter. Bind the covers to the index card frames. You may use notebook rings, colored yarn, or any other substance that will permit easy turning of the index cards. Be certain that the answers to each frame, which appear on the back of the previous frame, are easily readable and are not upside down. When the program has been completed, make it available to students whose learning styles are complemented by this resource.

Sample Programmed Learning Sequences

Examine the Programmed Learning Sequence samples that follow. They were developed by teachers and used successfully with primary youngsters whose learning styles matched the controlled sequencing intrinsic to this approach. These children needed structured, attractive visual and tactual materials that provided immediate feedback and could be used either alone or in a pair.

The universe is an exiting phenomenon to each of us, and particularly to young children. Perhaps some of them, someday, will experience flights to other planets and meetings with different species. We always have taught about space, but today, for our young charges, the idea of becoming an astronaut is not at all out of the question. Thus, Linda Harris wove a tale about taking a space flight and taught both the names of the planets and their sequential distance away from Earth through the tempting thought of "Exploring the Planets." Her global title? "Give Me Some Space"!

Exploring Planets: Give Me Some Space!

Exploring the Planets
or
Give Me Some Space

The PLS "Exploring the Planets: Give Me Some Space" was designed by Linda Harris, teacher and graduate student, St. John's University, New York.

Tom and Sally are friends. They live next door to
each other. They go to the same school and play together
after school. Both children have been chosen to be junior
astronauts. They are going to ride in a space shuttle and will
explore the solar system. But the children have a problem. They can't
remember the names of all nine (9) planets.

"Mercury, Venus, Earth, Mars, Jupiter, Saturn, Uranus, Pluto, and Neptune. Maybe if we keep
saying the names over and over we'll remember," said Tom.

"Sally come here please," called her mother. Sally ran to her mother, but she was soon back.

"Tom come quickly! My Very Educated Mother Just Served Us Pizza Now."

"That's it ," cried Tom. "Your mother just helped us solve our
problem. If we can remember the sentence "My Very
Educated Mother Just Served Us Pizza Now," we can
remember the names of the planets in the right order.
Oh Sally, it's going to be a great trip."

I am so happy that you are going to use this program.
By the time you have completed *Exploring the Planets*
or *Give Me Some Space*, you should be able to:

1. Define the following words:
   - Solar System–the sun and anything that
   goes around the sun
   - star–a hot ball of gas
   - orbit–a path
   - planet–a ball-shaped world
2. Identify the only star in our solar system.
3. Name the nine (9) planets.
4. Recognize the planets in their orbits.

Be certain to use this program on or near a large table.
This will give you enough room to use all the materials.

Please use the special pen attached to this program.
This will allow you to wipe off all your answers when you
are finished.

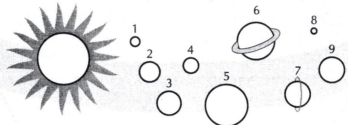

Read the statement on each frame.
Try to answer the question that follows.
Some may require you to put an X into a box.
For others you may be asked to fill in the blank or to
circle the answer.

It is very important to me that nobody gets "Lost in Space,"
If you need help, the answers can be found on
the back of each frame.

Put on your space suit. Get in the space shuttle.
Are you ready? 9–8–7–6–5–4–3–2–1–BLAST OFF!!!

Frame 1

Our solar system consists of the
sun, the planets, and anything that
travels around the sun.

The sun, planets, and anything traveling
around the sun make up our

☐ sun   ☐ solar system   ☐ moon

Answer: solar system
(Back of Frame 1)

Frame 2

The sun, the planets, and
anything traveling around the sun
make up our solar system.

Look at the picture below. It has a sun and planets.
Circle the correct answer.

This is a picture of our:

solar system   moons   stars

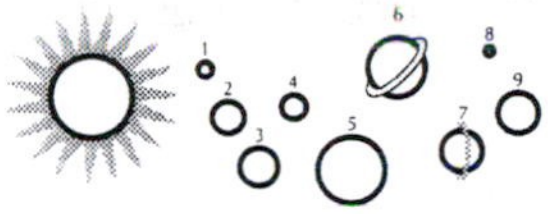

(Back of Frame 2)

Answer: solar system

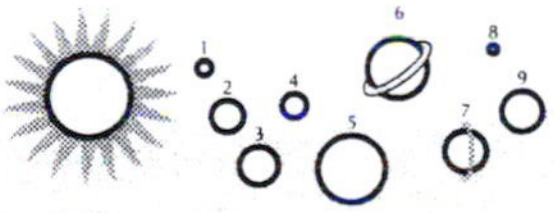

Frame 3

Stars are bright balls of gas
that twinkle in the night sky.

Circle the answer.
What are the stars made of?

water   gas   air

Answer: gas
This isn't the kind of gas that
gives you stomach pains!

(Back of Frame 3)

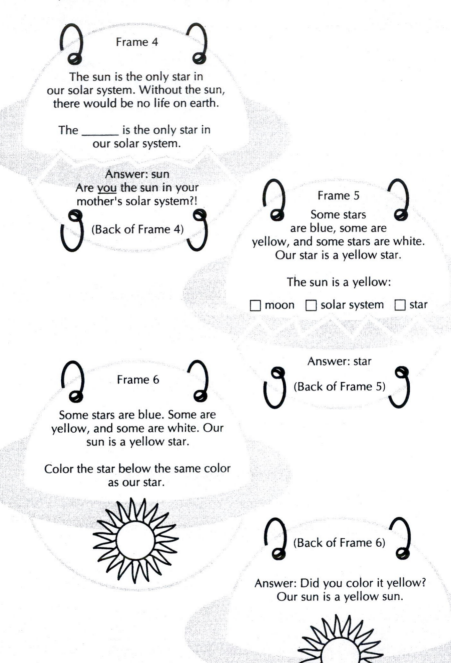

Frame 4

The sun is the only star in
our solar system. Without the sun,
there would be no life on earth.

The _____ is the only star in
our solar system.

Answer: sun
Are _you_ the sun in your
mother's solar system?!

(Back of Frame 4)

Frame 5
Some stars
are blue, some are
yellow, and some stars are white.
Our star is a yellow star.

The sun is a yellow:

☐ moon   ☐ solar system   ☐ star

Answer: star

(Back of Frame 5)

Frame 6

Some stars are blue. Some are
yellow, and some are white. Our
sun is a yellow star.

Color the star below the same color
as our star.

(Back of Frame 6)

Answer: Did you color it yellow?
Our sun is a yellow sun.

Frame 7

A planet is a ball-shaped world
that travels around the sun.

A _____ travels around the sun.

Answer: planet

The planet we live on is called Earth
We are residents of the planet Earth.
A resident of Earth is someone
who lives on Earth. How do you
do, Earth resident?

(Back of Frame 7)

Frame 8

There are nine (9) planets in our
solar system. Mercury, Venus, Earth,
Mars, Jupiter, Saturn, Uranus, Pluto,
and Neptune are planets.

How many planets are in our solar system?

9 (nine)   10 (ten)   5 (five)

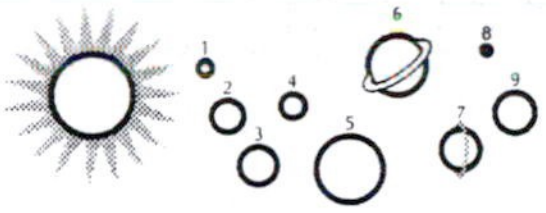

(back of Frame 8)

Answer: nine (9)
There are nine (9) planets in our
solar system.

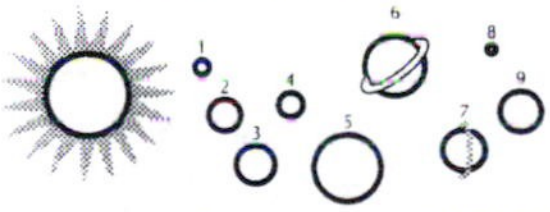

If you were an astronomer–someone who
studies the stars–and you discovered
a new tenth planet, what would you
name it? Would you name it after
you? (I would name it
after me!)

Frame 9

This is a picture of our solar system. Count the number of planets.

Be careful not to count the sun.

How many did you count? _____

(Back of Frame 9)

Answer: 9 (nine)

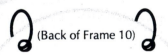

You count well if you counted nine (9) planets!

Frame 10

Each planet stays in its own path as it travels around the sun. This path is called an orbit.

An _____ is the path which a planet uses as it travels around the sun.

(Back of Frame 10)

Answer: orbit

What orbit do you take when you wander around this room?

Frame 11

The path a planet uses to travel
around the sun is called an orbit.
Connect the dots to make an orbit for
the planet in this picture.

(Back of Frame 11)

Answer: If you connect the
dots, the orbit looks like a circle
around the sun.

Frame 12

Some planets are very hot.
They are near the sun. Some planets
are very cold. They are far from the sun.

Planets near the sun are _____.

Planets far from the sun are _____.

(Back of Frame 12)

Answer:
Planets near the sun are __hot__ .

Planets far from the sun are __cold__ .

Do you think cold planets wish they
could wear a warm jacket?

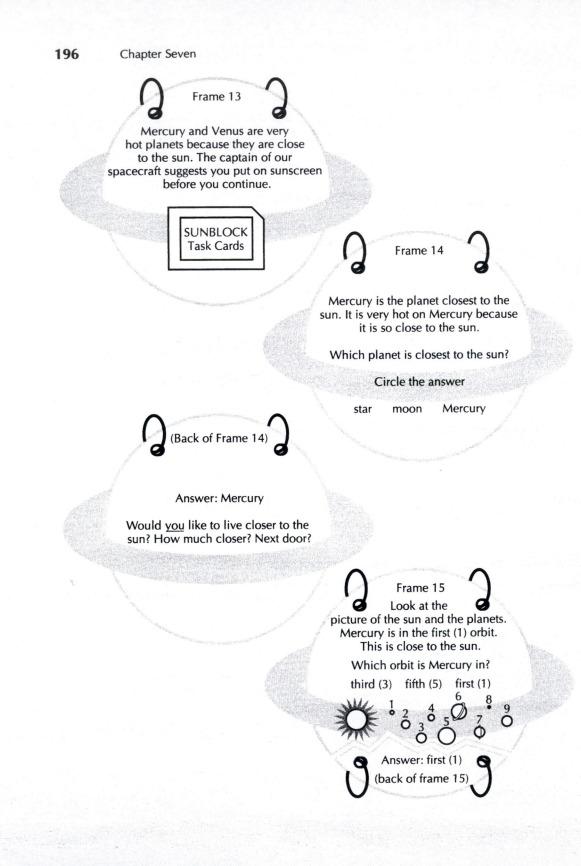

Frame 13

Mercury and Venus are very hot planets because they are close to the sun. The captain of our spacecraft suggests you put on sunscreen before you continue.

SUNBLOCK
Task Cards

Frame 14

Mercury is the planet closest to the sun. It is very hot on Mercury because it is so close to the sun.

Which planet is closest to the sun?

Circle the answer

star   moon   Mercury

(Back of Frame 14)

Answer: Mercury

Would <u>you</u> like to live closer to the sun? How much closer? Next door?

Frame 15

Look at the picture of the sun and the planets. Mercury is in the first (1) orbit. This is close to the sun.

Which orbit is Mercury in?

third (3)   fifth (5)   first (1)

Answer: first (1)
(back of frame 15)

Frame 16

Many clouds cover Venus as it travels in the second (2) orbit. It is always a cloudy day on Venus.

Which planet is in the second (2) orbit?

Circle the answer

Sun   Mercury   Venus

Frame 17

Venus is in the second (2) orbit. Venus is almost the same size as our planet Earth.

Look at the picture of the solar system.

Put a circle around Venus.

(Back of Frame 17)

Answer: This is Venus.

Cloudy days make me feel sad. People on Venus would feel sad almost all the time. Do you know why? (Because Venus has many, many cloudy days!)

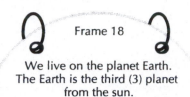

Frame 18

We live on the planet Earth.
The Earth is the third (3) planet
from the sun.

Circle the name of the planet where people live.

Mercury   Venus   Earth

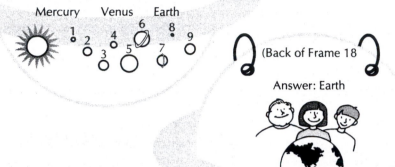

(Back of Frame 18)

Answer: Earth

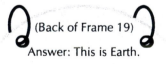

We are so lucky to be
residents of Planet Earth.

Frame 19

The Earth travels in the third (3)
orbit. It appears to be blue because
the Earth is the only planet known to
have water.

Look at the picture below.

Circle the planet Earth.

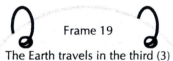

(Back of Frame 19)

Answer: This is Earth.

Our planet Earth has many sunny days
and is the only planet known to
have water. We Earth residents
really <u>are</u> lucky!

Frame 20

Mars is called the red planet. Mars travels in the fourth (4) orbit.

Look at the picture below.

Which planet is in the fourth (4) orbit?

☐ Mercury ☐ Mars ☐ Earth

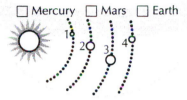

(Back of Frame 20)

Answer: Mars

I once ate a <u>Mars</u> candy bar!

Frame 21

Mars is called the red planet because it is covered with red dust. The red planet, Mars, is in the fourth (4) orbit.

This red planet travels around the sun in the fourth (4) orbit. _____

(Back of Frame 21)

Answer: Mars

My mom wouldn't want to live on Mars because of its red dust! She'd have me cleaning all the time!

Frame 22

Before we travel to other planets, the captain wants to take a walk in space.

We will look at what we have seen so far.

ball-shaped world

sun   planet   moon

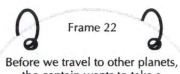

(Back of Frame 22)

"Captain, why is it so cold here?"

"We are now very far from the sun. These planets don't get heat and light from the sun like we do. Bundle up now. We are heading for the cold planets."

Frame 23

Jupiter is the fifth (5) planet from the sun. Jupiter is the largest planet. It has a red spot.

The planet in the fifth (5) orbit is:

Circle the answer:

Mars   Venus   Jupiter

(Back of Frame 23)

Answer: Jupiter

Frame 24

Jupiter travels in the fifth (5) orbit.

Put a red spot on Jupiter.

(Back of Frame 24)

Answer: Jupiter is recognized by
its large size and red spot.

Frame 25

The rings around Saturn are made
of bits of ice. We can reconize
Saturn in the sixth (6) orbit by its
colorful rings.

Saturn is in orbit number _____.

(Back of Frame 25)

Answer: six (6)

Can you imagine how lucky we Earth
residents are!? We are the only planet
residents with water! We do not have as many cloudy
days as residents of Venus have (if Venus has residents!).
We do not have red dust like Mars. We do not
have icy rings around us like Saturn! Of
course we are not as big as Jupiter,
but that doesn't bother me.

Frame 26

Saturn is the sixth (6) planet
from the sun. It has beautiful
flat rings around it.

Which planet has beautiful rings around it?

Circle the answer:

Saturn   Jupiter   Mercury

(Back of Frame 26)

Answer: Saturn

Those Saturn rings may be beautiful,
but if they are made from bits of ice, they
have to be very cold!

Frame 27

Uranus is called the oddball planet. Uranus
is tipped on its side so the ring goes straight up
and down. Uranus travels in the seventh (7) orbit.

The oddball planet, Uranus, travels in which orbit?

Circle the answer:

seventh (7)   fifth (5)   second (2)

(Back of Frame 27)

Answer: Uranus travels in the
seventh (7) orbit.

Frame 28

Uranus is in the seventh (7)
orbit. It has a ring, too. Uranus's
ring is made from big chunks of ice.

This planet has a ring made of big chunks of ice.

Underline the answer:

Jupiter   Saturn   Uranus

(Back of Frame 28)

Answer: Uranus

Saturn's rings are made from
bits of ice, and Uranus' rings are made
from big chunks of ice. I think I will remain
a resident of Earth!
Do <u>you</u> plan on moving?

Frame 29

Pluto is a snowball-like planet.
Its orbit sometimes crosses inside
Neptune's orbit. Until 1999, Pluto will
appear to be in the eighth (8) orbit.

Until 1999, this planet will appear to be
in orbit number eighth (8). _____

(Back of Frame 28)

Answer: Pluto

Pluto's orbit

Neptune's orbit

Neptune

Pluto

Frame 30

Pluto can be found in the eighth (8) orbit until 1999. Pluto is a very cold planet because it is so far from the sun.

Until 1999, this planet will travel inside of Neptune's orbit.

Underline the answer:

Saturn   Uranus   Pluto

Answer: Pluto

(Back of Frame 30)

Frame 31

When Pluto crosses Neptune's orbit, Neptune is the most distant planet.

What is the name of the most distant planet until 1999?

Circle the answer:

Neptune   Earth   Saturn

Answer: Neptune

Do you think that our astronauts will ever visit Neptune? Do you volunteer?

(Back of Frame 31)

Frame 32

Until 1999, Neptune will be the farthest planet from the sun.

Look at the picture below.

Neptune is in orbit number_____.

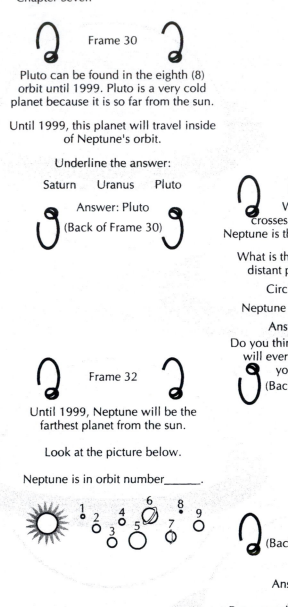

(Back of Frame 32)

Answer: nine (9)

But remember, Neptune is in this orbit only until 1999.

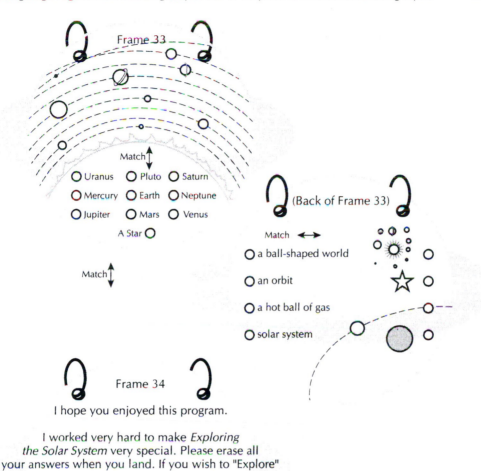

Frame 33

Match ↕

O Uranus   O Pluto   O Saturn

O Mercury   O Earth   O Neptune

O Jupiter   O Mars   O Venus

A Star O

Match ↕

(Back of Frame 33)

Match ↔

O a ball-shaped world

O an orbit

O a hot ball of gas

O solar system

Frame 34

I hope you enjoyed this program.

I worked very hard to make *Exploring the Solar System* very special. Please erase all your answers when you land. If you wish to "Explore" some more, you may start again.

We are ready to land—9–8–7–6–5–4–3–2–1–TOUCHDOWN!!!

WELCOME HOME!
You are a "star"!

Frame 33 is a review. Built into the frame is an Electroboard. The child using this Programmed Learning Sequence uses a Continuity Tester to see whether he or she knows the correct answers. The tester lights up when the correct answer is touched with one end and the question is touched with the other end—both at the same time!

Nutrition is also an integral part of every early childhood program. Carolyn Bovell translated a mundane, everyday academic unit into a Multisensory Instructional Package (MIP) (see Chapter 9) that excited her children's imaginations and made them *want* to handle the materials and learn through them. The MIP included all the approaches described in this book, and children were permitted to work *first* with those resources that best matched their strengths; *then* they were permitted to use any other resource included in the MIP—as long as no one else was using it at that time (unless the children opted to work together). Carolyn's MIP included this PLS, which was made in the shape of (and literally from) round plastic dinner plates. She housed the PLS, the CAP (see Chapter 8) and the tactual and kinesthetic components of each in an attractive wheelbarrow and merely asked her youngsters to be careful with it. She saw not a single case of abuse. Indeed, the youngsters cherished the MIP, used the parts of it with their accompanying tapes repeatedly, begged to have them available during Self-Teaching Time, and learned everything they were required to master.

Carolyn permitted peer-oriented students to work together when their LSI:P profiles indicated they needed to do so. However, she also allowed those who *wanted* to work with a classmate but who did not need to do so, to work together—*provided* they worked quietly, helped each other, did not interfere with anyone else's learning style, *and* earned a 90 or better on their unit test. They did all of the above, and both she and they were *very* pleased!

Nutrition: Neat Treat

NUTRITION

The PLS "Nutrition: Neat Treat" was designed by Carolyn Bovell, teacher, Portledge School, Locust Valley, New York.

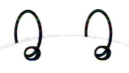

VOCABULARY

Here are some of the words you will
need to know to complete this program:

FOUR FOOD GROUPS: The groups that foods
   are put into; the groups are meat,
   bread-cereal, milk and fruit-vegetables.
NUTRIENT: A substance in food that keeps
   you healthy and alive.
CARBOHYDRATES: Nutrients made up of starch
   and sugar.
WELL-BALANCED DIET: Meals that contain at
   least one serving from each food group.
FOOD GROUP SYSTEM: Having at least
   one serving from the Four Food
   Groups at every meal.

Listen to the PLS tape as you read along. When you finish this program, you should be able to:

1. List three reasons why you should eat good food every day.
2. Name the four food groups.
3. List at least three foods in each group.
4. Describe six nutrients in food.
5. Name at least two foods that contain each nutrient.
6. Plan a healthful breakfast, lunch, or dinner by using the Food Group System.

Hi! I'm Betty Bag. I just love carrying home good food from the supermarket. I know a lot about good food because I spend a lot of time around it.

I'm sure that you know you should eat a well-balanced diet so that you can grow, have a lot of energy, and stay healthy. But do you know how to choose a well-balanced diet?

My friends, Thomas, the English
Muffin, and Granny Smith Apple are
always happy to provide you with quick
energy. Sir Loin Steak just told me that he was
happy that his fat and protein helped to keep
you warm and build your muscles. And the cheese,
Monte Ray Jack, just adores building strong
teeth and bones.

So the next time you plan a menu,
remember to include servings from
each food group. Now, read the
story of my friends, Amy and John,
as they go to the supermarket to
get food for their family.

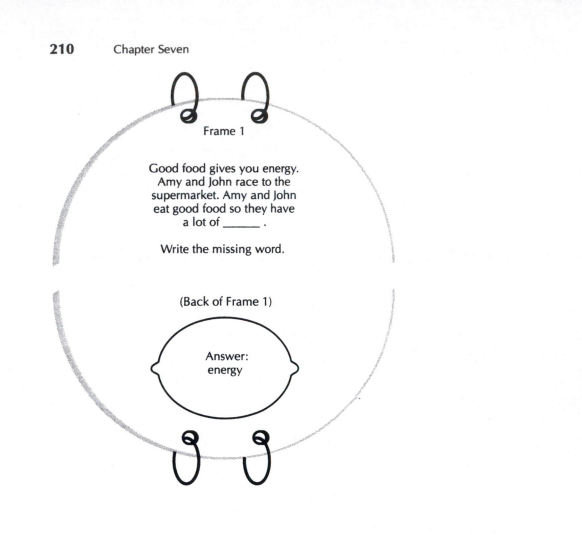

Frame 1

Good food gives you energy.
Amy and John race to the
supermarket. Amy and John
eat good food so they have
a lot of _____ .

Write the missing word.

(Back of Frame 1)

Answer:
energy

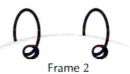

Frame 2

Good food keeps you healthy and
helps you grow. Amy and John have been
in school every day this year, and they are bigger in
the third grade than they were in the second grade.
Good food has kept them <u>tyhaelh</u> and helped
them <u>wrog</u>.

Unscramble the underlined words.

(Back of Frame 2)

Answers:

healthy
grow

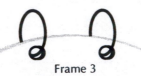

Frame 3

Carrots, apples, and tomatoes
are in the Fruit-Vegetable Food Group. Amy
and John need tomatoes for their sauce.
Tomatoes are in the
_____ _____ food group.

fruit-vegetable   meat   milk

Circle the correct answer.

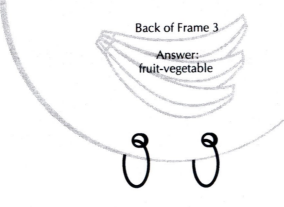

Back of Frame 3

Answer:
fruit-vegetable

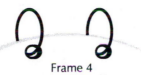

Frame 4

Amy and John want hamburgers
for their dinner. Hamburger is in the meat
food group. To buy their hamburger, Amy
and John go to the AEMT section of the supermarket.

Unscramble the correct answers
for the underlined word.

Back of Frame 4

Answer:
MEAT

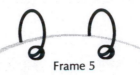

Frame 5

Amy and John want to make spaghetti
with meat sauce for their dinner. Spaghetti
is made from wheat. Wheat is in the
bread-cereal food group.
Spaghetti is in the _____ _____ food group.

meat   milk   bread-cereal

Circle the correct answer.

Back of Frame 5

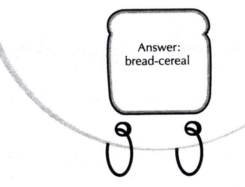

Answer:
bread-cereal

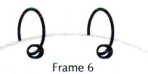

Frame 6

Amy and John like to sprinkle cheese on
their spaghetti and meat sauce. Cheese
is in the milk food group. So Amy and John went
to the _____ section of the supermarket.

Fill in the correct answer.

Back of Frame 6

Answer:
dairy

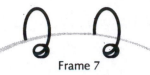

Frame 7

Connect each food with the
proper Food Group.

1. Spaghetti   A. Fruit-Vegetable

2. Cheese   B. Meat

3. Hamburger   C. Milk

4. Tomato   D. Bread-Cereal

Back of Frame 7

Answers:

1. Spaghetti   D. Bread-Cereal

2. Cheese   C. Milk

3. Hamburger   B. Meat

4. Tomato   A. Fruit-Vegetable

Frame 8

Protein and vitamins are nutrients
that keep you healthy and build muscles. Lean
steak has a lot of protein.

Amy and John should eat lean steak.

True   False

Circle the correct answer.

Back of Frame 8

Answer:
True

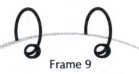

Frame 9

Minerals do a number of jobs
in your body. One job is
building strong teeth and
bones. Milk is rich in minerals.
Should Amy and John drink milk?

Yes   No

Circle the correct answer.

Back of Frame 9

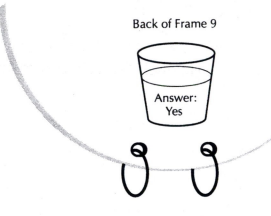

Answer:
Yes

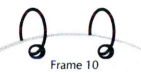

Frame 10

Carbohydrates give you quick energy.
Amy and John needed energy to run to
the supermarket. Amy and John must eat a lot of

C _ R B _ H _ D R _ T _ S

Fill in the missing letters.

Back of Frame 10

Answer:
CARBOHYDRATES

Frame 11

Water carries the other five
nutrients around your body. If John and Amy
want nutrients to be carried around their bodies,
they must drink a lot of <u>RATEW</u>.

Unscramble the underlined letters.

Back of Frame 11

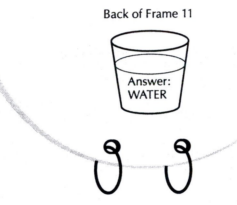

Answer:
WATER

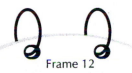

Frame 12

Fat can be used for energy in the body.
John and Amy used carbohydrates for energy.
They can also use fat for energy.

John and Amy can use fat for energy.

True   False

Circle true or false.

Back of Frame 12

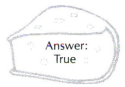

Answer:
True

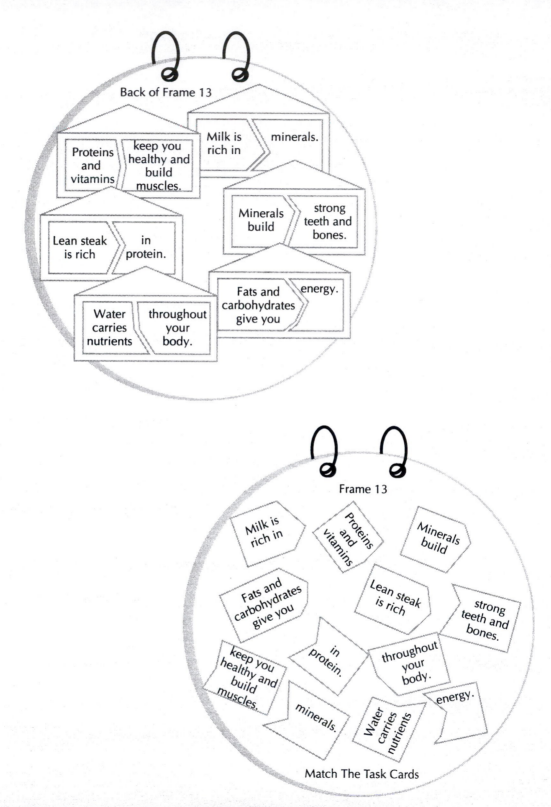

Back of Frame 13

Proteins and vitamins — keep you healthy and build muscles.

Milk is rich in — minerals.

Minerals build — strong teeth and bones.

Lean steak is rich — in protein.

Fats and carbohydrates give you — energy.

Water carries nutrients — throughout your body.

Frame 13

Milk is rich in

Proteins and vitamins

Minerals build

Fats and carbohydrates give you

Lean steak is rich

strong teeth and bones.

keep you healthy and build muscles.

in protein.

throughout your body.

minerals.

Water carries nutrients

energy.

Match The Task Cards

222

Frame 14

Amy invited her friend Susan for lunch.
Amy gave Susan a tuna fish sandwich
and apple juice. They had ice cream for
dessert. Did Amy prepare a well-balanced lunch?

Circle the correct answer.

True   False

Back of Frame 14

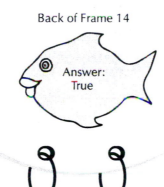

Answer:
True

Frame 15

John and Amy like to eat a well-balanced
breakfast. This morning they had eggs
and buttered toast.

Write another food they should have eaten so that
their breakfast would have been well-balanced.

Back of Frame 15

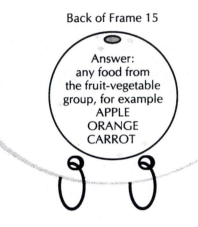

Answer:
any food from
the fruit-vegetable
group, for example
APPLE
ORANGE
CARROT

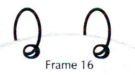

Frame 16

John and Amy planned a well-balanced
dinner for their mom and dad. They
served steak, a tossed salad, rice,
and cheese with crackers for dessert.

Write the names of two foods John and
Amy served from the bread-cereal group.

_____   _____

Back of Frame 16

Answers:
crackers
rice

Test Yourself

1. You should eat good food every day
   because good food

   1. _____

   2. _____

   3. _____

2. The Four Food Groups are:

   1. _____

   2. _____

   3. _____

   4. _____

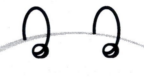

Answers:

1. 1. Gives you energy.

   2. Keeps you healthy.

   3. Helps you grow.

2. 1. Milk

   2. Meat

   3. Bread-Cereal

   4. Fruit-Vegetable

3. Carbohydrates give you quick
_____.

4. Hamburger and steak are in the
_____ food group.

5. A well-balanced diet has at
least one serving from each
_____ _____.

6. Name three foods in the
fruit-vegetable group.

1. _____

2. _____

3. _____

Answers:

3. energy

4. meat

5. food group

6. 1. tomato

   2. banana

   3. lettuce
   (or any fruits and vegetables
   that you have named)

7. Which nutrient(s) does a number of jobs in your body?

_____

8. Ice cream belongs to which food group?

_____

9. Spaghetti belongs to which food group?

_____

10. Rice and corn belong to the same food group, which is

_____ .

Answers:

7. minerals

8. milk

9. bread-cereal

10. bread-cereal

Keep going you're doing fine.

11. Fruits and vegetables are rich in which nutrients?

_____

12. Milk helps build strong teeth and bones.   True   False

13. Butter is rich in which nutrient?

_____

14. The nutrient water is found in all foods.   True   False

15. A well-balanced breakfast could have an egg, buttered toast, and orange juice.   True   False

Answers:

11. CARBOHYDRATES

12. True

13. FAT

14. True

15. True

1st PRIZE WINNER

This is super! You have finished a Programmed Learning Sequence about Nutrition. Please rewind the tape for the next person. Wipe away all your answers. Return everything to the Multisensory Instructional Package. Bye!

This Programmed Learning Sequence was designed by Phyllis Napolitano for a science unit. It can be reproduced, colored, and tried with children who are interested in butterflies, or with those who have completed basic requirements and want to move ahead of their classmates. It can also be used as part of a unit you might care to teach. The Contract Activity Package on "Discovering Butterflies" can be used for your independent children, whereas this PLS would be appropriate for those who require structure.

Discovering Butterflies: Come Fly with Me

DISCOVERING
BUTTERFLIES

COME FLY WITH ME

The PLS "Discovering Butterflies: Come Fly with Me," was designed by Phyllis Napolitano, teacher, Public School #135 Queens, Queens Village, New York.

Frame 1

If you wish to hear this Programmed Learning Sequence read to you, start the accompanying tape right after this card. Each time a question is read, turn the machine <u>off</u> (STOP BUTTON), write your answer, and then turn it back on to learn whether you were correct.

Frame 2

Instructions

Each card in this program is called a <u>frame</u>. On one side of each frame, information is presented, and a question is asked about it. Mark your answer on the frame itself with the pencil attached to this program.

Then look at the back of each frame to see if your answer was correct. If it was, move to the next frame. If it was incorrect, study the frame to find out why your answer was wrong. It is important that you understand your error before going ahead. When you are finished working with this book, go back and wipe off all the frames.

Turn to the next frame.

Frame 3

Hello! In this Programmed Learning Sequence, you will be learning about butterflies. By the time you finish this program, you will be able to: (1) recognize the four stages in the life cycle of a butterfly; and (2) name the body parts of a butterfly.

Imagine you are someone small hidden in a tiny egg growing bigger, until one hot morning you burst your shell and creep into brightness. Come with us on our journey of the butterfly...

Frame 4

Before you begin working on this program, you need to know how a butterfly is first created.

Every butterfly begins its life inside a very small egg.

What begins its life inside a very small egg?

bird   butterfly   dog

Circle your answer.
Turn over.

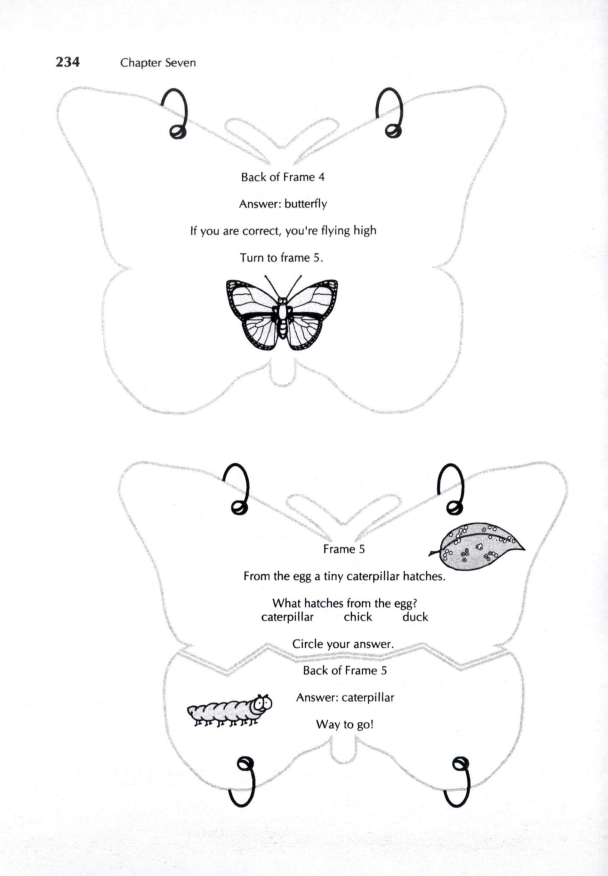

Back of Frame 4

Answer: butterfly

If you are correct, you're flying high

Turn to frame 5.

Frame 5

From the egg a tiny caterpillar hatches.

What hatches from the egg?
caterpillar   chick   duck

Circle your answer.

Back of Frame 5

Answer: caterpillar

Way to go!

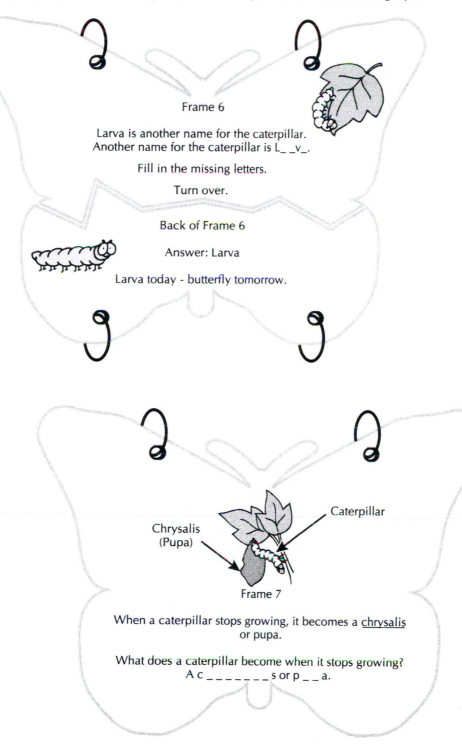

Frame 6

Larva is another name for the caterpillar.
Another name for the caterpillar is L_ _v_.

Fill in the missing letters.

Turn over.

Back of Frame 6

Answer: Larva

Larva today - butterfly tomorrow.

Chrysalis
(Pupa)

Caterpillar

Frame 7

When a caterpillar stops growing, it becomes a <u>chrysalis</u>
or pupa.

What does a caterpillar become when it stops growing?
A c _ _ _ _ _ _ _ s or p _ _ a.

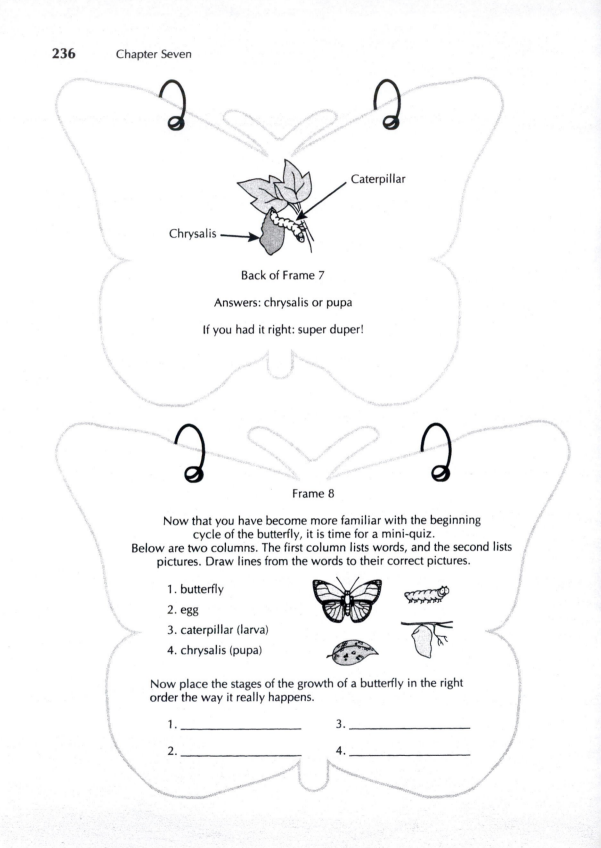

Caterpillar

Chrysalis

Back of Frame 7

Answers: chrysalis or pupa

If you had it right: super duper!

Frame 8

Now that you have become more familiar with the beginning
cycle of the butterfly, it is time for a mini-quiz.
Below are two columns. The first column lists words, and the second lists
pictures. Draw lines from the words to their correct pictures.

1. butterfly

2. egg

3. caterpillar (larva)

4. chrysalis (pupa)

Now place the stages of the growth of a butterfly in the right
order the way it really happens.

1. _____   3. _____

2. _____   4. _____

Back of Frame 8

The four (4) stages, in order, are:
1. EGG
2. CATERPILLAR (LARVA)
3. CHRYSALIS (PUPA)
4. BUTTERFLY-the prettiest stage!

Answers:

1. butterfly

2. egg

3. caterpillar (larva)

4. chrysalis (pupa)

If you had all those answers correct, go to the next frame and know that you are very, very intelligent! If you did *not* have all the answers correct, don't worry. Neither did *I*! If any were wrong, please go back, read the frame again, and see whether you can remember (a) the *first* stage (the egg; we *know* a baby starts with an egg); (b) the *second* stage (the caterpillar; the *caterpillar* stage follows the egg stage. Do you think it is because the caterpillar is hungry?); (c) the *third* stage (the chrysalis stage; *that's the hard one!* – but it is *crystal clear* that the chrysalis stage is third); and the (d) *fourth* stage – the beautiful *butterfly!*
Let's see: an egg into a caterpillar into a crystal clear chrysalis into a butterfly! I see it happening before my eyes! (Close your eyes and see if you can see the four stages!)

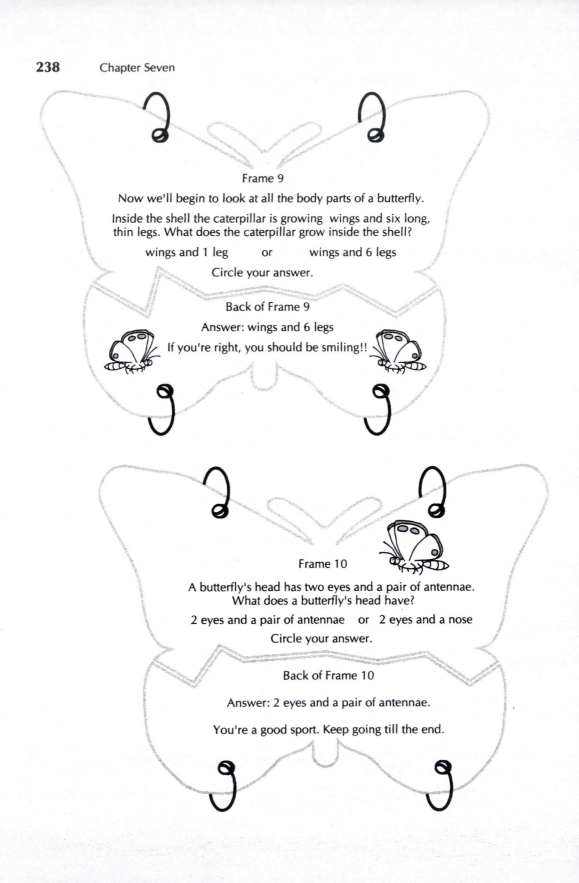

Frame 9

Now we'll begin to look at all the body parts of a butterfly.

Inside the shell the caterpillar is growing wings and six long, thin legs. What does the caterpillar grow inside the shell?

wings and 1 leg   or   wings and 6 legs

Circle your answer.

Back of Frame 9

Answer: wings and 6 legs

If you're right, you should be smiling!!

Frame 10

A butterfly's head has two eyes and a pair of antennae. What does a butterfly's head have?

2 eyes and a pair of antennae   or   2 eyes and a nose

Circle your answer.

Back of Frame 10

Answer: 2 eyes and a pair of antennae.

You're a good sport. Keep going till the end.

Frame 11

A pair of antennae help the butterfly's balance, touch, and smell.

Which of the following is not the job of the butterfly's antennae?

balance   touch   smell   talk

Circle the answer that <u>doesn't</u> belong.

Back of Frame 11

Answer: talk

Now you're talking!

Frame 12

The butterfly has a long tongue. It is rolled
up when at rest and unrolled to drink nectar from flowers.

What does a butterfly use to drink nectar?

teeth   mouth   tongue

Circle your answer, and <u>draw</u> it, too!

Back of Frame 12

Answer: tongue

It takes a "lickin."

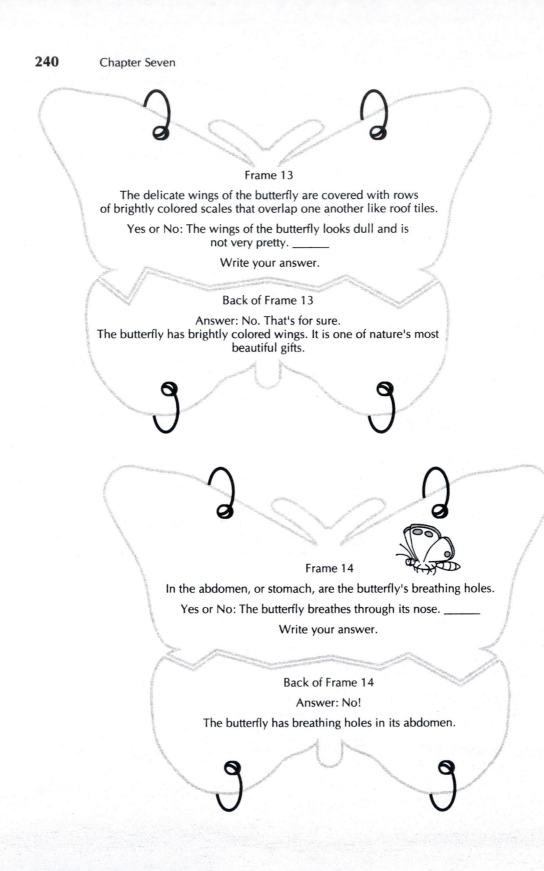

Frame 13

The delicate wings of the butterfly are covered with rows of brightly colored scales that overlap one another like roof tiles.

Yes or No: The wings of the butterfly looks dull and is not very pretty. _____

Write your answer.

Back of Frame 13

Answer: No. That's for sure.
The butterfly has brightly colored wings. It is one of nature's most beautiful gifts.

Frame 14

In the abdomen, or stomach, are the butterfly's breathing holes.

Yes or No: The butterfly breathes through its nose. _____

Write your answer.

Back of Frame 14

Answer: No!

The butterfly has breathing holes in its abdomen.

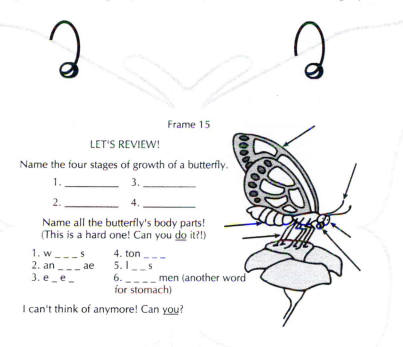

Frame 15

LET'S REVIEW!

Name the four stages of growth of a butterfly.

1. _____   3. _____

2. _____   4. _____

Name all the butterfly's body parts!
(This is a hard one! Can you <u>do</u> it?!)

1. w _ _ _ s   4. ton _ _ _
2. an _ _ _ ae   5. l _ _ s
3. e _ e _   6. _ _ _ _ men (another word
                          for stomach)

I can't think of anymore! Can you?

Back of Frame 15

Let's see how well you did! The four stages of the butterfly are:
1. Egg (I remembered that one! Did you?)
2. Caterpillar (larva). (I remembered that the caterpillar followed the egg-because he was hungry! Did you remember that one? That wasn't really easy!)
3. Chrysalis (pupa). (I remembered "crystal clear" but I couldn't remember the name of the stage! Did you? If you did, you are smarter than I am, and I wrote this Programmed Learning Sequence!)
4. Butterfly. That one was easy! Did you get all of these right?

Now let's see how many parts of a butterfly you could remember! Did you remember the:

Wings?
Antennae? (You have to be a <u>genius</u> to write that word correctly!)
Eyes?
Tongue? (It rolls up and down!)
Legs? (Why do butterflies need legs when they fly from place to place? Can <u>you</u> guess?)
Abdomen? (Abdomen <u>is</u> another word for stomach!) Does your abdomen hurt when you eat too much cake and ice cream? How about pizza and pickles?

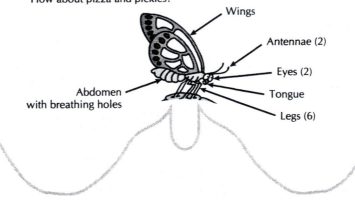

Children often have a fascination with—and little fear of—bugs and insects! This is a wonderful topic through which to expand vocabulary, improve spelling, develop writing skills, and excite the imagination. Books about insects of all species are available, and their illustrations often entice young minds and fantasies. Try asking the children to:

- Imagine you were an insect! Describe the places you'd go and the things you would see—that nobody else could know about!
- Write a story about a lonely insect who wants to be someone's pet. Describe the

The next time you see a butterfly, tell it about the four
stages it experienced to become what it is! I bet
that butterfly will be glad to know,
because it probably doesn't remember!

things he'd say to a person and that person's answers. What do you think your family would say—and do—if *you* agreed to keep an insect as your pet?!

- Imagine that a wicked magician has turned everyone you know into an insect of one kind or another. You look into the mirror and see an image. It no longer looks like you! Instead it looks like . . . Describe the insect you have become. Tell what you look like, how you feel, what you want to do.
- Write a poem about an insect.
- Draw an insect. Now, color the drawing and make it look very nice.
- Create an insect dance. What would it look like? Can you dance it for us? (I would love to see it!)
- Carve an insect out of soap. (Be *very* careful! Ask someone to help you if you need a helping hand. *Get permission from a grown-up in your family, PLEASE!)*

Eileen Clarke, a veteran New York teacher, began a unit with her first-graders, just to experiment with how much children could learn if she gave them initial directions and then permitted individuals to choose which instructional resources they preferred to learn through. Some chose the Contract Activity Package (CAP); she gave them a lot of guidance and assistance the first time. Some migrated immediately toward the Pic-A-Holes, Flip Chutes, Task Cards, and Floor Game. They worked very well on their own or with each other. Most of the little ones loved the Electroboard, and, before long, many were surrounding the children who were using it—watching, listening, learning!

Mrs. Clarke tried this PLS with a few youngsters who *always* needed *her;* they frequently wanted guidance, reassurance, and direct answers. Those children so enjoyed working with it that Eileen couldn't take the PLS away from them. They liked having the tape read to them, and before long those youngsters were reading the entire PLS on their own and to each other!

But the resource most in demand by these first-graders was the Floor Game. They loved it and learned everything they needed to know! At the end of the unit, Eileen Clarke asked the youngsters which items each liked best. *Everything* was enjoyed—but by different students. We think you'll find the same result. Although different children enjoy many ways of learning, each favors one strategy over another. Of course, some children like everything, and you may even have one or two who like nothing—until you wrap up the materials and pack them away. *Then* everyone begs for them—and uses them repeatedly!

Examine this PLS, which Mrs. Clarke developed on Insects!

All about Insects: Don't Bug Me

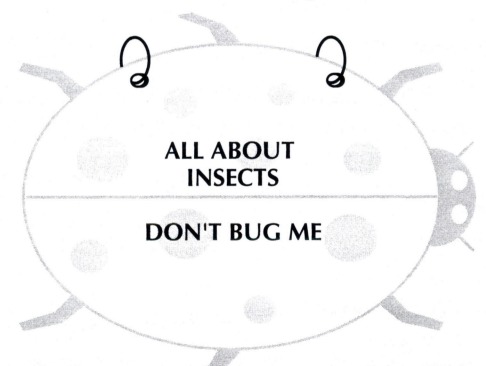

ALL ABOUT INSECTS

DON'T BUG ME

The PLS "All about Insects: Don't Bug Me!" was designed by Eileen Clark, teacher, Bayside, Queens, New York.

Frame 1

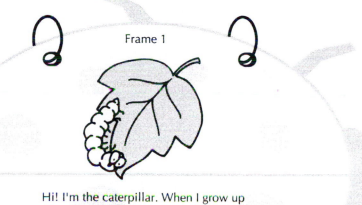

Hi! I'm the caterpillar. When I grow up
I'm going to turn into something else.
When ducks and hippopotamuses and people
get older, they get bigger. (especially
hippopotamuses!) But not caterpillars.
We turn into butterflies.

Frame 2

Caterpillars and butterflies are
insects. So are grasshoppers, ants,
bumblebees, and lots of other bugs.
But not all bugs are insects. As you
listen to this tape, and read along,
you will learn all about insects.

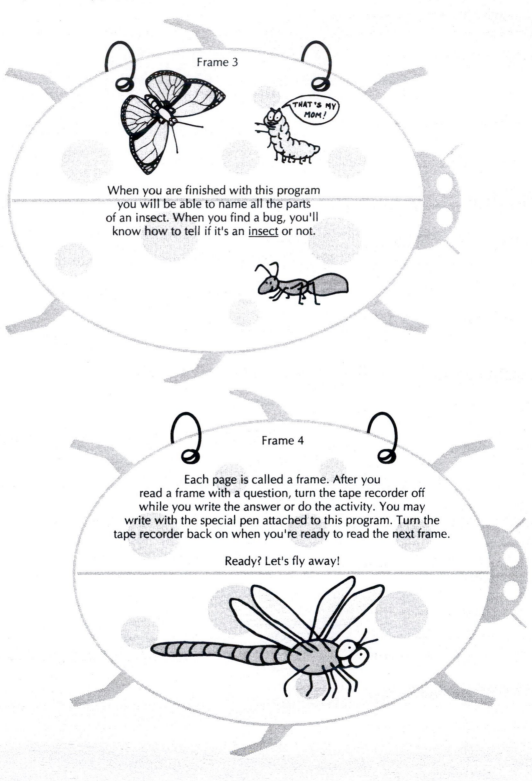

Frame 3

THAT'S MY MOM!

When you are finished with this program
you will be able to name all the parts
of an insect. When you find a bug, you'll
know how to tell if it's an <u>insect</u> or not.

Frame 4

Each page is called a frame. After you
read a frame with a question, turn the tape recorder off
while you write the answer or do the activity. You may
write with the special pen attached to this program. Turn the
tape recorder back on when you're ready to read the next frame.

Ready? Let's fly away!

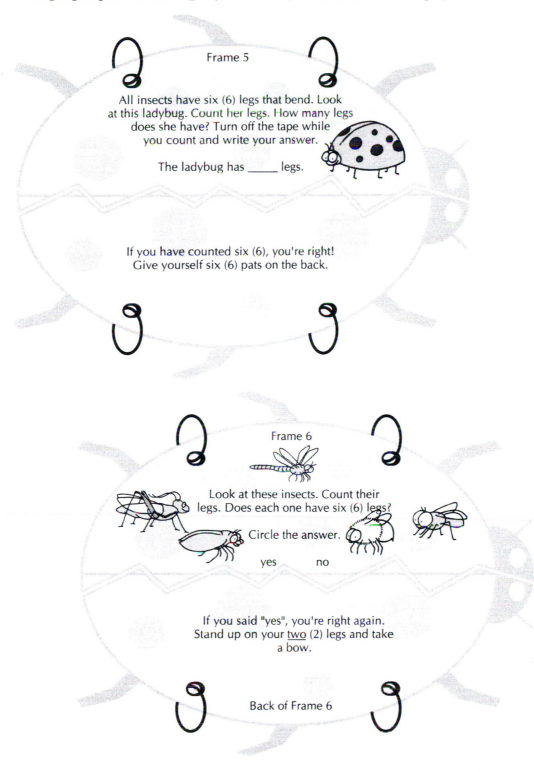

Frame 5

All insects have six (6) legs that bend. Look at this ladybug. Count her legs. How many legs does she have? Turn off the tape while you count and write your answer.

The ladybug has _____ legs.

If you have counted six (6), you're right! Give yourself six (6) pats on the back.

Frame 6

Look at these insects. Count their legs. Does each one have six (6) legs?

Circle the answer.

yes   no

If you said "yes", you're right again. Stand up on your <u>two</u> (2) legs and take a bow.

Back of Frame 6

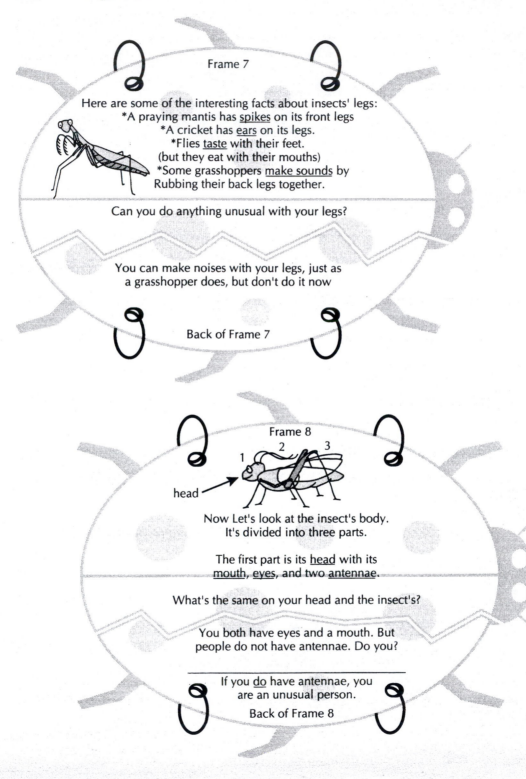

Frame 7

Here are some of the interesting facts about insects' legs:
*A praying mantis has <u>spikes</u> on its front legs
*A cricket has <u>ears</u> on its legs.
*Flies <u>taste</u> with their feet.
(but they eat with their mouths)
*Some grasshoppers <u>make sounds</u> by
Rubbing their back legs together.

Can you do anything unusual with your legs?

You can make noises with your legs, just as
a grasshopper does, but don't do it now

Back of Frame 7

Frame 8

head

Now Let's look at the insect's body.
It's divided into three parts.

The first part is its <u>head</u> with its
<u>mouth</u>, <u>eyes</u>, and two <u>antennae</u>.

What's the same on your head and the insect's?

You both have eyes and a mouth. But
people do not have antennae. Do you?

If you <u>do</u> have antennae, you
are an unusual person.

Back of Frame 8

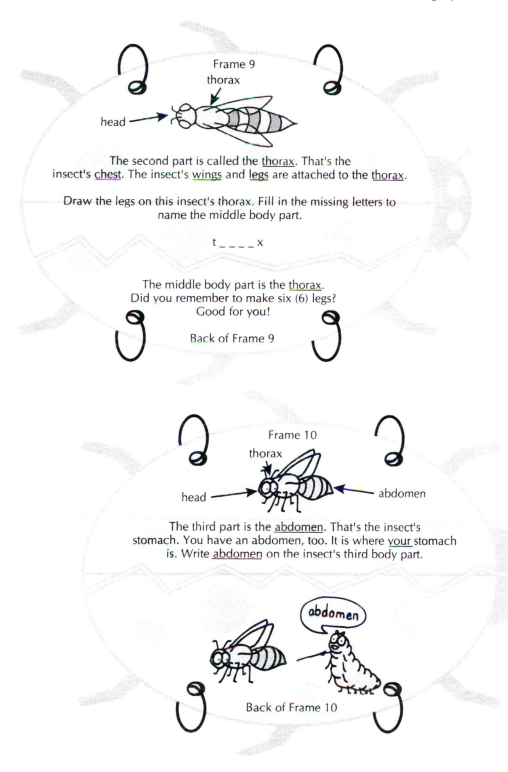

Frame 9
thorax

head

The second part is called the thorax. That's the insect's chest. The insect's wings and legs are attached to the thorax.

Draw the legs on this insect's thorax. Fill in the missing letters to name the middle body part.

t _ _ _ _ x

The middle body part is the thorax.
Did you remember to make six (6) legs?
Good for you!

Back of Frame 9

Frame 10
thorax

head   abdomen

The third part is the abdomen. That's the insect's stomach. You have an abdomen, too. It is where your stomach is. Write abdomen on the insect's third body part.

abdomen

Back of Frame 10

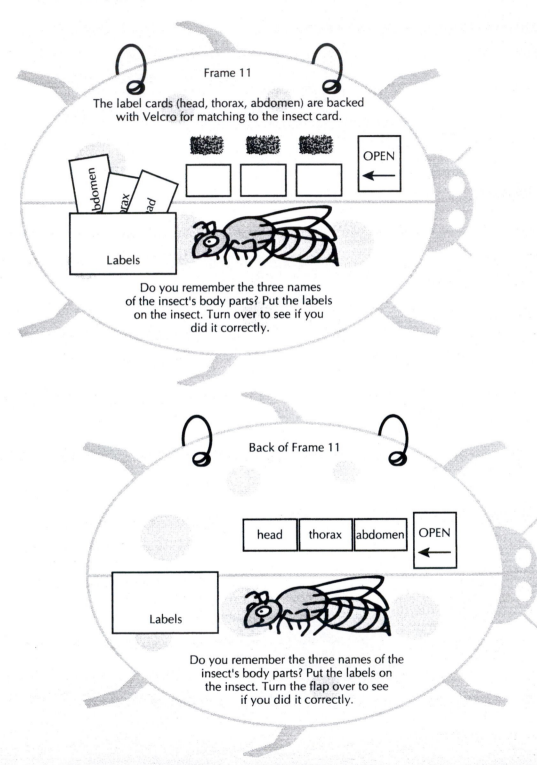

Frame 11

The label cards (head, thorax, abdomen) are backed with Velcro for matching to the insect card.

OPEN ←

Labels

Do you remember the three names of the insect's body parts? Put the labels on the insect. Turn over to see if you did it correctly.

Back of Frame 11

| head | thorax | abdomen |

OPEN ←

Labels

Do you remember the three names of the insect's body parts? Put the labels on the insect. Turn the flap over to see if you did it correctly.

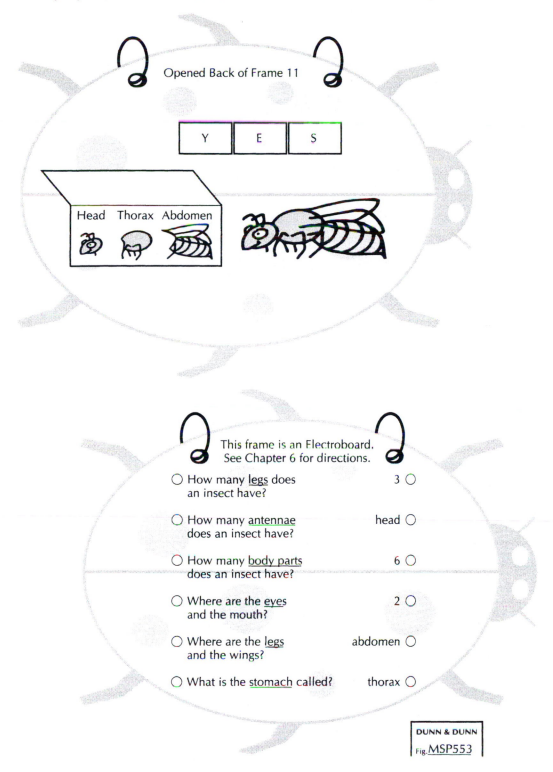

Opened Back of Frame 11

Y	E	S

Head   Thorax   Abdomen

This frame is an Electroboard.
See Chapter 6 for directions.

○ How many <u>legs</u> does   3 ○
   an insect have?

○ How many <u>antennae</u>   head ○
   does an insect have?

○ How many <u>body parts</u>   6 ○
   does an insect have?

○ Where are the <u>eyes</u>   2 ○
   and the mouth?

○ Where are the <u>legs</u>   abdomen ○
   and the wings?

○ What is the <u>stomach</u> called?   thorax ○

DUNN & DUNN
Fig. MSP553

If you have made the firefly light up, you
know all the important parts of an insect.
Hooray for you!

You should be beaming!

Whales, dinosaurs, dolphins, insects, elephants, felines of all types, and dogs are of great interest to little children. Irene Kozak designed this Programmed Learning Sequence on "The Humpback Whale" because it was *not* part of her curriculum. She thought that some of the brighter children would enjoy exploring a new topic when they had completed their required assignments. Much to her surprise, her good readers were not the only ones who loved the PLS. The accompanying tape allowed *everyone* to use it, and, to her surprise, almost every child in her class learned to read the entire PLS with no teacher direction or involvement! What was most interesting occurred when a few of them begged to take it home to "read" to their sisters, brothers, parents, grandparents, friends, or neighbors!

The Humpback Whale
or
Have a Whale of a Time

The Humpback Whale:
Have a Whale of a Time

The PLS "The Humpback Whale: A Whale of a Story" was designed by Irene Kosak, teacher, P.S. 107, Queens, New York.

Frame 1

Welcome aboard! We are going to take an exciting voyage across many oceans to search for information about the humpback whale. Whales are not big fish; they are mammals like you and me. Buckle up your life preserver and get ready for an exciting journey.

Frame 2

By the time you finish, you will be able to:

1. List the characteristics of mammals.
2. Name the types of food humpback whales eat.
3. Describe several interesting characteristics of humpback whales.

Frame 3

Before you begin this program, read each vocabulary word and its definition.

<u>Vocabulary</u>

1. <u>evolved</u>-to change, unfold or develop   2. <u>complex</u>-not simple

3. <u>plentiful</u>-a lot of   4. <u>krill</u>-shrimplike animal

Frame 4

After you read each frame of this program, a question will be asked.
Write the answer to each question on a separate sheet of paper.
Write the name of this program and your
name at the top of the paper.

Have Fun!

Frame 5

Whales are not fish, despite their appearance. They are mammals.
Mammals have four basic characteristics.

Mammals have _____ main characteristics.

Back of Frame 5

If you chose 4 as your answer, you
are correct. Go on to the next frame.

Frame 6

How long can you hold your breath? Some whales can hold their breath for
more than one hour. They must go to the surface, the top of the water,
eventually to get air. One of the characteristics of whales is that they
breathe air through their lungs.

Whales breathe _____.

Back of Frame 6

Air is the correct answer.

Riddle: What time is it when a whale swims in your pool?

(The answer will appear on another frame.)

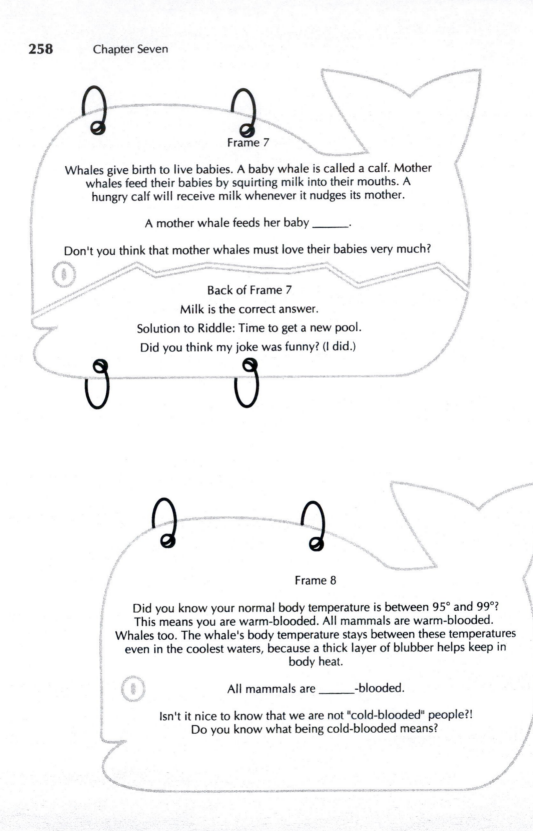

Frame 7

Whales give birth to live babies. A baby whale is called a calf. Mother whales feed their babies by squirting milk into their mouths. A hungry calf will receive milk whenever it nudges its mother.

A mother whale feeds her baby _____.

Don't you think that mother whales must love their babies very much?

Back of Frame 7

Milk is the correct answer.

Solution to Riddle: Time to get a new pool.

Did you think my joke was funny? (I did.)

Frame 8

Did you know your normal body temperature is between 95° and 99°? This means you are warm-blooded. All mammals are warm-blooded. Whales too. The whale's body temperature stays between these temperatures even in the coolest waters, because a thick layer of blubber helps keep in body heat.

All mammals are _____-blooded.

Isn't it nice to know that we are not "cold-blooded" people?! Do you know what being cold-blooded means?

Back of Frame 8

The correct answer is warm-blooded.

When people with warm blood are
called "cold-blooded," it means
they are not kind.

Frame 9

When you look at mammals, you will notice that they
have hair. Some mammals have tiny hairs that you may not
notice unless you are close to them.

All mammals have _____.

Back of Frame 9

All mammals have hair.

Riddle: What is a whale's favorite type of cake?

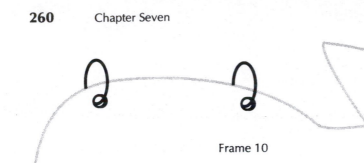

Frame 10

LET'S REVIEW

1. Mammals have _____ main characteristics.
2. The main characteristics of mammals are:
   They all breathe _____.
   All mammals have _____.
   All mammals are _____-blooded.
   A mammal feeds its baby _____.

Sea Star

Back of Frame 10

1. 4
2. air, hair, warm, and milk

Solution of Riddle: Fish cakes

If all your answers are correct, you receive a star.

Congratulations!

Are you eager for my riddle answer?
You must be patient!

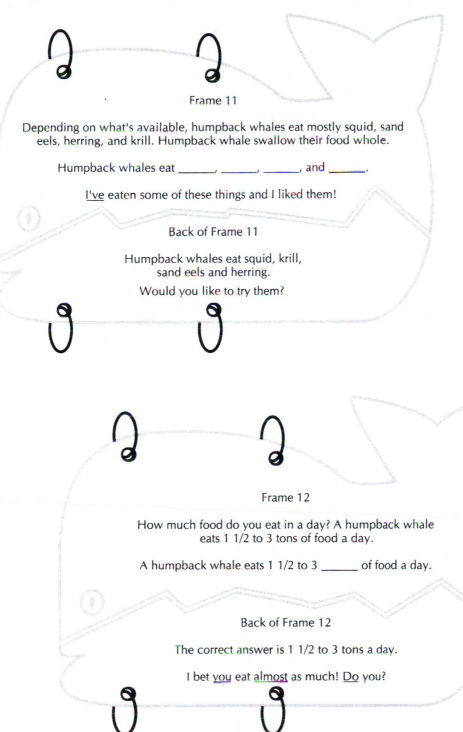

Frame 11

Depending on what's available, humpback whales eat mostly squid, sand eels, herring, and krill. Humpback whale swallow their food whole.

Humpback whales eat _____, _____, _____, and _____.

I've eaten some of these things and I liked them!

Back of Frame 11

Humpback whales eat squid, krill, sand eels and herring.

Would you like to try them?

Frame 12

How much food do you eat in a day? A humpback whale eats 1 1/2 to 3 tons of food a day.

A humpback whale eats 1 1/2 to 3 _____ of food a day.

Back of Frame 12

The correct answer is 1 1/2 to 3 tons a day.

I bet you eat almost as much! Do you?

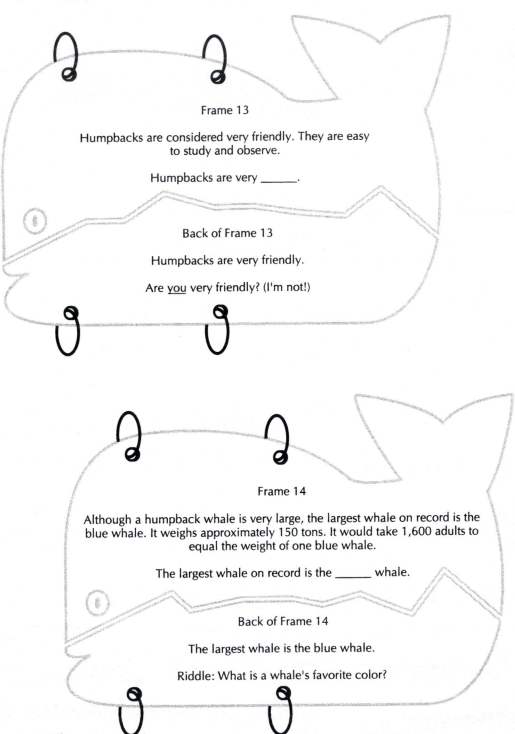

Frame 13

Humpbacks are considered very friendly. They are easy to study and observe.

Humpbacks are very _____.

Back of Frame 13

Humpbacks are very friendly.

Are <u>you</u> very friendly? (I'm not!)

Frame 14

Although a humpback whale is very large, the largest whale on record is the blue whale. It weighs approximately 150 tons. It would take 1,600 adults to equal the weight of one blue whale.

The largest whale on record is the _____ whale.

Back of Frame 14

The largest whale is the blue whale.

Riddle: What is a whale's favorite color?

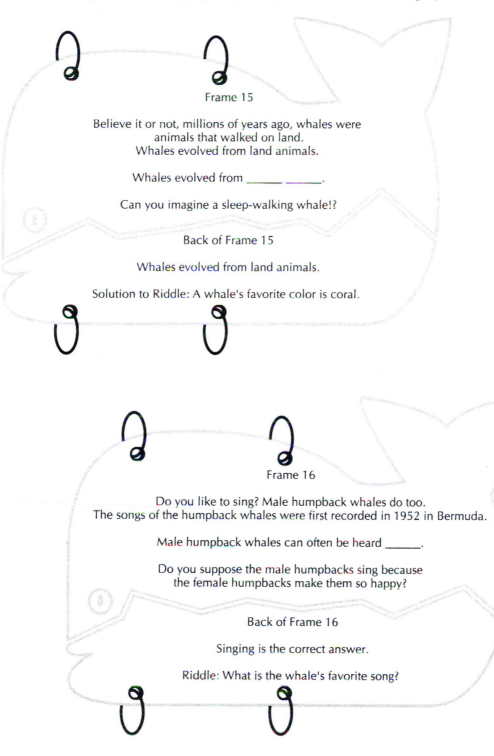

Frame 15

Believe it or not, millions of years ago, whales were
animals that walked on land.
Whales evolved from land animals.

Whales evolved from _____ _____.

Can you imagine a sleep-walking whale!?

Back of Frame 15

Whales evolved from land animals.

Solution to Riddle: A whale's favorite color is coral.

Frame 16

Do you like to sing? Male humpback whales do too.
The songs of the humpback whales were first recorded in 1952 in Bermuda.

Male humpback whales can often be heard _____.

Do you suppose the male humpbacks sing because
the female humpbacks make them so happy?

Back of Frame 16

Singing is the correct answer.

Riddle: What is the whale's favorite song?

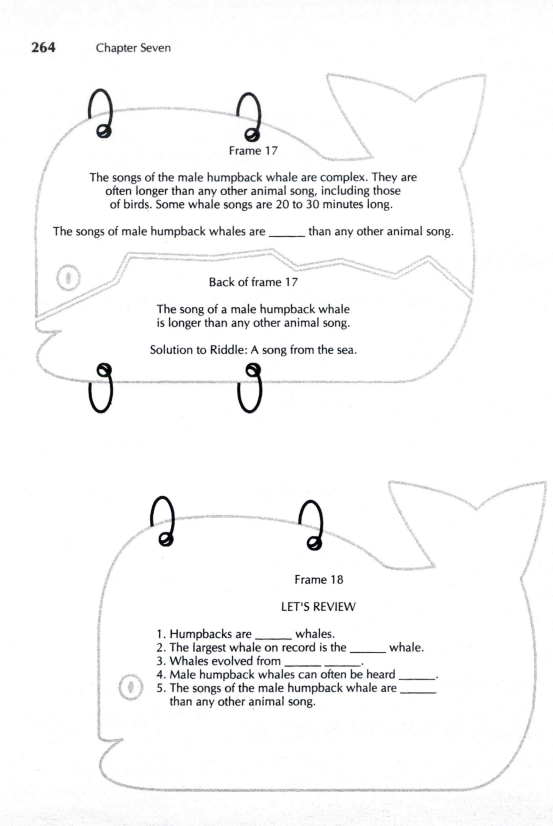

Frame 17

The songs of the male humpback whale are complex. They are
often longer than any other animal song, including those
of birds. Some whale songs are 20 to 30 minutes long.

The songs of male humpback whales are _____ than any other animal song.

Back of frame 17

The song of a male humpback whale
is longer than any other animal song.

Solution to Riddle: A song from the sea.

Frame 18

LET'S REVIEW

1. Humpbacks are _____ whales.
2. The largest whale on record is the _____ whale.
3. Whales evolved from _____ _____.
4. Male humpback whales can often be heard _____.
5. The songs of the male humpback whale are _____
   than any other animal song.

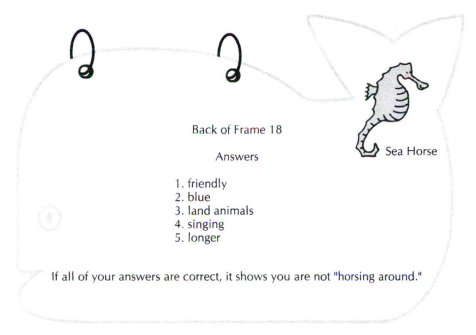

Back of Frame 18

Answers

Sea Horse

1. friendly
2. blue
3. land animals
4. singing
5. longer

If all of your answers are correct, it shows you are not "horsing around."

A Final Word about Programmed Learning Sequences

PLS are the closest thing we know to a tape-recorded story book. They are, however, based on the total school curriculum rather than only on literature. PLS enable children to learn to read rapidly; they introduce material globally—and most young children are global rather than analytic. PLS are structured but do not cause children tension or pressure. They may be used for children with any strengths. They stimulate interest; can be used without direct teaching; free the teacher to work with those who require immediate adult interaction; and can be made by parents, students, aides, and interested noneducators, as well as by teachers.

PLS are better than tape-recorded books because they: (1) begin globally, thus appealing to global children—the majority of our primary population; (2) incorporate tactual devices into the frames, thus helping low auditory and low visual children reinforce through another sense; (3) are sequential, appealing to analytic youngsters, too; (4) reinforce every seven or eight frames to revitalize learning on an ongoing basis; and (5) are accompanied by a tape so that nonreaders or poor readers can learn content, too. They also: (6) provide immediate feedback; (7) teach at each child's pace; (8) question, answer, reinforce; and (9) often joke a bit—such a change from everyday instruction!

You may photocopy the PLS in this chapter, duplicate them, and ask the children to experiment with them. You will, however, need to read them onto a tape so that the children who use them can hear the contents being read, quietly and in relative privacy. We hope you will decide to make a PLS for a unit you are planning to teach. If you do, check the following features to be certain you create a PLS that can teach effectively.

The PLS should include:

1. An attractive cover in a shape related to the content
2. Both an analytic and a global title (with humor, if possible, or a clever play on words)
3. Clearly stated objectives
4. Specific directions for the children to follow—read, answer, check, wipe off, erase, put back, use the accompanying tape, handle carefully, and so forth
5. A global beginning
6. When possible, the story woven through the entire PLS
7. Interesting, "upbeat" phrases rather than academic directives
8. Step-by-step sequencing
9. Actual teaching, with the identical concept/material repeated in different ways on several frames
10. Answers on the backs of the frame accompanied by humor, jokes, and illustrations
11. Illustrations related to the text, in color
12. Varied types of questions—"Circle," "Write in," "Fill in the missing letters," "Draw a line from the right side of the sheet to . . .", and so forth
13. An accompanying tape
14. Answers provided in complete statements
15. Few "yes" or "no" answers
16. An interdisciplinary theme for global students
17. Appropriate review frames
18. Built-in tactual reviews
19. Neatness, attractiveness, legibility
20. Correct spelling and grammar
21. Original and creative touches
22. Themes or ideas related to students' interests, life-style, or talents
23. A choice or two, at times
24. Laminated, easy-to-handle frames
25. Frames that turn in the correct position (not upside down)

We know, from experience, that kindergartners and first- and second-graders can create their own tactual materials—Flip Chutes, Electroboards, Pic-A-Holes, and Task Cards. We have seen many primary children create a short PLS. If you show parents how to do it, their children will learn by watching and assisting them. However, if you give the children the objectives, they will create simple, illustrated PLS and will *learn* the content as they create the resource. Allow two or three to work together *if they wish to do so. Don't* think that they can't do it; you will be pleasantly surprised!

8

Designing Contract Activity Packages to Respond to Individual Learning Styles

Contract Activity Packages (CAPs) are one of the three basic methods of individualizing instruction. The other two, Programmed Learning Sequences (PLSs) and Multisensory Instructional Packages (MIPs), are described in Chapters 7 and 9. Sample CAPs, PLSs, and MIPs all have been designed to teach the same objectives. Thus, three different strategies are available to respond to three different basic learning style patterns and different ability and performance levels. Generally, CAPs are appropriate for average or above-average, gifted and or nonconforming children (those with low LSI:P scores on Responsibility and Persistence). In addition to responding to specific learning style differences among students, Contract Activity Packages are more effective than large-group instruction or question-and-answer discussion for several reasons:

1. *Self-paced achievement.* When we stand before a group of young children and explain what we are trying to teach, they can absorb the content only as quickly as we are able to relate it. Given different resources through which to learn, many youngsters could achieve more rapidly than others. We teachers cover in each lesson what we believe the majority of students in that group are capable of assimilating, but we know that some are capable of learning much more than they are being exposed to in a given amount of time, whereas others are capable of learning only a fragment of what we are highlighting.

If we teach too much too quickly, we are bound to lose the less able child. If our pace is slow enough that less able students may keep abreast, we unwittingly irritate or bore the brighter youngsters. If we try to vary the pace to provide interest, both groups may miss important information during the presentation.

Contract Activity Packages allow children to learn as quickly—or as slowly—as they need to master new and difficult material. They are particularly responsive to the learning style characteristics of quickly achieving and nonconforming youngsters. (Photographs courtesy West Seneca Central School District, West Seneca, New York.)

In contrast to whole-group instruction, Contract Activity Packages permit individual pacing so that children may learn as quickly or as slowly as they are able to master the material. In addition, youngsters are neither embarrassed because others grasp the content more quickly than they do, nor bored because they must wait for classmates to catch up with them before the class is introduced to the next knowledge or skill area. Each learner works independently, but children may, by choice, team up with classmates who can pace themselves similarly.

2. *Varied academic levels.* Contract Activity Packages can be designed so that students can function on their current academic level but master concepts or facts through resources that clarify the content because of their style responsiveness. This may be accomplished in four ways: (a) Resource Alternatives teach the required objectives at different reading levels and through different perceptual modalities; (b) Activity Alternatives require application of the content; (c) Reporting Alternatives cause review of the content with peer interaction; and (d) Small-Group Techniques provide another instructional strategy through peer learning.

3. *Independent levels.* Usually, all youngsters are required to learn the same thing at the same time, to the same extent, and in the same way. Because children differ from one another in ability, achievement, interests, and learning styles, their dependence on us as a primary source seriously limits the academic progress of some. Finally, despite teachers' skill and sensitivity, it is important to recognize that some students learn better through multimedia approaches, computer programs, simulations, projects, or tactual/kinesthetic resources than they do from an articulate, knowledgeable adult. Large-group lectures enable few children to learn easily. Nature has endowed each person with unique sensory strengths and limitations, and many students are able to learn more and learn it better by beginning with visual, tactual, or kinesthetic resources rather than through an auditory approach such as a lecture or discussion.

The use of Contract Activity Packages makes youngsters personally responsible for learning what is required. Children receive specific objectives and, for young children, teachers structure a choice of media resources through which they may learn. Because of their exposure to a variety of materials, children obtain a great deal of ancillary knowledge. Often the required concepts are included in several resources—thus providing multisensory repetition.

Moreover, because youngsters may select from among the resources provided by their teacher, the self-selection factor improves their motivation, reduces their inclinations toward nonconformity, and permits them to work in ways in which they feel most comfortable. Self-pacing permits them to learn as quickly as they can, but well enough to retain what they have studied. As they become accustomed to exercising freedom of choice and assuming responsibility, they become increasingly independent of their teacher and learn to use resources to their personal advantage. They begin to recognize that they can learn easily and well by themselves and, gradually, many children develop sufficient confidence to design their own Contract Activity Packages and resources. They eventually take pride in their ability to teach themselves, and, ultimately, use the teacher as a guide and facilitator rather than as a fountain of knowledge from which to absorb information.

Teachers who believe that the greatest gifts they can give their students are a love of learning and the tools for teaching themselves will enjoy the effects of contracting. For optimal learning to occur, however, teachers need to identify who requires an authority figure; who learns by listening; who is most alert in the morning, afternoon, or evening; who can remain seated passively for a sustained length of time; and who is motivated enough to learn merely because the teacher imposes it.

4. *Reduced frustration and anxiety.* If education is important, as the compulsory education laws imply, then everyone should become educated. If everyone should be educated, everyone should be encouraged to learn as well and as quickly as is possible—for that person. Because the majority of youngsters are neither gifted nor extremely bright, imagine how discouraged they must feel every day of the week when they realize that they must use all their resources to live up to the teacher's expectations, whereas a few of their classmates exert little effort and invariably appear to know all the answers.

Although some successfully hide their anxiety, many verbalize that they don't like school, whereas others "drop out" even as they occupy seats in the classroom.

Many youngsters initially prefer to work with a teacher. Direction from an adult authority figure is essential to their comfort and ability to concentrate. Here, kindergarten teacher Bonnie Bryant is introducing a Contract Activity Package to kindergartner Brittani Dargan. (Photograph courtesy Brightwood Elementary School, Greensboro, North Carolina.)

Although both national and state commissions have recommended the development of alternative programs that respond to "the great diversity of students and needs . . . within the schools" (Rise Report, 1975), innovative approaches to learning often are suspect and are required to continually produce higher academic achievement and more positive student attitudes than are seen in traditional educational settings.

Contract Activity Packages reduce student anxiety and frustration without requiring extensive changes in the class organization. They can be used in a self-contained classroom, at any level, and with many students. Youngsters are permitted to learn by themselves in ways that they find most amenable—with a peer or two, in a small group, with the teacher, through resources of their choice, at their seats, on the floor, and so on.

Rules must be established to indicate clearly the behaviors that are acceptable when students are permitted to choose how they learn, and these regulations must be adhered to firmly. It also is important that students are trusted to proceed seriously and to accomplish their objectives. Their independence is enhanced when they self-select resources and Activity and Reporting Alternatives, or take CAPs to a Center, study area, or their home to pursue them at the *right* time of day, in quiet or with music, with parents, a classmate, or by themselves, with food or not, and so forth. Gradually, they become aware of how they learn best and how to teach themselves.

5. *Capitalizing on individual students' interests.* All students must learn to read, to write, to express themselves well, to compute, and to interpret data. Beyond these *musts,* there is no curriculum that every student everywhere *should* master. There is no need for every youngster to know the rainfall in exotic places or to commit to memory foreign products, capital cities, rivers, and other such facts that make up the required curriculum for many classes. The intent of extensive exposure to a variety of different subject matter disciplines is to expand the horizons and interests of students—but the opposite often occurs. When youngsters have no choice in what they are learning, they often become recalcitrant and negative.

Schools might experiment with a series of cluster subjects, like those that are found in most curricula, and offer their students a choice of any four from a core of seven, or five from among eight options. It is true that some students might never be exposed to selected segments in the social studies, literature, or the arts, but we suggest that most would learn in depth the areas in which they choose to focus. As Mager and McCann (1963) suggested, motivation increases with the amount of control exercised over what, when, and how students learn.

Children are permitted to work on Contract Activity Packages anywhere in the classroom as long as they are safe, they do not distract any classmate with a different learning style, their teacher can see them, they complete their work, and their grades are as good as or better than previously. Youngsters may sit at a desk, kneel at a table, sit on the floor, or sprawl on the carpet, as shown in the photograph. All can concentrate studiously. (Photograph courtesy West Seneca Central School District, West Seneca, New York.)

Learning Style Characteristics Responsive to Contract Activity Packages

Contract Activity Packages are responsive to most learning style characteristics, for they may be used flexibly with some students and with exacting structure for others, as described in the following examples:

1. If sound is needed, an earplug may be used to isolate radio or recorded music for those who benefit from it. If discussion is important, an instructional area (such as a Learning Station or Interest Center) can be established in a section of the room and blocked off by perpendicular dividers to provide a private place for its occupants and to protect their classmates from being distracted by movement or talk. Rules for discussion must be established so that no one outside the instructional area hears the words of anyone inside, but that management strategy will be necessary whenever you begin to accommodate the classroom to individual learning styles. The youngster who needs silence can use another Center where speaking is not permitted, adjacent to dens or alcoves that are used for essentially quiet activities.

2. When students are permitted to work on their CAPs anywhere in the classroom as long as they work quietly, do not interrupt others, and respect the rules that have been established, they automatically adjust light, temperature, and design to their learning style preferences.

3. Motivated, persistent, responsible, and self-structured students should be given (a) a series of objectives to complete; (b) resources they may use to obtain information; (c) suggestions for how and where to get help should they experience difficulty; and (d) an explanation of how they will be expected to demonstrate achievement of the objectives. They then should be permitted to begin working and to continue—with occasional spot checking—until each task has been completed. Children who are unmotivated, less persistent, less responsible, or in need of imposed structure should be given (a) only one or two objectives at a time; (b) specific resources to use; and (c) suggestions for obtaining assistance when necessary. These youngsters, however, need frequent supervision and constant encouragement and praise for their progress. You will need to circulate among them, help them use resources, ask questions, check on their understanding of what they are doing, and comment favorably when you observe their effort. If you treated the motivated, self-structured students in the same way, you would interrupt their concentration and distract them. But if you don't check on the nonpersistent, unmotivated children and the children who are having difficulty with an assignment, these children become frustrated, get involved in diversionary activities, or give up.

4. CAPs permit students to work alone, with a friend or two, or as part of a team through the small-group activities that are included. Youngsters also may work directly with the teacher when difficult objectives require adult assistance.

5. The Resource Alternatives of each CAP include auditory, visual, tactual, and/or kinesthetic resources at different levels that permit students to learn through their strongest perceptual strength and to reinforce what they have learned through the next strongest pair of senses. The CAP may be used during the morning or afternoon hours, either at home or at school, to match the learner's best time of day for concentrating and producing. Further, youngsters may snack on raw vegetables or other nutritious foods and take short breaks for relaxation—as long as they return to and continue working on their objectives (assignments) until they have been completed. Experiment with CAPs for students who have the potential to master objectives either alone or with a classmate or two.

Contracts in the Primary Classroom

When using Contract Activity Packages in kindergarten, at the beginning of first grade, or with children who are not yet independent readers, tape-record each chart included in a *group* contract. On large oaktag or chart paper illustrate a contract page (Figure 8–1).

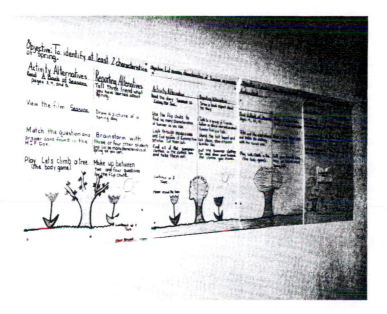

When beginning to use Contract Activity Packages (CAPs) with young children who may not yet be independent readers, use a group CAP so that classmates can help each other learn what heeds to be mastered. Print and then illustrate the CAP pages on large oak tag and mount them, in sequence, on the walls of the classroom. (Photograph courtesy Center for the Study of Learning and Teaching Styles, St. John's University, New York.)

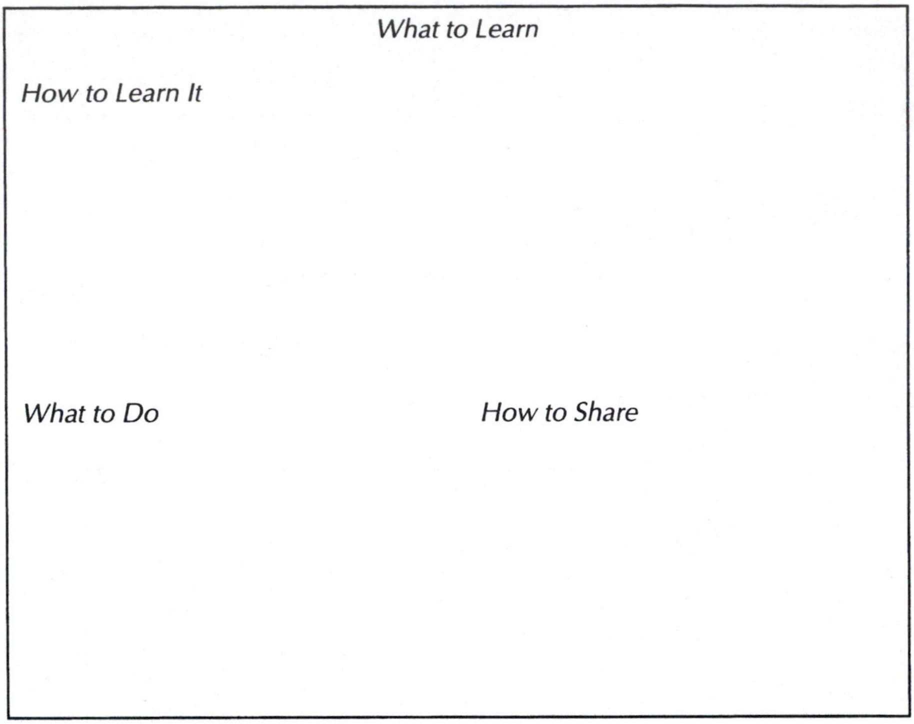

What to Learn

How to Learn It

What to Do   *How to Share*

FIGURE 8–1 Example of a Contract Page or chart that can be mounted on the classroom wall.

Discuss with the children what they will be learning, why it is important, and how it is related to what they already know—for example, "Boys and girls, we have been naming the letters of the alphabet for the past few weeks. Today, we will begin to recognize the sounds that some of those letters make." Read a familiar story, chant, or rhyme that highlights the specific sound/symbol relationship you want to teach. Here is an example:

Little Baby Bear
Little Baby Bear
Are you going somewhere?

To the beach with my ball
To the waves so tall.

Little Baby Bear
Are you going somewhere?

For berries on a farm
With a basket on my arm.

Little Baby Bear
Are you going somewhere?

On my bike over bumps
To bounce on bumpy lumps.

Little Baby Bear
Are you going somewhere?

To eat butter and bread
And jam colored red.

Little Baby Bear
Are you going somewhere?

To my blanket and bed
To rest my tired head.

Elicit responses from the children about why it is important to recognize the sounds that letters make. Then write the Behavioral Objective on the contract page under "What to Learn" (Figure 8–2). Next, discuss the resources children can use (Resource Alternatives) to master the objective. For example, "Some may listen to the Bb song on the tape; some may play the Alphabet Lotto Game, some may use the Hop-About Floor Game, some may use the Flip Chutes or Task Cards." As you suggest the resources that are available to the children, list them on the Contract page under "How to Learn" (Figure 8–3).

Next, introduce Activity Alternatives to the students.

Say:
Boys and girls, after you have used the resources you like most, you will be able to create something that teaches the sound of Bb to other children. You may choose to make a pictionary of Bb words or write a story [permit inventive spelling or a picture story]. Others may want to make Task Cards for our classroom Tactual Center or to use during Self-Teaching Time. Others may tape-record a story that has many Bb words in it. We could add those to the Listening Center.

As you suggest each Activity Alternative, the children may opt to do it, to show mastery of the objective, and to record it on the Contract page (Figure 8–4).

Ask the children to select an Activity Alternative to create from among the choices you have recorded. They should begin their Activity only after using the Resource Alternatives. At first, permit them to self-select any activity, but as you identify youngsters' perceptual patterns, assign them to an Activity that matches their perceptual strengths. Once your learning style program is fully implemented and children begin to see how comfortable they are with resources that match their strengths, they will self-select activities appropriate to their style. Also, at this early stage of using CAPs, allow the youngsters to complete their Activity Alternative with

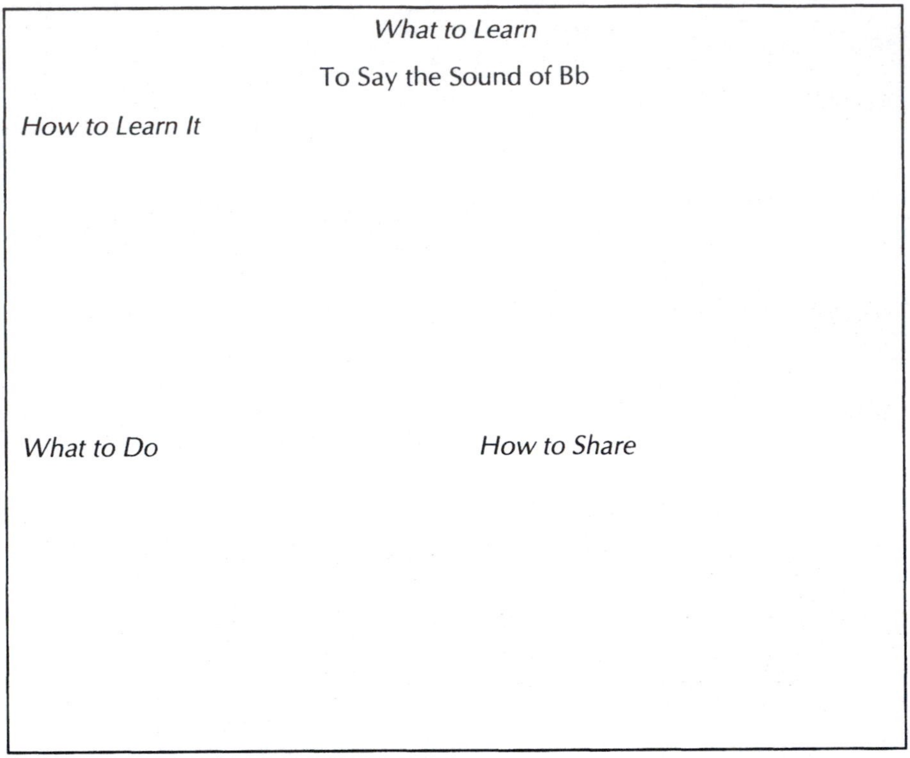

```
                                What to Learn
                           To Say the Sound of Bb

    How to Learn It










    What to Do                                    How to Share
```

FIGURE 8–2 Example of how objectives are added to the Contract Page or chart mounted on the classroom wall.

a classmate or two, by themselves, or with you, however they choose. Record their choices of Activity Alternatives and the persons with whom they select to work on a separate sheet of oaktag or posterboard (Figure 8–5).

Next, announce that, in a few days, there will be a special time for children to share and tell about their completed Activity Alternatives. Brainstorm with them the people they might like to invite to see their work. From their Brainstorming suggestions, select other teachers, classes, parents, and community members who might be asked to visit the classroom. Record each person's name or classification next to an Activity Alternative. When the children have completed their Activity Alternatives, schedule a time for those designated visitors to come and share the students' creative work.

It is not always necessary to invite visitors for sharing. Many children also enjoy sharing and telling with each other. When you have sharing in the classroom, assign half the class to be the visitors, while the other half shares and tells. Then reverse the roles. It is important that the student visitor initial the Activity Alternative that has been shared, because it is expected that the visitor will learn something new from the sharing. As the children share and talk with others, circulate about the classroom and ask the visitors to tell you something new that they have learned. This

What to Learn

To Say the Sound of Bb

How to Learn It
Bb Song Tape
Alphabet Lotto
Hop-About Floor Game
Flip Chute Alphabet Cards
Picture Letter Task Cards

What to Do   *How to Share*

FIGURE 8–3 Example of how alternative resources can be added to the Contract Page or chart mounted on the classroom wall.

What to Learn

To Say the Sound of Bb

How to Learn It
Bb Song Tape
Alphabet Lotto
Hop-About Floor Game
Flip Chute Alphabet Cards
Picture Letter Task Cards

What to Do   *How to Share*
Create a Pictionary   • with the principal
Tape a Story   • with 5 classmates
Make Task Cards   • with parents

FIGURE 8–4 Example of how alternative activities in which students use the new information they are learning (by creating a new original resource) ("What to Do") and share what they create with a classmate.

Make Task Cards	Tape a Story
Pamela	Meghan
Gary	Frank
James	Michael
Thomas	Nicholas
Create a Pictionary	*Draw a Picture-Story*
John	Liz
Susan	Matthew
Karen	Peter
Kelly	Krista

FIGURE 8–5 Chart on which children's choices of activities in which they will engage is recorded.

strategy will extend the learning experience for both the youngster who shares and the visitor with whom the product is shared.

Basic Principles of Contract Activity Packages

A Contract Activity Package is an individualized educational plan that helps children learn easily and rapidly because it includes each of the following elements:

Activity Alternatives provide creative ways in which children can reinforce difficult information learned through the resources. The creative applications should permit use of different perceptual strengths as shown in this photograph. (Photograph courtesy Sherridan Hill Elementary School, Williamsville, Texas.)

1. Simply stated Behavioral Objectives that itemize exactly what should be learned.

Do you recall studying for a test in college and trying to guess the important items that might be included? Teaching at all levels is often conducted in an atmosphere of mystery; we introduce many concepts, facts, and skills and then require students to intuit the ones that, in our opinion, are important enough to memorize. This approach, though common, is not logical. If specific knowledge is worthwhile, indicate that to children, and then encourage them to learn those specific things and remember them. Knowing what is expected of us is central to motivation.

Instead of continuing the pattern that says, "I'll teach many things, and you try to guess what is important," admit that every student cannot learn everything you teach—because of individual ability, experiences, interests, and learning style differences. Instead, diagnose each youngster to identify whether he or she is capable of learning many things independently (LSI:P analysis: The child does not require structure) or needs just a few things in a series of short, multiple assignments (LSI:P analysis: The child requires structure). Use the information you gain about the children in a lesson, a Contract Activity Package, a Programmed Learning Sequence, or any other approach described in this book to complement each child's learning style. Give motivated, persistent, responsible students longer tasks to complete; give their less motivated counterparts fewer, shorter, tasks. Assign brighter students a number of things to master; give slower students shorter prescriptions, one or two at a time.

When you tell youngsters what they are expected to achieve, you have given them their Objectives. When you also explain the ways in which they may demonstrate that they have mastered their objectives, you are giving them a statement that is called a Behavioral Objective.

The next section of this chapter has more information on how to write objectives for students.

2. Multisensory Alternative Resources teach the information that the objectives indicate must be mastered. Give students alternative resources that they may use to learn the information required by their objectives. The resources should be multisensory: visual materials such as books, films, filmstrips, study prints, computer programs, or transparencies; auditory materials such as records or tapes; tactual materials such as Task Cards, Learning Circles, Pic-A-Holes, Flip Chutes, and games; and interesting kinesthetic materials such as Body or Floor Games or extremely large tactual devices.

The resources are *suggested* sources of information. Because youngsters are free to select from among these sources, the choices are called Resource Alternatives. Help students recognize their perceptual strengths so that they use Resource Alternatives that respond to their strongest modality to *introduce* information. Then they should use materials that respond to their next strongest sense to reinforce what the first resource has introduced.

3. Activity Alternatives are child-made products through which the information that has been mastered is *used* in a creative way. When Rita and Ken Dunn first became involved in individualizing instruction in 1967, they used Learning Activity

Packages (LAPs) that included Behavioral Objectives, special and assigned readings, resources (then called "activities"), and a posttest for assessing students' progress. They found that students were able to examine their objectives, use the resources, acquire the necessary information, and pass the test at the end of the LAP—but three months later, the overall retention rate ranged between 38 and 58 percent.

When experimenting with alternatives to LAPs, the Dunns found that the addition of two procedures to the existing system increased students' ability to remember information by approximately 20 percent. The first was a series of activities in which students were required to *use* (apply) the information they had learned in a creative way. Based on Mager and McCann's studies, completed in 1963, they gave students a choice of activities to complete from among approved alternatives. This section of the CAP is thus called Activity Alternatives. Activity Alternatives may be labeled (A) for auditory, (V) for visual, (T) for tactual, or (K) for kinesthetic. They provide multisensory options that match perceptual strengths. The second addition to LAPs was named Reporting Alternatives.

4. Reporting Alternatives are a series of alternative ways in which creative products developed by one student may be shared with one or more—but no more than six to eight—classmates or outside visitors. When students develop a creative activity, they often want to share it with others. The sharing serves as either an introduction or a reinforcement of the material to the person who is being shown the product, but it also provides the person who created it with reinforcement and a sense of accomplishment and closure. This sharing—or reporting—increases retention of what has been learned, and, for some, serves as a self-fulfilling experience. Teaching others often promotes learning for the student "teacher."

5. Small-Group Techniques allow youngsters learning through a CAP to work with classmates—if they choose to do so. Individualization does not mean that children must learn in isolation. Identify each student's learning style and permit each learner to achieve in ways that complement his or her style strengths. Many students prefer to work in small groups or in a pair (DeBello, 1985; Dunn, Giannitti, Murray, Geisert, Rossi, & Quinn, 1990; Miles, 1987; Perrin, 1984; Poirier, 1970), and others evidence this preference only when their task becomes difficult. Thus, you should add at least three Small-Group Techniques (of your choice) to each Contract Activity Package so that students working together may attack (and conquer) difficult sections of the CAP. *Always* include a Team Learning to teach each difficult objective among the three Small-Group Techniques. Although the small-group requirements are not mandated for every youngster, they are helpful for those who find it difficult to complete tasks or learn concepts by themselves.

6. A Pretest, a Self-Test, and a Posttest also may be included in a CAP. Each CAP has a single test attached to it, which may be used to assess the student's knowledge of the information required by the CAP's Behavioral Objectives *before* the CAP is assigned, so that students who already have mastered those concepts and skills need not be burdened with the same subject matter again. Eliminate the pretest in all cases where you suspect scores will be very low—to avoid diminishing motivation or self-esteem.

This Pretest also may be used as a self-assessment by students to identify how much of the information required by the Behavioral Objectives they have mastered and how much remains to be learned even after they have ostensibly completed the CAP. Self-assessment reduces stress and promotes independence.

Finally, use the same assessment to test students *after* the resources have been used, the Activity Alternatives have been completed and shared with selected class-mates, and the three Small-Group Techniques have been mastered. If you wish, you may develop three separate assessment devices, but because the test questions are directly related to the individual Behavioral Objectives, it is just as valuable to use the identical test in all three situations. This approach establishes a pattern of reveal-ing what is expected, removes the mystery, and builds motivation. If you become concerned about rote memorization of answers, change the order of the questions on the final CAP test.

Step-by-Step Guide to Designing Contract Activity Packages

The first Contract Activity Package that you design takes time because you must adopt several new and unfamiliar techniques. The second CAP is much less difficult to write. By the time you embark on your third, you'll be helping colleagues and administrators by explaining the process and the reasons for each stage. Indeed, some second-graders can enthusiastically design their own CAPS with help from their teacher, their parents, or their classmates.

Step 1. Begin by identifying a topic, concept, or skill that you want to teach.

There are two kinds of CAPs. The first, a Curriculum CAP, covers a topic that you would like teach to all or most of the students in your class. The second, an

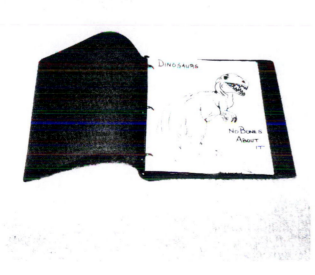

Develop a humorous or clever global subtitle for the Contract Activity Package topic. This sample is titled "Dinosaurs: No Bones about It!" (Photograph courtesy Center for the Study of Learning and Teaching Styles, St. John's University, New York.)

Add illustrations reflecting the Contract Activity Package topic throughout the text to make it attractive and motivating to youngsters. (Photograph courtesy Center for the Study of Learning and Teaching Styles, St. John's University, New York.)

Individual CAP, is designed for a topic that interests only one or a few students. If this is your first effort at CAP development, identify a topic that would be appropriate for most of your students. When you have completed this first CAP, you will have the skills to write as many as you wish—some for individuals, others for small groups, and the majority for use with an entire class at different times during the semester. St. John's University's Center for the study of Learning and Teaching Styles has excellent sample CAPs at cost for practitioners who prefer to use perfected ones (see Chapter 11).

Curriculum CAPs, once colored and laminated, remain useful for years. Sharing copied CAPs and building a CAP library on varied topics provide an expanding resource for schools and districts. Gifted students, parents, aides, and teacher education majors at local colleges can help stock a central "bank" of effective and valuable CAPs. All CAPs may be duplicated for multiple use by teachers in appropriate subject classrooms.

Step 2. Write the name of the topic, concept, or skill that you have decided to teach as a title at the top of blank sheet of paper.

Step 3. Develop a humorous or clever global subtitle. Here are some examples:

Knowing your ABC's: Let's Make Alphabet Soup!
Exploring the Planets: Give Me Some Space

Discovering Butterflies: Come Fly with Me!
Division: The Long and Short of It!

Step 4. List the things about this topic that you believe are so important that every student in your class should learn them. Then list those things about the topic that are important, but that slow achievers need not necessarily learn. Finally, consider those things about this topic that might appeal to special students—the musically talented, the artistic, the traveler, the carpenter, the cook, and so on. List these as special-interest items.

Examine your developing list of objectives. Be sure the most important ones are listed first, followed by objectives that are also of consequence but that everyone need not necessarily master. Finally, add those items you believe might be of interest to students with special talents or interests. Objectives concerning sports, dance, drama, music, or the culinary arts often increase interest when related to subject matter content.

All the most important items will become the required objectives for your students. Many of the secondary list of important items will be required, but students should have some choices among them. Thus, the way in which you assign the number of required objectives will help you personalize the CAP according to individual achievement and/or interest levels. When the CAP is completed and ready for use, assign the first group of required objectives to all. Motivation is increased by options; if you can give students some choices, even among the first objectives, even nonconformists will begin to show interest in the assignment. For example, you might say that the class must master "any seven of the following nine objectives." Some teachers suggest saying, "Complete the first three and any additional five of your choice." Another alternative is, "Do any three in the first group, numbers 1 through 3 in the second group, and any two in the third group." In short order, many gifted students will complete the most difficult questions, design two or three objectives of their own, or create an entire CAP!

Step 5. Translate the important items into Behavioral Objectives.

Years ago, Mager (1962) suggested that a behavioral objective should include (1) an identification and name of the overall behavioral act, (2) the conditions under which the behavior was to occur, and (3) the criterion of acceptable performance. After years of working with objectives, we are convinced that when all three items are included, the objectives become too long and complicated for most students to comprehend; are not individualized and therefore do not respond to learning style, interest, ability levels, or talents; and are not used as efficiently or as humanistically as possible.

Therefore, we suggest that behavioral objectives that list the behaviors that may demonstrate mastery of specific learning goals be written in the following *generalized* way, and that *specific* behaviors to demonstrate acquired knowledge or skills be *optional* through a series of Activity Alternatives. Further, the action prescribed at the beginning of the behavioral objectives should be direct and explicit—for example, *list, divide, collect, identify, predict.* Here is an example: *Identify the four parts of a plant—roots, stem, leaf, and flower.*

This objective clearly indicates what must be learned but does not restrict learners to explaining in a specific way. Because the four parts of a plant can be described in many different ways, you give the students a choice of how they will show that they know the answer by listing a series of Activity Alternatives directly below the Behavioral Objective and permitting each individual to decide which of the activities he or she prefers.

Step 6. Design at least three or four *Activity Alternatives* for each Behavioral Objective (or for a group of related objectives) so that students may choose how they demonstrate that they have learned what their objectives require of them. In effect, the Activity Alternatives permit students the *conditions* under which they will perform or will demonstrate their mastery.

Step 7. Create a Reporting Alternative for each of the Activity Alternatives that you have designed.

As indicated before, Activity Alternatives permit students to choose how they will apply information they have learned so that it is reinforced. Once they have completed a product, most students enjoy sharing it with others. Sharing an Activity Alternative with classmates or friends provides additional reinforcement for the person who developed it. In addition, it serves as either an introduction of new material or a repetition of previously studied material for the students who serve as the listeners, viewers, players, or participants. Furthermore, the sharing may be another way of demonstrating acquired knowledge or skill.

Example Behavioral Objective*

Describe what is necessary for a plant to grow—air, water, sun, and soil.

Activity Alternatives	*Reporting Alternatives*
1. Create a flower collage. Cut out pictures from a magazine of many kinds of flowers. Paste them onto a posterboard and write a story about what they need to grow.	1. Mount your collage. Talk about how the flowers are being cared for with two of your friends.
2. Use watercolors to paint a picture showing what plants need to grow.	2. Display your painting and talk to your teacher about it.
3. Plant a flower seed in soil in a plant box; water it, keep it near a window, and watch it grow!	3. Have three others join you each day to see how your plant changes; record your findings.
4. Make up a song about how we should care for plants. Be certain to include air, water, sun, and soil.	4. Teach the song to your friends. Have them sing it with you.

*This example "Plants, Animals, and Insects: For the Life of Us," was designed by Christine Bitalvo, graduate student, St. John's University, 1990.

What follows is a list of Activity and Reporting Alternatives that may be used to develop options for all students. Identify activities that are motivating for your students; adapt and rewrite them so that they are appropriate for the specific Contract Activity Package objectives that you are designing, and use them as part of the choices you permit. They may also be used as homework assignments to add interest to and provide applications of required items. Application through development of an original creation with the student's perceptual strengths and the sharing of it with classmates and adults contributes substantially to retention of the difficult information.

Examples

Activity Alternatives

1. Make a miniature stage setting with pipe-cleaner figures to describe the most important information you learned about your topic.
2. Make a poster "advertising" the most interesting information you have learned.
3. Describe costumes, people, or characters you have learned about.

4. Draw a series of pictures on a long sheet of paper fastened to two rollers. Write a script for them.
5. Describe in writing or on tape an interesting person or character that you learned about.
6. Write or tell a different ending to one of the stories you read.

7. Pantomime some information you found very interesting.
8. Construct puppets and perform a puppet show that explains an interesting part of the information you learned.

Reporting Alternatives

1. Display the stage setting and figures for three classmates. Explain what the scene represents and why you are showing it.
2. Display the poster and explain to three classmates why you found the information interesting.
3. Tell a group of classmates how you decided what the costumes should be, how you made them, and the people who would have worn them.
4. Show your paper movie to one or more classmates.

5. Ask a few classmates to tell you what they think of the person you portrayed.
6. After sharing your thoughts with a classmate or two, ask them to think of other ways the story could have ended.
7. Let a few classmates try to guess what you are pantomiming.
8. Present your puppet show to three friends. Have them tell you something interesting they learned from your performance.

Activity Alternatives

9. Make a map or chart representing information you have gathered.
10. Tape record a book review of what you read.

11. Make a clay, soap, or wooden model to illustrate some of the information you learned.
12. Construct a diorama to illustrate important information.
13. Dress paper dolls as people or characters in your topic.
14. Make a mural to illustrate the information you consider interesting.
15. Build a sand table setting to represent a part of your topic.

16. Make a time line, listing important dates and events in sequence.
17. Write a song including information you learned.
18. Make up a crossword puzzle.

19. Make up a game using information from your topic.
20. Direct and participate in a play or choral speaking about your topic.
21. Write a news story for a class newspaper explaining your views on any aspect of your topic.
22. Write an imaginary letter from one character to another. Tell about something that might have happened had they both lived in the time and place of your topic.
23. Make a filmstrip about your topic.

Reporting Alternatives

9. Display the map or chart and answer questions about it.
10. Permit others to listen to your tape and tell you if they would like to read the book.
11. Display the model and answer questions about it.

12. Display the diorama and answer questions as a teacher might.
13. Give a talk about the doll characters.
14. Display the mural and answer questions that others ask.

15. Explain the setting to other students. Ask them to evaluate your effort in a few short sentences.

16. Display the time line and be prepared to answer questions.
17. Sing the song in person or tape it for small groups of students.
18. Let other students try to complete it. Check and return their answers to them.
19. Play the game with other members of your class.
20. Present the dramatic or choral creation to a small group of classmates.

21. Ask three students to tell you something they learned from your story.
22. Ask three classmates to read your letter and respond to you.

23. Show your filmstrip to two classmates. Ask them to comment about it.

Activity Alternatives	*Reporting Alternatives*
24. Make a word search using at least ten words you learned from your topic.	24. Ask three classmates to solve your word search.
25. Write and illustrate a book about your topic.	25. Share your book with four classmates. Have them initial the back and tell you something they learned from it.
26. Make up riddles about information you learned.	26. Ask two classmates to solve your riddles.
27. Make three-part Task Cards about your topic.	27. Ask two classmates to use the Task Cards.
28. Make a set of Flip Chute cards on your topic.	28. Ask one classmate to use the Flip Chute cards.
29. Make a collage about your topic from magazine pictures.	29. Explain it to two classmates and then mount it on the bulletin board.
30. Draw a picture about your topic. Then cut the picture into pieces that form a puzzle.	30. Have a classmate put the puzzle together.
31. Make a Learning Circle or Learning Strip about your topic.	31. Have a few classmates work with the Learning Circle.
32. *Wild card activity.*	32. *Wild card reporting.*

(Have students design their own Activity and Reporting Alternative. Be certain to review and approve it before they proceed.)

Step 7. Gather all the *resources* you can locate that students may use to gain the information required by their Behavioral Objectives. In addition, assign students to gather resources on their own from the library or to write for information from associations.

Try to locate multisensory resources. Categorize them separately—for example, books, transparencies, tapes, records, magazines, games, and—if you have them—Programmed Learning Sequences, Instructional Packages, Pic-A-Holes, Flip Chutes, Electroboards, Task Cards, or Learning Circles. Students may use additional materials if they wish, but they should either show them to you or refer to them in their work. Because students may select which resources they use, these materials are called Resource Alternatives. For examples, see the Resource Alternatives included in the sample CAPs in this chapter.

If they are available, include materials at different reading levels responsive to the range of abilities in the class using the CAPs. For example, a CAP on plants, animals, and insects could include picture books as well as easy-to-read science texts.

Step 8. Add at least three Small-Group Techniques to the developing Contract Activity Package (see Chapter 5). Develop a Team Learning to introduce the topic of the CAP. Design a Circle of Knowledge to reinforce what you taught through Team

Learning. Use any of the remaining strategies—Brainstorming, Group Analysis, or Case Study—to help peer-oriented youngsters gain information. Circles of Knowledge are simple to create—try a few. Team Learnings require more time but are well worth the effort, for they enhance retention for many students while freeing you to work directly with those who are authority-oriented or need supervision and guidance. For examples, see the Small-Group Techniques included in Chapter 5 and in the sample CAPs in this chapter.

Step 9. Develop a test that is directly related to each of the Behavioral Objectives in your CAP. An assessment instrument that is directly related to stated objectives is called a *criterion-referenced test.* Form questions for such a test by either restating the objective or phrasing it in a different way. For example, if the Behavioral Objective is, "Identify the four parts of a plant," the test question should be, "List the four parts of a plant."

Be creative in the ways you test your students. Tests may include maps, puzzles, games, diagrams, drawings, and photos for those who learn best in those ways.

Step 10. Design an illustrated cover for the Contract Activity Package (see sample CAPs that follow).

Step 11. Develop an informational top sheet. On the page directly after the illustrated cover, provide important information. Items that may be included are:

- The analytic and global titles of the Contract Activity Package
- The student's name
- The student's class
- The objectives that have been assigned to or may be selected by that student
- The final date by which the CAP should be completed
- The dates by which selected parts of the CAP should be completed (for students who need structure)
- The dates for sharing the completed Activity Alternatives
- A place for a pretest grade if you administer a pretest
- A place for a self-test grade (the *child* corrects his/her answers)
- A place for a final test grade
- The names of the classmates who may work on this CAP as a team
- Special directions for working on or completing the CAP
- A place for signatures: student, teacher, and/or parent

Step 12. If possible, print each part of the CAP on large chart paper or oaktag and mount all the sections side by side on a classroom wall.

Step 13. Reread each of the parts of the Contract Activity Package to be certain they are clearly stated, well organized, in correct order, and grammatically correct. Check the spelling and punctuation.

Step 14. Add illustrations to the charts so that the CAP is attractive and motivating.

Step 15. Turn up the bottom of each chart to form a pocket. Staple the sides of the pockets so they can hold a tape that reads what is printed on that part of the CAP.

Step 16. Tape each chart of the CAP for beginning readers.

Step 17. If you choose to give each child or individual copy of the CAP, duplicate the original and encourage the children to color their own copy.

Step 18. Design a record-keeping form so that you know which students are using the Contract Activity Package and how much of it they have completed successfully (Figure 8–5).

Step 19. Try a CAP with those students who can work well with any two or three Small-Group Techniques. Be prepared to guide and assist the students through their first experiences with a CAP. Establish a system whereby they can obtain assistance if they need your help. You can place an "I Need You" column on the chalkboard or on a chart and have youngsters sign up for help when they are stymied. Direct children to place their names beneath the heading and to return to their places until you are free to come to them.

Suggestions for Perfecting Contract Activity Packages

1. Any time that you use a number in the objectives, spell out the number and then, in parentheses, also write the numeral. This technique accentuates the number for youngsters who may overlook specific details.

Example

Identify the four (4) main parts of a plant—roots, stem, leaf, and flower.

2. Use complete, grammatically correct sentences. Do not capitalize words that should not be capitalized. Contracts should be excellent examples of good usage, spelling, and grammar for students. If you wish to emphasize a word that may be new to the students' vocabulary, underline the word.

3. Use the phrase "at least" before any number of required responses to motivate selected students to achieve more than actually is necessary.

Example

Recognize at least five (5) zoo animals that live on land. (Can you identify seven (7)?)

4. Be certain that the objective does not become a Resource Activity or an Activity Alternative. The objectives state *what* the student should learn. The resources are *how* they learn the answers. The activities enable youngsters to show that they have learned the material by making a creative, original product. Using the new information by applying it creatively helps the children remember it.

Example

> *Objective:* Identify five (5) zoo animals and at least three (3) of their characteristics.
>
> *Resources:* Read or listen to the taped book *Animals at the Zoo* and/or look at the filmstrip "Junior Zoologist."

Activity Alternatives	*Reporting Alternatives*
1. Bend pipe cleaners into the shapes of at least five (5) different zoo animals. Be prepared to "share and tell" about three (3) characteristics of each.	1. Show your animals to three (3) classmates. Tell them about the different animals you created and at least three (3) characteristics of each.

5. For each small-group technique, begin at the top of a new page. Name the technique and then number from 1 through 4 and draw lines on which the students' names may be written. Add another line for the recorder's name.

Example

Team Learning

1. _____   3. _____

2. _____   4. _____

Recorder: _____

6. In the Reporting Alternatives, never ask a youngster to report to the entire class. Have an activity shared with one, two, or a few classmates, or a teacher. It is difficult for a child to hold the entire class's attention, and if one child is given that opportunity, it should be offered to all. Instead, have the students report to a small group of three classmates. If the activity is outstanding, ask the student to share it with a second small group. Either assign students or ask for volunteers to listen to the report.

7. Underline the title of each of the major parts of the CAP—for example, Behavioral Objectives or Activity Alternatives.

Sample Contract Activity Packages

Following are several samples of early childhood (grades K–2) Contract Activity Packages developed by teachers and used successfully at different levels with children whose learning styles matched the approach of this method.

If this is your pupils' first experience with CAPs, give them a few opportunities with a group CAP so they can feel secure with this method. Then, identify those youngsters with whom it is effective. For children who do not respond well to CAPs (even if they are permitted to work with one or two classmates), don't use the CAP system. Instead, introduce either Programmed Learning Sequences or Multisensory Instructional Packages to them.

Contract Activity Packages are most effective with youngsters who are motivated and either auditory or visual, *or* with nonconformists (low on Responsibility). It is an especially well organized system, although it permits flexibility and options for students.

Individual CAPs also may be designed by gifted, bright, and/or second-grade creative students who could pursue a specific interest unrelated to the required curriculum. Students need only think through and respond to the following curriculum questions.

1. What would I like to learn more about?
2. Is there something that really interests me that I can study on my own?
3. Which resource can I use? (A visit to the library or Media Resources Center will provide answers.)
4. How can I use what I need to learn in a creative, original way that I eventually can share with others?
5. If I rewrite the objectives (what I need to learn), how can I translate them into a self-test?

Read the following Contract Activity Packages and adapt those that seem appropriate to use with your students in their first group or whole-class CAP.

"Knowing your ABC's: Let's Make Alphabet Soup" is a Contract that every kindergarten and first-grade teacher should have on file. It is a generic contract into which every letter of the alphabet can be inserted. Kindergartners can be introduced to the sound–symbol relationships through the CAP; first-graders can use it to review the beginning and ending consonant sounds or to be introduced to vowel sounds or blends.

The example illustrates the letters *B*, *C*, and *D*, but any sound–symbol relationship can be substituted.

Example: "Knowing Your ABC's: Let's Make Alphabet Soup"

Objective: Identify the sounds and symbols of the letters Bb, Cc, and Dd.

Activity Alternatives	*Reporting Alternatives*
1. Use playdough to make a capital and small letter B, C, and D.	1. Show your playdough to four (4) friends and have them guess which letters you created.

Activity Alternatives

2. Think of three (3) words that begin with the sound of B, the sound of C, and the sound of D. Make a tape using those words.
3. Find pictures that begin with the letters B, C, or D. Cut them out. Paste them onto an oaktag chart and label their beginning sounds.
4. Identify two (2) objects in the classroom that begin with B, C, and D. Draw a picture of them. Label their beginning sounds.
5. Create a collage of B, C, and D pictures.

6. Make two-part Task Cards. On one part, write B, C, or D. On the other part draw or paste a picture that begins with that letter.
7. Make cookies shaped like a B, C, and D.

8. Make up a story containing as many B, C, and D words as you can. Tape-record the story.

9. Take a walk through the school. Make a list of things you see that begin with the sounds of B, C, D.
10. Create a decorative name tag for children you know whose names begin with a B, C, or D.
11. Look through a book from the classroom library; find as many words as you can that begin with a B, C, or D. Copy them onto paper. Ask your teacher to help you read them.

Reporting Alternatives

2. Play your tape for three (3) friends. Ask them to tell you the letter with which each word begins.
3. Display your chart on the bulletin board and have three (3) classmates tell you the letters with which each begins.
4. Show your pictures to three (3) classmates. Have them find the objects in the classroom.

5. Display the collage on the bulletin board. Ask three (3) classmates to tell you the beginning sounds of the pictures.
6. Ask two (2) classmates to put your Task Cards together.

7. Share the cookies with a small group of friends. Have them say a word that begins with the sound of the cookie letter before they eat it.
8. Ask three (3) classmates to listen to your story and clap their hands each time they hear a B, C, or D word.
9. Share your list with the teacher.

10. Ask the children to wear their name tags for a day.

11. Display your list on the bulletin board.

Activity Alternatives	*Reporting Alternatives*
12. Sort through the flannelboard letters for a B, C, and D. Cut out flannel characters for each letter and create a story.	12. Perform your flannelboard story for a small group of classmates.
13. Make alphabet soup for lunch. Say "yummy" each time you get a B, C, or D on your spoon.	13. Invite three (3) classmates to join you. Keep a tally of how many B's, C's, and Ds they find.

Small-Group Techniques

Team Learning (recorded on a tape)

Team Members:

1. _____   4. _____

2. _____   5. _____

3. _____   6. _____

Recorder: _____

Listen to the story on the tape and then answer the questions that follow.

> Barbara and Billy went on a picnic. They brought apples, peanut butter sandwiches, and berry juice. They packed it all in a big brown basket.

Questions:

1. Can you name at least five (5) words that begin with the letter Bb that were mentioned in this story? If you name six (6), that's great!
2. Name at least one (1) person in the story whose name begins with B.
3. Make up a sentence using as many Bb words as you can.
4. Draw a picture showing Barbara and Billy's picnic.
5. Make up a short skit about Barbara and Billy.

Team Members:

1. _____   4. _____

2. _____   5. _____

3. _____   6. _____

Recorder: _____

In three (3) minutes, list as many words or names as you can that begin with the letter B, C, or D.

Brainstorming
Call out all the Bb words you can. I'm going to start your list with:

bunny   big   Bernice   beautiful

Pretest/Self-test/Posttest

Name _____   Date _____

Pretest date _____   Number correct _____

Self-test date _____   Number correct _____

Posttest date _____   Number correct _____

1. List three (3) words that begin with the letters:

Bb	Cc	Dd
_____	_____	_____
_____	_____	_____
_____	_____	_____

2. Circle three (3) Bb words. Underline three (3) Cc words. Place a star (*) next to each Dd word.

baby	dog	Barbara	Don	car	classmate
big	cool	Cathy	Bill	basket	Dorothy
cat	daddy	Dick	Carl	boat	dot
cook	do	class	boy	dear	coat

Resource Alternatives
Books
Anno, Mitsumasa. *Anno's Alphabet.* New York: Crowell, 1975.
Beller, Janet. *A-B-C ing.* New York: Crown, 1984.
Charles, Donald. *Letters from Calico Cat.* Chicago: Children's Press, 1994.
Gag, Wanda. *The ABC Bunny.* New York: Coward McCann, 1975.
Hoban, Tana. *A B See!* New York: Greenwillow, 1982.
Lobel, Anita. *On Market Street.* New York: Greenwillow, 1983.
Roe, Richard. *Animal ABC.* New York: Random House, 1984.
Schreck, Susan. *I Know Letters.* Madison, WI: Western, 1985.
Wiley, David. *A Fishy Alphabet.* Chicago: Children's Press, 1983.

Records
    The Muppet Alphabet Album (Sesame Street)
    The Simon Says Alphabet Album
    Acting Out the ABC's

Filmstrips
    Curious George Learns about the Alphabet (Singer Films)
    What Comes after A? (Coronet Films)
    Alphabet Recognition (Eyegate Films)

Teacher-Made Resources and Games

ABC Cards

Picture Cards

Bottlecap Alphabet Game: Glue letters inside bottle caps and have the children put the caps into alphabetical order.

Alphabet Pockets: Sew or glue 26 pockets with one letter on each onto a piece of washable fabric. Let the children put the correct plastic or paper letter into the correct pocket.

B, C, D Task Cards (see Chapter 6)

B, C, D Flip Chute Cards (see Chapter 6)

B, C, D Pic-A-Hole Sets (see Chapter 6)

B, C, D Floor Games (see Chapter 6)

B, C, D Programmed Learning Sequences

B, C, D Multisensory Instructional Packages (see Chapter 9).

Exploring the Planets: Give Me Some Space is an excellent Contract for second-grade students to integrate with their science program. It also can be made available as an independent Contract for bright first-graders who are interested in the topic.

Exploring the Planets; Give Me Some Space

Behavioral Objectives

By the time you complete this contract, you should know a great deal about the sun and the planets. Complete objectives 1 through 4.

Behavioral Objective 1: Define the following four (4) words, and describe at least two (2) interesting facts about each word:

solar system	planet
star	orbit

Do at least one (1) of the following:

Activity Alternatives	*Reporting Alternatives*
1. Make a cassette tape that includes several sentences or a story that explains the four (4) words.	1. Let a small group of friends hear the tape and see if they can define the four (4) words.
2. Alphabetize the four (4) words above, and make a space dictionary. Include pictures.	2. Show your dictionary to three (3) or four (4) friends. Ask them to read it, initial it, and then display it on the reference shelf.

Activity Alternatives

3. Create a set of Task Cards matching the words with their definitions or illustrations.

Reporting Alternatives

3. Share the finished cards with one (1) or two (2) friends.

Behavioral Objective 2: Name the nine (9) planets in our solar system.

Please do at least two (2) of the following:

Activity Alternatives

1. Create a sentence that will help you remember the names of all nine (9) planets.
2. Write the names of all the planets in ABC order. Put the words into a space dictionary.
3. Construct a model of the planets. Label each planet.

4. Make up a Floor Game that helps teach the names of the planets to your classmates.
5. Make a chart listing all the planets. Start with the planet closest to the sun. Draw a picture of the planet next to its name.

Reporting Alternatives

1. Tell three (3) or four (4) friends the sentence. See if it is helpful to them.
2. Show your dictionary to a friend and display it on the bulletin board.
3. Display your model. Please be prepared to answer questions friends may have.
4. Play your game with two (2) friends.

5. Ask two (2) classmates to review your chart. Then display it on the bulletin board.

Behavioral Objective 3: Recognize the nine (9) planets in their orbit.

Please do at least two (2) of the following:

Activity Alternatives

1. Write a letter to a friend. Tell your friend about the planets in orbit.
2. Pretend you are an astronaut. Prepare a tape that will tell others about your trip to the planets in their orbits.
3. Make a puzzle of the planets in their orbits.

Reporting Alternatives

1. Read the letter to at least one (1) classmate.

2. Ask two (2) friends to listen to your tape. Then put it onto the reference shelf.

3. Ask two (2) friends to put it together.

Activity Alternatives	*Reporting Alternatives*
4. Pretend you are a member of a space team. Place nine (9) circles on the floor in the same order as the planets. As you walk around and land on each circle, name the planet.	4. Ask a friend to be a member of the space team and to participate. Tell each other something about each planet as you land on its circle.

Behavioral Objective 4:   Explain what an asteroid is and tell where the Asteroid Belt can be found in the solar system.

Please do at least one (1) of the following:

Activity Alternatives	*Reporting Alternatives*
1. Make a poster "advertising" the most important information you have learned about asteroids.	1. Display the poster and explain it to a few—three (3) or four (4)—classmates.
2. Pretend you are traveling in space. Create a skit that indicates your spacecraft has reached the Asteroid Belt.	2. Show your skit to a few friends.
3. Write the word *asteroid* and make a picture of it. Add the word to your space dictionary or Task Cards.	3. Display the dictionary on the bulletin board or show your Task Cards to a classmate.
4. Design a Wild Card Activity Alternative. Please ask the teacher for approval before you begin.	4. Share the activity with three (3) friends.

Small Group Techniques

Team Learning

Team Members

1. _____   2. _____

3. _____   4. _____

Recorder: _____

Many countries have a space program. Scientists all around the world are interested in learning more about the solar system. The United States has one of the best space programs in the world. Our space shuttle can go back and forth into space. It has carried weather satellites that help weather experts. It carries satellites that send back information about the planets and stars. It also has taken men and women into space and brought them home again.

The shuttle is attached to a giant fuel tank. There are two giant booster rockets next to the tank. After the shuttle blasts off from the launch pad, the booster rockets parachute into the sea. The giant fuel tank is then discarded in space.

Humans can survive in space only with the protection of the shuttle. There is enough room inside the shuttle for seven men and women. They wear ordinary clothes inside the shuttle. Some of the people are astronauts. Some are scientists or engineers. They eat, sleep, and work in a cabin in the front of the shuttle. There is room at the back of the cabin for a complete space laboratory. Experiments there will show how work in space can help people on earth.

When an astronaut leaves the shuttle to walk in space, it is important to wear a spacesuit. The spacesuit has oxygen tanks attached to it. Living things need oxygen. It is also very cold in space. The spacesuit helps keep the astronaut warm when he or she leaves the shuttle.

The people in our space agency, NASA, work very hard to learn more about our solar system. In a few years, they hope to put an astronaut colony on Mars. They have sent unmanned rockets to Jupiter and Saturn. They have sent satellites to study Neptune and Pluto. Maybe someday you will help explore the solar system too. If you do, please send me a letter and tell all about your trip.

1. What is the name of the U.S. spacecraft that carries astronauts into space and brings them home again?

_____

2. What is needed to help launch the spacecraft?

_____

_____

3. How many humans can travel in the spacecraft at one time?

_____

4. How do humans survive in space?

_____

_____

5. Which people have gone into space so far?

_____

_____

_____

Circle of Knowledge

Circle Members:

1. _____   3. _____

2. _____   4. _____

Recorder: _____

List as many facts as you can about our solar system in three (3) minutes.

Brainstorming

Group Members:

1. _____   3. _____

2. _____   4. _____

Recorder: _____

List all the reasons you think it might be important for scientists to know more about our solar system.

You have five (5) minutes and ten (10) seconds to complete your list.

Pretest, Self-Test, Posttest

1. The sun, planets, and anything else traveling around the sun make up our

_____

2. A ball-shaped world that travels around the sun is a

_____

3. How many planets are there in our solar system?

_____

4. The path a planet uses to travel around the sun is an

_____

True or False

5. Planets near the sun are hot. _____

6. Planets far from the sun are cold. _____

7. Many planets have water. _____

8. The earth is a good place for living things. _____

9. Match the planet with its orbit:

1.	first (1) orbit	1.	Mars
2.	second (2) orbit	2.	Jupiter
3.	third (3) orbit	3.	Venus
4.	fourth (4) orbit	4.	Earth
5.	fifth (5) orbit	5.	Pluto
6.	sixth (6) orbit	6.	Mercury
7.	seventh (7) orbit	7.	Neptune
8.	eighth (8) orbit	8.	Saturn
9.	ninth (9) orbit	9.	Uranus

10. All these planets travel around the _____ .

Resource Alternatives

Books

Adams, Richard. *Our wonderful solar system.* Madison, WI: Troll Associates, 1983.
Brandt, Keith. *Planets and our solar system.* Madison, WI: Troll Associates, 1985.
Earth, sun and stars, 1–3. Los Angeles: Milliken, 1988.
An educational book of planets. Santa Barbara, CA: Spizzirri, 1982.
Mosler, Ryan. *The astronauts.* New York: Random House, 1992.
Nance, Timothy. *Learning about the planets.* New York: Superscope, 1992.
Reed, Betty. *A book about planets.* New York: Scholastic Book Services, 1991.
Snowden, Sheila. *The young astronomer.* Chicago: EDC, 1992.

Multisensory Resources

Exploring the Planets: Programmed Learning Sequence (see Chapter 7)
Exploring the Planets: Pic-A-Hole (see Chapter 6)
Exploring the Planets: Task Cards (see Chapter 6)
Exploring the Planets: Flip Chute (see Chapter 6)
Exploring the Planets: Floor Game (see Chapter 6)

Video Cassettes

Spacewatch, *Foundations of the Solar System,* Encyclopedia Britannica Educational Corporation, 1990.

Whales, like dinosaurs, are fascinating creatures to children of all ages. The CAP "The Humpback Whale: Have a Whale of a Time," is an excellent motivation for a first- or second-grade unit on the study of mammals.

The Humpback Whale: Have a Whale of a Time

Objective 1: Identify at least five (5) characteristics of mammals.

Complete at least one (1) of the following activities

Activity Alternatives

1. Make a collage showing five (5) different characteristics of mammals.

2. Draw a whale on a large sheet of oaktag. Label the parts that are characteristic of mammals.

3. Design at least ten (10) pairs of Task Cards. Each pair must contain a characteristic of a mammal.

4. Create a mobile that displays at least five (5) characteristics of mammals.

Reporting Alternatives

1. Display your collage in the classroom. Ask four (4) friends to look at the collage and name at least four (4) characteristics of mammals.

2. Explain your picture to a small group of classmates. Answer their questions.

3. Play the Task Cards with two (2) friends. When the game is over, ask your friends to name four (4) characteristics of mammals. See if they are correct.

4. Hang the mobile in the classroom. Explain your mobile to three friends.

Objective 2: Name the types of food that humpback whales eat.

Activity Alternatives

1. Make a diorama showing humpback whales' favorite foods. Label each type of food.

2. Write a poem using all the humpback whales' favorite foods.

3. Make a word search puzzle using the foods of a humpback whale.

4. Write a play about a conversation among the sea creatures that humpback whales like to eat.

Reporting Alternatives

1. Share your diorama with two (2) friends. Ask them to identify the foods. Check their answers.

2. Read your poem to a small group of classmates. Display it on the bulletin board.

3. Give the word search puzzle to four (4) classmates. Check their answers.

4. Act out your play for a small group of classmates. You may make costumes.

Objective 3: Describe how a humpback whale eats its food.

Activity Alternatives

1. Make a filmstrip that describes how a humpback whale eats its food.

2. Write a book (at least ten [10] pages) that describes how a humpback whale eats its food.

Reporting Alternatives

1. Present the filmstrip to at least four (4) classmates. Be prepared to answer questions.

2. Give your book to a classmate to read. Ask her to give you a "book review" when she is finished.

Activity Alternatives

3. Create a slide presentation that shows the eating methods of humpback whales.

Reporting Alternatives

3. Have at least two (2) of your classmates view the slide show. Ask them questions about what they learned.

Circle of Knowledge

1. _____
2. _____
3. _____
4. _____
5. _____
6. _____

Recorder: _____

In five minutes, list as many characteristics of the humpback whale as you can.

Team Learning

Team Members:

1. _____
2. _____
3. _____
4. _____
5. _____
6. _____

Recorder: _____

Watch Expedition 2, "Whalewatch," of the *Voyage of the Mimi.* Answer the following questions:

1. Name three (3) differences between the way baleen whales and toothed whales eat.

   1. _____
   2. _____
   3. _____

2. How can humpback whales be identified?
3. What are some types of baleen whales?
4. What are some of the ways that humans cause *extinction* of an animal species?
5. Draw or create a *three-dimensional replica* of a toothed whale and a humpback whale.

Pretest/Self-Test/Posttest

1. How many distinctive characteristics do mammals have?
2. Name at least four (4) characteristics of mammals.

3. Name four (4) of the humpback whales' favorite foods.
4. What is another name for a humpback whale?
5. Describe how a humpback whale eats its food. Illustrate your answer in the space below.

Resource Alternatives
Filmstrips
> The Humpback Whale
> Our Friends in the Sea

Videotapes
> *The Voyage of the Mimi*

Computer Disks
> *The Voyage of the Mimi*

Records
> "Songs of the Sea"

Books
Cousteau, Jacques, and Dole, P. *The Whale, Mighty Monarch of the Sea.* Garden City, NY: Doubleday, 1975.
Ellis, Richard. *The Book of Whales.* New York: Knopf, 1980.
Hill, David. "Vanishing Giants," in *Audubon,* January 1975, Vol. 77, No. 1.

Institutions
> The Museum of National History, New York

Tactual/Kinesthetic Resources
> Flip Chutes
> Pic-A-Holes
> Task Cards
> Electroboard

Programmed Learning Sequence: The Humpback Whale: Have a Whale of a Time. (See Chapter 7.)

One of a first-grader's favorite activities is to take a walk, with magnifying glasses in hand, and look for insects. The following CAP, "All about Insects: Don't Bug Me" is one that your young students will complete with enthusiasm as they explore the fascinating world of insects.

All About Insects: Don't Bug Me

By the time you finish this CAP and complete each objective, you should be an expert on insects.

Name _____

Activity Alternatives completed _____

Date completed _____

Objective 1: Identify the parts of an insect.

Activity Alternatives

1. Make an insect from collage materials showing all the parts of an insect. You may use egg cartons, paper plates, pipe cleaners, yarn, buttons, and tissue paper.
2. Draw an insect and label its parts.

3. Make cookies in the shape of an insect. Include all its body parts. Use nuts, chips, raisins, M&M's, or other candies to show the different parts.
4. Write a poem about the parts of an insect. Record it onto a cassette.

Reporting Alternatives

1. Display your insect on our science table. Be prepared to identify its body parts to four (4) classmates.

2. Display the insect on the bulletin board. Be prepared to tell about it.
3. Make enough cookies to share with five (5) classmates.

4. Play the tape for a small group of friends.

Objective 2: Recognize the stages of development in the life cycle of insects.

Activity Alternatives

1. Make a mobile showing the four (4) stages in the life of a butterfly.

2. Make a shape book showing the stages of an insect's life.

3. Pantomime the life cycle of an insect.

4. Make up a song or poem that tells about the changes an insect goes through.

Reporting Alternatives

1. Hang the mobile over the science table. Be prepared to explain it to five (5) friends.
2. Read the book to two (2) classmates. Then add the book to our library.
3. Have a small group of classmates guess each stage as you act it out.
4. Recite your poem for five (5) classmates. Ask them questions about the stages of development.

Objective 3: Classify animals as insects or non-insects.

Activity Alternatives

1. Make an insect alphabet book. For each letter of the alphabet, write one or more words that have to do with insects.
2. Choose any three insects and complete the chart on worksheet #1.

3. Make up a crossword puzzle of insect names.
4. Make a diorama of a garden. Show all the creatures you could find in a garden. Tell which are insects and which are not.

Reporting Alternatives

1. Share your book with two (2) classmates. Allow them to suggest additions. Stand your book on the science table.
2. Mount the chart on construction paper and display it on the bulletin board. Be prepared to answer questions from the teacher.
3. Let five (5) friends complete the puzzle.
4. Describe your diorama to four (4) classmates and display it in the Science Center.

Worksheet #1

Name: _____   Date: _____

Insect Chart _____

   One interesting fact:

   _____

   Where it lives:

   _____

   What it eats:

   _____

   Insect's name:

   _____

Team Learning

Team Members:

1. _____   2. _____

3. _____   4. _____

            Recorder: _____

Butterflies and moths are insects. They also have their own special group called Lepidoptera (LEP e DOP te ra). Butterflies and moths are in this group because they have soft scales on their wings. Other insects do not have these soft scales. Because butterflies and moths are also different from each other, they each belong to their own group.

1. What special insect group do butterflies and moths belong to?

   _____

2. Why are butterflies and moths in this group?

   _____

3. Make a butterfly and moth poster. Show two (2) different ways that butterflies and moths are different.

   _____

4. Find two (2) ways that they are the same.

   _____

5. Make a butterfly or moth from materials in our scrapbox. Give it a name, but don't say if it is a butterfly or moth. Write a paragraph or poem describing it. Other teams will guess if it is a moth or butterfly from your description.

   _____

Circle of Knowledge

Team Members:

1. _____   2. _____

3. _____   4. _____

   Recorder: _____

In five (5) minutes, list as many insects as you can that have wings.

Brainstorming

Team Members:

1. _____   4. _____

2. _____   5. _____

3. _____   6. _____

   Recorder: _____

Imagine you are a butterfly or a moth just coming out of the chrysalis. In four minutes, name all the things you would need in your environment to have a safe, healthy, and happy life.

Pretest/Self-Test/Postest

Name _____

antennae   <u>wings</u>   <u>legs</u>   <u>body parts</u>

Fill in one of the underlined words.

1. All insects have two (2) _____.

2. The insect's _____ and legs are attached to the thorax.

3. Insects have six (6) _____.

4. Insects have three (3) _____ _____.

Write T (true) or F (false):

_____ 1. Insects hatch from eggs.

_____ 2. Another name for *larva* is *butterfly*.

_____ 3. A caterpillar becomes a grasshopper.

_____ 4. A larva changes to a butterfly.

_____ 5. A chrysalis is a soft shell.

_____ 6. A spider is an insect.

_____ 7. A bumblebee is an insect.

_____ 8. An earthworm is an insect.

Draw a line from the insect's body part to its name

Resource Alternatives

Books
Carle, Eric. *The grouchy ladybug.* New York: Scholastic, 1977.
Compton's Encyclopedia.
Goodman, Beth. *Bugs! bugs! bugs!* New York: Scholastic, 1990.
Day, Jennifer W. *What is an insect?*
Dorros, Arthur. *Ant cities.* New York, Scholastic, 1989.

Records
Weekly Reader Insect World Teaching Kit record

Teacher-Made Materials
      PLS: "All About Insects: Don't Bug Me"
      Flip Chute: "Beatrice B. Bug"
      Pic-A-Hole: Ladybug
      Floor Game: "All About Insects: Don't Bug Me"

Field Trips
      Your backyard
      A garden center
      The local library

Miscellaneous
> Butterflies and Moth Poster
> Insect Photo Gallery
> Life Cycles Sequencing Cards

Every early childhood curriculum contains objectives focused on nutrition. Try the CAP "Nutrition: Neat Treats" if you are interested in an exciting hands-on unit of study that leads children into the supermarket—with their parents, of course—to conduct research.

Nutrition: Neat Treats

By the time you finish this contract, you will have completed Objectives 1, 2, 3, and 4.

Date started: _____   Date completed: _____

Pretest grade: _____

Self-test grade: _____

Posttest grade: _____

Before you sign your contract, take the Pretest. Don't worry if you don't know all the answers. As you do this CAP, you will learn the answers. Then take the test again, and see your grade soar.

Pre-/Self-/Posttest

1. List three reasons that you should eat good food every day.

   a. _____

   b. _____

   c. _____

2. Name the four (4) food groups.

   a. _____

   b. _____

   c. _____

   d. _____

3. Which food group has cabbage, lemons, and carrots?

   _____

4. Which food group has turkey, peanut butter, and steak?

_____

5. Which food group has flour, rice, and wheat?

_____

6. Which food group has cheese, butter, and cream?

_____

7. Match the foods that are in the same food group.

1. hamburger   a. apples
2. bread   b. yogurt
3. peaches   c. lettuce
4. milk   d. fish
5. broccoli   e. oats

8. Which nutrients give you energy?

_____

9. Which nutrients build muscle and keep you healthy?

_____

10. Which nutrient is in all good foods and especially in fruits and vegetables?

_____

11. Which nutrient makes the other nutrients stronger?

_____

12. Name two (2) foods that give you energy.

_____

13. Name two (2) foods that build strong bones and teeth.

_____

14. You have an egg, toast, and milk for breakfast. What else do you need to have a well-balanced, nutritious breakfast?

1. Twinkie
2. orange juice
3. Pepsi Cola

Objective 1: List at least three (3) reasons that you should eat good food every day.

Activity Alternatives

1. Make a collage of at least fifteen (15) pictures of boys and girls doing different things that show why we need to eat good food every day.
2. Write a letter to a friend, and list three (3) reasons why you should eat good food.
3. Create a song that tells at least three (3) reasons why it is important to eat good food. Make a tape of your song.

Reporting Alternatives

1. Show your collage to four (4) friends. Ask them to name the things the children are doing. Display your collage on the bulletin board.
2. Mail your letter to your friend. Ask her to write to you and explain why she eats good food.
3. Play your song to four (4) friends.

Objective 2:   List the four (4) Food groups, and name at least three (3) foods in each group.

Activity Alternatives

1. Visit the supermarket with an adult. Find foods from each of the four (4) food groups. Make a list of them.
2. Make a chart of the four (4) food groups. Put at least three (3) foods in each group.
3. Make papier-mache models of three foods from each group.
4. Make a scrapbook of pictures of food. Put each food group on a separate page. Be certain to include at least three (3) foods in each group.

Reporting Alternatives

1. Show three (3) or four (4) classmates your list. Tell why each food belongs to its food group.
2. Display your chart in the classroom. Be prepared to answer questions from the teacher.
3. Show the models to three (3) classmates. Ask them to name each food group.
4. Share your scrapbook with three (3) classmates. Ask them to tell you their favorite foods in each group.

Objective 3:   Describe six (6) nutrients in good food, and list two (2) foods that contain each nutrient.

Activity Alternatives

1. Cut out pictures of at least fifteen (15) different foods. Group together at least two (2) foods that have the same nutrients. Make a scrapbook of your pictures.

Reporting Alternatives

1. Share your scrapbook with two (2) friends. Ask them to name the nutrients.

Activity Alternatives	*Reporting Alternatives*

Activity Alternatives

2. Visit the school cafeteria. Ask the dietitian to tell you all the foods he or she serves in one week. Make a list of the foods and the nutrients each supplies.
3. Make a chart of six (6) nutrients found in food. Draw at least two (2) foods for each nutrient.
4. Make a mobile of good foods. Put two (2) foods that have the same nutrients together.

Reporting Alternatives

2. Share your list with four (4) or five (5) classmates. Report to them what the dietitian said.

3. Show your chart to three (3) friends and have them ask you questions.

4. Display your mobile in the classroom, and tell three (3) classmates about it.

Objective 4: Plan a healthful breakfast, lunch, or dinner using the food group system.

Activity Alternatives

1. Pretend you own a restaurant. Write a menu for a balanced dinner. Include at least one (1) serving from each food group.
2. Go to a supermarket with an adult and buy foods for a well-balanced lunch. Include at least one (1) serving from each food group.
3. Write your own words to the tune of "Row, Row, Row Your Boat" using foods that make a well-balanced menu. Include at least one (1) serving from each food group.
4. Make a Learning Circle that shows a well-balanced breakfast, lunch, and dinner. Be certain you include at least one serving from each food group.

Reporting Alternatives

1. Show your menu to at least three (3) classmates. Ask them to make their own menu for a well-balanced meal.
2. Show the class what you bought. Present a report about why you bought certain foods.

3. Sing your song to the three (3) classmates. Have your classmates write their own words if they can!

4. Have four (4) or five (5) classmates complete the Learning Circle. Give them stickers if they do it correctly.

Brainstorming

Group Members

1. _____   3. _____   5. _____

2. _____   4. _____   6. _____

7. _____   8. _____   9. _____

Recorder: _____

Call out as many words as you can that have to do with good food. You have three (3) minutes.

Team Learning: Listen to the passage on tape and answer the questions that follow.

How can foods help you to stay healthy?

Your eating habits affect how you feel during the day. For example, what happens if you have no breakfast, or a poor breakfast? You are likely to be tired or cross. By midmorning you may be very hungry and unable to do your school-work.

Among the good food choices for breakfast are fruit, fruit juices, cereal, bread, milk, and eggs. Cheese, peanut butter, and potatoes are other good breakfast foods that can make the meal interesting. All these foods give you energy for the day's work and help you grow properly.

They have nourishing substances, or *nutrients,* that your body needs. Candy, cookies, and other very sweet foods and drinks do not furnish the nutrients you need.

1. List two (2) things that might happen if you do not eat a well balanced breakfast.
2. Another word for *nourishing substance* is _____.
3. Write a menu that would make a good breakfast.
4. Write a poem about the good foods a person needs to eat for breakfast.

Resource Alternatives

Books
Berenstein, Stan, and Berenstein, Jan. *The Berenstein bears/Too much junk food.* New York: Random House, 1985.
Sebell, William. *Food and nutrition.* Time Inc., 1980.
Simon, Seymour. *About the food you eat.* New York: McGraw-Hill, 1979.
Ward, Brian. *Diet and nutrition.* Watts, 1987.

Teacher-Made Materials
Flip-Chute, Pic-A-Holes, Electroboard, Task Cards on Nutrition
Programmed Learning Sequence: *Nutrition: Neat Eats* (see Chapter 7).

Filmstrip
Today's Food and Breakfast. San Francisco, Cereal Institute, 1992.

For young children to grasp science concepts, they must be involved in real, concrete scientific experiments. The CAP on *Discovering Butterflies: Come Fly With ME* provides such experiments that can be conducted right in the schoolyard.

Discovering Butterflies: Come Fly With Me

Name: _____

Objectives completed: _____

Date received: _____

Date completed: _____

By the time you complete this CAP, you should become an expert on the butterfly.

Objective 1: Identify four (4) stages in the life cycle of the butterfly.

Activity Alternatives

1. Make a movie-in-a-box about the life cycle of a butterfly. Draw pictures and write sentences about it.
2. Create a song about the life cycle of the butterfly. Record your song on the tape recorder.
3. Design a butterfly chart. Write the names of each stage of the life cycle in order. Draw a picture describing each stage.
4. Design a lotto game that matches a life cycle stage with a picture.
5. Make a set of Task Cards showing a butterfly's life cycle. Number the left side of each Task Card and draw that stage on its right side.

Reporting Alternatives

1. Display your movie to five (5) friends. Have them ask you questions about it.
2. Teach the song to four (4) friends. Use the tape you made to help you.
3. Display the chart and explain each stage of the cycle to three (3) classmates.
4. Let a group of four (4) or five (5) children play your game.
5. See if your father or mother can piece the Task Cards together correctly

Objective 2: Describe the process of the butterfly emerging from the chrysalis.

Activity Alternatives

1. Close your eyes and pretend you are a butterfly. Think, see, and feel from the butterfly's point of view. Write a story about emerging from the chrysalis.

Reporting Alternatives

1. Have three (3) classmates read your story. Record their reactions to it.

Activity Alternatives

2. Pretend you are a newscaster. Interview a butterfly after it comes out of the chrysalis. Tape your pretended newscast.
3. Take a walk outside of school and look for a chrysalis. Take or draw a picture of it.

Reporting Alternatives

2. Ask a small group of friends to listen to your tape. Answer any questions they might have.
3. Share your picture with a friend. Explain what is happening inside the chrysalis.

Objective 3: Identify and define at least ten (10) vocabulary words about the butterfly.

Activity Alternatives

1. Make a vocabulary list of ten (10) words about butterflies. Then create a word search. Ask the teacher to make five (5) copies for you.
2. Make a mobile of ten (10) vocabulary words and their definitions. You may add illustrations.
3. Design a Task Card game that matches ten (10) words and their definitions.
4. Design a crossword puzzle using at least ten (10) words that describe the butterfly.
5. Make a Flip Chute game using at least ten (10) words that describe the butterfly.

Reporting Alternatives

1. Share your word search with five (5) friends. Ask them to solve it.

2. Hang your mobile in the classroom. Ask four (4) classmates to look at your mobile.
3. Have four (4) children play the card game with you.

4. Ask five (5) classmates to solve the crossword puzzle. Check to see if they are correct.
5. Ask two (2) classmates to use your cards.

Objective 4: Name and locate the body parts of a butterfly.

Activity Alternatives

1. Make a labeled diagram showing the body parts of a butterfly.

2. Draw a picture of a butterfly and label its parts. Then cut your picture into puzzle pieces.

3. Make a chart describing the body parts of a butterfly and, if you can, what each part does. Use pictures to illustrate it.

Reporting Alternatives

1. Share your diagram with two (2) friends. Answer questions they may have.
2. Have three (3) classmates put your puzzle together. Describe the body parts to them when they are finished.
3. Tell two (2) classmates about your chart.

Activity Alternatives

4. Make up at least four (4) riddles about the body parts of a butterfly.

Reporting Alternatives

4. Ask three (3) friends to answer your riddles.

Team Learning

Team Members:

1. _____

2. _____

3. _____

4. _____

5. _____

6. _____

Recorder: _____

Read along with the tape of the following passage. Then, as a group, answer the questions that follow.

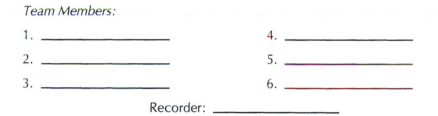

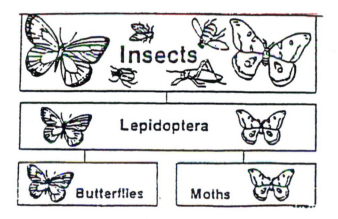

What Is a Butterfly?

Everyone knows what a *butterfly* looks like, but few people know what a butterfly really is. A butterfly has six legs, although the two front legs on some butterflies are so small that they are difficult to see. Think about other living creatures that have six legs. You might think about grasshoppers, crickets, and, of course, flies, bees, and beetles. All these creatures that have six legs belong to the same class of animal life. They are called *insects*. Some insects are wingless, but most of them, including butterflies, have two pairs of wings.

The second part of the word *butterfly* gives us a clue to where they can be found. Butterflies *fly* about, so they can be found in the air. Some butterflies, like birds, fly smoothly. Others flutter, and some make a jerky motion when they fly. They come down to feed or rest. Although they may land with wings outspread, they usually rest with their wings held upward and together over their back.

Look for butterflies in the daytime, for they like to fly about in the sunshine. You may see one land, or light, on the leaf of a tree, a flower, the stem of a plant, a blade of grass, or even on your windowsill.

1. Name an insect that has two pairs of wings and six legs.
2. Draw a butterfly.
3. Where might you see a butterfly at rest during the day?
4. Why is a butterfly pretty?
5. Make a butterfly puppet. You may use clay, pipe cleaners, coffee filters, clothespins, or any other material you choose. Be creative!

Circle of Knowledge   You have three (3) minutes to list as many insects as you can.

Team Members:

1. _____   4. _____

2. _____   5. _____

3. _____   6. _____

Recorder: _____

Pre-/Self-/Posttest

Name: _____   Date: _____

1. List, in order, the four stages in the life cycle of a butterfly.
2. Describe what happens when the butterfly begins to emerge from the *chrysalis.*
3. List and define three (3) vocabulary words related to the butterfly.
4. Draw a picture of a butterfly. Label the body parts.
5. Tell three (3) interesting things you know about butterflies.

Resource Alternatives

Books
Aliki. *My five senses.* New York: Thomas Y. Crowell, 1962.
Collier, Ethel. *Who goes there in my garden?* New York: Scott, 1963.
Conklin, Gladys. *We like bugs.* New York: Holiday House, 1962.
Florian, Douglas. *Discovering butterflies.* New York: Macmillan, 1986.
Hogner, Dorothy. *Butterflies.* New York: Thomas Y. Crowell, 1962.
Nash, Pamela. *The butterfly.* Ohio: Modern Curriculum Press, 1983.
Ryder, Joanne. *Where butterflies grow.* New York: E. P. Dutton, 1989.

Filmstrips
"How Insects Help Us" (Coronet Films)
"Little Animals" (Dowling Films)
"Spring Is an Adventure" (Coronet Films)
"Spring On the Farm" (E. B. F. Films)
"Spring Brings Changes" (Churchill-Wexler Films)

Teacher-Made Resources

The Butterfly Learning Circle

Life Cycle of the Butterfly Task Cards

Vocabulary Word Box

Pic-A-Hole on Butterfly Stages

Flip Chute on Butterfly Vocabulary Words

Electroboard on Butterfly Stages

Pic-A-Hole on Butterfly Vocabulary Words

Programmed Learning Sequence: "Discovering Butterflies: Come Fly with Me."

A Final Word on Contract Activity Packages

Although Contract Activity Packages (CAPs) are not appropriate for everyone, they *are* extremely responsive to bright, independent, and/or nonconforming children—*or* to youngsters with the *potential* for becoming independent. Many little ones are self-structured; they prefer to do things *their* way. For them CAPs are perfect.

Place the equivalent of each "page" of a CAP onto large oaktag charts. Mount them, and illustrate the charts in attractive colors. If you have folded and stapled the bottom of the oaktag chart to form a pocket, and inserted into it a short tape that "reads" what is on each chart, some of the children will want to play the tape repeatedly and hear what it says. A few will be inspired to begin working with the tape's directions. Once they succeed and become involved in the interesting Activity and Reporting Alternatives of the CAP, others also will wish to try using the CAP. Gradually, motivation to work independently or in pairs will increase, and approximately 20 percent of your class will develop several skills for teaching themselves and each other many interesting facts. Beyond that, they will be increasing their ability to learn independently—perhaps the most worthwhile skill we can teach students of any age!

9

Designing Multisensory Instructional Packages to Respond to Individual Learning Styles

Multisensory Instructional Packages (MIPs) are especially appealing to primary students who find it difficult to sit quietly for long periods of time or who cannot listen to a teacher without frequently interrupting or losing attention. Using MIPs allows these youngsters to concentrate for the amount of time that suits them, take breathers whenever they wish, and then continue with their work. MIPs are not effective for students who need continual direct interaction with either adults or peers, but often the same MIP on the identical objectives or topic may be suitable for several learners at the beginning of a school year, for others a few weeks later, for others at midterm, and so on. MIPs also may be designed so that one or two of the multisensory activities can be bypassed if less concentration on the topic is necessary.

Multisensory Instructional Packages are a boon to teachers who want to individualize instruction through direct appeal to personal learning styles but cannot stretch themselves thin enough for a class full of individuals with a variety of needs and problems. Because students work independently or with a friend and the materials are self-corrective, the MIP can meet the needs of learners on several academic levels—youngsters with learning problems who require special attention; slow learners who need more time to grasp new material; average youngsters who prefer working on their own or for shorter or longer periods of time; advanced students who are capable of progressing faster than their peers; and any interested student who wants to learn about a topic, concept, or skill at the moment he or she desires, not only when the teacher is able to get to the subject. The packages do not take up much classroom space, and they are particularly well suited to home study.

As an example of what is possible in a single classroom, six or seven highly visual students might be working on a PLS on vocabulary related to community help-

319

ers; three auditory students might be listening to a tape telling stories about police officers, firefighters, and so forth; five highly kinesthetic students might be playing a Floor Game to learn community helper words (*before* they hear the tape); four or five independent youngsters might be working on a CAP on the same lesson; three extremely tactual students would be *beginning* the lesson with an Electroboard, Flip Chute, or Pic-A-Hole; and students with low perceptual strengths would be using MIP items in their first exposure through their strongest modality. Then students may exchange resources for reinforcement, but they need to *begin* correctly.

Learning Style Characteristics Responsive to Multisensory Instructional Packages

Most students do not reach full visual acuity much before the third grade and do not acquire strong auditory learning power until fifth or sixth grade at the earliest. Indeed, slow learners rarely develop strength in those two perceptual modalities.

Therefore, because of their multisensory activities, MIPs are highly motivating to primary learners, who generally respond to tactual/kinesthetical materials and usually require repetition and varied approaches through many senses before they acquire and retain new and difficult knowledge and skills. The tape, written script, and tactual and kinesthetic materials may be used over and over again until the young-

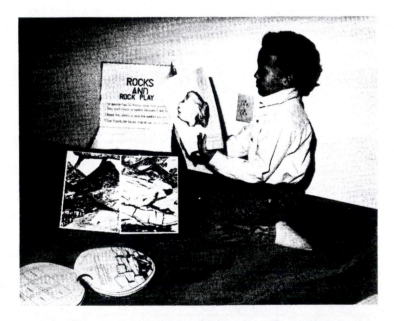

Students with either tactual/kinesthetic or no perceptual strengths, who enjoy multiple activities and find it difficult to sit still and listen, often perform extremely well with a Multisensory Instructional Package. (Photograph courtesy Center for the Study of Learning and Teaching Styles, St. John's University.)

sters master the objectives of the package.

Each MIP focuses on a single objective or concept to be taught. This isolated goal is well suited to the recalcitrant learner who often finds it difficult to concentrate on more than one thing at a time. Young high achievers may respond with strong interest to an MIP if challenging games and more difficult items are included.

MIPs are especially appropriate for those youngsters who require structure. The step-by-step procedures provide clear, sequenced directions that are repeated in a variety of ways until success is achieved.

Students who prefer working alone usually enjoy this multisensory method immensely. They can take the materials to an instructional area in the room, to the library, or even to their homes to work on intensively without the distractions of the classroom and their peers.

MIPs appeal to all perceptual strengths. By definition, they include visual, auditory, tactual, and kinesthetic activities. Even a student with only a single perceptual strength is likely to learn and to complete objectives because everything that is taught is introduced and reinforced through the four major learning senses.

Teachers should be aware of those children who prefer instructional packages but who lack responsibility. Piecemeal success on portions of the package should be promoted. Careful monitoring will help those students build responsibility. At times it may be necessary for the teacher or selected peers to work with those youngsters who require interaction with an authority figure or friends to stimulate learning.

Generally speaking, instructional packages are ideal for primary students who require structure and who can be sufficiently motivated by their multisensory activities to progress independently and successfully. MIPs may be signed out for home study. Instructions on the tapes guide students through each of four multisensory activities. The first one used should respond to each individual's perceptual strength—whichever has the highest score on the Learning Style Inventory: Primary (LSI:P) assessment.

Learning Style Characteristics to Which Multisensory Instructional Packages Can Be Accommodated

MIPs can be taken to wherever the light, temperature, and design of the physical environment are exactly as the student wishes them to be. Because they are portable and may be worked on alone, the choices of where to use this resource belong to the student, who may select the amount of light, the degree of temperature, and the kind of design in which he or she feels most comfortable. However, many primary students will need your guidance in selecting their best learning environments.

Motivation is often developed or stimulated through these packages because of (1) the choice that students have in their selection or in the topic to be studied, (2) the way the MIPs accommodate to the environmental and physiological elements of learning style, (3) the control that youngsters exercise over the amount and pace of learning in which they engage at a given time, and (4) the academic progress that is virtually assured by the package's multisensory repetition.

*Students who enjoy working with peers and/or find a particular topic
or subject difficult to master will learn most easily through a Multisensory Instructional Package. (Photograph courtesy Center for the Study
of Learning and Teaching Styles, St. John's University, New York).*

MIPs accommodate three other important aspects of learning style—intake,
time of day, and mobility. It is easy to take advantage of intake while working independently on an MIP. Raw vegetables, fruit, raisins, or other nutritious foods can be
available in a bowl wherever the youngster is working, provided that rules have been
established beforehand for access to, eating, and discarding them, and care of the
premises.

MIPs may be used at any time of the day or evening without interfering with
others and without interrupting other scheduled activities. Therefore, students can
select or be assigned the most appropriate and effective time to complete an MIP.

Many primary students cannot sit still or work in one place for a long time. A
student may take the package with him, spread it out, walk away, then come back,
sprawl, kneel, or just sit. Because the activities themselves provide action and movement, mobility also is well served by this method.

Case Studies Describing Students Whose Learning Styles Are Complemented by Multisensory Instructional Packages

*Billy looked around. He couldn't seem to follow the teacher's instructions. They were
printed on a sheet but they didn't make sense to him. He turned to his neighbor, Ed, and*

Auditory students may need to hear *instructions or directions; pictures or words alone may not be effective for them. Multisensory Instructional Packages provide a taped version of the written instructions. (Photograph courtesy of Brightwood Elementary School, Greensboro, North Carolina).*

asked what he was supposed to do after finishing the second problem. Before Ed could respond, the teacher called out impatiently, "Billy, the directions are printed for you. All you have to do is look at the pictures and the arrows. The sheet tells you what to do."

Auditory students may need to hear instructions or directions; pictures or words alone may not be effective for them. Instructional packages provide a taped version of the written instructions.

Amy was creative. She liked to put games together without reading their assembly directions. Most of the time she made them work well, but occasionally she ruined them when she did not read the instruction sheets. She repeated this pattern at school when she plunged ahead on assignments and answered questions that she had not really understood. Her projects, too, though inspired, frequently contained many errors or were not completed because of Amy's cavalier approach to directions.

Students who require experience with structure, direction, sequence, a single focus, and logical steps will benefit from the use of MIPs.

John slammed his book down. The others looked at him. The teacher called John to her and asked what was wrong. "It's the kids, I guess," explained John. "Every time I start working everybody talks to me. I can't get anything done!" Students who work best alone may find MIPs to their liking.

Multisensory Instructional Packages may be used alone, in a pair, or in a group of three or four. (Photograph courtesy Center for the Study of Learning and Teaching Styles, St. John's University, New York.)

Susie smiled. She played the tape again; her fingers traced the words in the written script as she listened. She understood perfectly! For the first time, reading had become fun. After she finished the touching and feeling game, she began to build the map with the pieces in the MIP. She told her teacher that she wanted a new package tomorrow.

Multisensory Instructional Packages are ideal for those who need to learn through a perceptual strength that is not usually complemented in classrooms and for those who require reinforcement through more than one modality.

How Multisensory Instructional Packages Facilitate Academic Achievement

Multisensory Instructional Packages are self-contained teaching units that appeal to students with no perceptual strengths who have previously been unmotivated. All packages have certain basic elements in common:

1. *Each package focuses on a single concept.* Whether the package focuses on a unit such as pets or dinosaurs or a theme such as "getting along," students know precisely what the focus is and can decide if it is appealing as a new topic or useful in

Students with tactual or kinesthetic strengths who are not succeeding in the auditory/visual mode—or who enjoy a variety of activities—eagerly embrace a Multisensory Instructional Package box filled with attractive instructional items. This one, "Whales: A Whale of a Tale!," is like a treasure chest of ways to discover answers to the objectives required for this topic. Note the Electroboard, Pic-A-Hole, Flip Chute with a whale on top, Floor Game, Programmed Learning Sequence, and script that enables the youngster to read what is provided on the audio tape. (Photograph courtesy Center for the Study of Learning and Teaching Styles, St. John's University, New York).

reinforcing a previously learned skill. The cover and dual title (analytic and global) always reveal what the package contains.

2. *At least four senses are used to learn the contents.* A typewritten script that is repeated by the teacher's taped voice gives clear directions to students to construct, manipulate, piece together, write, draw, complete, play, and in several ways use their sense of touch and their entire body in kinesthetic activities related to the package's objectives.

3. *Feedback and evaluation are built in.* The package includes tests, and students may respond by writing, taping, or showing results. Correct answers and responses may be checked as the items to be mastered are completed. The directions allow for immediate feedback and self-evaluation. Mistakes can be corrected through repetition of the taped and printed directions and by comparing the student's answers with ones prepared by the games and activities.

4. *Learning is private and is aimed at individual learning styles.* Only the teacher and student know how well the youngster is doing. Self-image and success are enhanced as progress increases without peer competition for the slower students. The multisensory approach; the colorful materials and packaging; the option of working alone; the motivating choices; the selection of when, where, and how to work; and the ability to move about and to eat if necessary make the instructional package an effective teaching aid for many students.

A Step-by-Step Guide to Designing a Multisensory Instructional Package

Step 1. Identify the topic. For example, you may want your students to understand concepts or acquire skills related to curriculum items such as nutrition, vowels, blends, farm animals, number facts, and so forth.

Step 2. List the information you want the student to learn about the topic.

Step 3. Plan to tape-record simple learning objectives for your students. Use verbs like *explain, describe, list,* and *name.* For example, if you were constructing a package on nutrition, the taped objective might be: "By the time you finish this package, you should be able to list all the good foods you could eat for breakfast. (For specific instructions, see the section of this chapter on 'How to Tape Directions for Instructional Packages.')"

Step 4. Pretend you are teaching your class the most important information concerned with the selected topic. Think through exactly how you would explain what the children need to remember and call that information "objectives." Tape-record the objectives.

Step 5. Develop a visual, a tactual, and a kinesthetic activity that emphasize these objectives in different ways. Write the directions for each of the activities exactly as they should be taped.

Step 6. Make up a short test that will reveal whether the student has learned the objectives (what they need to learn) after using the package. This may be recorded as well as shown on sheets with drawings and diagrams.

Step 7. Use a colorful box with an illustration or design that reveals the topic and contents. Cover the entire box, including the typewritten topic and contents, with clear contact paper, or laminate it to ensure longevity.

Examples of Appropriate Instructional Package Content

Language Arts:
Parts of speech, correct grammar, and selected skills, such as the following:

New Vocabulary Words	Capital Letters
Periods and Question Marks	Using New Words

Making up a Story	Vowels
How Did It End?	Blends
Following Directions	The Alphabet
Putting Things into the Right Order	Consonants

Social Studies:

Map skills, geographical locations, community workers, common interests, such as:

Safety	Transportation
Community Helpers	Stop and Go
Pets	Finding Your House
Your Family	What's in a Post Office?
Farm Animals	Native Americans
Dinosaurs	Doing Your Best

Mathematics:

Telling time, counting, using money, sets, shapes, or signs:

How Many?	Measurement
Clocks	A Set of Three
Telling Time	Money
Numbers	Shapes
Adding	Counting
Subtracting	Triangles

Science:

Explaining sources of power, food, growth, and health.

Healthful Foods	Colors
Nutrition	Seeds
Magnets	Your Teeth
The Seasons	Wind
Weather	Rain and Snow
Temperature	Flying

These topics constitute the analytic part of the title. You would need to develop a global counterpart for each.

How to Tape Directions for Instructional Packages

The cassette tape is perhaps the most important part of a Multisensory Instructional Package. To be effective, the tape must provide simple, concise directions and explanations so that students can use the package without your assistance. The following suggestions can help you to develop a good tape:

1. State the objectives clearly and simply.
2. Speak slowly, and vary your speech pattern, tone, and inflection to add listening interest. Be dramatic, but not overly so.
3. Avoid picking up background noises or taping where electrical appliances can cause interference.
4. Use explicit directions for each action that the child must take. For example, request that the package's cover be placed onto the table, that items be taken out carefully, that each envelope be returned to the box at the end, and so on.
5. Pause after giving directions so that the listener has time to consider them and carry them out. To allow longer periods of time, you could say, "Turn off the tape recorder while you are putting these materials away. Remember to turn the recorder back on when you are ready to continue."
6. Don't ask questions that require only "yes" or "no" responses. Avoid saying, "Are you ready to begin the next activity?" or "Did you know the answer to that riddle?" Instead, say, "I hope you are ready for the next activity! Please take out the blue box with the cotton cloud on it." Or, "I hope you knew that the answer to that riddle was a clock! A clock has 'hands' but never washes them!"
7. Be certain that the tape is completely self-instructional. Put yourself into the student's place and see if you can work alone without assistance or additional resources and without having to leave the area.
8. Repeat important directions or difficult passages in a slightly different way to reinforce them in an interesting manner.
9. Use good grammar and appropriate vocabulary.
10. Be certain that the tape and the materials are self-corrective. If you ask questions, pause sufficiently and then provide answers.
11. Use supplementary sounds (music, bells, animal imitations, other people's voices).
12. Use a good tape recorder and fresh batteries. Place the microphone in a comfortable position for you. Place a "Taping" sign on your door to avoid bells and other intrusions; take the telephone off the hook; leave enough footage at the beginning of the tape so that your introduction is recorded in its entirety. Watch that the tape does not run out while you are still speaking; check the volume; and test as you are recording to be certain the pickup is clear.

Contents of the MIP

The MIP looks like a gift box. The same analytic and global title that is on the PLS and CAP is also on the box cover. Inside, the box contains the PLS for the children who: (1) need structure and are visual or tactual or (2) are tactual and very motivated. The MIP box also includes the CAP for youngsters who are (1) auditory, visual, and independent; (2) tactual and highly motivated; or (3) nonconforming. The Pic-A-Hole, Flip Chute, Electroboard, Learning Circle, and Task Cards also are included for tactual children who normally progress more slowly than their classmates. Your students may be able to make tactual and kinesthetic items for additional MIPs. With

The Multisensory Instructional Package looks like a gift box. "Boats Float" has an attractive lighthouse tower and small boat on the top cover to attract children's attention. (Photograph courtesy Center for the Study of Learning and Teaching Styles, St. John's University, New York.)

help, they can create Task Cards, Learning Circles, Flip Chutes, Puzzles, Floor Games, and Electroboards. When they make their own resources, many young students become motivated and stimulated to keep learning. Finally there is a Floor Game for kinesthetic learners.

Sample Multisensory Instructional Package Scripts

A script, which would be on tape for young children who do not read well or who need to *hear* things to remember them, is included on the inside cover of the MIP box. The purpose of the tape is to explain to children with various perceptual strengths which activity each should use *first,* so that the material is *introduced* through the individual's strongest modality. Because the instructional resources in the box will be appealing to the children, it is important that the script (tape) explains that *after* the youngsters have used the most appropriate activity to *begin* learning about this topic, they may use any or all of the additional ones (*their* choice) to reinforce. Thus, the youngster who is:

1. auditory, visual, and independent, or nonconforming, may begin learning about the topic with the CAP, but will find all the other resources listed under the Resource Alternative section of the CAP, including the PLS, the Floor Game, and the tactual materials.
2. in need of structure *begins* with the PLS and has all the miniature tactual resources built into it on the frames, but also may follow up with the Floor Game, the CAP—including its Activity and Reporting Alternatives or small-group techniques—or the larger tactual resources *afterward.*
3. kinesthetic begins with the Floor Game but then should use either tactual resources or the PLS. When those have been worked through, that child may work with the CAP.

The following transcripts and photographs of MIPs offer samples to emulate and improve on. They are provided as a guide to help you explain how children should choose those activities in which to engage first, second, or third. A child who masters all the required objectives with just one activity is not *required* to use more; continuation is by choice. However, everyone takes the unit test on the same day. If you can alter the *time* of the test to respond to children's chronobiological highs, most will perform better and earn better grades than if they are required to take the test at their energy low.

"All about Insects: Don't Bug Me," designed by teacher Eileen Clarke, and "Discovering Butterflies: Come Fly with Me!" by Phyllis Napolitano Falco capitalize on young children's fascination with moving creatures. The "Bean Bug" game in the first, and the award of the two chances at the basketball hoop in the second, are likely to be interesting to them, too. Later, Denise Sullivan's script on whales provides a longer, more descriptive approach.

MIP Script for "All about Insects: Don't Bug Me!"

Hello, I'm very glad you chose to learn about insects. By the time you finish the activities in this package, you should be able to identify many insects and many facts about them.

There are seven activities in this package: the Flip Chute, Task Cards, a Pic-A-Hole, an Electroboard, a butterfly-shaped book called a PLS, a beanbag game, and a Contract Activity Package. Listen to this entire tape before you do any of the activities. It will help you decide the activity with which you begin learning about bugs. *Afterward,* you may use all the other activities that appeal to you.

Let's look at the Flip Chute first. There are 13 cards that will help you identify and learn the names of 13 different insects. The other activities will help you to learn other interesting facts about insects. Place the *picture* side of the card (facing you) into the top opening of the Flip Chute, and the *name* of that insect should come out from the bottom. If you study the name and the picture, I bet you remember at least two (2) that you didn't know before!

If you are *kinesthetic,* go to the beanbag game *first.* You may play this game with one other person or in teams. This is the way to play the game:

First place each fact card, fact side up, into the small rectangles on the game sheet. One player tosses the Bean Bug onto one of the insects. That player must choose a fact card about that insect. If the card does tell about the insect, the player keeps the card and the next person goes. If the fact is not correct for that insect, it is returned to the game sheet and then the next person goes. The game ends when all the cards have been taken. The winner is the one with the most cards. Have fun with the beanbags—I mean beanbugs!

If you are *tactual,* you will enjoy starting with the Electroboard, the Pic-A-Hole, the Flip Chute, and the Task Cards in any order you like. You have used these many times in this class and should feel comfortable learning through them.

If you like to work alone and *enjoy following directions,* go to the PLS first. It is *shaped* like a real insect! It has a tape to read a wonderful story to you and to tell you just what to do.

If you like to work alone and you want to do things your way, try the Contract Activity Package first. This package has tapes to help you work in *your* way. I can't wait to see all the creative things you do with the Contracts Activity Alternatives!

I hope you enjoy doing the activities you choose, because I really had fun making them for you. Remember, you may use the activities anywhere in the room that matches your learning style. I know you will take very good care of everything and that you will put each activity back into the MIP box carefully. Please remember to rewind this tape when you are finished. Goodbye for now, and I hope no one "bugs" you while you work!"

MIP Script for "Discovering Butterflies: Come Fly with Me"

Hello! I am very glad you chose this package on "Discovering Butterflies." I do hope you enjoy working with it! By the time you finish this package, you should be able to identify certain characteristics about butterflies. You should be able to: (1) *name the four stages in the life cycle of the butterfly;* (2) *identify and understand vocabulary words about the butterfly;* (3) *name the body parts of a butterfly, and* (4) *identify different types of butterflies.*

Now let's have some fun concentrating on important vocabulary about the characteristics of the butterfly. If you are tactual, look inside the "Discovering Butterflies" box and take out the Task Cards. Place them in front of you. You can choose to work with either the blue side or the red side. These Task Cards are a game that will help you remember butterfly characteristics. Separate them on the desk top or the floor—wherever you prefer! When you piece them together carefully, the parts will form a butterfly.

You also should plan to try the butterfly Flip Chute. This activity also will help you recognize important butterfly characteristics. You've used a Flip Chute many times in this class, and this one works the same way.

Another tactual activity is the Pic-A-Hole. Its cards will ask questions about the butterfly. It is self-correcting because, if you choose the correct answer, the card will slip out easily; if your answer was not correct, you'll need to try again until it is!

This photograph shows the Multisensory Instructional Package "Discovering Butterflies: Come Fly with Me!" (in this text). (Photograph courtesy Center for the Study of Learning and Teaching Styles, St. John's University, New York.)

Look at the Electroboard. The Electroboard will test your knowledge about the butterfly. Your answer is correct when the light lights and beeps! Won't *that* be fun?! How many beeps can you produce with this resource?

If you like structure and are visual or tactual, the Programmed Learning Sequence (PLS) will help you discover butterflies. You may use the tape in the box glued to its back cover if you would like to hear the PLS read to you.

If you like working alone and enjoy auditory or visual activities, take out the CAP. This gives you choices of activities to do *after* you learn about butterflies.

If you are kinesthetic, the Floor Game also teaches about butterflies. Place the butterfly cards in the center along with the salt and pepper in their places. Start at the pepper. Move from the napkin, to the dish, to the cup, and so on. Roll the die to see who goes first. Using the fork, knife, and spoon playing pieces, move the correct number of spaces on the die. A question is asked that you need to answer. If you answer correctly, you go again. If not, the next player goes. Every time you land on the napkin, you get two chances at the basketball hoop. Move ahead one space for each basket scored. The player who reaches the salt first, wins!

Now the choice is yours:

- If you are a highly *visual* learner and need *structure,* you should begin with the PLS. If you are *tactual and motivated,* you may begin with the PLS too.

- If you are a *motivated auditory* or *visual* learner and do *not prefer structure,* you may want to begin with the CAP. If you like to do things *your* way, a CAP might be just what the doctor ordered!
- If you enjoy *variety* and *tactual* and/or *kinesthetic* materials, you may want to begin with the Flip Chute, the Electroboard, the Pic-A-Hole, the Task Cards, and the Floor Game. You should use several of these tactual resources, because they will help you remember the important information in this unit.

Remember that you may begin with any material that matches your learning style. After that, you may use any other material in this MIP box. I hope you enjoy this package, because I enjoyed making it for you. Thank you, and goodbye for now. Please let me know how much you liked learning through these resources. When you take the test at the end of this unit, you'll be showing me how well you learned.

Looking at the sky and wondering about the planets, stars, constellations, and solar system captures the imagination of most young children. "Exploring the Planets: Give Me Some Space" by Linda Harris is certain to get and hold primary youngsters' attention. You might decide to Xerox the CAP, PLS, and tactual/kinesthetic instructional resources related to this MIP (see the appropriate chapters), have your students color them, and assign them as "Extra Special Learning" for those who show interest. That initial attention will expand, and, before long, many of your charges will be asking to learn about the distance between the planets and Earth. Mrs. Harris's first-graders were bright and interested in many things, and she used similar resources with them frequently; thus, this script represents minimal directions for children who have had experience with previous MIPs.

MIP Script for "Exploring the Planets: Give Me Some Space"

I am so happy that you have decided to work with this package. Inside this box, you will find enjoyable and interesting ways to learn about the planets. By the time you complete these activities, you should be able to define the words *solar system, star, planet,* and *orbit.* You also will be able to identify the *star in our solar system and name all nine* (9) *planets!* If you are especially interested in the planets, you may learn *how close* and *how far away* those planets are from the sun.

I think you will enjoy using the different activities in this package. If you need time to complete an activity or if you want to take a short break, you may stop the tape and relax. When you are ready to continue, turn the tape on again. You will need plenty of room to work when you use this package. Place the cover in a spot where it won't be in your way and won't be damaged. Now look inside the box.

In this box, you find a Flip Chute that looks like an *astronaut.* The cards for the Flip Chute are in the astronaut's *backpack.* You also will find an Electroboard, Task Cards, a Pic-A-Hole, a Planet Floor Game, a Programmed Learning Sequence, and a Contract Activity Package. Use these activities in the order that most matches *your* learning style. If you forgot *your* strengths, look at the Wall Chart on the side of our classroom, find your name, and read about your strengths. Please complete at least two (2) different tactual activities and one (1) other of your choosing. They will help you learn about the sun and the planets in our solar system.

After you have finished an activity, please carefully place it back inside this box. If you use the tape attached to an activity, rewind it and return it to the box, too. You may use as many activities as you like, but begin with the one that most matches your style. When you have completed at least two (2) activities, you can check to see how much you have learned by trying the test at the end. Ask your teacher to see how well you did. Now, if you are ready to explore the planets, hold your breath for a second and get ready to Blast Off! I think you will enjoy the trip!"

"Antonyms: Opposites Attract" was designed by Ann Battipaglio, Christine Rutigliano, and Ingred Von Lepal, three teachers who thought it would be more fun—and less time-consuming—to create this resource together than alone. They designed this Multisensory Instructional Package around a circus theme—always an interesting topic for youngsters. This MIP script is comprehensive and all-inclusive, perhaps a reflection of how well peer-oriented students of any age can achieve when they work together on something of mutual interest.

Intelligent six-, seven-, or eight-year-olds often enjoy learning about words that mean the opposite of each other. One way of introducing this topic globally is to ask: "Have you ever been in a 'nonconforming' mood and had someone ask you, 'Why do you do the *opposite* of what I tell you to do?' The next time that happens, just say, 'Because I feel like an *antonym!*' Can you guess what an *antonym* is?"

Before you begin to *talk* about antonyms (auditory learning for the children), open an MIP (which you can produce by copying this script), and use the guidelines in each of the appropriate chapters to create your own CAP, PLS, and tactual/kinesthetic materials. Then say, "This Multisensory Instructional Package will teach you all about *antonyms* and explain why you behave like one when you are in the mood to do so!"

MIP Script for "Antonyms: Opposites Attract"

(Turn on the MIP tape for children when they are ready to begin using this package.)

Hello! This package has many enjoyable and interesting activities that explain what *antonyms* are and how to identify them. The activities all center on the circus, and many of the antonyms that you will learn describe circus characters.

You will enjoy learning about antonyms through this package, but if you get tired and want to stop or rest, just turn off the tape and relax. When you complete at least two (2) different kinds of activities, or more if you wish, or if you care to stop between them, please turn off the tape you are using, rewind it, and carefully return it and the other materials that you are using to the box.

Let's begin! Get ready to "Step Right Up and See the Best Antonym Show on Earth!" Ah! But what if I'd said, "Step Right Up and See the *Worst* Antonym Show on Earth?" That would have been the *opposite* of the "best" show, and wouldn't it have made you feel very differently about using this package?

Or, suppose I'd said, "Step right *down*" instead of "Step right *up*"— wouldn't you be stepping in the *opposite* direction? Well, that's what antonyms are all about! Opposites!

Activity 1

Look into the box and find a booklet that is shaped like a circus tent. Go ahead! I will wait for you. (Pause) I hope you've found the tentlike book with red and white stripes and a little yellow flag on top that says, "The Circus Tent Antonym Book." Inside that booklet you will find information on antonyms.

Open the booklet and look at the first page; it has colored circus balloons all around it. (Pause) The word *Antonym* is printed at the top of the page in large letters. If you have *visual* or *auditory* strengths and enjoy *structure*, begin learning about antonyms with this programmed story. If your strength is *tactual*, start with the tactual resources—the Task Cards or the Electroboard—and *then* listen to this story. If you prefer to begin with the Floor Game because of your *kinesthetic* strength, start there and then use this programmed story afterward.

If you are beginning with this programmed story, let's read *The Circus Antonym Book* together.

Robby was tired of being told what to do. His mother always told him what to do. His dad did the same thing. So did his big brother Ricky and even Ricky's friend. Robby felt like being an *antonym*. Can you imagine what it means to "be like an antonym"?

A word that means the *opposite* of another word is an antonym. The first part of antonym, *ant,* comes from the Greek prefix *anti*, which means "against." The last part of antonym is the Greek word *onym*, which means "name." Thus, a word that is *against*, or opposite to, another word—or name—is called an *antonym*.

Do you remember when I said that the circus was the best show on earth, and then I changed it to the *worst* show on earth? *Best* and worst are *antonyms;* they mean exactly the *opposite* of each other. Stepping *down* would be the opposite of stepping *up*. *Down* and *up* are opposites; they are antonyms.

Look at the two sentences on the first page of *The Circus Antonym Book*. They have underlined antonyms in them:

- The <u>smallest</u> balloon is yellow.
- The <u>largest</u> balloon is red.

The word *smallest* is the opposite of the word *largest*. The word *largest* is the opposite of the word *smallest*. They are opposite to each other; they are *antonyms*.

Turn the page and let's read it together: The two sentences at the top of the second page each contain one underlined word. Those words are antonyms; they are the opposite of each other. (Pause)

- This clown is <u>happy.</u>
- This clown is <u>sad.</u>

Happy and *sad* are opposites; these two words are antonyms. You should be able to recognize the two antonyms in the next sentence. See whether you can!

A long time ago, Gonzola was the shortest gorilla in the circus, but now he is the tallest.

Which two words are antonyms? Which words are the *opposite* of each other? I hope you recognize that *tallest* and *shortest* are the two antonyms.

Gonzola was the *shortest* gorilla when he was a baby. He was born into a circus family of gorillas. Both his mother and father were very tall, and when he was a baby, they would jump from one trapeze to another with little Gonzola snuggled tightly in their arms. Now, many years later, Gonzola is the *tallest* circus gorilla that anyone has ever seen!

Please turn to the next page. Let's read:

- The tiger looks like a wild animal, but George, the monkey, appears to be tame. (Pause)

Name the antonyms. Are you ready for the answer? (Pause) The word *wild* is the opposite, or the antonym, of the word *tame*. You would not want a wild tiger *or* a wild monkey nearby!

Please turn to the next page. Let's read:

- Proud Piggy is standing on his hind legs, but Pinkey Poodle is walking on his front legs. (Pause)

The antonyms in that sentence are *hind* and *front*. Hind means *back* and is the opposite of *front*. I wonder whether you knew that!

Turn to the next page. Let's read:

- Rocco the Great is a muscular man.
- Elephant Ella has a flabby tummy. (Pause)

Do you know which words are the antonyms? (Pause). Those are not easy! If you thought *muscular* and *flabby* were opposites of each other, you were able to recognize the correct antonyms in those two sentences. When your flesh or muscles sag, you are *flabby!* When you have big muscles, you are *muscular.*

Please turn to the next page. Let's read:

- Jimmy juggles while leaning on his left leg.
- Ringmaster Ricardo jumps through hoops on only his right foot. (Pause)

The words (Pause) and (Pause) were the antonyms in this example. What were they? (Pause) *Left* and *right* are the antonyms.

Let's read further: See if you can find two words in the first sentence that are antonyms to two words in the second sentence.

- Flying Fran swings high in the sky.
- Ivan, the bear, rides his bicycle low on the ground. (Pause)

I hope you are able to discover all four antonyms. In the first sentence, *high* is the opposite of the word *low* in the second sentence. In addition, the word *sky* is an antonym for the word *ground* in the second sentence. *Sky* and *ground* are opposites.

Turn to the last page in our book. Look at the list of words on the right. Can you think of antonyms for each of them? Let's see. What would be the opposite of:

black horses	_____ horses
jumping high	jumping _____
happy elephants	_____ elephants
big hoops	_____ hoops
a noisy barker	a _____ barker
a packed or filled tent	an _____ tent
midget cars	_____ cars
baby boys	baby _____

Have you made your decisions? Let's see whether you really know what antonyms are!

- The opposite of *black* horses would be *white* horses.
- The opposite of jumping *high* would be jumping *low.*
- An antonym for *happy* is *sad,* or *unhappy.* Therefore, the opposite of *happy* elephants would be *sad,* or *unhappy,* elephants.
- The opposite of *noisy* would be *quiet.* Therefore, an antonym for a *noisy* barker would be a *quiet* barker.

- An antonym for a *packed* or *filled* tent would be an *empty* tent.
- An antonym for a *midget* car would be just the opposite—a *giant* car!

Finally,

- The opposite of a baby *boy* would be a baby *girl. Girl* is the antonym for *boy!*

Now we are at the end of *The Circus Tent Antonym Book.* I hope you enjoyed reading this book and learning about antonyms.

Please return the book to the big box. (Pause) After you turn off the tape recorder, be certain you rewind the tape. Then return the tape to the tape box. Return the script, too, by placing it into the big box. You now may turn off this tape, but look for the cassette labeled #2. If you feel ready to continue learning about antonyms, insert it into the tape recorder and get ready for another activity.

Activity 2

Hello again! You now are ready for the tactual activity in this box. Look into the big box again, and you will see a colorful small box with a label that reads, "Circus Ring Task Cards." Please take the smaller box out of the big box, and take the cover off it; then put it to one side away from you. (Pause)

Take out the cards that are in this smaller box. Place them in front of you. These Task Cards are a game that will give you a chance to practice matching pairs of antonyms.

There should be 16 different cards. Spread them out in front of you. (Pause) You really have 8 sets of Task Cards because your task is to fit the parts together to form both question and answer sections. Let's try to match one pair together. (Pause).

Pick up the card that has the word *late* (spell: *l-a-t-e*) written on it. (Pause) Try to find the *antonym,* or the word that has the *opposite meaning of late.* (Pause) I hope you found the correct word. The antonym for *late* is *early.* If you found the word *early* and placed it side by side with its antonym, *late,* you formed a circus tent. If you did, you found the correct answer. *Early* is e-a-r-l-y (Spell).

See if you can match each pair of antonyms correctly. If you do, each matched pair will fit together to form a circus tent. Turn off the tape recorder while you are matching the Task Cards, but remember to turn the tape back on after you have finished. You may now turn off the tape recorder. (Pause)

Now that you've turned the tape on again, I guess you've matched the Task Card sets. You also may have noticed that it was fairly easy to match the antonyms correctly because they are *shape-coded.* Also, on the back of each matching pair of cards was a matching symbol—like clown hats or monkey faces.

Did you match the following antonyms?

- *water* and *land*
- *fat* and *thin*
- *weak* and *strong*
- *tall* and *short*
- *rich* and *poor*
- *smile* and *frown*
- *love* and *hate*
- *light* and *dark*

It would be wonderful if you had almost *all* those antonyms correctly matched! But that is not easy to do the first time!

Please put the Task Cards back into the small box and place the cover carefully on top. (Pause) Put the small box into the bigger one. (Pause) After you turn off this tape recorder, be certain to rewind the Task Card tape. Then return the tape to the big box.

You may now turn off the tape—unless you would like to try another activity to be *certain* that you can explain what antonyms are. If you would, continue. If you have had enough about antonyms, ask your teacher for the antonym posttest, and see how well you can do!

Activity 3

Hi! This activity will be more difficult than the first two—but, of course, you know more now than you did before! Try it! See how well you do!

You do not have to look into the large box to play this game, because it is right here on the tape. All you need to do is to sit back, listen carefully, and relax. You are going to hear several difficult words. See if you can find words that are their opposites. We are looking for antonyms for the words that you hear. I hope you are ready to begin!

Now listen carefully.

What do you think an antonym for the word *beautiful* would be? (Pause) What is the opposite of *beautiful?* Can you think of a word? *I* can! *Ugly* is the opposite of *beautiful*—or maybe even *homely.*

Listen for the next word.

- An antonym for *noisy* is _____. (Pause)
- The answer is *quiet* or *still.*

Let's try another.

- The next word is *soft*. What would be an antonym for *soft?* (Pause)
- If you thought of *hard,* you are correct.

Get ready for the next word.

- Asleep. What is an antonym for *asleep?*
- Do you know? I would choose *awake.* If you are not *asleep,* you are *awake.*

Let's try a very difficult sentence. I will say part of it, and you give me the remainder by saying an antonym. Let's try.

- *Dog* is to *cat* as *round* is to _____.
- What do you think the answer is? What *could* it be? (Pause)

What is the opposite of something that is *round?* It might be *square,* or *oblong,* or *long,* or *straight.* There are several antonyms for *round*—and all would be correct. *Any* word that is the opposite of another word is an antonym.
Let's try one more.

- *High* is to *low* as *wide* is to _____. (Pause)
- That answer is *narrow,* because narrow is the opposite of wide.

Here is another example.

- *Crying* is to *laughing* as *frowning* is to _____. (Pause)
- Did you say *smiling?* If you did, you were correct.

This will be the last exercise in this activity. Listen carefully.

- The antonym for *clean* is _____. (Pause)
- *Dirty,* or *filthy,* or any other word that has the opposite meaning of *clean* would be the answer.

We are now at the end of this activity. I hope you learned from working with this tape, and were able to identify more antonyms. After you turn off the tape recorder, be certain you rewind the tape and return it to the tape box. Then return the script to the big box. You now may turn off the tape.

Activity 4

If you remain interested in seeing whether you can explain what antonyms are and whether you can recognize words that are opposite from each other, you will enjoy this last activity.
Find the large plastic sheet that is folded inside the large box and take it out. Carefully spread it onto the floor. You can see the large drawing of Simba the Lion on the sheet, but notice that Simba is divided into many sections. Each of those sections has a word on it.

Look into the big box once more and take out the colorful envelope that is labeled "Puzzle Pieces for Activity 4." (Pause) Open the envelope and take out all the pieces. These pieces also have words written on them. Those words are *antonyms* to the words you see written on the plastic sheet. If you can match the words on the loose pieces to their correct antonyms of "Simba the Lion" correctly, the pieces of the puzzle will fit exactly onto Simba.

You may turn off the tape recorder until after you have completed the puzzle. However, remember to turn it back on when you have finished! Now turn off the tape recorder. (Pause)

I'm glad you came back to this tape. I hope you were able to find the correct pairs of antonyms and to put poor Simba back together. If you did, Simba must be very happy.

Please return all the loose puzzle pieces to their envelope and close the envelope flap. (Pause) After that, place the envelope back into the big box. (Pause) Now take the large plastic sheet and fold it carefully so that it can fit back into the box. (Pause)

After you turn off this tape recorder, be certain that you rewind the tape. Then return the tape to its box. Finally, return the script to the big box. Now— turn this tape off . . . and remember what antonyms are! Goodbye!

Assessment

This is a test to see how much you know about antonyms. If you know a great deal, then you really do not need to use this package. If you need to know more than you do, this package may be an interesting and enjoyable way for you to learn: (1) what antonyms are and (2) how to identify them. Answer these questions as well as you can!

1. What does the word *antonym* mean? _____

2. Draw a line from the word in the *left*-hand column (far away from the circus tent) to its *antonym* in the *right*-hand column.

small	low
scarce	sour
expensive	beautiful
homely or ugly	full
filthy	cheap
empty	plentiful
sweet	clean
high	big

3. Write an antonym for the underlined word in the following sentences:

   a. The bread tasted quite *stale.* _____

   b. The river was very *swift* _____

    c. Bob put a *thin* coat of paint on his model plane. _____

    d. The doctor said that Susan was a *healthy* girl. _____

    e. The circus tent was *dark* inside. _____

4. In which country did the word *antonym* originate (begin)? _____

Bonus question—for *Extremely* knowledgeable people only!

5. The prefix of the word antonym is *anti*—which means _____

    Irene Kozak used a sea-adventure theme to capture her students' attention to study "The Humpback Whale: Have a Whale of a Time!" Almost all the instructional resources she designed—the PLS, the Task Cards, the Floor Game—were designed in the shape of a whale, and the other materials each had illustrations of whales on them. Children fondled the materials and were observed running their fingers and hands around the whale replicas. Imagine how they would react to materials shaped like dinosaurs, flying witches, ghosts. Imagine teaching addition or subtraction through 7 with characters of the Seven Dwarfs! Here is how Mrs. Kozak introduced the concept.

MIP Script for "The Humpback Whale: Having A Whale of a Time!"

Welcome aboard! You are going to take an exciting journey across many oceans to search for information on the humpback whale. Buckle up your life preserver and get ready for a thrilling voyage!

    If you prefer to work alone and enjoy following directions, begin with the PLS. It is a storybook shaped like a whale. If you like to work alone but you enjoy doing things *your* way, start with the CAP. It looks a little bit like a thin notebook. If you know you are kinesthetic, you will enjoy beginning with the Floor Game. If you are tactual, you may want to begin with the Electroboard, Pic-A-Hole, Task Cards, or Flip Chute. Happy sailing!—and do *not* be afraid. I promise that you will not get seasick on this ocean trip!"

    Denise Sullivan initiated a totally different approach to teaching her young pupils about whales. She created a large, soft, cuddly, appealing whale and its little calf and used them as characters. She mounted one on the top of the MIP box and the other on the Flip Chute. Those two personalities told the story of whales and simultaneously captured the children's interest and hearts.

    Capitalizing on children's fascination with large animals, particularly those with "personality," and on their natural yearning for adventurous "things to do," provided an interesting unit without any danger of boredom or loss of attention. Denise permitted her students to begin with the Flip Chute because most were strongly tactual. She encouraged them to use the remaining reinforcement activities by choice, as long as each child used the tactual resources *and* the Programmed Learning Sequences.

MIP Script for "The S.S. Whale Watch: Come to Sea with Winnie and Me!"

(Teacher or student turns on Introductory Tape. The MIP box is closed and closeted inside a big colored plastic bag on a table in one of the instructional areas in the classroom. It is hidden from view. The student sees the plastic bag but begins by hearing only the words on the tape.)

Welcome aboard the S.S. Whale Watch! We are about to begin a sea voyage, and we hope you will stay and join us! This voyage will be a great adventure, for it is all about whales! All ashore that's going ashore! But stay aboard if you want to see the biggest Mamma that ever lived!

> If you want to hide under your coat,
> I suggest you leave this boat.
> But if you're brave and will not fuss,
> I suggest you come along with us!

I have made a very special MIP seafaring box, for you from me! It is a treasure chest, and inside this treasure chest I have hidden many wonderful things for you to play with. They all have different names—which I will explain—but each is called an *activity*. Each activity will teach interesting things about a friend of mine—the biggest Mamma in the whole world!

Open the large plastic bag on this table. Look inside. Carefully slide the box out. This treasure chest is called an MIP Box. Look at what is on the MIP Box cover! It is Winnie the Whale! Winnie looks exactly like one of the biggest Mammas in the whole wide world—a *Whale Mamma!* Winnie is a Mamma whale, and she is my friend.

I will introduce you to Winnie, and you need not be afraid. She is a loving Mamma, and she loves all children, especially her own. *You* are called a child because you are a human baby. Winnie's child is called a *calf.* If you are interested, you can meet Winnie's calf.

You and Winnie and her calf will be shipmates on this voyage—unless you get seasick and need to stop. If you *want* to stop, just stop the tape recorder (press the red button), rewind the tape (press the yellow "Go-Back" button), take the tape out of the recorder, and place it back into its pocket on the outside of the MIP box—right below Winnie's tail.

If you want to go to sea with Winnie and me—and Winnie's calf—settle down, relax, and get your imaginary rainwear clothing ready! If you have any questions or need some help, you can get some from me. I am the Captain of this Classroom, and I am never *really* "at sea"! I am always nearby when you need me. If you get tired, you can take a rest. Just stop the tape, rewind it, take it out of the recorder, and put it into its pocket so that the next sailor can use the MIP Box.

If you remain on board with us, you will learn many interesting things on this ship. For example, the activities in this MIP Box will teach you through a storybook, the Flip Chute, the Pic-A-Hole, and the Electroboard. Then you should be able to describe:

1. What makes whales different from fish
2. How whales and you are alike
3. What *warm-blooded* means
4. How and what whales breathe
5. The kinds of babies whales have, and what they are called
6. Some of the whales' relatives
7. How whales feed themselves
8. Some things that whales do that you and *your* relatives do
9. The largest whale of all—and its name

If you are remaining on board with us, you should meet Winnie. Thar she blows! I spot Winnie the Whale on the top of the MIP Box! Gently pat her back. She likes that.

(New voice) Carefully take the large box out of the plastic bag. You will see Winnie on top.

Whale: Hello! My name is Winnie the Whale. Of course, I am a whale. I am a Mamma whale. Did you know that we whales are the largest animals in the world? We are very, very big when we are real—bigger than a truck, bigger than a tree—sometimes, bigger than a building.

If you would like to hold me, you may carry me as you work with the activities in this MIP Box. I am "Velcroed" onto the top of this box, so if you pull gently, you can carry me away with you as you work. If I were a *real* whale, however, I would be much too big for you—or anybody else—to carry! Big *and* heavy! Please remember to put me back onto the Velcro patch on the MIP Box when you stop learning through this package. Let's *dive in!*

Open the MIP Box. On the inside cover you can see a boy holding a sea shell. Carefully look for the sea shell in the box and find it. When you find the sea shell, hold it close to your ear. When you place a sea shell close to your ear and listen quietly, you should be able to hear the ocean. The ocean is where my calf and I and all our relatives live. Listen carefully. Do you hear the ocean? (Pause) If you concentrate a little more, you may be able to hear some of my relatives talking or singing. We whales are called the "Gentle Giants of the Deep," and we talk among ourselves and sing just as human animals do. When you no longer want to hear our Whale Music, place the shell back into the box.

Now carefully look for a blue box with my baby calf on top of it. That is *my* calf; her name is Gigi. The box that Gigi is sitting on is called a Flip Chute. I think you used Flip Chutes in your class before, so you probably recognize what it is. Look into the pocket on the side of the Flip Chute. Take out the cards in the pocket. On one side of each card is a question.

Let's do the first Flip Chute card together. Take the card on the top of the pile. Look at it. It reads, "Mammals breathe _____". What do *you* think mammals breathe? *You* are a mammal. What do you breathe? Whales *and* humans are both mammals. They breathe the same thing. Do you know what it is without looking at the back of the Flip Chute card?

Now hold the card so that the cut-off end is at the top (where the arrow is pointing down), and gently push the card, with the arrow pointing down, into the top slit of the Flip Chute. Let it go; it will come out the bottom slit with the answer on it. Gigi's flippers will help the perfect answer slide out the bottom slit. Be ready to catch it! Look at the answer.

Mammals breathe air.

Did you like the way Gigi flipped her flipper to get you the right answer? I hope so! You may use all the Flip Chute cards, one at a time, to learn the answers to many interesting questions about whales and our life in the ocean with our calves and our other relatives. This tape will read the correct question to you if you would like to hear the questions read. If not, you may turn the tape off. If you wish to learn about whales all by yourself, you may do that. If you prefer to work with one other friend, two of you may work together on this topic.

Try to remember as many answers as you can. This is fun, but it is very grown up. So, if you have some concern, just ask your teacher, a classmate, or Winnie. She will help you if she can. When you have finished using all the Flip Chute cards, and remember just what you can for today, turn the tape off. For now, you are on your own—with either your teacher, a friend, or Winnie!

If a child chooses to listen to the tape, it covers the entire series of Flip Chute cards; if not, the tape stops and is turned on again and moved ahead to the point indicated when the child has completed the activity. When the tape is turned on again and moved ahead, or the Flip Chute activity has been completed, it will say:

Please put all the Flip Chute cards back into their pocket. Turn me off while you do that, and turn me on again when you are ready to move on to the next activity.

(When the tape is turned on again) There are many activities in this MIP Box. Each will teach you many interesting things about Winnie the Whale and her relatives. If you like learning best tactually and remember complicated things that way, use the Pic-A-Hole or Electroboard—whichever you wish—and the tape. Insert the tape into this recorder carefully, and follow its directions. When you finish the next activity, you may take another if you would like to do so. When you have completed the Pic-A-Hole and the Electroboard, please try the Programmed Learning Sequence (PLS) storybook, "The S.S. Whale Watch." I know you will enjoy it.

If you are visual and like structure—or if you are tactual, like structure, and are really interested in whales—*begin* with the PLS storybook, then the Pic-A-

Hole, and then the Electroboard. The Captain is on deck if you need help, and you may keep Winnie near your side if you wish. Otherwise, place her back on top of the MIP box.

(Tape introducing PLS) You are holding a storybook in the shape of a big whale. I am going to read this storybook to you.

"Thar she blows! Whale Watch!" called the Captain.

This story will teach you many interesting things about whales. If you would like to hear it read to you, use this tape. If you would rather read the story by yourself, turn the tape off, "Be kind, rewind!" and place it into the plastic box glued onto the back of this storybook.

We call the pages in this book *frames.* Many frames will teach something new about whales and then ask a question about what they taught. If you wish to answer, just mark your answers with the special crayon attached to this story-book. Be certain to wipe all your answers off every frame when you have finished the book. That is important, because someone else will need to use it when you are through, and you do not want to give *your* answers away. Wipe your answers off at the end with a paper towel so the next shipmate can use the book.

(The tape will continue to read the story about whales)

(Tape for Pic-A-Hole) You have found the Pic-A-Hole!—or at least you have the Pic-A-Hole tape! The Pic-A-Hole has a red sea creature on the front. Don't be scared. It is a friendly sea creature! Tickle him gently and watch him change colors. (The sea creature is a phosphorescent stick-on, which can be purchased in many large greeting card stores.)

The Pic-A-Hole cards have questions and answers about whales on them. By now, you may even know some of the answers. Use the golf tee on the string attached to the Pic-A-Hole to show which answer you think is right. Just place the pointed end of the gold tee into the answer that looks, feels, or seems to be correct. If your answer *is* right, you will be able to gently lift the card up. If it is not the right answer, try again until you *do* find it. Let's try the first card together.

The first card reads, "Whales are _____ ." We will need to find a word that gives us a correct answer. Down at the bottom of the card are three holes. There is one possible answer above each hole. The word on the right says "fish"; the word in the middle says "mammals"; the word on the left says "dino-saurs." Do you know what whales are? Are they fish? Are they mammals? Are they dinosaurs?

Put the point of the golf tee into the hole below the word that you think is the right answer. Hold the golf tee firmly, and gently lift the card. If the card does not lift easily, you may have chosen the wrong answer. Think about the choices: *fish, mammals,* or *dinosaurs.* If your card did not lift, try another answer. Move the golf tee to your second choice and then, holding it in the hole firmly, try to lift the card. Does the large card lift? If it did, you have chosen the correct answer. If the card still does not lift, you had better try the third possibility. If the card still does not lift, bring the entire Pic-A-Hole to the Captain on the Bridge—your teacher! We will get to the bottom of this mystery!

If the card did lift, you know the answer is "mammals"; whales are mammals. Work through the remainder of the cards in the Pic-A-Hole and see how much you can learn about whales. Remember the objectives (what you should try to remember) for this unit. You should be able to describe: (1) what makes whales different from fish; (2) how whales and you are alike; (3) what *warm-blooded* means; (4) how and what whales breathe; (5) the kinds of babies whales have and what they are called; (6) who is related to whales; (7) how whales feed themselves; and (8) what the biggest whale of all is named.

You may work with this activity by yourself or with a classmate, as you choose. Concentrate on trying to "swim through" the answers to the objectives. This is like a puzzle; the pieces need to fit together—like Winnie and the top of the MIP Box! Keep working until you either know many of the answers or are tired. You do not need to learn all the answers today. Tomorrow is another day. See how many you can learn and remember this time! Next time you will remember more.

(Tape for Electroboard) You have used an Electroboard many times in this classroom. You know how it works. Find the Electroboard in the MIP Box; it is in the shape of a whale. Using the continuity tester in the box, look at the questions on the left side of the Electroboard and see whether you can find the correct answer to each question on the right side. If you remember three (3) or four (4) answers today, that will be *good!*

1. Can you describe what makes whales different from fish?
2. Also, can you describe how you and whales are alike?
3. Do you know how—and what—whales breathe? (*You* breathe the *same* thing!)
4. What are whale babies called? And what are they like?
5. Can you name the *biggest* whale of all?
6. Do you know how whales feed themselves?
7. Can you remember what whales do that human beings do too? (Maybe even *you* do some of those things, too!)

When you have found many of the answers on the Electroboard and can remember at least three (3) or four (4), stop if you wish to do so. Did you read the story book on whales? When you are finished, be certain to "Be kind—rewind!" Then put the tape, the Electroboard, and the continuity tester back inside the box. By then, it may be time to put Winnie back too. Be certain that:

- Every page in the storybook has been wiped off.
- All the tapes have been rewound and returned to the box. *This is important!*

- All the activities have been returned to the box.
- The activities are all neatly inside the box.
- Winnie is back on top.

I hope you enjoyed using this MIP! I bet you do well on the test on whales!

(Tape on Floor Game). If you are kinesthetic, the Whale Floor Game should be the *first* activity you use to begin learning about whales. If you are not kinesthetic, you can use the Whale Floor Game to review some of the information you have read or heard about whales through other activities in the MIP Box.

Place the Whale Floor Game carefully on the floor. Place it where classmates will not need to step on it. Spread out all the corners. One or two sailors can play this game, so if you would like, ask someone working on this same unit to join you. If you prefer to play it alone, you may!

Begin at "START." Answer the questions under the first whale and then move to the next whale in turn. If you are competing against yourself, call your brain "Brain Child" and your mind "Mind Child." See which part of you "wins"!

(Final tape in package, just prior to the test) I hope you enjoyed learning about whales through this Multisensory Instructional Package (the box's *real* name). I hope that Winnie is back safely on top of the box, and Gigi, her baby calf, is safely on top of the Flip Chute. Winnie likes to know that her calf is safe inside the box.

The Captain suggests that you try as many of these activities as you need to be certain that you know all the answers to the objectives for this unit. The objectives also are printed on a sheet of oaktag on the wall of our classroom. Review the answers, and, if you have forgotten a few, go back and check. You may use the storybook or the tactual or kinesthetic activity as often as you need to be certain that you remember the answers.

It is smart to *begin* with the activity that most matches your learning style. Then review the information through *different* activities. That should make this information fairly easy to remember. If you are having a problem, please see the Captain. We want all our sailors to really understand whales so that they are kind to them when they meet them jumping in the ocean, dancing with the waves, or singing. No one knows *why* whales jump. Maybe they jump because it feels good to be a whale. No one knows why they sing or dance, but they must be having a good time. We know that most whale mothers love their babies (their little calves) very much and take good care of them, just as most human mothers do.

Get ready to take the Whale of a Test. I bet you jump for joy when you see how much you remember. That happens when we enjoy learning and learn through our learning style. When you finish your test, you may just jump into the air and sing—the way whales do. *Why* do whales sing? Well, *no* one really knows, but that's another story!

Happy sailing!
Your Captain

A Final Word on Multisensory Instructional Packages

Teachers often do not have the time or patience to teach and reteach each student who needs individualized attention. Multisensory Instructional Packages can do both and offer a variety of other benefits too. They develop listening skills, encourage independent work, and teach students to follow directions. They make children aware of their own growth and, gradually, build positive self-image and confidence. They provide a new teaching method when all else has failed. MIPs may be used anywhere in the classroom, and thus they respond to individual preferences for sound versus quiet, soft or bright light, temperature, and design. They permit students who wish to work by themselves to do so while simultaneously allowing peer-oriented students to work cooperatively with one or two classmates. They minimize direct interaction between

Multisensory Instructional Packages respond to all perceptual modalities. Their activities can be sequenced so that each student learns initially *through his or her first strength and then is reinforced through two* different *senses. Note the variety of resources in the MIPs on "The Four Seasons." (Photograph courtesy Center for the Study of Learning and Teaching Styles, St. John's University, New York).*

the learner and the teacher when a poor or negative relationship exists. When students are teacher-oriented, however, the teacher's voice on the tape or directions for usage provide a temporary substitute for direct personal proximity. They provide alternative activities for youngsters who enjoy variety and ensure a specific pattern for those who feel secure with familiar strategies.

These Instructional Packages are multisensory and thus respond to all perceptual modalities. Their activities can be sequenced so that each student learns *initially* through his or her strengths and then is *reinforced* through two different senses. They are private; no one except the learner and the teacher knows who is learning what and how. This resource permits students to move while learning and be directly involved in their own instruction. All children can proceed at a pace with which they can cope—and succeed.

MIPs provide structure; youngsters who are extremely self-structured (low LSI:P scores on structure) will not enjoy Multisensory Instructional Packages as a routine, unless the content is interesting to them. Conforming students will be willing to use them; nonconformists will enjoy the choices and variety of the activities.

Gifted students can capitalize on their special creativity and talents to make MIPs for use by others. Parents can be involved by designing and developing packages, too. Once completed, these resources may be used year after year by students who enjoy learning through multisensory materials. In effect, Multisensory Instructional Packages produce a pleasant, nonconfrontational, constructive environment in which teachers who previously could not individualize instruction can do so. In addition to all these benefits, instructional packages are fun!

Notes

1. "All about Insects: Don't Bug Me" was designed by Eileen Clarke, teacher, P.S. #169, Queens, New York.
2. "Discovering Butterflies: Come Fly with Me!" was designed by Phyllis Napolitano Falco, teacher, P.S. #135, Queens, New York.
3. "Exploring the Planets: Give Me Some Space!" was designed by Linda Harris, graduate student, St. John's University, New York.
4. "Antonyms: Opposites Attract" was designed by Ann Batigpaglia, Christine Rutigliano, and Ingrid Von Lepal, three New York teachers.
5. "The Humpback Whale: Have a Whale of a Time" was designed by Irene Kozak, teacher, P.S. #107, Flushing, New York.
6. "The S.S. Whale Watch: Come to Sea with Winnie and Me!" was designed by Denise Reichter Sullivan, teacher and graduate student, St. John's University, New York.

__10__

Teaching Young Children to Read through Their Learning Style Strengths

Matching Methods to Learning Style Perceptual and Processing Styles

Prior to Urbschat's (1977) pioneering investigation, few educators would have believed that most elementary children are *not* auditory. An auditory student is able to remember approximately three-quarters of what is heard during a normal classroom period of 40 to 50 minutes, something that *most* youngsters cannot do. (Neither can most adults!) Years ago, studies concerned with teaching children to read assumed that a majority learned by listening or seeing; few researchers experimented with teaching through tactual resources. When they *did* examine tactual learning, many:

1. Confused tactual and kinesthetic instruction
2. Did not recognize that writing with a pencil is not tactual enough below third or fourth grade
3. Used unreliable instruments to identify tactual strengths
4. Did not *teach* through tactual, hands-on approaches. Often they *reinforced* tactually—and usually after the child had already experienced failure through other introductory approaches.
5. Did not *introduce* new and difficult material tactually and then reinforce through the student's secondary or tertiary strength in sequence
6. Did not understand that some children *become* underachievers because their teachers teach by talking whereas those youngsters learn through experiencing, handling, and active doing (Restak, 1979)
7. Never experimented with teaching through tactual/visual or kinesthetic/visual

approaches that did *not* include talking—to avoid initial failure because of many primary children's low auditory ability.

It is crucial that every teacher and reading specialist recognize that many children who previously were poor students have reversed underachievement and became perfectly normal C, B, and B+ learners when taught through their perceptual strengths. That occurred both in well-controlled studies (Bauer, 1991; Carbo, 1980*; Dunn, 1990; Gardiner, 1986; Garrett, 1991; Hill, 1987; Ingham, 1989*; Jarsonbeck, 1984; Kroon, 1985; Martini, 1986*; Weinberg, 1983; Wheeler, 1983) *and* in regular everyday classrooms (Andrews, 1990; Brunner & Majewski, 1990; Dunn, 1990; Dunn & Griggs, 1988; Harp & Orsak, 1990; Orsak, 1990a, 1990b; Perrin, 1990; Sinatra, 1990).

Despite those data from school systems in many states, some authors continue to report on older studies, conducted during the 1970s and earlier, *before* we learned that:

1. Most people cannot remember much of what they hear, particularly if the information is difficult or uninteresting (to them).
2. Tactual learners remember by *handling or manipulating resources that teach required information;* kinesthetic learners remember by moving and experiencing.
3. Certain instruments such as the Learning Style Inventory (LSI) (Dunn, Dunn, & Price) or the Learning Style Inventory: Primary Version (LSI:P) (Perrin, 1981), reveal how students prefer to learn and, simultaneously, describe how those same individuals are likely to show improved test scores, attitudes, and behavior.
4. Just as runners, joggers, and walkers often find that they experience mental breakthroughs and solve problems *while* engaged in these activities, kinesthetic learners understand better while they are moving and are actively involved in learning than when they are sitting "still"—a requirement that many conventional teachers impose on them.
5. Flip Chutes, Electroboards, Pic-A-Holes, and multipart Task Cards help tactual learners remember new and difficult information better than lectures do; the pictures on them help global learners.
6. Floor Games, trips, and real-life experiences help kinesthetic learners remember new and difficult academic information better than lectures do.
7. Many tactual and kinesthetic children need to be *introduced* to new material through their perceptual strength *first;* then the information can be reinforced through a lecture;
8. Children with academic problems do not remember much of what they hear and do not read well. They are likely to achieve best when new information is introduced through a combined tactual/visual/kinesthetic approach. With such youngsters, talk *last,* after they have been exposed to the concept and have had

---

*Prize-winning research.

Children who remember new and difficult vocabulary best tactually *should use resources like the two-part elephant Task Cards that Ryan and Katie placed on the floor in this photograph, or an Electroboard with dinosaur names and matching illustrations, or a Flip Chute. (Photograph courtesy Center for the Study of Learning and Teaching Styles, St. John's University, New York.)*

a chance to process it their way. Thus, teachers should identify which young children are:

a. Auditory, visual, tactual, kinesthetic, nonpreferred, or multipreferred
b. Global, analytic, or nonpreferred (some learn both ways)
   and then design a program in which those youngsters can be taught to read through approaches that best match their strengths.

Designing a Beginning Reading Program Based on Young Children's Perceptual and Processing Strengths

Identifying Individual Perceptual and Processing Styles

Before organizing a classroom, schoolwide, or districtwide reading program for grades K–2, read *Elephant Style* to the children (see Chapter 11). This storybook for young children explains the concept of learning style—that people learn and remem-

Just as runners, joggers, and walkers often find that they experience mental breakthroughs and solve problems while they are running, jogging, or walking, kinesthetic learners under-stand better while they are moving and are actively involved in learning than when they are sitting still. Some children learn best through kines-thetic Floor Games, whereas others prefer a rocking chair to provide the action-oriented learning they need. (Photograph courtesy Center for the Study of Learning and Teaching Styles, St. John's University, New York.)

ber information in very different ways. It describes the experiences of two elephant friends who love each other and enjoy playing together but cannot learn their lessons in the same room or in the same way.

Next, administer the Learning Style Inventory: Primary Version[1] to identify the styles of children in grades K–2. The LSI:P describes each child's environmental, emotional, sociological, and physiological preferences for the conditions in which new and difficult information should be mastered. It is easy to administer and inter-pret; intelligent parents or high school students can do it successfully. Although the LSI:P takes less than an hour to complete, it is better to administer it to young chil-dren in several short sittings than in one long one. When the children's styles have been identified, share with them the information concerning their style and their classmates' styles. Then read *Kids in Style* to them so that they understand that each processing style is perfectly fine.

Grouping for Instruction Based on Style

Examine the LSI:P results. On paper, establish a column in which you can list those students whose perceptual preferences are highest for: (1) auditory, (2) visual, (3) tactual, or (4) kinesthetic learning (see Figure 10–1).

[1]The instrument for identifying individual students' learning styles, and the storybooks for preparing the students for administration of the learning style diagnostic assessment are avail-able from the Center for the Study of Learning and Teaching Styles, St. John's University, Utopia Parkway, Jamaica, NY 11439 (see Chapter 11).

Auditory	Visual	Tactual	Kinesthetic	Nonpreferenced

$\overline{A}$ $\overline{G}$ $\overline{NP}$ $\overline{A}$ $\overline{G}$ $\overline{NP}$ A $\overline{G}$ $\overline{NP}$ A $\overline{G}$ $\overline{NP}$ A $\overline{G}$ $\overline{NP}$

FIGURE 10–1 Initial Grouping by Perceptual Strength

Code: A = Analytic; G = Global; NP = Nonpreferenced

Examine the auditory children's profiles. If they have at least three of the following characteristics, they are likely to have analytic inclinations (Dunn, Bruno, Sklar, & Beaudry, 1990; Dunn, Cavanaugh, Eberle, & Zenhausern, 1982).

1. Prefers quiet.
2. Prefers bright light.
3. Prefers a formal design.
4. Is persistent.
5. Does not prefer intake while learning.

Count the number of auditory youngsters with at least three analytic traits and write their initials into the space on Figure 10–1 under "Auditory" in the A (for "Analytic") column.

Count the number of auditory youngsters with at least three of the following characteristics:

1. Prefers sound.
2. Prefers low light.
3. Prefers an informal design.
4. Is not persistent (low on persistence).
5. Prefers intake while learning.
6. Often likes learning with peers.

Count the number of auditory youngsters with at least three global traits and write their initials into the space on Exhibit 1 under "Auditory" in the G (for "Global") column.

Count the number of auditory children who have fewer than three analytic *or* three global characteristics; they may have two of both or none of either, or any such combination. Consider those pupils *nonpreferenced,* and write their initials under "Auditory" and "NP."

Conduct the same procedure for the visual, then the tactual, and then the kinesthetic children. When the Figure 10–1 chart has been completed, you will *know* which children in the group would profit most from the major approaches to teaching young children to read: phonics, word recognition, whole language, or none of the above.

Phonics is an excellent way to teach auditory analytic *children to read.* Begin *by introducing the alphabetical letters and their sounds. Then read a story that emphasizes words beginning with the same letters and sounds. Elizabeth and Jennifer are using a Learning Circle to "sound out" beginning letters and match them to pictures of words that begin with those letters. (Photograph courtesy Sheridan Hill Elementary School, Williamsville, New York).*

Matching Style and Reading Approaches

Use the following guidelines as a beginning matching strategy:

1. *For auditory analytics:* Begin with phonics. Focus on alphabet letters and their sounds. Read stories to the children and emphasize words within them. Have the children read back to you. Provide alphabet letters with matching words that begin with the same letter and help the children play games recognizing them. Have the children write initial letters in shaving cream, with water on a chalkboard, in slightly warm chocolate pudding, in sand, or using sandpaper letters. Make up songs with the letters of the alphabet and words that begin with them; sing the songs with the children. Reinforce letters and words with tactual resources such as Electroboards, Flip Chutes, Pic-A-Holes, or Task Cards.

2. *For auditory globals:* Begin by reading stories often and dramatically. Emphasize comprehension and emotions, not sequences or specific data. Follow with games, dramatizations, discussions, translations of content into drawings, and role playing. Use tactual reinforcements for words (see Chapter 6). Provide large task cards with the words and their picture representations on opposite sides of the shape-coded or picture-coded card. Also use Pic-A-Holes, Flip Chutes, and Electroboards

Whole language is an excellent way to teach auditory global children. Begin by introducing a story and then emphasizing the important and interesting words in it. These children may sit anywhere in the classroom where they feel comfortable and hear their teacher's voice reading to them on head sets. (Photograph courtesy Fred L. Wilson Elementary School, Kannapolis, North Carolina.)

Read often to visual analytics. *As you do, point to unique words that look visually different from others (e.g., with two vowels in sequence, with letters that reach above and/or below the line, with shorter words within the longer one). Ask children to find the same vocabulary in another story or to write an original story with many of the words and phrases you introduced. (Photograph courtesy Fred L. Wilson Elementary School, Kannapolis, North Carolina.)*

to review *words and happenings*—not letters. Sing songs with the words spelled out in them.

3. *For visual analytics:* Read to the children often while simultaneously pointing to unique and different-looking words. The longer the word and the more difficult in adults' estimation, the more intriguing it is to the youngster, particularly if the word is considered "scary": *dinosaur, dragon, witch, bloody.* You can point out the letters of difficult words and match them with related pictures, but (a) have the children find the same word on other pages in the same book and in other books, and (b) *avoid* asking them to convert the letters into sounds. Reward for success (a penny, a sugar-free gumdrop, dinosaur stickers, etc.). Make a fuss over the accomplishment when the word is located successfully in another paragraph or page. Reinforce by having the children draw and then, later, write the words on murals, stories, signs, and so forth.

4. *For visual globals:* Read to the children often, but emphasize story context and dramatic events. Ask questions: "What did you like most about this story? What did you like least about Sneezy?" Let them express feelings and wishes. Reinforce with tactual resources. Do *not* try to get the children to convert alphabet letters or words into sounds. That should *follow* this initial exposure. Instead, emphasize visual recognition. Later, when the children recognize words in different contexts, begin to use phonics—but don't *demand* their response; instead, expose them to it.

Use Electroboards, Flip Chutes, Pic-A-Holes, and Task Cards to introduce reading to tactual analytics. For example, emphasize words that begin with the same letters and develop three-part Task Cards where the child can place the consonant on the first section of the card next to the remaining letters in that word on the second half of the card, and attach both front sections to the matching picture of that word on the third section. Read many stories that include those same words and point to the words as you read them. (Photograph courtesy Joe Wright Elementary School, Jacksonville, Texas).

5. *For tactual analytics:* This style is rare. If you do locate a few, however, begin reading lessons with the tactual resources, but emphasize letters (like initial consonants and the words that begin with them) and matched pictures. Focus on Electroboards, Pic-A-Holes, Flip Chutes, and Task Cards, but use them in the beginning to get smaller parts of the whole—words, not concepts; characters, not events; sequences, not the summary. Then try phonics, but every day start the new lesson with the tactual resources and supplement with phonics.

6. *For tactual globals:* This may be the largest group of young students you identify. *Begin* with the tactual resources described in Chapter 6. Emphasize this approach until the children feel comfortable with a specific vocabulary (a week or two). Then read stories together. Have them create their own stories by using the vocabulary with which they have become familiar. Make up songs and poems with the vocabulary, but emphasize ideas (e.g., "The witch is flying high tonight; her broom is very long; the witch is flying high tonight, she sings her scary song!")—not details.

Tactual globals have to feel comfortable with information before they are tested with more difficult passages. Three or four days of tactual resources emphasizing the same words should do before you begin the "reading" of the story that encompasses those words (the same words they have been "playing" with on the Electroboard and other hands-on manipulatives). *Don't* focus on the alphabet with this group until much later; don't let reading become either a chore or a threat. They should succeed with the tactual manipulatives before they begin to feel stress. Once they recognize the words (and they'll learn to do that through the tactual resources) and feel comfortable, they will succeed with the actual reading and recognition. These children like to "play" and often have a short attention span when confronted with a "reading lesson" and a textbook. But wait until you see what happens when they can use the resources we suggest.

7. *For kinesthetic analytics:* This is another small group. Start with body action Floor Games, dramatizations, assigning parts they need to memorize in a play, singing stories, and the RITA reading method suggested later in this chapter.

Allow such youngsters to stand or sprawl while you are reading a story; these children cannot sit "still"; they don't understand what you mean when you tell them

Begin *reading instruction for* kinesthetic analytics *with Floor Games, dramatizations, and dancing and marching to word songs. Encourage these children to "teach" themselves and others words, phrases, letters, and information that must be mastered while standing, walking, and role playing. (Photograph courtesy West Seneca Central School District, West Seneca, New York.)*

to do that. Don't pressure them; instead, love them and encourage them. Don't force them to behave conventionally; instead, require that they complete their work, but permit them to do it as they feel comfortable.

8. *Kinesthetic globals:* Follow all of the above advice for kinesthetics, but don't give multiple directions to these children. "Take out your crayons, find the red one, and hold it in your right hand" is too much at one time. Speak slowly, and *demonstrate* every thing you do; These children do not follow multiple, sequential steps; they *feel* life and survive holistically.

Require that their tasks be completed, but allow them to sit comfortably and wherever they wish in the classroom (as long as you can see them). Permit them to work with another child or two, as long as they do their assignments and do them well. That is how many global youngsters learn best. Emphasize acting, dramatizing, visits, trips, role playing, huge body action Floor Games, huge storybooks, huge tactual materials. Laugh with these children; they need you to do that.

Questions Concerning Beginning Reading Strategies for Young Children

Can all children learn to read? Our experiences with learning style programs strongly indicate that children within a normal IQ range of 90 and above *can,* but some need one method and others need another. In addition, learning style specialists have obtained excellent reading results with many children with IQs in the 80–90 range (Bauer, 1991; Brunner & Majewski, 1990; Weinberg, 1983; Wheeler, 1980, 1983). We need to keep probing and experimenting with all the strategies we have learned that *do* work, but we now know that many youngsters who previously could *not* read well have totally reversed their underachievement when taught through their learning style strengths (Andrews, 1990; Brunner & Majewski, 1990; Dunn, 1990; Perrin, 1990).

Can teachers use several different methods at the same time? Yes, but many need to be shown how to do that. Or you might want to experiment on your own until you find procedures with which *you* feel comfortable—procedures that may differ dramatically from those with which the teacher next door may be successful. Or perhaps you wish to work with a colleague, sharing both developing ideas and responsibilities until a satisfactory, totally new system is found. Or you might care to revise the strategies suggested herein and make them your own. What works best for you is highly personal—dependent on your own learning and teaching *style*. Until you *do* learn how to introduce to each group correctly, however, experiment with one of the following:

1. Ask a colleague to take one of your larger perceptual groups for one hour each day while, at the same time, you take one of her or his larger groups (divided as indicated in Figure 10–1). Each of you do with the entire class whatever is suggested for the larger group you have taken. Follow that same pattern for six weeks. If you don't see phenomenal improvement and growth for the larger group to whose strengths you are responding, *stop!* But we believe you will!

2. Ask your principal to reorganize classes on a single grade level (K–2) for reading next year. Each of the larger perceptually strong groups should be assigned to specific teachers, and, if necessary, smaller groups should be used to fill in the register to secure fairly equal class sizes. Watch what happens within six weeks. If the groups whose perceptual strengths are being responded to are not learning better than they ever have before, STOP!

3. Because reading is so important, teach half an hour each day with each method described here, but *start* with the tactual/global approach, followed by the kinesthetic/global, then the visual global, and then the other approaches (with the *same* words/concepts) as indicated. Of course, you will be spending a *lot* of time teaching the children to read, but they *will* learn, and that is what is really important for K–2 children.

If responding to individual children's learning style strengths is more than you can undertake at this time, consider another alternative. Most teachers are comfortable with at least one standard approach to reading. Consider examining your students' learning style strengths and adapting your favorite method to them. Though not as effective as teaching students to read through their strengths, this system will produce better learning than would occur if children were introduced to reading incorrectly.

Adapting Each Teacher's Favorite Reading Method to Students' Learning Style Strengths

Teaching Students to Read through Their Individual Learning Styles (Carbo, Dunn, & Dunn, 1986) described extensive research that supported matching students' characteristics with the reading method that best complemented their individual strengths. After its publication, many teachers reported that (1) they felt comfortable with only one, or possibly two, basic approaches to reading—not the six that the book had analyzed; (2) they could not understand how anyone could use several different methods with 20 or more beginning readers in the same class at the same time; and (3) assigning children with matched learning styles to reading seemed too complicated to undertake.

Although many teachers *did* successfully match students with complementary reading methods and obtain rapid and unusual success (Andrews, 1990; Dunn, 1990; Lemmon, 1985), underachieving children in the classes of those who were fearful— or incapable—of experimenting with the suggested techniques continued to experience either failure or frustration. Children *enjoy* reading when they learn through their strengths; they find it either difficult or tiresome when they do not.

Many primary children require an informal environment while reading. Some sit on a wooden floor in a softly lit area against a wall. Others sprawl in carpeted nooks away from their classmates. A few find a special friend—human or otherwise—to share their stories. (Photograph courtesy West Seneca Central School District, West Seneca, New York.)

Thus, the purpose of this section is to explain how to *introduce* reading correctly to each youngster—*regardless of the method with which either the teacher or the administrator feels most comfortable.* What is the ideal? That each child be exposed to reading through strategies that best complement his or her learning style strengths—with an accent on perceptual sequencing, responsiveness to environmental and physiological requisites, and the "right" processing style (global or analytic) for each. The likelihood, however, is that any primary program will include many more global, tactual, kinesthetic children who need mobility, informality, variety, and activity than it will analytic, auditory, passive youngsters who prefer routines. Despite that last statement, in every class, there will be some children who need both.

Step 1: Explaining the Process to Children

Use the specific reading method you prefer, but begin by explaining to the children that everyone has strengths, but each person has different strengths. In your class, children are going to be taught how to teach themselves through their own unique learning style strengths!

Two short storybooks, *Elephant Style* (Perrin, 1980) and *Kids with Style* (Lenahan, 1991) should be read to the youngsters to explain what *learning style* means. Then each child's processing (global or analytic) and perceptual (auditory, visual, tactual, kinesthetic, or multiple) strengths should be identified by the Learning Style Inventory: Primary Version (LSI:P) (Perrin, 1978).

After you have identified the children's learning styles, print each youngster's name, processing style, and perceptual strength(s) on a Class Wall Chart. Wall Charts for recording an entire class's learning style data are available from St. John's University Center for the Study of Learning and Teaching Styles, Utopia Parkway, Jamaica, NY 11439 (see Chapter 11). Discuss the differences and similarities among individuals within the class. Emphasize that (1) all styles are good; (2) everyone has strengths—just *different* strengths; and (3) your own style and that of your spouse (or the principal's style or that of another teacher) differ. It is important that the children understand that no style is better or worse than any other; what is important is that each person learns through his or her strengths.

Explain that, most of the time, global children learn most easily with short stories, illustrations (pictures), jokes, or symbols (like a "$" sign instead of the word *dollar*). By contrast, analytic children find it easier to learn through a step-by-step approach—one detail after another until everything is understood. Thus, globals should always begin learning new or difficult material with a story or pictures; analytics should always begin with the important details. Each will *review* (reinforce) through the opposite method. To learn the new reading or spelling words for this week, global students will *begin* with a story that includes and explains its new words in context. Analytics will begin with the words—what they mean, how they are spelled—and then either hear them or use them in a story, depending on their style!

Step 2: Adapting Different Reading Methods to Individual Learning Style Strengths

When the Teacher Favors Phonics

Phonics is the best way to teach young children with analytic and auditory strengths—less than 15 percent of primary-aged children. Phonics, however, should *not* be discarded merely because it is not the *most* effective method for everyone—*no method* is! A teacher who favors phonics should say to the class:

> *Today we all are going to learn some new,* difficult *(see "A Final Word," page 375) reading and writing words, but each of you will learn them differently. Each of you will learn in your* own learning style.
>
> *Look at this Wall Chart. Every student's name is printed here [point] in this column. Your perceptual strength is listed right next to your name. Next to that is your processing style—whether you are mostly global or mostly analytic—or both—or integrated! You all have strengths, but each of you has* different *strengths. You each will learn new words today through* your special *strengths.*

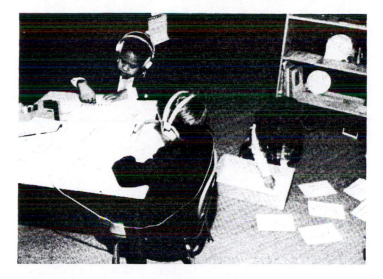

Once they are comfortable with the procedures, global analytic
*students can use a tape recorder to read a new story aloud to
them while they listen and focus on interesting new words. At the
same time, tactual students can trace the new words in sand or
cut out matching words and pictures to create their own Task
Cards. Then they hear the taped story. (Photograph courtesy Sa-
cred Heart Seminary, Hempstead, New York.)*

Explain to the global learners that they need to begin with a story that includes
the new words; *analytic* learners would start with the words and review with the
story. Direct them to look at the Wall Chart so as to remember whether they are
mostly global or mostly analytic, and whether they remember best by *hearing, seeing, touching,* or *experiencing.* Direct the children's attention to the class chart
mounted on the wall and point out which youngsters have which processing
strengths.

1. When the children are *global and auditory,* they will be placed into the
global/auditory (GA) group. They should sit near the tape recorder and, when you say
that group should start, the person wearing most of the color _____ (insert any color that a child in that group might be wearing) will carefully turn on the
recorder. The GA Group will *begin* by listening to a story about _____
(insert the topic). The story will be short, so they will need to listen carefully for the
words. Show the GA Group a list of neatly printed *and illustrated* words that are in
the story that should have been tape-recorded. These are the new words for that week.

When the story is over, the child who turned on the tape recorder will serve as
the group leader. That child should run his or her finger slowly over each word on this

list and see whether the group can figure out the words. When most of the children *can* recognize at least ten words, each should make a set of Task Cards for those words. They should print each word neatly on one side of the Task Card and draw a picture of what that word means to that child on the other side. Show them a sample. As they complete a set of ten Task Cards, working either alone or with one other classmate, they should use each other's Task Cards to see how many of the new words they can recognize—either *with* or *without* the picture half of the card. They should be urged to work quietly so that they do not disturb classmates with different learning styles.

2. Children who are *visual and global* should *start* learning new words by looking at overhead transparencies that are copies of the pages of the story you read to them. They should watch for the words when they hear you begin to read the story. Then look carefully at the Word-and-Picture Cards you have made. The pictures on the card tell what the printed letters "say," and the letters on the card tell how to write the words that represent the pictures.

The children should be told to look at the Word-and-Picture Cards carefully and remember which words match which pictures. When they think they can remember a word, they should make a Task Card for it. They also should see if someone else in their group can recognize the word *without* the matching picture. Then, after they can remember at least ten of the words, they should separate the word part from the picture part and see how many they actually *do* remember! The words should be visually different from each other, and the youngsters really need to concentrate and learn all the words they can in ten minutes. Then they should find a partner (unless they prefer to study alone!) and use both sets of Task Cards to see how many words they each can teach the other! One day of that week, play another game with their Task Cards so they learn as many words as they can.

3. Global and tactual children should begin studying the new words with Task Cards. The words and their matching pictures should be all mixed up. The children may work alone if they prefer or with a partner if that is their style. They should match the words and pictures and try to remember how the words look—or the letters in each word—as they begin to remember which words and pictures go together. After ten minutes, read a story to them that includes the new and difficult words. Show them the story on transparencies (on an overhead projector) as they hear it.

4. Children who are *global and kinesthetic* should try standing or walking on a Floor Game as they study new words. If they are *global, kinesthetic, and tactual,* they should try combining the Task Cards and a Floor Game to learn the words. Then they should act out the parts of the story and use pantomime to explain the meanings of the words. They also could form a team with large alphabetical letters distributed evenly among the members. As one member calls out a word, those who have the letters should move into the proper sequence so that the word is spelled correctly when the letters are held up. They also might write the word on the chalk board and illustrate it, or print it on acetate and make a transparency of it for others to see.

5. Children who are *global, kinesthetic, and visual* should first hear the story and see its pages on the transparencies while standing; then they should use Task

Cards to see how many words they can remember. They also should experiment with walking while they are concentrating. If they get tired of walking, they should sit down, but walking may help them remember. They also should try learning with a Floor Game as another beginning strategy!

6. Children who are *global, kinesthetic, and auditory* should act out the parts of the story being read to them *as* they listen to it. They also might experiment with standing or moving in place while they are making the Task Cards.

7. *Analytic auditory* students should hear the words and see them first, before hearing the story. They are permitted to concentrate on the words for approximately ten minutes in whichever sociological pattern they prefer—alone, in pairs, or in a small group. They then hear the story and make the Task Cards—using them, again, alone or with others.

8. *Analytic visual* children should see the list of words first, then be permitted to study them, and then hear the story as they read its pages on transparencies.

9. *Analytic tactual* children should begin by using the Task Cards. They then should see and hear the story simultaneously.

10. *Analytic kinesthetic* children should play sequential Floor Games and follow the pattern for analytics prescribed above based on their *second* perceptual strength. Kinesthetics stand, move in place, or walk and follow the pattern suggested for their next strongest modality. They also may dramatize words, meanings, and ideas.

Organizing for Phonics

Up to this point, the procedures may sound complicated, but they are not. Examine them graphically and see how easy it is to organize reading groups based on learning style strengths if you wish to teach through phonics (Figure 10–2).

Thus, if phonics is your favored reading approach, organize the students so that they *begin* studying the new words through their learning style strengths, as indicated above. After focusing on the Wall Chart (which graphically reminds the youngsters of each of their strengths and the sequence each should follow), tell them:

> *Auditory Analytics and visual Analytics will be* introduced *to this week's* words *first. We will spend a few minutes going over them before you hear and see a story that uses those words. The auditory children should concentrate on hearing the words. If seeing them makes it difficult to concentrate, you can try closing your eyes and saying them to your-self "inside your head." Experiment—see what works best for you.*

Auditory global and visual global children should begin learning the week's new words by hearing and seeing them in a *story.* Auditory children should concentrate on listening. Those who are visual should concentrate on looking at the words on the page (or on the transparency).

Tactual analytic and tactual global children should *begin* studying the week's

Introduction: Step 1	Reinforcement: Step 2	Reinforcement: Step 3
Auditory analytics	*Hear* and see words first; accent on letters in sequence.	Then hear story that includes words; then make Task Cards[a] with words and practice[b]. Also use Floor Game.
Visual analytics	*See* and hear words first; accent on visual formation.	Then hear story which includes words; then make Task Cards[a] with words and practice[b]. Also use Floor Game.
Tactual analytics	*Use* Task Cards first, matching pictures and words.	Then hear story which includes words while seeing storybook or page transparency. Then use Floor Game.
Kinesthetic analytics	*Walk,* use Floor Game or real activity to begin, follow procedures for children with the same secondary perceptual strength.	Follow the procedures for children with the same tertiary perceptual strength. Use Task Cards[a]
Auditory globals	*Hear* story first, but look at storybook pages or transparencies of them while listening to story.	Then use Task Cards[a] and practice.[b] Then use Floor Game.
Visual globals	*See* storybook pages or transparencies of them while listening to story.	Then use Task Cards[a] and practice.[b] Then use Floor Game.
Tactual globals	*Handle* Task Cards of pictured story sequence combined with words first; then see and hear story.	Then make Task Cards[a] and practice.[b]
Kinesthetic globals	*Walk, use Floor Game,* and then follow the procedures for children with the same secondary perceptual strength.	Follow the procedures for children with the same tertiary perceptual strength.

FIGURE 10–2 Organizing for Phonics

[a]Electroboards, Pic-A-Holes, or Flip Chutes can and *should* be substituted alternatively.
[b]Practice should be based on each child's preference—alone, in a pair, or in a small group.

words by using Task Cards (or Pic-A-Holes, Electroboards, or Learning Circles). Kinesthetic analytics and Kinesthetic globals should stand, move in place, or walk while they follow the pattern for students with their processing style and their *second* strongest *modality.* In addition, they should use Floor Games to learn the information.

Some will start with the words, then hear the story, and then use the Task Cards. Others will start with the story and then use the Task Cards. The next day they will dramatize and pantomime the words (kinesthetic). For homework, with a choice of assignments, they may use the words in something they create, such as a poem, a story of their own, an Electroboard or Pic-A-Hole, a picture dictionary, or a game they create with the words. The next day, they should share the creative homework they did—in pairs or in small groups—to see how many of them *really* learned the words. On the day after that, give an award to the person or pair who makes up the best song with the words—but the song has to include spelling them!

When the Teacher Favors Whole Language

A whole language approach to reading is most responsive to global students who need to understand the entire concept before they can begin to relate to its fragments (the words and/or their meanings and/or how to spell or write them). Auditory globals should do well with this method; if the children can see the story and its words *while* the teacher is reading, the approach becomes responsive to global visual students. If there are not enough copies of the story for everyone, a transparency of each page projected onto a wall will be a wonderful supplement for visuals as they hear the story being read.

However, tactual globals should be able to use a picture of the story or, preferably, a pictured story sequence (as in a puzzle form) *first;* they *then* should hear and see the story. Giving tactual children a ten-minute interval in which to work with the manipulatives related to the story before they actually are exposed to it will help such children master the content and enjoy learning it more.

Organizing for Whole Language

Thus, when organizing a whole language reading lesson, teachers should encourage the following:

- Tactual analytics should work with the words through matched picture and word Task Cards or Flip Chutes for a short interval (approximately 10 to 12 minutes).
- Tactual globals should piece together a story sequence related to the material. Multipart Task Cards, Flip Chute Cards, or a word picture puzzle would do for this group. At the same time, auditory visuals could be hearing about the words (either directly from the teacher or on a tape).
- Visual analytics could be looking at the words in a list supplemented by pictures.
- Auditory analytics could be listening to the words and hear them being spelled and supplemented by pictures. *Then* the entire class could hear the story, but the auditory and visual analytics would have focused on the words first and would be reinforced globally, whereas the globals would start with the story and be reinforced afterward analytically (through an assignment).

The entire class could be listening to the story at the same time, but, as with the phonics procedures above, the tactuals will have been *introduced* correctly, the auditory children will be advised to focus on the listening, and the visual children will be advised to focus on the seeing and reading along with the teacher. The kinesthetics are also with the group—but they are standing while engaged in concentration and move from one matched word and picture of it to the next as the teacher refers to them in the story. If the story lends itself to creative activities *and* the kinesthetic students have specific talents (which they often do!), *while* hearing the story they could engage in activities such as: (1) sketching the characters or drawing their costumes if artistic, pantomiming the events if they are dramatic; (2) "mapping" the events in water on a chalkboard or developing Task Cards or Pic-A-Hole cards if tactual; or (3) creating a new version of an existing Floor Game to use the story information.

What do the nontactuals *do* for the first ten minutes while their classmates are using manipulatives? If you are working with young children, the *majority* will be tactual, tactual/kinesthetic, or visual/tactual. Thus, only a few youngsters will need to be supervised during that short interval. They could be permitted to glance through the book (or look at the transparencies) and see how much of the story they can "read" (work through), whether alone, in pairs, or in small groups. In effect, they can prepare themselves for listening or reading alone a little later.

When the Favored Approach Is Word Recognition, Orton-Gillingham, or Any Other Method

Use the guidelines above to *introduce* whatever is being taught—concept, skill, or vocabulary—through each child's perceptual strength and processing style. Ten minutes is all that is needed for a basic understanding and comfort level to develop. Then use whichever method is favored, but remind the children to concentrate on using their "best" (strongest) learning style characteristics. If you are willing, also permit them to sit anywhere they feel comfortable in the classroom. Of course they must: (1) complete their work, (2) not interfere with anyone else's style, and (3) earn better grades than they have heretofore. Within six weeks, you will see children reading better and enjoying it more than they ever did before.

The next section suggests a new, experimental approach to reading that incorporates many of these combined suggestions in a new way. You can try this new method with many young children but, like any approach, it will not be effective with *all* youngsters. This one, however, will reach the ones who are unsuccessful with phonics, whole word, and whole language approaches—as good as they all are. Why? Because it is responsive to tactual and kinesthetic global students—and *starts* that way!

Are You Willing to Experiment with a Tactual, Visual, and Global Approach to Reading?

For several years, St. John's University's Center for the Study of Learning and Teaching Styles has been concerned with identifying those methods that were likely

Experiment with permitting children to sit anywhere they feel comfortable in the class-
room provided they behave nicely, do not distract anyone with a different learning style,
complete their assignment, and learn more than they did previously. You will find some
inevitably read: at their desks, whereas others vie for informal seating; in the brightest
light available, whereas others prefer a darkened, cozy nook; and in the tepee, bathtub,
or Reading Raft you created or in whatever is enclosed, snug, and away from the main
traffic and intrusions. (Photograph courtesy Otsego Elementary School, Half Hollow
Hills, New York.)

to be effective with poor readers. That focus prompted two New York City teachers
to explore a combined approach that showed promise of responding to the learning
style characteristics of many K–2 children.

In the spring of 1990, Lorraine Sena and Mary Jane Hazelton (see Note 1)
identified the perceptual strengths of children in one kindergarten class and designed
a pretest–posttest experiment in which they taught the children vocabulary with the
phonics (decoding) approach. As had occurred throughout that academic year, a majority of children either failed or achieved very low grades. In addition, many youngsters behaved poorly during the reading lessons. They were inattentive, restless, and
hyperactive. This is the approach the two teachers subsequently tried.

1. Each day, on a large sheet of oaktag, they printed an original "scary" story.
It is important that:

Create and print an original *story about something scary, an animal with personality, or money on a large sheet of oaktag. Continue adding a new phase of the story each day for several weeks. Each day, after the introduction on the first day, the children walk in small groups from one chart to the other, in sequence along each wall, as they read every chart from the beginning one and continue all the way through until they reach the most recently added segment. (Photograph courtesy Fred L. Wilson Elementary School, Kannapolis, North Carolina.)*

- The story should be created on a day-to-day basis and be original, so that no one in the class actually knows what will happen to the major characters in each new "sequel"—the part introduced each subsequent day.
- The story should center on unusual characters or items of an attention-holding quality, such as dragons, witches, ghosts, animals with personalities, or money. A previous research project had revealed that those were the things that elementary school children found most interesting!

2. Every time a character's name, or a word that leant itself to illustration, was used—and the same words were used repeatedly—it was drawn directly above where it was printed. For example, if *crocodile* was a word in the story, every time *crocodile* was printed, a drawing (or picture) of a crocodile appeared directly above it.

3. Each day's story was short, only two or three sentences. But each day the story ended on a hair-raising note—for example, "The crocodile opened its enormous mouth and moved closer to the monkey!" or "The monkey began to cry as the crocodile crawled closer and closer."

4. Lorraine told the class that she *knew* everyone wanted to learn how to read, but that she could teach only five or six children each day. She told them not to worry and not to cry, because they all *would* learn to read, but not at the same time. She then asked for "volunteers" for that first afternoon. The volunteers were placed in a small semicircle facing the chalkboard. The first part of the story sequence had been mounted on that board.

5. She pointed to the first word on the story chart, where she had placed a small colored dot, and said that the child in each day's Story Chart Group—the group that was learning to read—who also was wearing the *most* of the color on the dot would be that day's Team Leader. The Team Leader (with the entire group watching) was taught how to;

- Operate the tape recorder
- Carefully find the tape secreted in a pocket at the bottom of the story chart
- Find the tactual resources (Task Cards, Electroboard, Pic-A-Hole, or matched picture/word puzzle cards) that had been placed into the same chart pocket
- Distribute fairly among the five or six members of the Story Chart Group whatever other items had been placed into the pocket, such as crayons, drawing paper, or rulers. Everyone in the group saw and heard what the Team Leader had been taught, but the teaching was ostensibly directed only toward the Leader.

6. In the meantime, Mary Jane had seated the remaining 12 children in a second-row semicircle directly behind that day's first Story Chart Group volunteers. The youngsters *not* in the reading group were cautioned to "rest, relax, daydream, stare at the ceiling, or look out the window"—but *not* to learn to read that day. *They* would be taught another day!

7. Lorraine showed the reading group an Electroboard with the words *crocodile, monkey,* and *cry* on one side and pictures representing those items on the other—but in mixed-up, unmatched positions. She told them that they probably didn't know the words but, by using a continuity tester (which she showed them), they could find the word that was matched with each picture. She allowed the reading group members to handle the Electroboard and the tester and to experiment by placing the tester's point onto the holes. When the tester bulb lit up because the matched pair had been correctly identified, she admiringly said things like, "You've found the word that says *crocodile!*" Thus, the children were *introduced* to the vocabulary in the story initially by handling the tactual Electroboard and finding the matched pictures and words.

In the meantime, the nonvolunteering children in back of the reading group were straining to observe the Electroboard bulb flashing and the pictures and printed matches to each word. Periodically, Mary Jane and Lorraine teasingly cautioned them. "You are not supposed to be learning to read today. You will learn tomorrow. Just close your eyes and try to rest!"

8. Lorraine then directed that day's Team Leader to carefully extract the tape from the Story Chart's pocket and place it into the tape recorder. The child then was told to turn the recorder on. The teacher placed her index finger on the colored dot next to the first word and moved it horizontally, from left to right, as the teacher's voice on the recording dramatically read the first chart in the story: "The crocodile saw the monkey. The crocodile crawled toward the monkey. The crocodile opened its mouth. The monkey began to cry."

9. Every time the word *crocodile* was read, Lorraine pointed to the word *and* the picture of the crocodile. She did the same thing for the words *monkey* and *cry* (next to which she glued a small packet of clear plastic wrap filled with water to suggest tears). After the story had been read on the tape, she asked the children (in that day's Story Chart Group) to examine the Electroboard again and see if they could find the word *crocodile* and its matching picture. The next day, she showed them Task cards with the words and matched pictures, and the following day she asked them if they could recognize the words *without* the pictures. Those who could were praised; those who couldn't were told, "It is difficult to recognize long words without their matching pictures, but you will be able to do that very soon! You'll see!"

10. After their experience with the second tactual resource, the members of the reading group were asked to draw *why* they thought the monkey began to cry. They then were asked to explain their drawings.

11. Periodically during the lesson, either Lorraine or Mary Jane would caution the children in the second (or third) outer circle *not* to pay attention, *not* to listen, and *not* to learn to read that day. Their turn would come tomorrow—or another day.

The more the youngsters were cautioned *not* to pay attention, the more they did. When the first day's reading lesson was over and the reading group was told to draw why the monkey cried, Mary Jane said to the children who had *not* been taught to read, "Don't worry! Many of you will learn to read tomorrow! Today just was not your day!" (To which many of the children responded, "*I* learned to read today anyway!" or "I *know* the words!"—to which the teachers responded, "But you were not *supposed* to learn today! Today was *not* your day!"

12. The next day, the first day's Story Chart Group had to "read" the first Story Chart together, out loud and standing up, before they could proceed to the new chart. The teachers assisted, but most of the children could say the words because of the matched pictures. After reading the previous day's chart, the first day's group proceeded to the subsequent chart, where one of the teachers helped them: (a) begin by seeing, and handling, or manipulating the words with a tactual resource (Electroboard, Task Cards, etc.); (b) hear the story being read to them on the teacher-made tape (which, again, had been stored in the Story Chart's bottom pocket) as the youngsters followed the content of the story with their eyes; (c) reinforce the vocabulary through a second tactual device, such as a Learning Circle; (d) review the vocabulary of the previous day, and (e) engage in some form of higher-level critical thinking in terms of either *why* something had happened, what *might* happen, what might be done to prevent something from happening, and so forth.

13. Each day lead to a kinesthetic activity related to the previous day's vocabulary and story content. The ladies also designed a "Crocodile Crawl" in which the children danced to the spelling of the emphasized words and a "Monkey Mountain Mimic" where they erected a monkey village and labeled correctly and dramatized all the characters and events in the story.

14. Each day, for four days in a row, the "next reading group" (new teams of five or six) was introduced to the *beginning* of the story (the first chart). Each group read every chart daily before it was permitted to continue and, gradually, worked its way through each new sequence of the continuing story—which always ended with a tension-provoking note that made every child discuss and predict what would happen in the next day's story events. Thus, every day, every group reads and rereads every chart.

15. The children grew to love the charted story and raced to it each day *before* it was "time to read." They conjectured about what had happened after the previous day's scary ending. They stood in small groups trying to read the new words. Some would try to "sound them out," whereas others would refer to previous charts and try to recognize words they remembered from earlier parts of the story. A few would take commercial storybooks and search through them for hints of picture-related meanings. Many would take out the tactual resources from previous chart pockets and search them for clues to meanings of new words. Gradually, one by one, the youngsters would surround the charts, deciphering new words and evidencing that they recognized familiar ones. A few began teaching the others.

16. At the end of the story—after the twenty-third day—children were reading its words out of context in other sources. The Story Charts eventually were numbered, rolled up, ribboned, and placed into a corner where, periodically, individuals, pairs, or small groups would beg to be permitted to unroll them and read them again. Small groups of four or five would find a section of the room, unroll the charts, sit around them on the floor, and reread the story to themselves and to everyone else who would listen. Eventually, the teachers allowed a "Self-Teaching Reading Period"—fifteen minutes each day when individuals, pairs, or small groups could read anything they wanted. The Story Charts were in constant demand, but, interestingly, *some* children consistently preferred the "old" (previous) stories, whereas others consistently preferred the (then) "new" one.

17. The Story Charts continued throughout the remainder of the semester, one after the other. The children *loved* reading them and *begged* for time to do it. The global children read beautifully, and so did the analytics. But what impressed Ms. Sena and Ms. Hazelton most was that the children who had achieved well with the initial phonics lessons (who happened to be more analytic than global and more auditory than most of the others), continued to decode words all semester, even when using the tactual resources. The ones who had achieved poorly with phonics were ecstatic about the manipulatives and the Story Charts and rarely showed any interest in decoding.

*"Self-Teaching Time," ten- to fifteen-minute periods two or three
times each day when children can read either alone, in pairs, or
with their teacher, becomes one of the most sought-after intervals
of the day. Youngsters may read any book in the classroom with
whomever they wish, or listen to their teacher reading it to them
on the tape glued to the back of each book. (Photograph courtesy
Center for the Study of Learning and Teaching Styles, St. John's
University, New York.)*

As a result, the teachers thereafter taught the auditory analytics phonics at the
beginning of each lesson, when they first used the tactual resources *before* actually
hearing the story. They then permitted those youngsters to read the Story Charts.
Conversely, the tactual children were introduced to the vocabulary with the tactual
materials first, then were exposed to the Story Charts and the accompanying resources and, *after* they were able to recognize the words, were then taught how to
decode them with phonics.

18. During a three-week interval, Lorraine and Mary Jane taught all the children new vocabulary with phonics and pretested and posttested for each of the three
weeks. They recorded each child's scores and made notations concerning which children were: (a) auditory, (b) visual, (c) tactual, (d) kinesthetic, (e) analytic, and/or
(f) global. During the subsequent three weeks, they again pretested, then unfolded a
new Story Chart, which, during the entire sequence, included as many words as
would normally be taught during three separate weeks of reading. That number was
equivalent to what had been taught during the three-week phonics study. At the end
of the second three-week period, they posttested.

The students who had achieved well with phonics did *not* obtain similarly high grades with this method. However, the students who had *not* done well with phonics—the visual, tactual, and kinesthetic kindergartners—achieved beautifully with it. The two groups had almost *reversed* achievement levels in the same classroom, but with different methods!

Because Professor Rita Dunn had suggested these steps to them in a graduate, field-based learning style research course, Lorraine Sena and Mary Jane Hazelton named this approach to beginning reading, "Reading-Is-The-Answer," which they promptly shortened to "RITA." If the RITA approach appeals to you, you might consider experimenting with it with your global/tactual primary students.

A Final Word on Teaching Young Children to Read

We often tell children that they could learn easily if they would "only pay attention." They *do* pay attention, but learning to read is *not* easy when the reading approach we use is unresponsive to *how* the child learns. In addition, when children are told that what they need to learn is not difficult, *and they cannot learn it,* they certainly must feel inadequate.

Consider the reverse. When children are told that what they need to learn is difficult, competitive, motivated youngsters rise to the occasion; underachievers do not suffer reduced self-image because they have been forewarned that mastery is not easy, and thus they can rationalize; and if the teacher permits students to learn either alone, in a pair, or in a small group on the basis of their individual styles, the youngsters have a good chance of helping each other succeed. Of course, if the teacher channels children toward concentrating through their learning style strengths, they all should perform better than ever before!

Another point to consider is that certain global children cannot "spell" words easily because spelling requires mental recall of alphabetical letters in sequence—an analytic skill. Tell those youngsters to "write" (rather than "spell") the words. Tell them to try to "see" the word in their mind's eye and then just to copy it onto a paper. As long as they do not think they have to "spell" it, they often can envision the "whole image" of the word.

Try explaining this to young children. Tell them that they have a choice—they may learn either to "spell" the words or to "write" them. Describe the sequencing that is involved in spelling and the visualization required for writing. (In truth, each method requires both processes; what matters is how the youngster *begins* to remember.)

[2]Lorraine Sena and Mary Jean Hazelton are graduate students at St. John's University, New York. They teach at St. Raphael's School in Sunnyside, Queens, New York.

11

Resources for Primary Teachers and Trainers Getting Started with Learning Styles Instruction

Dr. Angela Klavas

Whether you are a teacher beginning to respond to learning styles in your classroom, an administrator eager to interest teachers in the concept, or a trainer helping teachers in the implementation process, you ask yourself, "What resources are available to get started?" You are fortunate in that the Center for the Study of Learning and Teaching Styles at St. John's University in New York has many resources specifically designed to help you begin a learning styles instructional program.

Background Information

Your first step is to become thoroughly acquainted with the Dunn and Dunn model by reading this book. You might want to attend the eight-day Leadership Institute sponsored by St. John's University's Center for the Study of Learning and Teaching Styles each July in New York.

You also can join the National Network on Learning Styles cosponsored by the National Association of Secondary School Principals (NASSP) and St. John's University. For a yearly subscription, you receive information about developments in the fields of learning and teaching styles. Services include three annual newsletters that provide summaries of the latest research, practical applications, and experimental

Angela Klavas, Ed.D., is Assistant Director of the Center for the Study of Learning and Teaching Styles, St. John's University, New York. Her previous publications include articles in *Educational Leadership* and the *Journal of Reading, Writing, and Learning Disabilities: International*.

programs; information about conferences, institutes, and inservice workshops for teachers and administrators; descriptions of publications and dissertations in the field; identification of resources, personnel, and exemplary school sites; an updated bibliography of publications and films; and responses to written or telephone requests for information.

Publications for Adults

Listed next are publications available from the Center for the Study of Learning and Teaching Styles that provide background information to teachers, administrators, and trainers interested in learning styles instruction.

• *Teaching Elementary Students through Their Individual Learning Styles* by Dr. Rita Dunn and Dr. Kenneth Dunn is a practical, hands-on guide to implementing learning styles in elementary schools. Similarly, *Teaching Secondary Students through Their Individual Learning Styles* is a practical, hands-on guide to implementing learning styles with adolescents. Both explain how to teach students to teach themselves and include a Teaching Style identification instrument.

• *Teaching Students to Read through Their Individual Learning Styles* by Dr. Marie Carbo, Dr. Rita Dunn, and Dr. Kenneth Dunn provides a diagnostic-prescriptive approach for teaching children to read. It involves the identification of individual learning styles and the subsequent matching of complementary reading strategies, resources, and environments.

• *A Review of Articles and Books* is a compilation of articles and research studies and their implications for gifted, special education, and regular instruction. This publication also provides proposals for funding and extensive documentation needed for writing term papers, theses, proposals for funding, and dissertations on learning styles, hemisphericity, and brain behavior.

• *The Curry Report* is a psychometric review of the major instructional preference, information-processing, and cognitive personality instruments that bear on individuals' learning styles.

• *The DeBello Report* compares learning style models and the psychometric analyses of their instruments. It contains an audiotape, script, extensive reference list, and diagram comparing eleven models, with variables, appropriate populations, validity of instrumentation, and the research behind each.

• *Annotated Bibliography* is an updated review of articles, books, dissertations, and research on learning style. This, too, is a valuable resource for writing term papers, theses, proposals for funding, or manuscripts.

Videotapes

Videotapes are excellent resources for educating administrators, trainers, and teachers by providing an overview of the Dunn and Dunn model, the research, and the step-by-step strategies and techniques in its implementation process. Each of Tapes I and II provides a complete inservice course for introducing faculty to beginning steps for teaching students through their individual learning styles.

• *Videotape Set #1: Teaching Students through Their Individual Learning Styles* is a six-hour complete training program narrated by Dr. Rita Dunn. It introduces the Dunn and Dunn learning style model by explaining the environmental, emotional, sociological, physiological, and psychological elements of style. It describes how to identify individual strengths, redesign classrooms to respond to diversified styles, and teach students to do their homework through their learning style strengths.

• *Videotape Set #2: Teaching At-Risk Students through Their Individual Learning Styles* is a complete training program narrated by Dr. Rita Dunn and Dr. Kenneth Dunn. It is a six-hour, hands-on, how-to description that provides the research and all the methods for teaching at-risk students through their individual learning styles.

• *Videotape Set #3 (Elementary) and Set #4 (Secondary): The Look of Learning Styles* are excellent resources for anyone interested in observing learning style techniques and strategies in classrooms. It can be used either as an introduction to the concept or as a culminating workshop activity. Each videotape presents learning style programs in four different elementary or secondary schools in the United States and demonstrates how students' unique characteristics are matched with appropriate en-

The most reliable and valid instrument for identifying the learning styles of children in grades K–2 is the Learning Style Inventory: Primary (LSI:P). Before administering the Learning Style Inventory: Primary Version, the concept of learning style should be explained to young children through the storybook Elephant Style. *(Photograph courtesy Brightwood Elementary School, Greensboro, North Carolina.)*

vironments, resources, and methods in the classroom. This also serves as an excellent explanation of learning styles for students.

- *Videotape #5: How to Conduct Research in Your Own Classroom* is a three-hour presentation by Dr. Rita Dunn to enable practitioners to determine the effects of innovation on students with diverse learning styles.
- *Videotape #6: How to Write and Get Published* is a two-hour videotape for classroom teachers and is directly related to its title.
- *Videotape #7: Personal Learning Power* is a ten-minute rap video for older elementary and secondary students. It explains the value of using each student's learning style strengths.
- *Videotape #8: Learning Styles and Brain Behavior: What Schools Do Not Know about Learning* is a one-half hour presentation by Professor Rita Dunn on what schools can do to increase student achievement.
- *Videotape #9, Part I, II: Teaching Young Children to Read through Their Individual Learning Style Strengths* is a three-hour presentation by Professor Rita Dunn describing a step-by-step instructional process for teaching young children to read through their individual learning styles.
- *Videotape #10: Providing Staff Development through Teachers' Learning Styles* is a three-hour presentation by Dr. Rita Dunn and Dr. Ken Dunn describing how to conduct effective inservice through *teachers'* learning styles.
- *Videotape #11: Teaching Multicultural Students through Their Learning Style Strengths* is a three-hour presentation by Professor Rita Dunn describing the learning styles of multicultural students and how to teach diverse groups through their strengths.

Instrumentation

- Before assessing students' learning styles, teachers and administrators should identify their own learning styles with the Productivity Environmental Preference Survey (PEPS). They will discover how *they* prefer to function, learn, concentrate, and perform when trying to master difficult academic material. Analyzing their personal style allows them to understand the process, thus helping them to interpret students' learning styles. More important, when teachers realize that *they* have unique learning characteristics, they better understand and accept the diversity among their students' styles.

Administrators and trainers find that staff development sessions become more effective after they have administered and interpreted the PEPS to the participants. The PEPS (Dunn, Dunn, & Price) is available in a specimen set, a computerized program, and/or a scan-and-score program for on-site processing.

- The only instrument of its kind that can identify the learning styles of primary (grades K–2) students is available from the Center for the Study of Learning and Teaching Styles. The Learning Style Inventory: Primary (LSI:P) (Perrin) is a pictorial questionnaire with a manual that provides (1) information concerning the

An equally important resource to help youngsters understand the differences between global *and* analytic *learners is the storybook* Kids in Style. *Principal Roland Andrews discusses this book with second-graders prior to testing them with the Learning Style Inventory: Primary. (Photograph courtesy Brightwood Elementary School, Greensboro, North Carolina.)*

development of the instrument, (2) directions for administration, and (3) instructional strategies for responding to specific learning style characteristics. This package includes reproducible answer forms and research information that provides reliability and validity data. Before administering the LSI:P, the learning style concept should be explained to students in grades K–2 through the storybook *Elephant Style* (Perrin & Santora) or *Kids in Style* (Lenahan).

Publications for Students

The following storybooks, especially written for young children, are available to assist teachers in preparing students to take the LSI or LSI:P. They should be read by or to the youngsters before identifying their styles to explain the concept of learning style strengths.

• *Elephant Style* (Perrin and Santora) is an excellent resource with which to prepare primary youngsters (K–2) to take the LSI:P assessment. It explains the concept of learning style to young children by describing the various ways two elephants learn and remember new and difficult information.

• *Mission from Nostyle* (Braio) is a storybook explaining the concept of learning style to students in grades 2 through 6. It describes the search of space children for information concerning how to learn new and difficult information. Earthlings join them and eventually unravel how to achieve well in school. This high-interest story should be read *before* diagnosing learning styles, so that students understand that everyone has different strengths.

• *Return to Nostyle* (Braio) explains the concept of learning style to elementary youngsters in *Special Education*. It should be read to or by students before they are assessed for their learning style.

• *Kids with Style* (Lenahan) is a coloring book that explains the differences between analytic and global processing styles of a brother and sister. In this story, Kate and Tom like many of the same things and often do them together. However, when it comes to doing schoolwork or projects, they perform differently. This is an excellent book to be read to or by students before diagnosing their learning styles (grades 1–6).

Doing Homework

Research indicates that improved academic achievement occurs when students do their homework through their individual learning styles. Available at the Center for

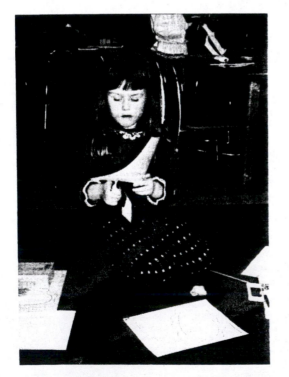

Youngsters can capitalize on their tactual abilities by following directions for creating shapes from a Programmed Learning Sequence on the topic, as shown, or by constructing an Electroboard through which they can master vocabulary words. (Photograph courtesy Brightwood Elementary School, Greensboro, North Carolina.)

the Study of Learning and Teaching Styles are resources relating to homework and learning style for teachers, parents, and students.

• *Learning How to Learn* is a Programmed Learning Sequence (PLS) concerning how to learn, study, and do homework through one's own perceptual strengths. In 36 frames, it explains how to learn more easily and remember better by introducing new information or skills through each person's strongest modality and then reinforcing through others. This PLS can be duplicated and then colored and laminated by students who read on a third-grade level or above.

• *How to Do Homework through Learning Style* is a colorful, animated filmstrip and cassette tape showing students in grade 2 or above how to do homework. This resource also can be shown to parents or Parent–Teacher Associations (PTAs) so that they provide their children with the proper home environment while studying and doing homework.

• *Perceptual Strength Homework Charts* are inexpensive posterboard charts for both teachers and students. The Learning Style Instructional Charts list the correct sequence of instruction for the tactual, visual, auditory, or kinesthetic student in teacher-directed lessons. The Learning Style Class Charts cite the six-step perceptual sequence of instruction for students in teacher-directed or whole-group lectures. Using the primary perceptual strength, the charts show appropriate personal sequencing for self-instruction during homework assignments.

Teacher Inservice Packages

The four Teacher Inservice Packages (TIPs) available at the Center for the Study of Learning and Teaching Styles are designed to provide staff development through teachers' learning style preferences.

• The *TIP on Contract Activity Packages* (CAPs) demonstrates alternative methods of instructing gifted students in ways that many research studies suggest high-IQ, creative youngsters learn. The TIP includes: (1) a series of explicit, colored slides and a cassette tape that shows teachers how to design Contract Activity Packages (CAPs); (2) a Programmed Learning Sequence (PLS) on how to develop and use CAPs to accommodate selected learning style characteristics; and (3) three reproducible CAPs.

• The *TIP on PLSs* is designed for teaching motivated, persistent, visual students who need structure and like to work alone or in pairs. Environmental preferences, time of day, and intake also can be accommodated. This package includes a PLS on the design and use of a PLS, a cassette tape, overhead transparencies, and a script.

• *TIP on Alternatives to Lecture* is designed to show teachers better ways to teach than talking and discussing. Four small-group instructional strategies (Team Learning, Circle of Knowledge, Brainstorming, and Group Analysis) are taught through three activities accommodating teachers' learning style preferences. The resources include: (1) scripts, worksheets, and samples; (2) transparencies and an audiotape; and (3) a PLS that may be reproduced.

  • *TIP on Conducting Staff Development Workshops* contains ideas and materials for conducting inservice with the Dunn and Dunn model with suggested resources and strategies. This package includes transparencies, a research list, an audiotaped overview, and other materials to assist teachers when implementing.

  • *Only Overheads* is a looseleaf folder comprising all the important transparencies that accommodate teaching adults how to design the methods involved with teaching to learning styles.

Instructional Resources for Students

  • Stimulating resources for students include Contract Activity Packages (CAPs) on the primary level. These CAPs are self-contained units of study for motivated, persistent students. They include (1) clearly stated Behavioral Objectives; (2) suggested multisensory Resource Alternatives through which students may learn the information required by the objectives; (3) Activity Alternatives for creative ways in which students apply the information acquired through the resources; (4) Reporting Alternatives (in which the Activity Alternatives are shared); (5) at least three small-group techniques such as Circle of Knowledge, Team Learning, Brainstorming, and the like; and (6) related assessments. These reproducible CAPs are an excellent resource for gifted and nonconforming students.

Stimulating resources for students (K–2) include Contract Activity Packages (CAPs). One of the most effective tactual resources is the Electroboard, which works with a continuity tester, a battery device that lights up when a correct answer on one side of the Electroboard is matched to a question on the opposite side. (Photograph courtesy Christa McAuliffe Elementary School, Lewisville Independent School District, Lewisville, Texas.)

Additional resources specifically designed to teach students through their individual learning styles include:

- *Contract Activity Package and Programmed Learning Sequence Sets* provide a CAP and a PLS on the same topic with the same objectives. They can be used for experimental studies for youngsters with different learning styles. They are also an excellent resource for use as workshop samples and are extremely motivating for students.
- *Comics in the Classroom: A Learning Style Approach* (McCoubrey) is a 175-page kit that uses comics as a practical and enjoyable resource for teaching basic skills to underachievers. It spans all grade levels (K–12) and covers a wide range of subject areas, including language arts, mathematics, creative arts, dramatic arts, social studies, and others. It also introduces and explains the concept of individual learning style—enhancing its value as a unique and comprehensive resource. It contains 150 suggested activities and a Teacher's Manual.
- *Touch and Learn Alphabet* is a kit that meets the sensory stimulation needs of the preschool and K–2 tactual learner. It contains upper- and lower-case alphabet letters, a set of numerals, a Teacher's Guide, and ten suggested hands-on activities.
- *Wrap-ups,* plastic bars with self-correcting features, are designed for visual/tactual students to master basic skills in various sociological settings. They are available in early childhood and elementary levels and teach computation and language arts.
- *Continuity Tester.* This is used with an Electroboard, a gamelike resource that both teaches and reinforces information through an interesting and dramatic approach. It is an effective instructional device for the tactually and visually oriented students. This industrial heavy-duty tester has two AA batteries and a large red lens.
- *Thinking Network (TN) Software Kits* (Narration for reading levels 2–6 and Theme Writing for reading levels 3–9) are Apple microcomputer software programs for improving thinking, reading, and writing skills. TN combines computer technology with high-interest, grade-appropriate reading selections through a variety of hands-on, global reading activities not available in other software programs.

Resources for Parents

The following resources are designed specifically for parents to help them understand their children's learning styles.

- *Learning Style—An Explanation for Parents* contains a filmstrip and audiotape explaining the concept of learning style. If followed by a discussion of learning style, it is an excellent resource for parent–teacher conferences or meetings.
- *Learning Styles: A Guide for Parents* is a booklet explaining the concept and includes a written account of how children's styles can be accommodated at home.
- *Videotape: What Parents Need to Know about Their Children's Individual Learning Styles* is a half-hour presentation by Professor Rita Dunn.

- *Bringing Out the Giftedness in Your Child: Nurturing Every Child's Unique Strengths* by Drs. Rita and Ken Dunn, and Dr. Donald Treffinger is a guide for parents on how to identify, redefine, and build each child's unique style of learning to develop giftedness and how to monitor progress with checklists and assessment scales.

Resource for Counselors

The Center for the Study of Learning and Teaching Styles also has an excellent resource specifically designed for counselors.

- *Learning Styles Counseling* (Griggs) is a monograph that offers counselors, teachers, and human services personnel a practical approach for customizing and reaching K–2 students through their strengths. Counselors are shown how to diagnose learning style, utilize compatible interventions, and consult with teachers about accommodating diverse styles in the classroom. This book should be read *before* troubled and difficult-to-teach students are assigned to alternative programs, psychologists, or county agencies. Though written specifically for counselors, it also should be read by teachers and parents.

Where to Obtain Resources for Getting Started

If interested in obtaining any of the resources listed, please write to the Center for the Study of Learning and Teaching Styles, St. John's University, Utopia Parkway, New York, NY 11439.

A Final Word on Implementing the Dunn and Dunn Model

Dr. Angela Klavas, assistant director, Center for the Study of Learning and Teaching Styles, St. John's University, visited elementary schools that had implemented the Dunn and Dunn learning styles model in geographic locations throughout the United States. Her report (Klavas, 1991) describes those factors that both helped and hindered the development of their successful learning styles programs. Hindering factors revolved around Central Office mandates and intrusions, supervisors with a different agenda, and in some cases lack of financial resources for staff development. Helpful factors revolved around the understanding and insight that both staff and students developed once they became familiar with the research and theory concerned with this model and the statistically higher achievement and attitude scores that resulted from implementation.

Figure 11–1 is a graph that Dr. Klavas designed to represent the four stages of implementation of the Dunn and Dunn model. Although many of the schools had been involved in learning styles instruction for five or more years, few had moved into in-depth evaluations as indicated in the fourth stage. All had completed stages 1

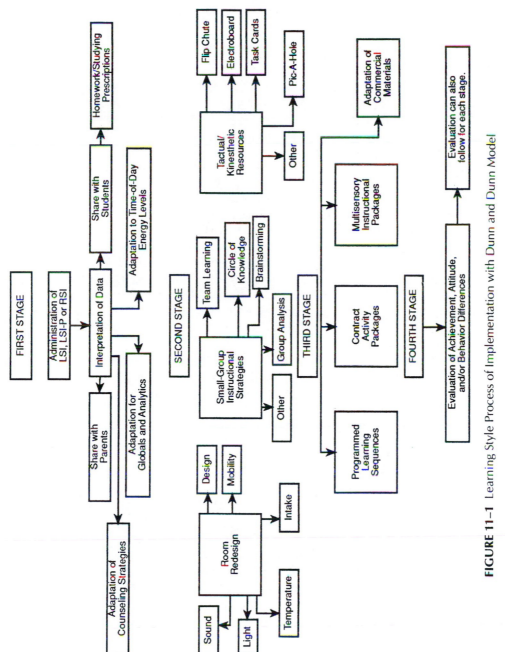

FIGURE 11–1 Learning Style Process of Implementation with Dunn and Dunn Model

Designed by Angela Klavas, Ed.D.

and 2 to varying degrees; many had moved into stage 3. *All had obtained increased test achievement.* Of those that had tested for attitudinal improvement, all had obtained significantly higher attitude test scores based on how the students felt about learning in this type of program. *All* reported improved behavior and fewer incidences (if any) of the need for referrals because of discipline problems.

Thus, follow the Klavas design as closely as possible (see Figure 11–1). Begin with the administration of the appropriate instrument to identify each student's learning style; see Appendix A for a listing of learning style instruments and the grade levels for which each is recommended. Share the children's learning style strengths with the youngsters and their parents. Interpret the results in terms of how you will alter the classroom, resources, and/or instruction to respond better to students' identified strengths. Use the St. John's University Homework Disc to give each child and parent a prescription for how the youngster should study and do assignments based on individual learning style strengths. Be certain to explain that (1) in each family, parents and siblings often have styles that are dramatically different from each other's, and (2) all styles are equally valuable. Do what you can to teach globals globally and analytics analytically (see Chapter 4), and remind students to do their most demanding cognitive work at the time of day that best matches their energy highs.

Next consider the elements in stage 2 with which you feel most comfortable. If redesigning the room does not appear overwhelming, choose those aspects that make sense to you and begin improving the instructional environment. If you are willing to experiment with introducing new and difficult material through Team Learning and then reinforcing through Circle of Knowledge, begin with those. If you are concerned about underachievers or bored students, begin with tactual/kinesthetic instructional resources—the Flip Chute, Pic-A-Hole, Task Cards, Electroboards, Learning Circles, and so forth. Permit intake (water, juice, vegetables) if you are so inclined. You do *not* need to adopt all facets of learning styles instruction; do what you can!

The third stage entails translating your objectives—what you want the students to master—into appropriate methods—CAPs, PLSs, or MIPs. You can adapt commercial materials to reflect similar approaches. At each stage, determine the effectiveness of the approach you are implementing with each child. Thus, compare individuals' grades during a three-week interval immediately *before* and *after* you begin each phase of the learning styles approach. Youngsters should perform better with learning styles methods and resources than they did previously. Share your comparison of the students' before-and-after test scores with them. Discuss how to change instruction to better appeal to each. The final stage should be teaching students to develop their own materials.

Move into learning styles instruction slowly; take only one step at a time into those stages you believe you can manage. Do not undertake too much, but *do* keep trying new things. You will be amazed at how well certain methods work for certain youngsters and not for others. With each new stage you move into, your students will achieve better, like school more, and behave better than before. In addition, they will develop a healthy appreciation of their own—and others'—styles, and will feel better about themselves, their classmates, and their teachers than they have for a long, long time! And they will owe it all to you.

—— APPENDIX A ——

Instruments for Identifying Learning or Teaching Styles

- *Adults' Learning Styles: Productivity Environmental Preference Survey* (PEPS). Specimen Set, Tests, and Processing. Price Systems, Box 1818, Lawrence, KS 66044–1818.
- *Students' Learning Styles (Grades 3–12): Learning Style Inventory* (LSI). Specimen Set, Tests, and Processing. Price Systems, Box 1818, Lawrence, KS 66044–1818.
- *Students' Learning Styles (Grades K–2): Learning Style Inventory: Primary Version* (LSI:P). Center for the Study of Learning and Teaching Styles, St. John's University, Utopia Parkway, Jamaica, NY 11439.
- *Teachers' Teaching Styles: Teaching Style Inventory* (TSI) (Chapter 10) of R. Dunn & K. Dunn, *Teaching Elementary Students Through Their Individual Learning Styles,* Allyn and Bacon, 1992, and R. Dunn & K. Dunn, *Teaching Secondary Students Through Their Individual Learning Style Strengths,* Allyn & Bacon, 1993.

APPENDIX B

LSI:P Illustrations

Sound

Light

Temperature

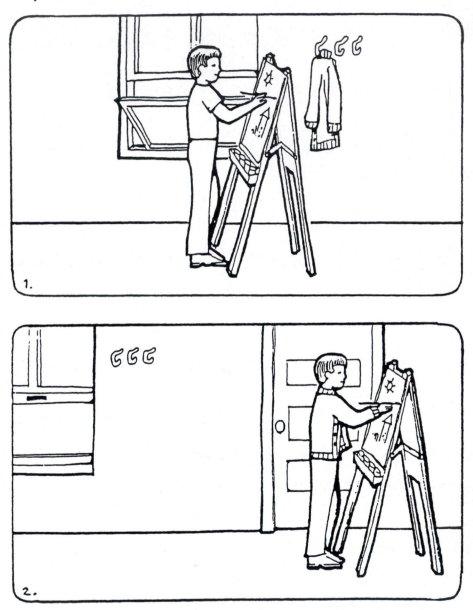

Design

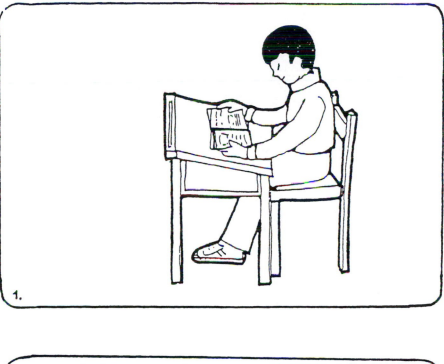

1.

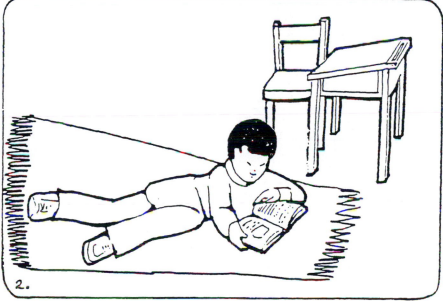

2.

Motivation

Responsibility and Persistence

Structure

Sociological

Perception

Intake

Time

Mobility

REFERENCES

Alberg, J., Cook, L., Fiore, T., Friend, M., Sano, S., et al. (1992). *Educational approaches and options for integrating students with disabilities: A decision tool.* Triangle Park, NC: Research Triangle Institute.

Andrews, R. H. (1990, July–September). The development of a learning styles program in a low socioeconomic, underachieving North Carolina elementary school. *Journal of Reading, Writing, and Learning Disabilities International.* New York: Hemisphere Publishing Corporation, *6*(3), 307–314.

Andrews, R. H. (1991). Insights into education: An elementary principal's perspective. *Hands on approaches to learning styles: Practical approaches to successful schooling.* New Wilmington, PA: Association for the Advancement of International Education.

Argyris, C. (1957). *Personality and organization.* New York: Harper.

Atkinson, S. L. (1988). A longitudinal study: The effect of similar and non-similar student/teacher learning styles on academic achievement in fourth- and fifth-grade mathematics. Doctoral dissertation, Temple University.

Avise, M. J. (1982). The relationship between learning styles and grades of Dexfield junior and senior high school students in Redfield, Iowa. Doctoral dissertation, Drake University. *Dissertation Abstracts International, 43*(09), A, 2953.

Bailey, G. K. (1988). Examination of the relationship between hemispheric preferences and environmental characteristics of learning style in college students. Doctoral dissertation, University of Southern Mississippi. *Dissertation Abstracts International, 49*(08), A, 2151.

Bass, B. M. (1965). *Organizational psychology.* Boston: Allyn and Bacon.

Bauer, E. (1991). The relationships between and among learning styles, perceptual preferences, instructional strategies, mathematics achievement, and attitude toward mathematics of learning disabled and emotionally handicapped students in a suburban junior high school. Doctoral dissertation, St. John's University.

Beaty, S. A. (1986). The effect of inservice training on the ability of teachers to observe learning styles of students. Doctoral dissertation, Oregon State University. *Dissertation Abstracts International, 47,* 2530A.

Biggers, J. L. (1980). Body rhythms, the school day, and academic achievement. *Journal of Experimental Education, 49*(1), 45–47.

Billings, D., & Cobb, K. (1992). Effects of learning style preference, attitude, and GPA on learner achievement using computer-assisted interactive videodisc instruction. *Journal of Computer-Based Instruction, 19*(1), 12–16.

Bonham, L. A. (1987). Theoretical and practical differences and similarities among selected cognitive and learning styles of adults: An analysis of the literature (Volumes I and II). Doctoral dissertation, University of Georgia. *Dissertation Abstracts International, 48,* 2530A.

Braio, A. (1988). *Mission from nostyle.* St. John's University. Center for the Study of Learning and Teaching Styles. Jamaica, NY 11439.

Brennan, P. K. (1984). An analysis of the relationships among hemispheric preference and analytic/global cognitive style, two elements of learning style, method of instruction, gender, and mathematics achievement of tenth-grade geometry students. Doctoral dissertation, St. John's University, 1984. *Dissertation Abstracts International, 45,* 3271A.

Brown, M. D. (1991). The relationship between traditional instrumental methods, Contract Activity Packages, and mathematics achievement of fourth-grade gifted students. Doctoral dissertation, University of Southern Mississippi. *Dissertation Abstracts International,* A, The Humanities and Social Sciences, *52*(6), 1999A–2000A.

Brunner, C. E., & Majewski, W. S. (1990, Occtober). Mildly handicapped students can succeed with learning styles. *Educational Leadership.* Alexandria, VA: Association for Supervision and Curriculum Development, *48,* 21–23.

Brunner, R., & Hill, D. (1992, April). Using learning styles research in coaching. *Journal of Physical Education, Recreation and Dance, 63*(4), 26–61.

Bruno, J. (1988). An experimental investigation of the relationships between and among hemispheric processing, learning style preference, instructional strategies, academic achievement, and attitudes of developmental mathematics students in an urban technical college. Doctoral dissertation, St. John's University. *Dissertation Abstracts International, 48*(5), 1066A.

Buell, B. G., & Buell, N. A. (1987). Perceptual modality preference as a variable in the effectiveness of continuing education for professionals. Doctoral dissertation, University of Southern California. *Dissertation Abstracts International, 48,* 283A.

Buhler, J. (1990). A study of the relationship between selected learning styles and achievement of kindergarten language arts objectives in a local school district. Doctoral dissertation, University of North Texas. *Dissertation Abstracts International, 51*(09), A, 2978.

Cafferty, E. (1980). An analysis of student performance based upon the degree of match between the educational cognitive style of the teachers and the educational cognitive style of the students. Doctoral dissertation, University of Nebraska. *Dissertation Abstracts International, 41*(07), A, 2908.

Calvano, E. J. (1985). The influence of student learning styles on the mathematics achievement of middle school students. Doctoral dissertation, East Texas State University. *Dissertation Abstracts International, 46,* 10A.

Carbo, M. (1980). An analysis of the relationship between the two elements of learning style, method of instruction, gender, and mathematics achievement of tenth-grade geometry students. Doctoral dissertation, St. John's University. *Dissertation Abstracts International, 45,* 3271A.

Carns, A. W., & Carns, M. R. (1991, May). Teaching study skills, cognitive strategies, and metacognitive skills through self-diagnosed learning styles. *The School Counselor, 38,* 341–346.

Carruthers, S. A., & Young, A. I. (1979). Do time preferences affect achievement or discipline? *Learning Styles Network Newsletter, 1*(2), 1. St. John's University and the National Association of Secondary School Principals.

Cholakis, M. M. (1986). An experimental investigation of the relationships between and among sociological preferences, vocabulary instruction and achievement, and the attitudes of New York, urban, seventh and eighth grade underachievers. Doctoral dissertation, St. John's University. *Dissertation Abstracts International, 47,* 4046A.

Clark-Thayer, S. (1987). The relationship of the knowledge of student-perceived learning style preferences, and study habits and attitudes to achievement of college freshmen in a small urban university. Doctoral dissertation, Boston University. *Dissertation Abstracts International, 48,* 872A.

Clay, J. E. (1984). *A correlational analysis of the learning characteristics of highly achieving and poorly achieving freshmen at A&M University as revealed through performance on standardized tests.* Normal: Alabama A&M University.

Cody, C. (1983). Learning styles, including hemisphericity: A comparative study of average, gifted, and highly gifted students in grades five through twelve. Doctoral dissertation, Temple University. *Dissertation Abstracts International, 44,* 1631A.

Cohen, L. (1986). Birth order and learning styles: An examination of the relationships between birth order and middle school students' preferred learning style profiles. Doctoral dissertation, Temple University. *Dissertation Abstracts International, 47,* 2084A.

Coleman, S. J. (1988). An investigation of the relationships among physical and emotional learning style preferences and perceptual modality strengths of gifted first-grade students. Doctoral dissertation, Virginia Polytechnic Institute and State University.

Cook, L. (1989). Relationships among learning style awareness, academic achievement, and locus of control among community college students. Doctoral dissertation, University of Florida. *Dissertation Abstracts International, 50*(07), A, 1996.

Cooper, T. J. D. (1991). An investigation of the learning styles of students at two contemporary alternative high schools in the District of Columbia. Doctoral dissertation, George Washington University, School of Education and Human Development.

Coperhaven, R. (1979). The consistency of student learning styles as students move from English to mathematics. Doctoral dissertation, Indiana University. *Dissertation Abstracts International, 40,* 3735A. (University Microfilms No. 80-00610)

Cramp, D. C. (1990). A study of the effects on student achievement of fourth- and fifth-grade students' instructional times being matched and mismatched with their particular time preference. Doctoral dissertation, University of Missouri.

Crampton, N. A. S. (1990). Learning style (modality) preferences for students attending private residential alternative schools (at risk). Doctoral dissertation, University of South Dakota, 1991. *Dissertation Abstracts International, 52*(02), A, 407.

Crino, E. M. (1984). An analysis of the preferred learning styles of kindergarten children and the relationship of these preferred learning styles to curriculum planning for kindergarten children. Doctoral dissertation, State University of New York at Buffalo. *Dissertation Abstracts International, 45,* 1282A.

Cross, J. A. (1982). Internal locus of control governs talented students (9–12). *Learning Styles Network Newsletter, 3*(3), 3. St. John's University and the National Association of Secondary School Principals.

Currence, J. A. (1991). High school dropouts as learners: A comparative analysis of schooling experiences and school behaviors, school climate perceptions, learning style preferences, and locus-of-control orientation of persisters and high school dropouts in a rural Eastern Shore county school system. Doctoral dissertation, University of Maryland, College Park. *Dissertation Abstracts International,* A, The Humanities and Social Sciences, *52*(7), 2388A.

Damian, A. (1988). Designing instructional strategies using individual learning styles diagnosis and prescriptions to improve reading in third grade elementary school children. Master's thesis, Dowling College, New York.

Davis, M. A. (1985). An investigation of the relationship of personality types and learning style preferences of high school students (Myers-Briggs Type Indicator). Doctoral dissertation, George Peabody College for Teachers of Vanderbilt University. *Dissertation Abstracts International, 46,* 1606A.

Dean, W. L. (1982). A comparison of the learning styles of educable mentally retarded students and learning disabled students. Doctoral dissertation, University of Mississippi. *Dissertation Abstracts International, 43,* 1923A.

DeBello, T. (1985). A critical analysis of the achievement and attitude effects of administrative assignments to social studies writing instruction based on identified eighth grade students' learning style preferences for learning alone, with peers, or with teachers. *Dissertation Abstracts International, 47,* 68–01A.

DeBello, T. (1990, July–September). Comparison of eleven major learning styles models: Variables, appropriate populations, validity of instrumentation, and the research behind them. *Journal of Reading, Writing, and Learning Disabilities International.* New York: Hemisphere Publishing Corporation, *6*(3), 203–222.

DeGregoris, C. N. (1986). Reading comprehension and the interaction of individual sound preferences and varied auditory distractions. Doctoral dissertation, Hofstra University, 1986. *Dissertation Abstracts International, 47,* 3380A.

Delbrey, A. (1987, August). The relationship between the Learning Style Inventory and the

Gregorc Style Delineator. Doctoral dissertation, University of Alabama. *Dissertation Abstracts International, 49*(2).

Della Valle, J. (1984). An experimental investigation of the word recognition scores of seventh grade students to provide supervisory and administrative guidelines for the organization of effective instructional environments. Doctoral dissertation, St. John's University, 1984. *Dissertation Abstracts International, 45*, 359A. Recipient: Phi Delta Kappa National Award for Outstanding Doctoral Research, 1984; National Association of Secondary School Principals' Middle School Research Finalist citation, 1984; and Association for Supervision and Curriculum Development Finalist for Best National Research (Supervision), 1984.

DellaValle, J. (1990, July–September). The development of a learning styles program in an affluent, suburban New York elementary school. New York: Hemisphere Publishing Corporation, *6*(3), 315–322.

Drew, M. W. (1991). An investigation of the effects of matching and mismatching minority underachievers with culturally similar and dissimilar story content and learning style and traditional instructional strategies. Doctoral dissertation, St. John's University.

Dunn, K., & Dunn, R. (1987). Dispelling outmoded beliefs about student learning. *Educational Leadership, 44*(6), 55–62.

Dunn, R. (1984). How should students do their homework? Research vs. opinion. *Early Years, 14*(4), 43–45.

Dunn, R. (1985). A research-based plan for doing homework. *The Education Digest, 9,* 40–42.

Dunn, R. (1987, Spring). Research on instructional environments: Implications for student achievement and attitudes. *Professional School Psychology, 2*(1), 43–52.

Dunn, R. (1988). Commentary: Teaching students through their perceptual strengths or preferences. *Journal of Reading, 31*(4), 304–309.

Dunn, R. (1989a, May–June). Can schools overcome the impact of societal ills on student achievement? The research indicates—yes! *The Principal.* New York: Board of Jewish Education of Greater New York, *34*(5), 1–15.

Dunn, R. (1989b). Capitalizing on students' perceptual strengths to ensure literacy while engaging in conventional lecture/discussion. *Reading Psychology: An International Quarterly, 9*(4), 431–453.

Dunn, R. (1989c, Summer). Do students from different cultures have different learning styles? *International Education.* New Wilmington, PA: Association for the Advancement of International Education, *16*(50), 40–42.

Dunn, R. (1989d). Individualizing instruction for mainstreamed gifted children. In R. R. Milgram (Ed.), *Teaching gifted and talented learners in regular classrooms* (Chapter 3, pp. 63–111). Springfield, IL: Charles C Thomas.

Dunn, R. (1989e). Recent research on learning and seven applications to teaching young children to read. *The Oregon Elementary Principal, 50*(2), 29–32.

Dunn, R. (1989f, February). A small private school in Minnesota. *Teaching K–8.* Norwalk, CT: Early Years, Inc., *18*(5), 54–57.

Dunn, R. (1989g, Fall). Teaching gifted students through their learning style strengths. *International Education.* New Wilmington, PA: Association for the Advancement of International Education, *16*(51), 6–8.

Dunn, R. (1990a, January). Bias over substance: A critical analysis of Kavale and Forness' report on modality-based instruction. *Exceptional Children, 56*(4), 354–356.

Dunn, R. (1990b, October). Rita Dunn answers questions on learning styles. *Educational Leadership.* Alexandria, VA: Association for Supervision and Curriculum Development, *48*(15), 15–19.

Dunn, R. (1990c, Winter). Teaching underachievers through their learning style strengths. *International Education.* New Wilmington, PA: Association for the Advancement of International Education, *16*(52), 5–7.

Dunn, R. (1990d, Summer). Teaching young children to read: Matching methods to learning style perceptual processing strengths, Part 1. *International Education.* New Wilmington, PA: Association for the Advancement of International Education, *17*(54), 2–3.

Dunn, R. (1990e, Fall). Teaching young children to read: Matching methods to learning style perceptual processing strengths, Part 2. *International Education*. New Wilmington, PA: Association for the Advancement of International Education, *17*(55), 5–7.

Dunn, R. (1990f, July–September). Understanding the Dunn and Dunn learning styles model and the need for individual diagnosis and prescription. *Journal of Reading, Writing, and Learning Disabilities International*. New York: Hemisphere Publishing Corporation, *6*(3), 223–247.

Dunn, R. (1990g, Spring). When you really have to lecture, teach students through their perceptual strengths. *International Education*. New Wilmington, PA: Association for the Advancement of International Education, *17*(53), 1, 6–7.

Dunn, R. (1991a, Winter). Are you willing to experiment with a tactual/visual/auditory global approach to reading? Part 3. *International Education*. New Wilmington, PA: Association for the Advancement of International Education, *18*(56), 6–8.

Dunn, R. (1991b). *Hands on approaches to learning styles: A practical guide for successful schooling*. New Wilmington, PA: Association for the Advancement of International Education.

Dunn, R. (1991c). Instructional leadership in education: Limited, diffused, sporadic, and lacking in research. *CSA Leadership*. New York: American Federation of School Administrators, pp. 30–41.

Dunn, R. (1992a, April–June). Strategies for teaching word recognition to the disabled readers. *Reading and Writing Quarterly*. New York: Hemisphere Publishing Corporation, *8*(2) 157–177.

Dunn, R. (1992b, Spring). Teaching the "I-was-paying-attention-but-I-didn't-hear-you-say-it learner." *International Education*. New Wilmington, PA: Association for the Advancement of International Education, *19*(61), 1, 6.

Dunn, R. (1993, Winter–Spring). The learning styles of gifted adolescents in nine culturally diverse nations. *International Education*. New Wilmington, PA: Association for the Advancement of International Education, *20*(64), 4–6.

Dunn, R. (in press a). Research report: The learning styles of students from different cultural backgrounds. *Canadian Emergency Librarian*. British Vancouver: Emergency Librarians' Association.

Dunn, R. (in press b). Teaching gifted students through their individual learning style strengths. In R. M. Milgram, R. Dunn, & G. E. Price (Eds.), *Teaching and counseling gifted and talented adolescents for learning style: An international perspective* (Chapter 7). Praeger.

Dunn, R. (1993). Teaching the "I don't like school and you can't make me like it" learner. *International Education*. New Wilmington, PA: Association for the Advancement of International Education, *20*(65),4–5.

Dunn, R., Beaudry, J. A., & Klavas, A. (1989). Survey of research on learning styles. *Educational Leadership, 46*(6), 50–58.

Dunn, R., & Bruno, A. (1985). What does the research on learning styles have to do with Mario? *The Clearing House, 59*(1), 9–11.

Dunn, R., Bruno, J., Sklar, R. I., Zenhausern, R., & Beaudry, J. (1990, May–June). Effects of matching and mismatching minority developmental college students' hemispheric preferences on mathematics scores. *Journal of Educational Research*. Washington, DC: Heldref Publications, *83*(5), 283–288.

Dunn, R., Cavanaugh, D., Eberle, B., & Zenhausern, R. (1982). Hemispheric preference: The newest element of learning style. *The American Biology Teacher, 44*(5), 291–294.

Dunn, R., DeBello, T., Brennan, P., Krimsky, J., & Murrain, P. (1981). Learning style researchers define differences differently. *Educational Leadership*. Alexandria, VA: Association for Supervision and Curriculum Development, *38*(5), 382–392.

Dunn, R., Deckinger, E. L., Withers, P., & Katzenstein, H. (1990, Winter). Should college students be taught how to do homework? The effects of studying marketing through individual perceptual strengths. *Illinois School Research and Development Journal*. Normal: Illinois Association for Supervision and Curriculum Development, *26*(3), 96–113.

Dunn, R., Della Valle, J., Dunn, K., Geisert, G., Sinatra, R., & Zenhausern, R. (1986). The effects of matching and mismatching students' mobility preferences on recognition and memory tasks. *Journal of Educational Research, 79*(5), 267–272.

Dunn, R., & Dunn, K. (1972). *Practical approaches to individualizing instruction: Contracts and other effective teaching strategies.* Nyack, NY: Parker Publishing Company—A Prentice-Hall Division.

Dunn, R., & Dunn, K. (1975). *Educator's self-teaching guide to individualizing instructional programs.* Nyack, NY: Parker Publishing Company—A Prentice-Hall Division.

Dunn, R., & Dunn, K. (1979). Using learning style data to develop student prescriptions. In *Student Learning Styles: Diagnosing and Prescribing Programs* (Chapter 12, pp. 109–122). Reston, VA: National Association of Secondary School Principals.

Dunn, R., & Dunn, K. (1992). *Teaching elementary students through their individual learning styles.* Boston: Allyn and Bacon.

Dunn, R., & Dunn, K. (1993). *Teaching secondary students through their individual learning styles.* Boston: Allyn and Bacon.

Dunn, R., Dunn, K., & Freeley, M. E. (1984). Practical applications of the research: Responding to students' learning styles—Step one. *Illinois State Research and Development Journal, 21*(1), 1–21.

Dunn, R., Dunn, K., & Price, G. E. (1977). Diagnosing learning styles: Avoiding malpractice suits against school systems. *Phi Delta Kappan, 58*(5), 418–420.

Dunn, R., Dunn, K., Primavera, L., Sinatra, R., & Virostko, J. (1987). A timely solution: A review of research on the effects of chronobiology on children's achievement and behavior. *The Clearing House, 61*(1), 5–8.

Dunn, R., Dunn, K., & Treffinger, D. (1992). *Bringing out the giftedness in every child: A guide for parents.* New York: Wiley.

Dunn, R., Gemake, J., Jalali, F., Zenhausern, R., Quinn, P., & Spiridakis, J. (1990, April). Cross-cultural differences in the learning styles of elementary-age students from four ethnic backgrounds. *Journal of Multicultural Counseling and Development, 18*(2), 68–93.

Dunn, R., Gemake, J., & Zenhausern, R. (1990, January). Cross-cultural differences in learning styles. *Missouri Association for Supervision and Curriculum Development Journal, 1*(2), 9–15.

Dunn, R., Giannitti, M. C., Murray, J. B., Rossi, I., Geisert, G., & Quinn, P. (1990). Grouping students for instruction: Effects of learning style on achievement and attitudes. *Journal of Social Psychology.* Washington, DC: American Educational Research Association, *130*(4), 485–494.

Dunn, R., & Griggs, S. A. (1988a). High school dropouts: Do they learn differently from those who remain in school? *The Principal.* New York: Jewish Board of Education of Greater New York, *34*(1), 1–8.

Dunn, R., & Griggs, S. (1988b). *Learning styles: Quiet revolution in American secondary schools.* Reston, VA: National Association of Secondary School Principals.

Dunn, R., & Griggs, S. A. (1989a, January). Learning styles: Key to improving schools and student achievement. *Curriculum Report.* Reston, VA: National Association of Secondary School Principals.

Dunn, R., & Griggs, S. A. (1989b, October). The learning styles of multicultural groups and counseling implications. *Journal of Multicultural Counseling and Development.* Alexandria, VA: American Association for Multicultural Counseling and Development, *7*(4), 146–155.

Dunn, R., & Griggs, S. A. (1989c). Learning styles: Quiet revolution in American secondary schools. *Momentum.* Washington, DC: Heldref Publications, *63*(1), 40–42.

Dunn, R., & Griggs, S. A. (1989d, April). A matter of style. *Momentum.* Washington, DC: National Catholic Education Association, *20*(2), 66–70.

Dunn, R., & Griggs, S. A. (1989e, January). A quiet revolution in Hempstead. *Teaching K–8.* Norwalk, CT: Early Years, Inc., *18*(5), 54–57.

Dunn, R., & Griggs, S. A. (1989f). A quiet revolution: Learning styles and their application to secondary schools. *Holistic Education.* Greenfield, MA: Holistic Education Review, *2*(4), 14–19.

Dunn, R., & Griggs, S. A. (1990). Research on the learning style characteristics of selected racial and ethnic groups. *Journal of Reading, Writing, and Learning Disabilities.* Washington, DC: Hemisphere Press, *6*(3), 261–280.

Dunn, R., Griggs, S. A., & Price, G. E. (1993). Comparison of the learning styles of fourth-, fifth-, and sixth-grade male and female Mexican-American students in southern Texas and same-grade students in the general population of the United States. *Journal of Multicultural Counseling and Development, 21,* (4), 237–247.

Dunn, R., Krimsky, J., Murray, J., & Quinn, P. (1985). Light up their lives: A review of research on the effects of lighting on children's achievement. *The Reading Teacher, 38*(9), 863–869.

Dunn, R., Pizzo, J., Sinatra, R., & Barretto, R. A. (1983, Winter). Can it be too quiet to learn? *Focus: Teaching English Language Arts, 9*(2), 92.

Dunn, R., & Price, G. E. (1980). The learning style characteristics of gifted children. *Gifted Child Quarterly, 24*(1), 33–36.

Dunn, R., Price, G. E., Dunn, K., & Griggs, S. A. (1981). Studies in students' learning styles. *Roeper Review, 4*(2), 38–40.

Dunn, R., Shea, T. C., Evans, W., & MacMurren, H. (1991). Learning style and equal protection: The next frontier. *The Clearing House.* Washington, DC: Heldref Publications, *65*(2), 93–96.

Dunn, R., & Smith, J. B. (1990). Learning styles and library media programs. In J. B. Smith (Ed.), *School Library Media Annual.* Englewood, CO: Libraries Unlimited, Inc., Chapter 4, pp. 32–49.

Dunn, R., White, R. M., & Zenhausern, R. (1982). An investigation of responsible versus less responsible students. *Illinois School Research and Development, 19*(1), 19–24.

Eitington, N. J. (1989). A comparison of learning styles of freshmen with high and low reading achievement in the Community Scholars Liberal Studies Program at Georgetown University, Washington, DC. *Dissertation Abstracts International, 50*(05), A, 1285.

Elliot, I. (1991, November–December). The reading place. *Teaching K–8.* Norwalk, CT: Early Years, Inc., *21*(3), 30–34.

Emery, L. (1990). A descriptive comparison at the kindergarten level of two methods of identifying student learning style preferences. Master's thesis, Northern State University, South Dakota.

Ewing, N., & Yong, L. F. (1992). A comparative study of the learning style preferences among gifted African-American, Mexican-American, and American-born, Chinese middle-grade students. *Roeper Review, 14*(3), 120–123.

Fadler, J. L., & Hosler, V. (1979). *Understanding the alpha child at home and at school.* Springfield, IL: Charles C Thomas.

Ferrell, B. G. (1981). Factor analytic validation of the learning styles paradigm. Doctoral dissertation, Southern Illinois University of Carbondale. *Dissertation Abstracts International, 42*(07), A, 3069.

Fitt, S. (1975). The individual and his environment. In T. G. David & B. D. Wright (Eds.), *Learning environments.* Chicago: University of Chicago Press.

Fleming, V. J. (1989, August). Vocational classrooms. *Vocational Education Journal.* Alexandria, VA: Vocational Association, *10*(1), 36–39.

Freeley, M. E. (1984). An experimental investigation of the relationships among teachers' individual time preferences, inservice workshop schedules, and instructional techniques and the subsequent implementation of learning style strategies in participants' classrooms. Doctoral dissertation, St. John's University. *Dissertation Abstracts International, 46,* 403A.

Gadwa, K., & Griggs, S. A. (1985). The school dropout: Implications for counselors. *The School Counselor, 33,* 9–17.

Galvin, A. J. (1992). An analysis of learning and productivity styles across occupational groups in a corporate setting (learning styles, corporate training). Doctoral dissertation, Boston University. *Dissertation Abstracts International, 53*(04), A, 1027.

Garcia-Otero, M. (1987). Knowledge of learning styles and the effect on the clinical performance of nurse anesthesiology students. Doctoral dissertation, University of New Orleans. *Dissertation Abstracts International, 49*(05), B, 1602.

Gardiner, B. (1983). Stepping into a learning styles program. *Roeper Review, 6*(2), 90–92.

Gardiner, B. (1986). An experimental analysis of selected teaching strategies implemented at specific times of the school day and their effects on the social studies achievement test scores and attitudes of fourth grade, low achieving students in an urban school setting. Doctoral dissertation, St. John's University. *Dissertation Abstracts International, 47,* 3307A.

Garger, S. (1990, October). Is there a link between learning style and neurophysiology? *Educational Leadership.* Alexandria, VA: Association for Supervision and Curriculum Development, *48*(2), 63–65.

Garrett, S. L. (1991). The effects of perceptual preference and motivation on vocabulary and attitude test scores among high school students. Doctoral dissertation, University of La Verne, CA.

Geisert, G., & Dunn, R. (1991a, March). Computers and learning style. *Principal.* Reston, VA: National Association of Secondary School Principals, *70*(4), 47–49.

Geisert, G., & Dunn, R. (1991b, March). Effective use of computers: Assignments based on individual learning style. *The Clearing House.* Washington, DC: Heldref Publications, *64*(4), 219–224.

Geisert, G., Dunn, R., & Sinatra, R. (1990). Reading, learning styles, and computers. *Journal of Reading, Writing, and Learning Disabilities.* Washington, DC: Hemisphere Press, *6*(3), 297–306.

Giannitti, M. C. (1988). An experimental investigation of the relationships among the learning style sociological preferences of middle-school students (grades 6, 7, 8), their attitudes and achievement in social studies, and selected instructional strategies. Doctoral dissertation, St. John's University. *Dissertation Abstracts International, 49,* 2911A.

Glasner, J., & Ingham, J. (1993). Learning styles and literacy. *The Bookmark.* Albany, NY: State Education Department, New York State Library, *50*(111), 218–223.

Gould, B. J. (1987). An investigation of the relationships between supervisors' and supervisees' sociological productivity styles on teacher evaluations and interpersonal attraction ratings. Doctoral dissertation, St. John's University. *Dissertation Abstracts International, 48,* 18A.

Griggs, S. A. (1989, November). Students' sociological grouping preferences of learning styles. *The Clearing House.* Washington, DC: Heldref Publications, *63*(3), 135–139.

Griggs, S. A. (1991a). Counseling gifted children with different learning-style preferences. In R. M. Milgram (Ed.), *Counseling talented gifted children: A guide for teachers, counselors, and parents.* New Jersey: Ablex, pp. 53–74.

Griggs, S. A. (1991b). *Counseling students through their individual learning styles.* Ann Arbor: University of Michigan. Obtainable from Center for the Study of Learning and Teaching Styles, St. John's University, Jamaica, NY 11439.

Griggs, S. A., & Price, G. E. (1980). A comparison between the learning styles of gifted versus average junior high school students. *Phi Delta Kappan, 61,* 361.

Griggs, S. A., & Price, G. E. (1982). A comparison between the learning styles of gifted versus average junior high school students. *Creative and Gifted Child Quarterly, 7,* 39–42.

Griggs, S. A., Price, G. E., Koepl, S., & Swaine, W. (1984). The effects of group counseling with sixth-grade students using approaches that are compatible versus incompatible with selected learning style elements. *California Personnel and Guidance Journal, 5*(1), 28–35.

Guild, P. O'R. (1980). Learning styles: Knowledge, issues and applications for classroom teachers. Doctoral dissertation, University of Massachusetts. *Dissertation Abstracts Internationa, 41*(03), A, 1033.

Guinta, S. F. (1984). Administrative considerations concerning learning style and the influence of instructor/student congruence on high schoolers' achievement and educators' perceived stress. Doctoral dissertation, St. John's University. *Dissertation Abstracts International, 45,* 32A.

Guzzo, R. S. (1987). Dificuldades de apprenddizagem: Modalidade de atencão e analise de tarefas em materials didaticos. Doctoral dissertation, University of São Paulo, Institute of Psychology, Brazil.

Hankins, N. E. (1973). *Psychology for contemporary education.* Columbus, OH: Charles E. Merrill, Chapter 7.

Hanna, S. J. (1989). An investigation of the effects on achievement test scores of individual time preferences and time of training in a corporate setting. Doctoral dissertation, St. John's University.

Harp, T. Y., & Orsak, L. (1990, July–September). One administrator's challenge: Implementing a learning style program at the secondary level. *Journal of Reading, Writing, and Learning Disabilities International.* New York: Hemisphere Publishing Corporation, 6(3), 335–342.

Hart, L. A. (1983). *Human brain and human learning.* New York: Longman.

Harty, P. M. (1982). *Learning styles: A matter of difference in the foreign language classroom.* Unpublished master's dissertation, Wright State University.

Hawk, T. D. (1983). A comparison of teachers' preference for specific inservice activity approaches and their measured learning styles. Doctoral dissertation, Kansas State University. *Dissertation Abstracts International, 44*(12), A, 3557.

Hickerson-Roberts, V. L. (1983). Reading achievement, reading attitudes, self-concept, learning styles and estimated high school grade-point average as predictions of academic success for 55 adult learners at Kansas State University. Doctoral dissertation, Kansas State University. *Dissertation Abstracts International, 44*(05), A, 1295.

Hill, G. D. (1987). An experimental investigation into the interaction between modality preference and instructional mode in the learning of spelling words by upper-elementary learning disabled students. Doctoral dissertation, North Texas State University. *Dissertation Abstracts International, 48,* 2536A.

Hodges, H. (1985). An analysis of the relationships among preferences for a formal/informal design, one element of learning style, academic achievement, and attitudes of seventh and eighth grade students in remedial mathematics classes in a New York City junior high school. Doctoral dissertation, St. John's University. *Dissertation Abstracts International, 45,* 2791A. Recipient: Phi Delta Kappa National Finalist Award for Outstanding Doctoral Research, 1986.

Homans, G. (1950). *The human group.* New York: Harcourt Brace.

Hutto, J. R. (1982). The association of teacher manipulation of scientifically acquired learning styles information to the achievement and attitudes of second and third grade remedial students. Doctoral dissertation, University of Southern Mississippi. *Dissertation Abstracts International, 44*(01), A, 30.

Ignelzi-Ferraro, D. M. (1989). Identification of the preferred conditions for learning among three groups of mildly handicapped high school students using the Learning Style Inventory. Doctoral dissertation, University of Pittsburgh. *Dissertation Abstracts International, 51*(3), 796A.

Ingham, J. (1989). An experimental investigation of the relationships among learning style perceptual preference, instructional strategies, training achievement, and attitudes of corporate employees. Doctoral dissertation, St. John's University. *Dissertation Abstracts International, 51*(02), A. Recipient: American Society for Training and Development National Research Award, 1990.

Ingham, J. (1991). Matching instruction with employee perceptual preferences significantly increases training effectiveness. *Human Resource Development Quarterly, 2*(1), 53–64.

Jacobs, R. L. (1987). An investigation of the learning style differences among Afro-American and Euro-American high, average, and low achievers. Doctoral dissertation, George Peabody University, Tennessee. *Dissertation Abstracts International, 49*(01), 39A.

Jalali, F. (1988). A cross cultural comparative analysis of the learning styles and field dependence/independence characteristics of selected fourth-, fifth-, and sixth-grade students of Afro, Chinese, Greek, and Mexican heritage. Doctoral dissertation, St. John's University. *Dissertation Abstracts International, 50*(62), 344A.

Jarsonbeck, S. (1984). The effects of a right-brain and mathematics curriculum on low achieving, fourth grade students. Doctoral dissertation, University of South Florida. *Dissertation Abstracts International, 45*, 2791A.

Jenkins, C. (1991). The relationship between selected demographic variables and learning environmental preferences of freshman students of Alcorn State University. Doctoral dissertation, University of Mississippi. *Dissertation Abstracts International, 92*, 16065.

Johnson, C. D. (1984). Identifying potential school dropouts. Doctoral dissertation, United States International University. *Dissertation Abstracts International, 45*, 2397A.

Johnson, D. W., & Johnson, R. T. (1975). Learning together and alone: Cooperation, competition, and individualization. Englewood Cliffs, NJ: Prentice-Hall.

Johnston, R. J. (1986). A comparative analysis between the effectiveness of conventional and modular instruction in teaching students with varied learning styles and individual differences enrolled in high school industrial arts manufacturing. Doctoral dissertation, North Carolina State University. *Dissertation Abstracts International, 47*(08), A, 2923.

Kahre, C. J. (1985). Relationships between learning styles of student teachers, cooperating teachers, and final evaluations. Doctoral dissertation, Arizona State University. *Dissertation Abstracts International, 45*, 2492A.

Kaley, S. B. (1977). Field dependence/independence and learning styles in sixth graders. Doctoral dissertation, Hofstra University. *Dissertation Abstracts International, 38*, 1301A.

Keefe, J. W. (1982). Assessing student learning styles: An overview of learning style and cognitive style inquiry. *Student Learning Styles and Brain Behavior.* Reston, VA: National Association of Secondary School Principals.

Kelly, A. P. (1989). Elementary principals' change-facilitating behavior as perceived by self and staff when implementing learning styles instructional programs. Doctoral dissertation, St. John's University.

Kizilay, P. E. (1991). The relationship of learning style preferences and perceptions of college climate and performance on the National Council Licensure Examination for registered nurses in associate degree nursing programs. Doctoral dissertation, University of Georgia.

Klavas, A. (1991). Implementation of the Dunn and Dunn learning styles model in United States elementary schools: Principals' and teachers' perceptions of factors that facilitated or impeded the process. Doctoral dissertation, St. John's University.

Kleinfeld, J., & Nelson, P. (1991). Adapting instruction to Native Americans' language styles: An iconoclastic view. *Journal of Cross Cultural Psychology, 22*(2), 273–282.

Koester, L. S., & Farley, F. H. (1977). *Arousal and hyperactivity in open and traditional education.* Paper presented at the annual convention of the American Psychological Association, San Francisco. ERIC Document Reproduction Service No. ED 155 543.

Kreitner, K. R. (1981). *Modality strengths and learning styles of musically talented high school students.* Unpublished master's dissertation, The Ohio State University.

Krimsky, J. (1982). A comparative analysis of the effects of matching and mismatching fourth grade students with their learning style preference for the environmental element of light and their subsequent reading speed and accuracy scores. Doctoral dissertation, St. John's University. *Dissertation Abstracts International, 43*, 66A. Recipient: Association for Supervision and Curriculum Development First Alternate National Recognition for Best Doctoral Research (Curriculum), 1982.

Kroon, D. (1985). An experimental investigation of the effects on academic achievement and the resultant administrative implications of instruction congruent and incongruent with secondary industrial arts students' learning style perceptual preferences. Doctoral dissertation, St. John's University. *Dissertation Abstracts International, 46*, 3247A.

Kulp, J. J. (1982). A description of the processes used in developing and implementing a teacher training program based on the Dunns' concept of learning style. Doctoral dissertation, Temple University. *Dissertation Abstracts International, 42*, 5021A.

Kussrow, P. G., & Dunn, K. (1992, Summer). Learning styles and the community educator. *Community Education Journal.* Alexandria, VA: National Community Education Association, *19*(4), 16–19.

Kuznar, E., Falciglia, G. A., Grace, A., Wood, L., & Frankel, J. (1991). Learning style preferences: A comparison of younger and older adult females. *Journal of Nutrition for the Elderly, 10*(3), 213–233.

LaMothe, Billings, D. M., Belcher, A., Cobb, K., Nice, A., & Richardson, V. (1991). Reliability and validity of the productivity environmental preference survey (PEPS). *Nurse Educator, 16*(4), 30–34.

Lam-Phoon, S. (1986). A comparative study of the learning styles of Southeast Asian and American Caucasian college students of two Seventh-Day Adventist campuses. Doctoral dissertation, Andrews University. *Dissertation Abstracts International, 48*(09), 2234A.

Lan Yong, F. (1989). Ethnic, gender, and grade differences in the learning style preferences of gifted minority students. Doctoral dissertation, Southern Illinois University at Carbondale.

LeClair, T. J. (1986). *The preferred perceptual modality of kindergarten aged children.* California State University. *Master's Abstracts, 24, 324.*

Lemmon, P. (1985). A school where learning styles make a difference. *Principal, 64*(4), 26–29.

Lenahan, M. (1991). *Kids in style.* New York: St. John's University's Center for the Study of Learning and Teaching Styles.

Lengal, O. (1983). Analysis of the preferred learning styles of former adolescent psychiatric patients. Doctoral dissertation, Kansas State University. *Dissertation Abstracts International, 44,* 2344A.

Levy, J. (1979). Human cognition and lateralization of cerebral function. *Trends in Neuroscience,* 220–224.

Levy, J. (1982, Autumn). What do brain scientists know about education? *Learning Styles Network Newsletter, 3*(3), 4. St. John's University and the National Association of Secondary School Principals.

Li, T. C. (1989). The learning styles of the Filipino graduate students of the evangelical seminaries in metro Manila. Doctoral dissertation, Asia Graduate School of Theology, Philippines.

Lookwood, S. (1987). Learning styles and the learning disabled. Master of Special Education thesis, Graduate College of Northeastern State University, Oklahoma.

Lorge, I., Fox, D., Davitz, J., & Brenner, M. (1958). A survey of studies contrasting the quality of group performance and individual performance, 1920–1957. *Psychological Bulletin 55,* 337–372.

Lux, K. (1987). Special needs students: A qualitative study of their learning styles. Doctoral dissertation, Michigan State University. *Dissertation Abstracts International, 49*(3), 421A.

Lynch, P. K. (1981). An analysis of the relationships among academic achievement, attendance, and the learning style time preferences of eleventh and twelfth grade students identified as initial or chronic truants in a suburban New York school district. Doctoral dissertation, St. John's University. *Dissertation Abstracts International, 42,* 1880A. Recipient: Association for Supervision and Curriculum Development, First Alternate National Recognition for Best Doctoral Research (Supervision), 1981.

MacMurren, H. (1985). A comparative study of the effects of matching and mismatching sixth-grade students with their learning style preferences for the physical element of intake and their subsequent reading speed and accuracy scores and attitudes. Doctoral dissertation, St. John's University. *Dissertation Abstracts International, 46,* 3247A.

Madison, M. B. (1984). A study of learning style preferences of specific learning disability students. Doctoral dissertation, University of Southern Mississippi. *Dissertation Abstracts International, 46,* 3320A.

Mager, R. F. (1962). *Preparing instructional objectives.* Palo Alto, CA: Fearson, pp. 1–2, 53.

Mager, R. F., & McCann, J. (1963). *Learner-controlled instruction.* Palo Alto, CA: Varian.

Marcus, L. (1977a). How teachers view learning styles. *NASSP Bulletin, 61*(408), 112–114.

Marcus, L. (1977b, April). Learning style and ability grouping among seventh-grade students. *The Clearing House, 52*(8), 377–380.

Mariash, L. J. (1983). *Identification of characteristics of learning styles existent among students attending school in selected northeastern Manitoba communities.* Unpublished master's dissertation, University of Manitoba, Winnipeg.

Martini, M. (1986). An analysis of the relationships between and among computer-assisted instruction, learning style perceptual preferences, attitudes, and the science achievement of seventh grade students in a suburban, New York school district. Doctoral dissertation, St. John's University. *Dissertation Abstracts International, 47,* 877A. Recipient: American Association of School Administrators (AASA) First Prize National Research, 1986.

McEwen, P. (1985). *Learning styles, intelligence, and creativity among elementary school students.* Unpublished master's dissertation, State University of New York at Buffalo, Center for Studies in Creativity.

McFarland, M. (1989). An analysis of the relationship between learning style perceptual preferences and attitudes toward computer assisted instruction. Doctoral dissertation, Portland State University. *Dissertation Abstracts International, 50*(10), 3143A.

Mein, J. R. (1986). Cognitive and learning style characteristics of high school gifted students. Doctoral dissertation, University of Florida. *Dissertation Abstracts International, 48*(04), 880A.

Melone, R. A. (1987). The relationship between the level of cognitive development and learning styles of the emerging adolescent. Doctoral dissertation, State University of New York at Buffalo. *Dissertation Abstracts International, 38,* 607A.

Mickler, M. L., & Zippert, C. P. (1987). Teaching strategies based on learning styles of adult students. *Community/Junior College Quarterly, 11,* 33–37.

Miles, B. (1987). An investigation of the relationships among the learning style sociological preferences of fifth and sixth grade students, selected interactive classroom patterns, and achievement in career awareness and career decision-making concepts. Doctoral dissertation, St. John's University. *Dissertation Abstracts International, 48,* 2527A. Recipient: Phi Delta Kappan Eastern Regional Research Finalist, 1988.

Miller, L. M. (1985). *Mobility as an element of learning style: The effect its inclusion or exclusion has on student performance in the standardized testing environment.* Unpublished master's dissertation, University of North Florida.

Monheit, S. L. (1987). An analysis of learning based upon the relationship between the learning style preferences of parents and their children. Doctoral dissertation, The Fielding Institute. *Dissertation Abstracts International, 50*(2), 395A.

Monsour, S. E. M. (1991). The relationship between a prescribed homework program considering learning style preferences and the mathematics achievement of eighth-grade students. Doctoral dissertation, University of Southern Mississippi. *Dissertation Abstracts International,* A, The Humanities and Social Sciences, *52*(6), 1630A.

Moore, R. C. (1991). Effects of computer-assisted instruction and perceptual preference(s) of eighth-grade students on the mastery of language arts and mathematics (CAI, Perceptual Preferences). Doctoral dissertation, South Carolina State University. *Dissertation Abstracts International, 53*(06), 1876.

Morgan, H. L. (1981). Learning styles: The relation between need for structure and preferred mode of instruction for gifted elementary students. Doctoral dissertation, University of Pittsburgh. *Dissertation Abstracts International, 43,* 2223A.

Morris, V. J. P. (1983). The design and implementation of a teaching strategy for language arts at Chipley High School that brings about predictable learning outcomes. Doctoral dissertation, Florida State University. *Dissertation Abstracts International, 44,* 3231A.

Moss, V. B. (1981). The stability of first-graders' learning styles and the relationship between selected variables and learning style. Doctoral dissertation, Mississippi State University. *Dissertation Abstracts International, 43*(3), 665A.

Murrain, P. G. (1983), Administrative determinations concerning facilities utilization and instructional grouping: An analysis of the relationships between selected thermal environments and preferences for temperature, an element of learning style, as they affect word recognition scores of secondary students. Doctoral dissertation, St. John's University. *Dissertation Abstracts International, 44,* 1749A.

Murray, C. A. (1980). The comparison of learning styles between low and high reading achievement subjects in the seventh and eighth grades in a public middle school. Doctoral dissertation, United States International University. *Dissertation Abstracts International, 41,* 1005.

Naden, R. C. (1992). Prescriptions and/or modality-based instruction on the spelling achievement of fifth-grade students. Doctoral dissertation, Andrews University. *Dissertation Abstracts International, 53*(04), A, 1051.

Napolitano, R. A. (1986). An experimental investigation of the relationships among achievement, attitude scores, and traditionally, marginally, and underprepared college students enrolled in an introductory psychology course when they are matched and mismatched with their learning style preferences for the element of structure. Doctoral dissertation, St. John's University. *Dissertation Abstracts International, 47,* 435A.

Neely, R. O., & Alm, D. (1992, November–December). Meeting individual needs: A learning styles success story. Washington, DC: Heldref Publications, *2,* 109–113.

Neely, R. O., & Alm, D. (1993). Empowering students with styles. *Principal.* Reston, VA: National Association of Elementary School Principals, *72*(4), 32–35.

Nelson, B. N. (1991). An investigation of the impact of learning style factors on college students' retention and achievement. Doctoral dissertation, St. John's University.

Nganwa-Baguma, M. J., & Mwamenda, T. S. (1991). Effects on reading comprehension tests of matching and mismatching students' design preferences. *Perceptual and Motor Skills, 72*(3, Part 1), 947–951.

Nganwa-Baguma, M. J. (1986). Learning styles: The effects of matching and mismatching students' design preferences on reading comprehension tests. Bachelor's dissertation, University of Transkei, South Africa.

Nides, A. G. (1984). The effect of learning style preferences on achievement when an advance organizer is employed. Doctoral dissertation, Georgia State University College of Education. *Dissertation Abstracts International, 45*(05A), 1288.

Ogato, B. G, (1991). A correlational examination of perceptual modality preferences of middle school students and their academic achievement. Doctoral dissertation, Virginia Polytechnic Institute, Northern Virginia Graduate Center.

Orsak, L. (1990a). Learning styles and love: A winning combination. *Journal of Reading, Writing, and Learning Disabilities International.* NY: Hemisphere Publishing Corporation, *6*(3), 343–346.

Orsak, L. (1990b, October). Learning styles versus the Rip Van Winkle syndrome. *Educational Leadership.* Alexandria, VA: Association for Supervision and Curriculum Development, *48*(2), 19–20.

Ostoyee, C. H. (1988). The effects of teaching style on student writing about field trips with concrete experiences. Doctoral dissertation, Columbia University, Teachers College. *Dissertation Abstracts International, 49,* 2916A.

Paskewitz, B. U. (1985), A study of the relationship between learning styles and attitudes toward computer programming of middle school gifted students. Doctoral dissertation, University of Pittsburgh. *Dissertation Abstracts International, 47*(03), 697A.

Pederson, J. K. (1984). The classification and comparison of learning disabled students and gifted students. Doctoral dissertation, Texas Tech University. *Dissertation Abstracts International, 45*(09), A, 2810.

Perrin, J. (1979, 1981). *Learning Style Inventory: Primary.* Learning Styles Network, St. John's University, New York 11439.

Perrin, J. (1983). *Learning Style Inventory: Primary manual for administration, interpretation and teaching suggestions.* Learning Styles Network, St. John's University, Center for the Study of Learning and Teaching Styles, Jamaica, NY.

Perrin, J. (1984). An experimental investigation of the relationships among the learning style sociological preferences of gifted and non-gifted primary children, selected instructional strategies, attitudes, and achievement in problem solving and rote memorization. Doctoral dissertation, St. John's University. *Dissertation Abstracts International, 46,* 342A. Recipient: American Association of School Administrators (AASA) National Research Finalist, 1984.

Perrin, J. (1990, October). The learning styles project for potential dropouts. *Educational Leadership, 48*(2), 23–24.

Perrin, J., & Santora, S. (1982). *Elephant style.* St. John's University, Center for the Study of Learning and Teaching Styles, Jamaica, NY 11439.

Pizzo, J. (1981). An investigation of the relationships between selected acoustic environments and sound, an element of learning style, as they affect sixth grade students' reading achievement and attitudes. Doctoral dissertation, St. John's University. *Dissertation Abstracts International, 42,* 2475A. Recipient: Association for Supervision and Curriculum Development First Alternate National Recognition for Best Doctoral Research (Curriculum), 1981.

Pizzo, J. (1982, December). Breaking the sound barrier: Classroom noise and learning style. *Orbit, 64.* Ontario: Ontario Institute for Studies in Education, *13*(4), 21–22.

Pizzo, J., Dunn, R., & Dunn, K. (1990, July–September). A sound approach to reading: Responding to students' learning styles. *Journal of Reading, Writing, and Learning Disabilities International.* Washington, DC: Hemisphere Publishing Corporation, *6*(3), 249–260.

Poirier, G. A. (1970). Students as partners in team learning. Berkeley, CA: Center of Team Learning, Chapter 2 (1975).

Ponder, D. (1990). An analysis of the changes and gender differences in preferences of learning styles at adolescence and the relationship of the learning styles of adolescents and their parents when matched and mismatched according to gender. Doctoral dissertation, East Texas State University. *Dissertation Abstracts International, 64*(4), 1170A.

Price, G. E. (1980). Which learning style elements are stable and which tend to change over time? *Learning Styles Network Newsletter, 1*(3), 1.

Price, G. E., Dunn, K., Dunn, R., & Griggs, S. A. (1981). Studies in students' learning styles. *Roeper Review, 4,* 223–226.

Ragsdale, C. S. (1991). The experiences and impressions of tenth-grade students in a modern European history class designed as a collaborative, heuristic learning environment. *Dissertation Abstracts International, 52*(03), A, 796.

Rahal, B. F. (1986). The effects of matching and mismatching the diagnosed learning styles of intermediate level students with their structure preferences in the learning environment. Doctoral dissertation, West Virginia University. *Dissertation Abstracts International, 47*(6), 2010A.

Ramirez, A. I. (1982). Modality and field dependence/independence: Learning components and their relationship to mathematics achievement in the elementary school. Doctoral dissertation, Florida State University. *Dissertation Abstracts International, 43,* 666.

Raviotta, C. F. (1988). A study of the relationship between knowledge of individual learning style and its effect on academic achievement and study orientation in high school mathematics students. Doctoral dissertation, University of New Orleans. *Dissertation Abstracts International, 50*(05), A, 1204.

Rea, D. C. (1980). Effects on achievement of placing students in different learning environments based upon identified learning styles. Doctoral dissertation, University of Missouri.

Reid, J. M. (1987, March). The learning style preferences of ESL students. *TESOL Quarterly, 21,* 87–105. Available to members only from TESOL, 1118 22nd Street, N.W., Georgetown University, Suite 205, Washington, DC 20037.

Restak, R. (1979). *The brain: The last frontier.* New York: Doubleday.

Review of research on sociological preferences. (1991, Summer). *Learning Styles Network Newsletter.* New York: St. John's University and the National Association of Secondary School Principals, *12*(2).

Reynolds, J. (1988). A study of the pattern of learning style characteristics for adult dependent decision-makers. Doctoral dissertation, Virginia Polytechnic Institute and State University. *Dissertation Abstracts International, 50*(04), A, 854.

Reynolds, J. (1991, December). Learning style characteristics of adult dependent decision makers: Counseling and instructional implications. *The Career Development Quarterly, 40*, 145–154.

Ricca, J. (1983). Curricular implications of learning style differences between gifted and non-gifted students. Doctoral dissertation, State University of New York at Buffalo. *Dissertation Abstracts International, 44*, 1324A.

The Rise Report: Report of the California Commission for Reform of Intermediate and Secondary Education. Sacramento: California State Department of Education.

Roberts, O. A. (1984). Investigation of the relationship between learning style and temperament of senior high students in the Bahamas and Jamaica. Graduate dissertation, Andrews University.

Rodrigo, R. A. (1989). A comparison of the profiles of the learning styles of first-grade pupils at the Ateneo DeManila Grade School for the school year 1988–1989. Master's degree, Graduate School Atteneo DeManila University.

Rogers, D. S. (1983). The effect of teacher inservice about learning styles on students' mathematics and reading achievement. Doctoral dissertation, Bowling Green State University.

Sage, C. O. (1984). The Dunn and Dunn learning style model: An analysis of its theoretical, practical, and research foundations. Doctoral dissertation, University of Denver. *Dissertation Abstracts International, 45*(12), 3537A.

Shands, R., & Brunner, C. (1989, Fall). Providing success through a powerful combination: Mastery learning and learning styles. *Perceptions.* New York: New York State Educators of the Emotionally Disturbed, *25*(1), 6–10.

Shea, T. C. (1983). An investigation of the relationship among preferences for the learning style element of design, selected instructional environments, and reading achievement of ninth grade students to improve administrative determinations concerning effective educational facilities. Doctoral dissertation, St. John's University. *Dissertation Abstracts International, 44*, 2004A. Recipient: National Association of Secondary School Principals' Middle School Research Finalist Citation, 1984.

Siebenman, J. B. (1984). An investigation of the relationship between learning style and cognitive style in non-traditional college reading students. Doctoral dissertation, Arizona State University. *Dissertation Abstracts International, 45*, 1705A.

Sims, J. E. (1988). Learning styles: A comparative analysis of the learning styles of black-American, Mexican-American, and white-American third and fourth grade students in traditional public schools. Doctoral dissertation, University of Santa Barbara.

Sinatra, C. (1990, July–September). Five diverse secondary schools where learning style instruction works. *Journal of Reading, Writing, and Learning Disabilities International.* New York: Hemisphere Publishing Corporation, *6*(3), 323–342.

Sinatra, R., Hirshoren, A., & Primavera, L. H. (1987). Learning style, behavior ratings and achievement interactions for adjudicated adolescents. *Educational and Psychological Research, 7*(1), 21–32.

Sinatra, R., Primavera, L., & Waked, W. J. (1986). Learning style and intelligence of reading disabled students. *Perceptual and Motor Skills, 62*, 1243–12.

Slavin, R. E. (1983). *Cooperative learning.* New York: Longman.

Slavin, R. E. (1988). Synthesis of research on cooperative learning. *Educational Leadership, 38*(8), 655–660. Alexandria, VA: Association for Supervision and Curriculum Development.

Smith, S. (1987). An experimental investigation of the relationship between and among achievement, preferred time of instruction, and critical-thinking abilities of tenth- and eleventh-grade students in mathematics. Doctoral dissertation, St. John's University. *Dissertation Abstracts International, 47,* 1405A.

Smith, T. D. (1988). An assessment of the self-perceived teaching style of three ethnic groups of public school teachers in Texas. Doctoral dissertation, East Texas University. *Dissertation Abstracts International, 49*(08), A, 2062.

Snider, K. P. (1985). A study of learning preferences among educable mentally impaired, emotionally impaired, learning disabled, and general education students in seventh, eighth, and ninth grades as measured by response to the Learning Styles Inventory. Doctoral dissertation, Michigan State University. *Dissertation Abstracts International, 46*(05), SECA, 1251.

Solberg, S. J. (1987). An analysis of the Learning Style Inventory, the Productivity Environmental Preference Survey, and the Iowa Test of Basic Skills. Doctoral dissertation, Northern Arizona University. *Dissertation Abstracts International, 48,* 2530A.

Spires, R. D. (1983). The effect of teacher inservice about learning styles on students' mathematics and reading achievement. Doctoral dissertation, Bowling Green State University. *Dissertation Abstracts International, 44,* 1325A.

Stahlnecker, R. K. (1988). Relationships between learning style preferences of selected elementary pupils and their achievement in math and reading. Doctoral dissertation, Loma Linda University. *Dissertation Abstracts International, 50*(11), A, 3471.

Steinauer, M. H. (1981). Interpersonal relationships as reflected in learning style preferences: A study of eleventh grade students and their English teachers in a vocational school. Doctoral dissertation, Southern Illinois University. *Dissertation Abstracts International, 43,* 305A.

Stiles, R. (1985). Learning style preferences for design and their relationship to standardized test results. Doctoral dissertation, University of Tennessee. *Dissertation Abstracts International, 46,* 2551A.

Stokes, B. M. (1989). An analysis of the relationship between learning style, achievement, race, and gender. Doctoral dissertation, University of Akron. *Dissertation Abstracts International, 49,* 757A.

Stone, P. (1992, November). How we turned around a problem school. *The Principal.* Reston, VA: National Association of Elementary School Principals, *71*(2), 34–36.

Sullivan, M. (1993). A meta-analysis of experimental research studies based on the Dunn and Dunn learning styles model. Doctoral dissertation, St. John's University.

Svreck, L. J. (1990). Perceived parental influence, accommodated learning style preferences, and students' attitudes toward learning as they relate to reading and mathematics achievement. Doctoral dissertation, St. John's University, 1990.

Sykes, S., Jones, B., & Phillips, J. (1990, October). Partners in learning styles at a private school. *Educational Leadership.* Alexandria, VA: Association for Supervision and Curriculum Development, *48*(2), 24–26.

Tanenbaum, R. (1982). An investigation of the relationships between selected instructional techniques and identified field dependent and field independent cognitive styles as evidenced among high school students enrolled in studies of nutrition. Doctoral dissertation, St. John's University. *Dissertation Abstracts International, 43,* 68A.

Tappenden, V. J. (1983). Analysis of the learning styles of vocational education and nonvocational education students in eleventh and twelfth grades from rural, urban, and suburban locations in Ohio. Doctoral dissertation, Kent State University. *Dissertation Abstracts International, 44,* 1326A.

Thies, A. P. (1979). A brain behavior analysis of learning style. In *Student learning styles: Diagnosing and prescribing programs.* Reston, VA: National Association of Secondary School Principals.

Thrasher, R. (1984). A study of the learning-style preferences of at-risk sixth and ninth graders. Pompano Beach: Florida Association of Alternative School Educators.

Tingley-Michaelis, C. (1983). Make room for movement. *Early Years, 13*(6), 26–29.

Trautman, P. (1979). An investigation of the relationship between selected instructional techniques and identified cognitive style. Doctoral dissertation, St. John's University. *Dissertation Abstracts International, 40,* 1428A.

Turner, N. D. (1992). Prescriptions and/or modality-based instruction on the spelling achievement of fifth-grade students. Doctoral dissertation, Andrews University. *Dissertation Abstracts International, 53*(04), 1051.

Urbschat, K. S. (1977). A study of preferred learning modes and their relationship to the amount of recall of CVC trigrams. Doctoral dissertation, Wayne State University, 1977. *Dissertation Abstracts International, 38,* 2536-5A.

Vaughan, J. L., Underwood, V., House, G., Schroth, G., Weaver, S. L., Bienversie, N., & Durkin, M. (1992, Spring). The learning style characteristics of Tohono O'Odham students in the Indian Oasis-Baboquivari Unified School District #40, Sells, Arizona. Mesquite: East Texas State University.

Vaughan, J. L., Underwood, V. L., House, G. L., Weaver, S. W., & Dotson, S. (1992). *Learning styles and TAAS scores: Preliminary results.* Research Report No. 3. Commerce: Texas Center for Learning Styles, East Texas State University.

Vaughan, J. L., Weaver, S. L., Underwood, V. L., Binversie, N., House, G., Durkin, M., & Schroth, G. (1992). *The learning style characteristics of Tohono O'Odham students: An executive summary.* Research Report No. 1. Commerce: Texas Center for Learning Styles, East Texas State University.

Vaughan, J. L., Weaver, S. L., Underwood, V. L., & House, G. (1992). *A comparison of students' learning styles as determined by Learning Style Inventory and Personal Learning Power.* Research Report No. 2. Commerce: Texas Center for Learning Styles, East Texas State University.

Vazquez, A. W. (1985). Description of learning styles of high risk adult students taking courses in urban community colleges in Puerto Rico. Doctoral dissertation, Union for Experimenting Colleges and Universities, Puerto Rico.

Vignia, R. A. (1983). An investigation of learning styles of gifted and non-gifted high school students. Doctoral dissertation, University of Houston. *Dissertation Abstracts International, 44,* 3653A.

Virostko, J. (1983). An analysis of the relationships among academic achievement in mathematics and reading, assigned instructional schedules, and the learning style time preferences of third, fourth, fifth, and sixth grade students. Doctoral dissertation, St. John's University. *Dissertation Abstracts International, 44,* 1683A. Recipient: Kappa Delta Pi International Award for Best Doctoral Research, 1983.

Wallace, J. (1990). The relationship among preferences for learning alone or with peers, selected instructional strategies, and achievement of third-, fourth-, and fifth-grade social studies students. Doctoral dissertation, Syracuse University. *Dissertation Abstracts International, 51*(11), 3626A.

Wegner, W. A. (1980). Opsimathic styles of adults. Doctoral dissertation, University of Southern Mississippi. *Dissertation Abstracts International, 41*(05), A.

Weinberg, F. (1983). An experimental investigation of the interaction between sensory modality preference and mode of presentation in the instruction of arithmetic concepts to third grade underachievers. Doctoral dissertation, St. John's University. *Dissertation Abstracts International, 44,* 1740A.

Wheeler, R. (1980). An alternative to failure: Teaching reading according to students' perceptual strengths. *Kappa Delta Pi Record, 17*(2), 59–63.

Wheeler, R. (1983). An investigation of the degree of academic achievement evidenced when second grade, learning disabled students' perceptual preferences are matched and mismatched with complementary sensory approaches to beginning reading instruction. Doctoral dissertation, St. John's University. *Dissertation Abstracts International, 44,* 2039A.

White, R. (1981). An investigation of the relationship between selected instructional methods and selected elements of emotional learning style upon student achievement in seventh grade social studies. Doctoral dissertation, St. John's University. *Dissertation Abstracts International, 42,* 995A. Recipient: Kappa Delta Gamma International Award for Best Doctoral Research Prospectus, 1980.

Wild, J. B. (1979). *A study of the learning styles of learning disabled students and non-learning disabled students at the junior high school level.* Unpublished master's dissertation, University of Kansas, Lawrence.

Wilburn, H. R. (1991). An invsetigation of interaction among learning styles and computer-assigned instruction with synthetic speech. Doctoral dissertation, University of Texas at Austin. *Dissertation Abstracts International,* A, The Humanities and Social Sciences, *52*(7), 2398A–2399A.

Williams, G. J. (1989). A study of the learning styles of urban black middle school learning-disabled and non-learning-disabled students. Doctoral dissertation, Southern Illinois Univesrity, 1990. *Dissertation Abstracts International, 51*(6), A.

Williams, G. L. (1984). The effectiveness of computer assisted instruction and its relationship to selected learning style elements. Doctoral dissertation, North Texas State University. *Dissertation Abstracts International, 45,* 1986A.

Willis, M. G. (1989). Learning styles of African-American children: A review of the literature and interventions. *Journal of Black Psychology, 16*(1), 47–65.

Wingo, L. H. (1980). Relationships among locus of motivation, sensory modality and grouping preferences of learning style to basic skills test performance in reading and mathematics. Doctoral dissertation, Memphis State University. *Dissertation Abstracts International, 41,* 2923.

Wittenberg, S. K. (1984). A comparison of diagnosed and preferred learning styles of young adults in need of remediation. Doctoral dissertation, University of Toledo. *Dissertation Abstracts International, 45,* 3539A.

Wittig, C. (1985). Learning style preferences among students high or low on divergent thinking and feeling variables. Unpublished master's dissertation, State University of New York College at Buffalo, Center for Studies in Creativity.

Wolfe, G. (1983). Learning styles and the teaching of reading. Doctoral dissertation, Akron University. *Dissertation Abstracts International, 45,* 3422A.

Yeap, L. L. (1987). Learning styles of Singapore secondary students. Doctoral dissertation, University of Pittsburgh. *Dissertation Abstracts International, 48,* 936A.

Yong, F. L., & McIntyre, J. D. (1992). A comparative study of the learning styles preferences of students with learning disabilities and students who are gifted. *Journal of Learning Disabilities, 25*(2), 124–132.

Young, B. M. P. (1985). Effective conditions for learning: An analysis of learning environments and learning styles in ability-grouped classes. Doctoral dissertation, University of Massachusetts. *Dissertation Abstracts International, 46,* 708A.

Young, D. B., Jr. (1986). Administrative implications of instructional strategies and student learning style preferences of science achievement on seventh-grade students. Doctoral dissertation, University of Hawaii. *Dissertation Abstracts International, 48*(01), A, 27.

Zak, F. (1989). Learning style discrimination between vocational and nonvocational students. Doctoral dissertation, University of Massachusetts. *Dissertation Abstracts International, 50*(12), A, 3843A.

Zenhausern, R. (1980). Hemispheric dominance. *Learning Styles Network Newsletter, 1*(2), 3. St. John's University and the National Association of Secondary School Principals.

Zikmund, A. B. (1988). The effect of grade level, gender, and learning style on responses to conservation type rhythmic and melodic patterns. Doctoral dissertation, University of Nebraska. *Dissertation Abstracts International, 50*(1), 95A.

Index